Living With the Winnebagos

Juliette A. Kinzie

Living With the Winnebagos
Experiences of Wisconsin During the Early 19th Century

ILLUSTRATED

Wau-Bun
Mrs. John H. Kinzie

The History of Fort Winnebago
Andrew Jackson Turner

The Winnebago War of 1827
Charles R. Tuttle

Living With the Winnebagos
Experiences of Wisconsin During the Early 19th Century
Wau-Bun
by Mrs. John H. Kinzie
The History of Fort Winnebago
by Andrew Jackson Turner
The Winnebago War of 1827
by Charles R. Tuttle

ILLUSTRATED

FIRST EDITION

Leonaur is an imprint of Oakpast Ltd
Copyright in this form © 2022 Oakpast Ltd

ISBN: 978-1-915234-86-5 (hardcover)
ISBN: 978-1-915234-87-2 (softcover)

http://www.leonaur.com

Publisher's Notes

The views expressed in this book are not necessarily those of the publisher.

Contents

Preface	9
Departure from Detroit	11
Michilimackinac	13
Green Bay	19
Voyage Up Fox River	26
Winnebago Lake—Miss Four-Legs	36
Breakfast at Betty More's	41
"Butte Des Morts"—Lake Puckaway	44
Fort Winnebago	49
Housekeeping	55
Indian Payment—Mrs. Washington	58
Louisa—Day-Kau-Ray on Education	63
Preparations for a Journey	71
Departure From Fort Winnebago	74
William S. Hamilton—Kellogg's Grove	81
Rock River—Hours of Trouble	88
Relief	96
Chicago in 1831	102
Massacre at Chicago	115
Narrative of the Massacre, Continued	125

Captivity of J. Kinzie, Sen.—An Amusing Mistake	140
A Sermon	146
The Captives	150
Second-Sight—Hickory Creek	162
Return to Fort Winnebago	168
Return Journey, Continued	176
Four-Legs, the Dandy	187
The Cut-Nose	192
Indian Customs and Dances	197
Story of the Red Fox	204
Story of Shee-Shee-Banze	209
A Visit to Green Bay—Ma-Zhee-Gaw-Gaw Swamp	214
Commencement of the Sauk War	221
Fleeing From the Indians	229
Fort Howard—Our Return Home	238
Surrender of Winnebago Prisoners	248
Escape of the Prisoners	254
Agathe—Tomah	260
Conclusion	265
Appendix	270
A Note	279
The History of Fort Winnebago	289
The Winnebago War of 1827	325

To the
Hon. Lewis Cass,
In the "Early Day" the tried friend of
The pioneer and the red man
The following Memorials
Are
Respectfully inscribed

Preface

Every work partaking of the nature of an autobiography is supposed to demand an apology to the public. To refuse such a tribute, would be to recognise the justice of the charge, so often brought against our countrymen—of a too great willingness to be made acquainted with the domestic history and private affairs of their neighbours.

It is, doubtless, to refute this calumny that we find travellers, for the most part, modestly offering some such form of explanation as this, to the reader:

> That the matter laid before him was, in the first place, simply letters to friends, never designed to be submitted to other eyes, and only brought forward now at the solicitation of wiser judges than the author himself.

No such plea can, in the present instance, be offered. The record of events in which the writer had herself no share, was preserved in compliance with the suggestion of a revered relative, whose name often appears in the following pages. She would say:

> My child, write these things down, as I tell them to you. Hereafter our children, and even strangers, will feel interested in hearing the story of our early lives and sufferings."

And it is a matter of no small regret and self-reproach, that much, very much, thus narrated was, through negligence, or a spirit of procrastination, suffered to pass unrecorded.

With regard to the pictures of domestic life and experience (preserved, as will be seen, in journals, letters, and otherwise), it is true their publication might have been deferred until the writer had passed away from the scene of action; and such, it was supposed, would have been their lot—that they would only have been dragged forth hereafter, to show to a succeeding generation what "The Early Day" of our Western homes had been.

It never entered the anticipations of the most sanguine that the march of improvement and prosperity would, in less than a quarter of a century, have so obliterated the traces of "the first beginning," that a vast and intelligent multitude would be crying out for information in regard to the early settlement of this portion of our country, which so few are left to furnish.

An opinion has been expressed, that a comparison of the present times with those that are past, would enable our young people, emigrating from their luxurious homes at "the East," to bear, in a spirit of patience and contentment, the slight privations and hardships they are at this day called to meet with. If, in one instance, this should be the case, the writer may well feel happy to have incurred even the charge of egotism, in giving thus much of her own history.

It may be objected that all that is strictly personal, might have been more modestly put forth under the name of a third person; or that the events themselves and the scenes might have been described, while those participating in them might have been kept more in the background. In the first case, the narrative would have lost its air of truth and reality—in the second, the experiment would merely have been tried of dressing up a theatre for representation, and omitting the actors.

Some who read the following sketches may be inclined to believe that a residence among our native brethren and an attachment growing out of our peculiar relation to them, have exaggerated our sympathies, and our sense of the wrongs they have received at the hands of the whites. This is not the place to discuss that point. There is a tribunal at which man shall be judged for that which he has meted out to his fellow-man.

May our countrymen take heed that their legislation shall never unfit them to appear "with joy, and not with grief," before that tribunal!

Chicago, July, 1855.

CHAPTER 1

Departure from Detroit

It was on a dark, rainy evening in the month of September, 1830, that we went on board the steamer *Henry Clay*, to take passage for Green Bay. All our friends in Detroit had congratulated us upon our good fortune in being spared the voyage in one of the little schooners which at this time afforded the ordinary means of communication with the few and distant settlements on Lakes Huron and Michigan.

Each one had some experience to relate of his own or of his friends' mischances in these precarious journeys—long detentions on the St. Clair flats—furious headwinds off Thunder Bay, or interminable calms at Mackinac or the Manitous. That which most enhanced our sense of peculiar good luck, was the true story of one of our relatives having left Detroit in the month of June and reached Chicago in the September following, having been actually three months in performing what is sometimes accomplished by even a sail-vessel in four days.

But the certainty of encountering similar misadventures would have weighed little with me. I was now to visit, nay, more, to become a resident of that land which had, for long years, been to me a region of romance. Since the time when, as a child, my highest delight had been in the letters of a dear relative, (the author's uncle, Dr. Alexander Wolcott), describing to me his home and mode of life in the "Indian country," and still later, in his felicitous narration of a tour with General Cass, in 1820, to the sources of the Mississippi—nay, even earlier, in the days when I stood at my teacher's knee, and spelled out the long word Mich-i-li-mack-i-nac, that distant land, with its vast lakes, its boundless prairies, and its mighty forests, had possessed a wonderful charm for my imagination. Now I was to see it!—it was to be my home!

Our ride to the quay, through the dark by-ways, in a cart, the only vehicle which at that day could navigate the muddy, unpaved streets of Detroit, was a theme for much merriment, and not less so, our descent of the narrow, perpendicular stair-way by which we reached the little apartment called the Ladies' Cabin. We were highly delighted with the accommodations, which, by comparison, seemed the very climax of comfort and convenience; more especially as the occupants of the cabin consisted, beside myself, of but a lady and two little girls.

Nothing could exceed the pleasantness of our trip for the first twenty-four hours. There were some officers, old friends, among the passengers. We had plenty of books. The gentlemen read aloud occasionally, admired the solitary magnificence of the scenery around us, the primeval woods, or the vast expanse of water unenlivened by a single sail, and then betook themselves to their cigar, or their game of euchre, to while away the hours.

For a time, the passage over Thunder Bay was delightful, but, alas! it was not destined, in our favour, to belie its name. A storm came on, fast and furious—what was worse, it was of long duration. The pitching and rolling of the little boat, the closeness, and even the seasickness, we bore as became us. They were what we had expected, and were prepared for. But a new feature of discomfort appeared, which almost upset our philosophy.

The rain, which fell in torrents, soon made its way through every seam and pore of deck or moulding. Down the stairway, through the joints and crevices, it came, saturating first the carpet, then the bedding, until, finally, we were completely driven, "by stress of weather," into the Gentlemen's Cabin. Way was made for us very gallantly, and every provision resorted to for our comfort, and we were congratulating ourselves on having found a haven in our distress, when, lo! the seams above opened, and down upon our devoted heads poured such a flood, that even umbrellas were an insufficient protection.

There was nothing left for the ladies and children but to betake ourselves to the berths, which, in this apartment, fortunately remained dry; and here we continued ensconced the livelong day. Our dinner was served up to us on our pillows. The gentlemen chose the driest spots, raised their umbrellas, and sat under them, telling amusing anecdotes, and saying funny things to cheer us, until the rain ceased, and at nine o'clock in the evening we were gladdened by the intelligence that we had reached the pier at Mackinac.

We were received with the most affectionate cordiality by Mr. and Mrs. Robert Stuart, at whose hospitable mansion we had been for some days expected.

The repose and comfort of an asylum like this, can be best appreciated by those who have reached it after a tossing and drenching such as ours had been. A bright, warm fire, and countenances beaming with kindest interest, dispelled all sensations of fatigue or annoyance.

After a season of pleasant conversation, the servants were assembled, the chapter of God's word was solemnly read, the hymn chanted, the prayer of praise and thanksgiving offered, and we were conducted to our place of repose.

It is not my purpose here to attempt a portrait of those noble friends whom I thus met for the first time. To an abler pen than mine should be assigned the honour of writing the biography of Robert Stuart, (a native of Perthshire, Scotland who migrated to Canada.) All who have enjoyed the happiness of his acquaintance, or, still more, a sojourn under his hospitable roof, will carry with them to their latest hour the impression of his noble bearing, his genial humour, his untiring benevolence, his upright, uncompromising adherence to principle, his ardent philanthropy, his noble disinterestedness. Irving in his Astoria, and Franchere in his *Narrative*, give many striking traits of his early character, together with events of his history of a thrilling and romantic interest, but both have left the most valuable portion unsaid, his after-life, namely, as a Christian gentleman.

Of his beloved partner, who still survives him, mourning on her bereaved and solitary pilgrimage, yet cheered by the recollection of her long and useful course as a "Mother in Israel," we will say no more than to offer the incense of loving hearts, and prayers for the best blessings from her Father in heaven.

Chapter 2

Michilimackinac

Michilimackinac! that gem of the Lakes! How bright and beautiful it looked as we walked abroad on the following morning! The rain had passed away, but had left all things glittering in the light of the sun as it rose up over the waters of Lake Huron, far away to the east. Before us was the lovely bay, scarcely yet tranquil after the storm, but dotted with canoes and the boats of the fishermen already getting out their nets for the trout and whitefish, those treasures of the deep. Along the beach were scattered the *wigwams* or lodges of the Ottawas who had come to the island to trade. The inmates came forth to gaze upon us. A shout of welcome was sent forth, as they recognised *Shaw-nee-aw-kee* (name given to John Kinzie by the Indians), who, from a seven years' residence among them, was well known to each individual.

A shake of the hand, and an emphatic "*Bon-jour—bon-jour,*" is the customary salutation between the Indian and the white man.

"Do the Indians speak French?" I inquired of my husband.

"No; this is a fashion they have learned of the French traders during many years of intercourse."

Not less hearty was the greeting of each Canadian *engagé*, as he trotted forward to pay his respects to "Monsieur John," and to utter a long string of felicitations, in a most incomprehensible *patois*. I was forced to take for granted all the good wishes showered upon "Madame John," of which I could comprehend nothing but the hope that I should be happy and contented in my "*vie sauvage.*"

The object of our early walk was to visit the Mission-house and school which had been some few years previously established at this place by the Presbyterian Board of Missions. It was an object of especial interest to Mr. and Mrs. Stuart, and its flourishing condition at this period, and the prospects of extensive future usefulness it held out, might well gladden their philanthropic hearts. They had lived many years on the island, and had witnessed its transformation, through God's blessing on Christian efforts, from a worldly, dissipated community to one of which it might almost be said, "Religion was every man's business."

This mission establishment was the beloved child and the common centre of interest of the few Protestant families clustered around it. Through the zeal and good management of Mr. and Mrs. Ferry, (who established a Presbyterian church at Mackinac), and the fostering encouragement of the congregation, the school was in great repute, and it was pleasant to observe the effect of mental and religious culture in subduing the mischievous, tricky propensities of the half-breed, and rousing the stolid apathy of the genuine Indian.

These were the palmy days of Mackinac. As the headquarters of the American Fur Company, and the *entrepôt* of the whole Northwest, all the trade in supplies and goods on the one hand, and in furs and products of the Indian country on the other, was in the hands of the parent establishment or its numerous outposts scattered along Lakes Superior and Michigan, the Mississippi, or through still more distant regions.

Probably few are ignorant of the fact, that all the Indian tribes, with the exception of the Miamis and the Wyandots, had, since the transfer of the old French possessions to the British Crown, maintained a firm alliance with the latter. The independence achieved by the United States did not alter the policy of the natives, nor did our government succeed in winning or purchasing their friendship. Great Britain, it is true, bid high to retain them. Every year the leading men of the Chippewas, Ottawas, Pottowattamies, Menomonees, Winnebagoes, Sauks, and Foxes, and even still more remote tribes, journeyed from their distant homes to Fort Malden in Upper Canada, to receive their annual amount of presents from their Great Father across the water. It was a master-policy thus to keep them in pay, and had enabled those who practised it to do fearful execution through the aid of such allies in the last war between the two countries.

The presents they thus received were of considerable value, consisting of blankets, broadcloths or *strouding*, calicoes, guns, kettles, traps, silver-works (comprising arm-bands, bracelets, brooches; and ear-bobs), looking-glasses, combs, and various other trinkets distributed with no niggardly hand.

The magazines and store-houses of the Fur Company at Mackinac were the resort of all the upper tribes for the sale of their commodities, and the purchase of all such articles as they had need of, including those above enumerated, and also ammunition, which, as well as money and liquor, their British friends very commendably omitted to furnish them.

Besides their furs, various in kind and often of great value—beaver, otter, marten, mink, silver-grey and red fox, wolf, bear, and wild-cat, musk-rat, and smoked deer-skins—the Indians brought for trade maple-sugar in abundance, considerable quantities of both Indian corn and *petit-blé* (corn parboiled, shelled from the cob, and dried in the sun), beans and the *folles avoines* (literally, crazy oats, it is the French name for the Menomonees), or wild rice; while the squaws added to their quota of merchandise a contribution in the form of *moccasins*, hunting-pouches, *mocucks*, or little boxes of birch-bark embroidered with porcupine-quills and filled with maple-sugar, mats of a neat and durable fabric, and toy-models of Indian cradles, snow-shoes, canoes, etc., etc.

It was no unusual thing, at this period, to see a hundred or more canoes of Indians at once approaching the island, laden with their articles of traffic; and if to these we add the squadrons of large Mackinac boats constantly arriving from the outposts, with the furs, peltries, and buffalo-robes collected by the distant traders, some idea may be formed of the extensive operations and important position of the American Fur Company, as well as of the vast circle of human beings either immediately or remotely connected with it.

It is no wonder that the philanthropic mind, surveying these, races of uncultivated heathen, should stretch forward to the time when, through an unwearied devotion of the white man's energies, and an untiring sacrifice of self and fortune, his red brethren might rise in the scale of social civilization—when Education and Christianity should go hand in hand, to make "the wilderness blossom as the rose."

Little did the noble souls at that day rejoicing in the success of their labours at Mackinac, anticipate that in less than a quarter of a century there would remain of all these numerous tribes but a few scattered bands, squalid, degraded, with scarce a vestige remaining of their former lofty character—their lands cajoled or wrested from them, the graves of their fathers turned up by the ploughshare—themselves chased farther and farther towards the setting sun, until they were literally grudged a resting-place on the face of the earth!

Our visit to the Mission-school was of short duration, for the *Henry Clay* was to leave at two o'clock, and in the meantime, we were to see what we could of the village and its environs, and after that dine with Mr. Mitchell, an old friend of my husband. As we walked leisurely along over the white, gravelly road, many of the residences of the old inhabitants were pointed out to me. There was the dwelling of Madame Laframboise, an Ottawa woman, whose husband had taught her to read and write, and who had ever after continued to use the knowledge she had acquired for the instruction and improvement of the youth among her own people. (She was born about the year 1780 to a French trader and a native woman.)

It was her custom to receive a class of young pupils daily at her house, that she might give them lessons in the branches mentioned, and also in the principles of the Roman Catholic religion, to which she was deeply devoted. She was a woman of a vast deal of energy and enterprise—of a tall and commanding figure, and most dignified deportment. After the death of her husband, who was killed while away at his trading-post by a Winnebago named White Ox, she was accustomed to visit herself the trading-posts, superintend the clerks and *engagés*, and satisfy herself that the business was carried on in a regular and profitable manner. (Her husband was murdered early summer of 1807 in the vicinity of Grand Rapids, Michigan).

The Agency-house, with its unusual luxuries of *piazza* and gardens, was situated at the foot of the hill on which the fort was built. It was a lovely spot, notwithstanding the stunted and dwarfish appearance of all cultivated vegetation in this cold northern latitude.

The collection of rickety, primitive-looking buildings, occupied by the officials of the Fur Company, reflected no great credit on the architectural skill of my husband, who had superintended their construction, he told me, when little more than a boy.

There were, besides these, the residences of the Dousmans, the Abbotts, the Biddles, the Drews, and the Lashleys, (all prominent American merchants of Mackinac), stretching away along the base of the beautiful hill, crowned with the white walls and buildings of the fort, the ascent to which was so steep that on the precipitous face nearest the beach staircases were built by which to mount from below.

My head ached intensely, the effect of the motion of the boat on the previous day, but I did not like to give up to it; so, after I had been shown all that could be seen of the little settlement in the short time allowed us, we repaired to Mr. Mitchell's.

We were received by Mrs. M., an extremely pretty, delicate woman, part French and part Sioux, whose early life had been passed at Prairie du Chien, on the Mississippi. She had been a great *belle* among the young officers at Fort Crawford; so much so, indeed, that the suicide of the post-surgeon was attributed to an unsuccessful attachment he had conceived for her. I was greatly struck with her soft and gentle manners, and the musical intonation of her voice, which I soon learned was a distinguishing peculiarity of those women in whom are united the French and native blood.

A lady, then upon a visit to the Mission, was of the company. She insisted on my lying down upon the sofa, and ministered most kindly to my suffering head. As she sat by my side, and expatiated upon the new sphere opening before me, she inquired:

"Do you not realise very strongly the entire deprivation of religious privileges you will be obliged to suffer in your distant home?"

"The deprivation," said I, "will doubtless be great, but not *entire*; for I shall have my Prayer-Book, and, though destitute of a church, we need not be without a *mode* of worship."

How often afterwards, when cheered by the consolations of that precious book in the midst of the lonely wilderness, did I remember this conversation, and bless God that I could never, while retaining it, be without "religious privileges."

We had not yet left the dinner-table, when the bell of the little steamer sounded to summon us on board, and we bade a hurried farewell to all our kind friends, bearing with us their hearty wishes for a safe and prosperous voyage.

A finer sight can scarcely be imagined than Mackinac, from the water. As we steamed away from the shore, the view came full upon us—the sloping beach with the scattered *wigwams*, and canoes drawn up here and there—the irregular, quaint-looking houses—the white walls of the fort, and, beyond, one eminence still more lofty crowned with the remains of old Fort Holmes. The whole picture completed, showed the perfect outline that had given the island its original Indian name, *Mich-i-li-mack-i-nac*, the Big Turtle.

Then those pure, living waters, in whose depths the fish might be seen gliding and darting to and fro; whose clearness is such that an object dropped to the bottom may be discerned at the depth of fifty or sixty feet, a dollar lying far down on its green bed, looking no larger than a half dime! I could hardly wonder at the enthusiastic lady who exclaimed: "Oh! I could wish to be drowned in these pure, beautiful waters!"

As we passed the extreme western point of the island, my husband pointed out to me, far away to the northwest, a promontory which he told me was Point St. Ignace. It possessed great historic interest, as one of the earliest white settlements on this continent. The Jesuit missionaries had established here a church and school as early as 1607, the same year in which a white settlement was made at St. Augustine, in Florida, and one year before the founding of Jamestown, Virginia.

All that remains of the enterprises of these devoted men, is the remembrance of their labours, perpetuated, in most instances, only by the names of the spots which witnessed their efforts of love in behalf of their savage brethren. The little French church at Sandwich, opposite Detroit, alone is left, a witness of the zeal and self-sacrifice of these pioneers of Christianity.

Passing "Old Mackinac," on the main land, which forms the southern border of the straits, we soon came out into the broad waters of Lake Michigan. Every traveller, and every reader of our history, is familiar with the incidents connected with the taking of the old fort by the Indians, in the days of Pontiac. How, by means of a game of ball, played in an apparently friendly spirit outside the walls, and of which the officers and soldiers had come forth to be spectators, the ball was dexterously tossed over the wall, and the savages rushing in, under pretext of finding it, soon got possession and massacred the garrison.

The little Indian village of L'Arbre Croche gleamed far away south, in the light of the setting sun. With that exception, there was no sign of living habitation along that vast and wooded shore. The gigantic forest-trees, and here and there the little glades of prairie opening to the water, showed a landscape that would have gladdened the eye of the agriculturist, with its promise of fertility; but it was evidently untrodden by the foot of man, and we left it, in its solitude, as we took our course westward across the waters.

The rainy and gusty weather, so incident to the equinoctial season, overtook us again before we reached the mouth of Green Bay, and kept us company until the night of our arrival upon the flats, about three miles below the settlement. Here the little steamer grounded "fast and hard." As almost everyone preferred braving the elements to remaining cooped up in the quarters we had occupied for the past week, we decided to trust ourselves to the little boat, spite of wind, and rain, and darkness, and in due time we reached the shore.

Chapter 3

Green Bay

Our arrival at Green Bay was at an unfortunate moment. It was the time of a treaty between the United States Government and the Menomonees and Wau-ba-na-kees, (latter is the term applied to New York Indians who migrated to Wisconsin in the twenties). Consequently, not only the commissioners of the treaty, with their clerks and officials, but traders, claimants, travellers, and idlers innumerable were upon the ground. Most of these were congregated in the only hotel the place afforded. This was a tolerably-sized house near the riverside, and as we entered the long dining-room, cold and dripping from the open boat, we were infinitely amused at the motley assemblage it contained. Various groups were seated around. Newcomers, like ourselves, stood here and there, for there were not seats enough to accommodate all who sought entertainment. The landlord, Judge Arndt of German descent, sat calm and indifferent, his hands in his pockets, exhibiting all the phlegm of a Pennsylvania Dutchman.

His fat, notable spouse was trotting round, now stopping to scold about someone who, "burn his skin!" had fallen short in his duty; now laughing good-humouredly until her sides shook, at some witticism addressed to her.

She welcomed us very cordially, but to our inquiry, "Can you accommodate us?" her reply was, "Not I. I have got twice as many people now as I know what to do with. I have had to turn my own family out of their quarters, what with the commissioners and the lot of folks that has come in upon us."

"What are we to do, then? It is too late and stormy to go up to Shanty-town to seek for lodgings."

"Well, sit you down and take your supper, and we will see what we can do."

And she actually did contrive to find a little nook, in which we were glad to take refuge from the multitudes around us.

A slight board partition separated us from the apartment occupied by General Root, of New York, one of the commissioners of the treaty. The steamer in which we came had brought the mail, at that day a rare blessing to the distant settlements. The opening and reading of all the dispatches, which the general received about bed-time, had, of course, to be gone through with, before he could retire to rest. His eyes being weak, his secretaries were employed to read the communications. He was a little deaf withal, and through the slight division between the two apartments the contents of the letters, and his comments upon them, were unpleasantly audible, as he continually admonished his secretary to raise his voice.

"What is that, Walter? Read that over again."

In vain we coughed and hemmed, and knocked over sundry pieces of furniture. They were too deeply interested to hear aught that passed around them, and if we had been politicians, we should have had all the secrets of the *working-men's party* at our disposal, out of which to have made capital.

The next morning it was still rain! rain! nothing but rain! In spite of it, however, the gentlemen would take a small boat to row to the steamer, to bring up the luggage, not the least important part of that which appertained to us being sundry boxes of silver for paying the annuities to the Winnebagoes at the Portage.

I went out with some others of the company upon the *piazza*, to witness their departure. A gentleman pointed out to me Fort Howard, on a projecting point of the opposite shore, about three-quarters of a mile distant—the old barracks, the picketed enclosure, the walls, all looking quaint, and, considering their modern erection, really ancient and venerable. Presently we turned our attention to the boat, which had by this time gained the middle of the river. One of the passengers was standing up in the stern, apparently giving some directions.

"That is rather a venturesome fellow," remarked one; "if he is not careful, he will lose his balance." And at this moment we saw him actually perform a summerset backward, and disappear in the water.

"Oh!" cried I, "he will be drowned!"

The gentlemen laughed. "No, there he is; they are helping him in again."

The course of the boat was immediately changed, and the party returned to the shore. It was not until one disembarked and came dripping and laughing towards me, that I recognised him as my own peculiar property. He was pleased to treat the matter as a joke, but I thought it rather a sad beginning of Western experience.

He suffered himself to be persuaded to intrust the care of his effects to his friends, and having changed his dress, prepared to remain quietly with me, when just at this moment a vehicle drove up to the door, and we recognised the pleasant, familiar face of our old friend, Judge Doty.

He had received the news of our arrival, and had come to take us at once to his hospitable mansion. We were only too happy to gather together our bags and travelling-baskets and accompany him without farther ceremony.

Our drive took us first along the edge of Navarino, next through Shanty-town (the latter a far more appropriate name than the former), amid mud and mire, over bad roads, and up and down hilly, breakneck places, until we reached the little brick dwelling of our friends. Mrs. Doty received us with such true, sisterly kindness, and everything seemed so full of welcome, that we soon felt ourselves at home.

We found that, expecting our arrival, invitations had already been prepared to assemble the whole circle of Green Bay society to meet us at an evening party—this, in a new country, being the established mode of doing honour to guests or strangers.

We learned, upon inquiry, that Captain Harney, who had kindly offered to come with a boat and crew of soldiers from Fort Winnebago, to convey us to that place, our destined home, had not yet arrived; we therefore felt at liberty to make arrangements for a few days of social enjoyment at "the Bay."

It was pleasant to people, secluded in such a degree from the world at large, to bear all the news we had brought—all the particulars of life and manners—the thousand little items that the newspapers of that day did not dream of furnishing—the fashions, and that general gossip, in short, which a lady is erroneously supposed more *au fait* of, than a gentleman.

I well remember that, in giving and receiving information, the day passed in a pretty uninterrupted stream of communication. All the party except myself had made the journey, or rather voyage, up the

Fox River and down the Wisconsin to the Mississippi.

There were plenty of anecdotes of a certain trip performed by the three, in company with a French trader and his two sisters, then making their debut as Western travellers. The manner in which Mademoiselle Julie would borrow, without leave, a fine damask napkin or two, to wipe out the ducks in preparation for cooking—the difficulty of persuading either of the sisters of the propriety of washing and rinsing their table apparatus nicely before packing it away in the messbasket, the consequence of which was, that another nice napkin must be stealthily whisked out, to wipe the dishes when the hour for meals arrived—the fun of the young gentleman in hunting up his stray articles, thus misappropriated, from the nooks and corners of the boat, tying them with a cord, and hanging them over the stern, to make their way down the Wisconsin to Prairie du Chien.

Then there was a capital story of M. Rolette himself, (a native of Canada who arrived in 1806 and engaged in the Indian trade). At one point on the route (I think in crossing Winnebago Lake) the travellers met one of the Company's boats on its way to Green Bay for supplies. M. Rolette was one of the agents of the Company, and the people in the boat were his *employés*. Of course, after an absence of some weeks from home, the meeting on these lonely waters and the exchanging of news was an occasion of great excitement.

The boats were stopped—earnest greetings interchanged—question followed question.

"*Eh bien*—have they finished the new house?"

"*Oui, Monsieur.*"

"*Et la cheminée, fume-t-elle?*" (Does the chimney smoke?)

"*Non, Monsieur.*"

"And the harvest—how is that?"

"Very fine, indeed."

"Is the mill at work?"

"Yes, plenty of water."

"How is Whip?" (his favourite horse.)

"Oh! Whip is first-rate."

Everything, in short, about the store, the farm, the business of various descriptions being satisfactorily gone over, there was no occasion for farther delay. It was time to proceed.

"*Eh bien—adieu! bon voyage!*"

"*Arrachez, mes gens!*" (Go ahead, men!)

Then suddenly—"*Arrêtez! arrêtez!*" (Stop, stop!)

"*Comment se portent Madame Rolette et les enfans?*" (How are Mrs. Rolette and the children?)

****

This day, with its excitement, was at length over, and we retired to our rest, thankful that we had not General Root and his secretary close to our bed's head, with their budget of political news.

My slumbers were not destined, however, to be quite undisturbed. I was awakened, at the first slight peep of dawn, by a sound from an apartment beneath our own—a plaintive, monotonous chant, rising and then falling in a sort of mournful cadence. It seemed to me a wail of something unearthly—so wild—so strange—so unaccountable. In terror I awoke my husband, who reassured me by telling me it was the morning salutation of the Indians to the opening day.

Some Menomonees had been kindly given shelter for the night in the kitchen below, and, having fulfilled their unvarying custom of chanting their morning hymn, they now ceased, and again composed themselves to sleep. But not so their auditor. There was to me something inexpressibly beautiful in this morning song of praise from the untaught sons of the forest. What a lesson did it preach to the civilized, Christianised world, too many of whom lie down and rise up without an aspiration of thanksgiving to their Almighty Preserver—without even a remembrance of His care, who gives His angels charge concerning them! Never has the impression of that simple act of worship faded from my mind. I have loved to think that, with some, these strains might be the outpouring of a devotion as pure as that of the Christian when he utters the inspiring words of the sainted Ken—

> *Awake, my soul! and with the sun*, etc.
> *****************

Among the visitors who called to offer me a welcome to the West, were Mr. and Miss Cadle, who were earnestly engaged in the first steps of their afterwards flourishing enterprise for the education of Indian and half-breed children. (Rev. Richard Cadle came to Detroit in 1824, as a missionary of the Protestant Episcopal Church). The schoolhouses and chapel were not yet erected, but we visited their proposed site, and listened with great interest to bright anticipations of the future good that was to be accomplished—the success that was to crown their efforts for taming the heathen and teaching them the knowledge of their Saviour and the blessings of civilized life. The sequel has shown how little the zeal of the few can accomplish, when opposed to the cupidity of the many.

Our evening party went off as parties do elsewhere. The most interesting feature to me, because the most novel, was the conversation of some young ladies to whom I was introduced, natives of Green Bay or its vicinity. Their mother was a Menomonee, but their father was a Frenchman, a descendant of a settler some generations back, and who, there is reason to believe, was a branch of the same family of Grignon to which the daughter of Madame de Sévigné belonged. At least, it is said there are in the possession of the family many old papers and records which would give that impression, although the orthography of the name has become slightly changed. Be that as it may, the Miss Grignons were strikingly dignified, well-bred young ladies, and there was a charm about their soft voices, and original, unsophisticated remarks, very attractive to a stranger.

They opened to me, however, a new field of apprehension; for, on my expressing my great impatience to see my new home, they exclaimed, with a look of wonder,—

"*Vous n'avez donc pas peur des serpens?*"

"Snakes! was it possible there were snakes at Fort Winnebago?"

"At the Portage! oh! yes—one can never walk out for them—rattle-snakes—copper-heads—all sorts!"

I am not naturally timid, but I must confess that the idea of the *serpens sonnettes* and the *siffleurs* was not quite a subject of indifference.

There was one among these young ladies whose tall, graceful figure, rich, blooming complexion, and dark, glancing eye, would have distinguished her in any drawing-room—and another, whose gentle sweetness and cultivated taste made it a matter of universal regret that she was afterwards led to adopt the seclusion of a convent.

Captain Harney and his boat arrived in due time, and active preparations for the comfort of our journey commenced under the kind supervision of Mrs. Doty. The mess-basket was stowed with good things of every description—ham and tongue—biscuit and plum-cake—not to mention the substantiate of crackers, bread, and boiled pork, the latter of which, however, a lady was supposed to be too fastidious to think of touching, even if starving in the woods.

We had engaged three Canadian *voyageurs* to take charge of our tent, mess-basket, and matters and things in general. Their business it was to be to cut the wood for our fires, prepare our meals, and give a helping hand to whatever was going forward. A messenger had also been sent to the *Kakalin*, or rapids, twenty-one miles above, to notify

Wish-tay-yun, (*Le Forgeron*, or Blacksmith, a Menomonee chief), the most accomplished guide through the difficult passes of the river, to be in readiness for our service on a specified day.

In the meantime, we had leisure for one more party, and it was to be a "real Western hop." Everybody will remember that dance at Mrs. Baird's. All the people, young and old, that would be gathered throughout, or, as it was the fashion to express it, *on* Green Bay, were assembled. The young officers were up from Fort Howard, looking so smart in their uniforms—treasures of finery, long uncalled forth, were now brought to light—everybody was bound to do honour to the strangers by appearing in their very best. It was to be an entertainment unequalled by any given before.

All the house was put in requisition for the occasion. Desks and seats were unceremoniously dismissed from Mr. B.'s office, which formed one wing, to afford more space for the dancers. Not only the front portion of the dwelling, but even the kitchen was made fit for the reception of company, in case any primitive visitor, as was sometimes the case, should prefer sitting down quietly there and smoking his cigar. This was an emergency that, in those days, had always to be provided for.

Nothing could exceed the mirth and hilarity of the company. No restraint, but of good manners—no excess of conventionalities—genuine, hearty good-humour and enjoyment, such as pleasant, hospitable people, with just enough of the French element to add zest to anything like amusement, could furnish, to make the entertainment agreeable. In a country so new, and where, in a social gathering, the number of the company was more important than the quality, the circle was not always, strictly speaking, select.

I was aware of this, and was therefore more amused than surprised when a clumsy little man, with a broad, red, laughing face, waddled across the room to where I had taken my seat after a dance, and thus addressed me:

"*Miss* K——, nobody hain't never introduced you to me, but I've seen you a good many times, and I know your husband very well, so I thought I might just as well come and speak to you—my name is A——."

"Ah! Mr. A——, good-evening. I hope you are enjoying yourself. How is your sister?"

"Oh! she is a great deal worse—her cold has got into her eye, and it is all *shot up*."

Then turning full upon a lady, (niece of James Fenimore Cooper), who sat near, radiant with youth and beauty, sparkling with wit and genuine humour:

"Oh! Mrs. Beall," he began, "what a beautiful gown you have got on, and how handsome you do look! I declare you're the prettiest woman in the room, and dance the handsomest."

"Indeed, Mr. A——," replied she, suppressing her love of fun and assuming a demure look, "I am afraid you flatter me."

"No, I don't—I'm in earnest. I've just come to ask you to dance." Such was the penalty of being too charming.

CHAPTER 4

Voyage Up Fox River

It had been arranged that Judge Doty should accompany us in our boat as far as the Butte des Morts, at which place his attendant would be waiting with horses to convey him to Mineral Point, where he was to hold court.

It was a bright and beautiful morning when we left his pleasant home, to commence our passage up the Fox River Captain Harney was proposing to remain a few days longer at "the Bay," but he called to escort us to the boat and instal us in all its comforts.

As he helped me along over the ploughed ground and other inequalities in our way to the riverbank, where the boat lay, he told me how impatiently Mrs. Twiggs, the wife of the commanding officer, (Major David E. Twiggs, a Georgian, entered the army as captain in 1812), who since the past spring had been the only white lady at Fort Winnebago, was now expecting a companion and friend. We had met in New York, shortly after her marriage, and were, therefore, not quite unacquainted. I, for my part, felt sure that when there were two of our sex—when my piano was safely there—when the Post Library which we had purchased should be unpacked—when all should be fairly arranged and settled, we should be, although far away in the wilderness, the happiest little circle imaginable. All my anticipations were of the most sanguine and cheerful character.

It was a moderate-sized Mackinac boat, with a crew of soldiers, and our own three *voyageurs* in addition, that lay waiting for us—a dark-looking structure of some thirty feet in length. Placed in the centre was a frame-work of slight posts, supporting a roof of canvas, with curtains of the same, which might be let down at the sides and ends, after the manner of a country stagecoach, or rolled up to admit the light and air.

In the midst of this little cabin or saloon was placed the box containing my piano, and on it a mattress, which was to furnish us a divan through the day and a place of repose at night, should the weather at any time prove too wet or unpleasant for encamping. The boxes of silver, with which my husband was to pay the annuities due his red children, by treaty-stipulation, were stowed next. Our mess-basket was in a convenient vicinity, and we had purchased a couple of large square covered baskets of the Waubanakees, or New York Indians, to hold our various necessary articles of outward apparel and bedding, and at the same time to answer as very convenient little work or dinner-tables.

As a true daughter of New England, it is to be taken for granted I had not forgotten to supply myself with knitting-work and embroidery. Books and pencils were a matter of course.

The greater part of our furniture, together with the various articles for housekeeping with which we had supplied ourselves in New York and Detroit, were to follow in another boat, under the charge of people whose business it professed to be to take cargoes safely up the rapids and on to Fort Winnebago. This was an enterprise requiring some three weeks of time and a great amount of labour, so that the owners of the goods transported might think themselves happy to receive them at last, however wet, broken, and dilapidated their condition might be. It was for this reason that we took our choicest possessions with us, even at the risk of being a little crowded.

Until now I had never seen a gentleman attired in a coloured shirt, a spotless white collar and bosom being one of those "notions" that "Boston," and consequently New England "folks," entertained of the becoming in a gentleman's *toilette*. Mrs. Cass had laughingly forewarned me that not only calico shirts but patchwork pillowcases were an indispensable part of a travelling equipment; and, thanks to the taste and skill of some tidy little Frenchwoman, I found our divan-pillows all accommodated in the brightest and most variegated garb.

The judge and my husband were gay with the deepest of blue and pink. Each was prepared, besides, with a bright red cap (a *bonnet rouge,* or *tuque,* as the *voyageurs* call it), which, out of respect for the lady, was to be donned only when a hearty dinner, a dull book, or the want of exercise made an afternoon nap indispensable.

The judge was an admirable travelling companion. He had lived many years in the country, had been with General Cass on his expedition to the headwaters of the Mississippi, and had a vast fund of anecdote regarding early times, customs, and inhabitants.

Some instances of the mode of administering justice in those days, I happen to recall.

There was an old Frenchman at the Bay, named Réaume, excessively ignorant and grasping, although otherwise tolerably good-natured. This man was appointed justice of the peace. Two men once appeared before him, the one as plaintiff, the other as defendant. The justice listened patiently to the complaint of the one and the defence of the other; then rising, with dignity, he pronounced his decision:

"You are both wrong. You, Bois-vert," to the plaintiff, "you bring me one load of hay; and you, Crély," to the defendant, "you bring me one load of wood; and now the matter is settled." It does not appear that any exceptions were taken to this verdict.

This anecdote led to another, the scene of which was Prairie du Chien, on the Mississippi.

There was a Frenchman, a justice of the peace, who was universally known by the name of "Old Boilvin." His office was just without the walls of the fort, and it was much the fashion among the officers to lounge in there of a morning, to find sport for an idle hour, and to take a glass of brandy-and-water with the old gentleman, which he called "taking a little *quelque-chose.*"

A soldier, named Fry, had been accused of stealing and killing a calf belonging to M. Rolette, and the constable, a bricklayer of the name of Bell, had been dispatched to arrest the culprit and bring him to trial.

While the gentlemen were making their customary morning visit to the justice, a noise was heard in the entry, and a knock at the door.

"Come in," cried Old Boilvin, rising and walking toward the door.

Bell,—Here, sir, I have brought Fry to you, as you ordered.

Justice—Fry, you great rascal! What for you kill M. Rolette's calf?

Fry,—I did not kill M. Rolette's calf.

Justice (shaking his fist).—You lie, you great —— rascal! Bell, take him to jail. Come, gentlemen, come, let us take a leetle *quelque-chose.*

★★★★★★★★★★★★★★★★

The Canadian boatmen always sing while rowing or paddling, and nothing encourages them so much as to hear the "*bourgeois*" (Master—or, to use the emphatic Yankee term, boss), take the lead in the music. If the passengers, more especially those of the fair sex, join in the refrain, the compliment is all the greater.

Their songs are of a light, cheerful character, generally embodying some little satire or witticism, calculated to produce a spirited, sometimes an uproarious, chorus.

The song and refrain are carried on somewhat in the following style:

BOURGEOIS.—*Par-derrière chez ma tante,*
Par-derrière chez ma tante.

CHORUS.—*Par-derrière chez ma tante,*
Par-derrière chez ma tante.

BOURGEOIS.—*Il y a un coq qui chante,*
Des pommes, des poires, des raves, des choux,
Des figues nouvelles, des raisins doux.

CHORUS.—*Des pommes, des poires, des raves, des choux,*
Des figues nouvelles, des raisins doux.

BOURGEOIS.—*Il y a un coq qui chante,*
Il y a un coq qui chante.

CHORUS.—*Il y a un coq qui chante, etc.*

BOURGEOIS.—*Demande une femme à prendre,*
Des pommes, des poires, des raves, des choux, etc.

CHORUS.—*Des pommes, dos poires, etc.*

BOURGEOIS.—*Demande une femme à prendre,*
Demande une femme à, etc.
And thus, it continues until the advice is given successively,
Ne prenez pas une noire,
Car elles aiment trop à boire,
Ne prenez pas une rousse,
Car elles sont trop jalouses.

And by the time all the different qualifications are rehearsed and objected to, lengthened out by the interminable repetition of the chorus, the shout of the *bourgeois* is heard—

"*Whoop la! à terre, à terre—pour la pipe!*"

It is an invariable custom for the *voyageurs* to stop every five or six miles to rest and smoke, so that it was formerly the way of measuring distances—"so many pipes," instead of "so many miles."

The Canadian melodies are sometimes very beautiful, and a more exhilarating mode of travel can hardly be imagined than a voyage over these waters, amid all the wild magnificence of nature, with the measured strokes of the oar keeping time to the strains of "*Le Rosier Blanc,*"

"*En roulant ma Boule,*" or "*Lève ton pied, ma jolie Bergère.*"

The climax of fun seemed to be in a comic piece, which, however oft repeated, appeared never to grow stale. It was somewhat after this fashion:

BOURGEOIS.—*Michaud est monté dans un prunier,*
Pour treiller des prunes.
La branche a cassé—
CHORUS.—*Michaud a tombé?*
BOURGEOIS.—*Ou est-ce qu'il est?*
CHORUS.—*Il est en bas.*
BOURGEOIS.—*Oh! reveille, reveille, reveille,*
Oh! reveille, Michaud est en haut!

(Michaud climbed into a plum-tree, to gather plums. The branch broke. Michaud fell! Where is he? He is down on the ground. No, he is up in the tree.)

It was always a point of etiquette to look astonished at the luck of Michaud in remaining in the tree, spite of the breaking of the branch, and the joke had to be repeated through all the varieties of fruit-trees that Michaud might be supposed able to climb.

By evening of the first day, we arrived at the *Kakalin*, where another branch of the Grignon family resided. We were very pleasantly entertained, although, in my anxiety to begin my forest life, I would fain have had the tent pitched on the bank of the river, and have laid aside, at once, the indulgences of civilization. This, however, would have been a slight, perhaps an affront; so, we did much better, and partook of the good cheer that was offered us in the shape of hot venison steaks and *crêpes*, and that excellent cup of coffee which none can prepare like a Frenchwoman, and which is so refreshing after a day in the open air.

The *Kakalin* is a rapid of the Fox River, sufficiently important to make the portage of the heavy lading of a boat necessary; the boat itself being poled or dragged up with cords against the current. It is one of a series of rapids and *chûtes*, or falls, which occur between this point and Lake Winnebago, twenty miles above.

The next morning, after breakfast, we took leave of our hosts, and prepared to pursue our journey. The *bourgeois*, from an early hour, had been occupied in superintending his men in getting the boat and its loading over the *Kakalin*. As the late rains had made the paths through the woods and along the banks of the river somewhat muddy and uncomfortable for walking, I was put into an ox-cart, to be jolted over the unequal road; saluting impartially all the stumps and stones that lay in our way, the only means of avoiding which seemed to be when the little, thick-headed Frenchman, our conductor, bethought him of suddenly guiding his cattle into a projecting tree or thorn-bush, to the great detriment not only of my straw bonnet, but of my very eyes.

But we got through at last, and, arriving at the head of the rapids, I found the boat lying there, all in readiness for our re-embarking.

Our Menomonee guide, Wish-tay-yun, a fine, stalwart Indian, with an open, good-humoured, one might almost say *roguish* countenance, came forward to be presented to me.

"*Bon-jour, bon-jour, maman,*" was his laughing salutation. Again, I was surprised, not as before at the French, for to that I had become accustomed, but at the respectable title he was pleased to bestow upon me.

"Yes," said my husband, "you must make up your mind to receive a very numerous and well-grown family, consisting of all the Winnebagoes, Pottowattamies, Chippewas, and Ottawas, together with such Sioux, Sacs and Foxes, and Iowas, as have any point to gain in applying to me. By the first-named tribe in virtue of my office, and by the others as a matter of courtesy, I am always addressed as '*father*'—you, of course, will be their '*mother*.'"

Wish-tay-yun and I were soon good friends, my husband interpreting to me the Chippewa language in which he spoke. We were impatient to be off, the morning being already far advanced, and, all things being in readiness, the word was given:

"*Pousse au large, mes gens!*" (Push out, my men).

At this moment a boat was seen leaving the opposite bank of the river and making towards us. It contained white men, and they showed by signs that they wished to detain us until they came up. They drew near, and we found them to be Mr. Marsh, a missionary among the Waubanakees, or the New York Indians, lately brought into this country, and the Rev. Eleazar Williams, (the supposed *Dauphin* of France), who was at that time living among his red brethren on the right bank of the Fox River.

To persons so situated, even more emphatically than to those of the settlements, the arrival of visitors from the "east countrie" was a godsend indeed. We had to give all the news of various kinds that we had brought—political, ecclesiastical, and social—as well as a tolerably detailed account of what we proposed to do, or rather what we hoped to be able to do, among our native children at the Portage.

I was obliged, for my part, to confess that, being almost entirely a stranger to the Indian character and habits, I was going among them with no settled plans of any kind—general good-will, and a hope of making them my friends, being the only principles, I could lay claim to at present. I must leave it for time and a better acquaintance to show me in what way the principle could be carried out for their greatest good.

Mr. Williams was a dark-complexioned, good-looking man. Having always heard him spoken of, by his relations in Connecticut, as "our Indian cousin," it never occurred to me to doubt his belonging to that race, although I now think that if I had met him elsewhere, I should have taken him for a Spaniard or a Mexican. His complexion had decidedly more of the olive than the copper hue, and his countenance was grave, almost melancholy. He was very silent during this interview, asking few questions, and offering no observations except in reply to some question addressed to him.

It was a hard pull for the men up the rapids. Wish-tay-yun, whose clear, sonorous voice was the bugle of the party, shouted and whooped—each one answered with a chorus, and a still more vigorous effort. By-and-by the boat would become firmly set between two huge stones—

"*Whoop la! whoop! whoop!*"

Another pull, and another, straining every nerve—in vain.

"She will not budge!"

"Men, overboard!" and instantly every rower is over the side and into the water.

By pulling, pushing, and tugging, the boat is at length released from her position, and the men walk along beside her, helping and guiding her, until they reach a space of comparatively smooth water, when they again take their seats and their oars.

It will be readily imagined that there were few songs this day, but very frequent pipes, to refresh the poor fellows after such an arduous service.

It was altogether a new spectacle to me. In fact, I had hardly ever before been called upon to witness severe bodily exertion, and my sympathies and sensibilities were, for this reason, the more enlisted on the occasion. It seemed a sufficient hardship to have to labour in this violent manner; but to walk in cold water up to their waists, and then to sit down in their soaking garments without going near a fire! Poor men! this was too much to be borne! What, then, was my consternation to see my husband, who, shortly after our noon-tide meal, had surprised me by making his appearance in a pair of duck trowsers and light jacket, at the first cry of "Fast, again!" spring over into the water with the men, and "bear a hand" throughout the remainder of the long stretch!

When he returned on board, it was to take the oar of a poor, delicate-looking boy, one of the company of soldiers, who from the first had suffered with bleeding at the nose on every unusual exertion. I was not surprised, on inquiring, to find that this lad was a recruit just entered the service. He passed by the name of Gridley, but that was undoubtedly an assumed name. He had the appearance of having been delicately nurtured, and had probably enlisted without at all appreciating the hardships and discomforts of a soldier's life. This is evident from the dissatisfaction he always continued to feel, until at length he deserted from his post. This was some months subsequent to the time of which I am writing. He was once retaken, and kept for a time in confinement, but immediately on his release deserted again, and his remains were found the following spring, not many miles from the fort. He had died, either of cold or starvation. This is a sad interlude—we will return to our boating.

With all our tugging and toiling, we had accomplished but thirteen miles since leaving the *Kakalin*, and it was already late when we arrived in view of the "Grande Chûte," near which we were to encamp.

★★★★★★★★★★★★★★★★

We had passed the "Little Chûte" (the spot where the town of Appleton now stands) without any further observation than that it required a vast deal of extra exertion to buffet with the rushing stream and come off, as we did, victorious.

The brilliant light of the setting sun was resting on the high wooded banks through which broke the beautiful, foaming, dashing waters of the *chûte*. The boat was speedily turned towards a little headland projecting from the left bank, which had the advantage of a long strip of level ground, sufficiently spacious to afford a good encamping ground. I jumped ashore before the boat was fairly pulled up by the men, and with the judge's help made my way as rapidly as possible to a point lower down the river, from which, he said, the best view of the *chûte* could be obtained. I was anxious to make a sketch before the daylight quite faded away.

The left bank of the river was to the west, and over a portion less elevated than the rest the sun's parting rays fell upon the boat, the men with their red caps and belts, and the two tents already pitched. The smoke now beginning to ascend from the evening fires, the high wooded bank beyond, up which the steep portage path could just be discerned, and, more remote still, the long stretch of waterfall now darkening in the shadow of the overhanging forests, formed a lovely landscape, to which the pencil of an artist could alone do justice.

This was my first encampment, and I was quite enchanted with the novelty of everything about me.

The fires had been made of small saplings and underbrush, hastily collected, the mildness of the weather rendering anything beyond what sufficed for the purposes of cooking and drying the men's clothes, superfluous. The soldiers' tent was pitched at some distance from our own, but not too far for us to hear distinctly their laughter and apparent enjoyment after the fatigues of the day.

Under the careful superintendence of Corporal Kilgour, however, their hilarity never passed the bounds of respectful propriety, and, by the time we had eaten our suppers, cooked in the open air with the simple apparatus of a tea-kettle and frying-pan, we were, one and all, ready to retire to our rest.

The first sound that saluted our ears in the early dawn of the following morning, was the far-reaching call of the *bourgeois*:

"How! how! how!" uttered at the very top of his voice.

All start at that summons, and the men are soon turning out of their tents, or rousing from their slumbers beside the fire, and preparing for the duties of the day.

The fire is replenished, the kettles set on to boil, the mess-baskets opened, and a portion of their contents brought forth to be made ready for breakfast. One Frenchman spreads our mat within the tent, whence the bedding has all been carefully removed and packed up for stowing in the boat. The tin cups and plates are placed around on the new-fashioned table-cloth. The heavy dews make it a little too damp for us to breakfast in the open air; otherwise, our preparations would be made outside, upon the green grass. In an incredibly short time, our smoking coffee and broiled ham are placed before us, to which are added, from time to time, slices of toast brought hot and fresh from the glowing coals.

There is, after all, no breakfast like a breakfast in the woods, with a well-trained Frenchman for master of ceremonies.

It was a hard day's work to which the men now applied themselves, that of dragging the heavy boat up the *chûte*. It had been thought safest to leave the piano in its place on board, but the rest of the lading had to be carried up the steep bank, and along its summit, a distance of some hundreds of rods, to the smooth water beyond, where all the difficulties of our navigation terminated.

The judge kindly took charge of me while "the *bourgeois*" superintended this important business, and with reading, sketching, and strolling about, the morning glided away. Twelve o'clock came, and still the preparations for starting were not yet completed.

In my rambles about to seek out some of the finest of the wild flowers for a bouquet, before my husband's return, I came upon the camp-fire of the soldiers. A tall, red-faced, light-haired young man in fatigue dress was attending a kettle of soup, the savoury steams of which were very attractive.

Seeing that I was observing his occupation, he politely ladled out a tin-cupful of the liquid and offered it to me.

I declined it, saying we should have our dinner immediately.

"They left me here to get their dinner," said he, apparently not displeased to have someone to talk to; "and I thought I might as well make some soup. Down on the German Flats, where I come from, they always like soup."

"Ah! you are from the German Flats—then your name must be Bellinger or Weber."

"No, it isn't—it's Krissman."

"Well, Krissman, how do you like the service?"

"Very well. I was only recruited last summer. I used to ride horse on the *Canawl*, and, as I can blow a horn first-rate, I expect I will soon be able to play on a bugle, and then, when I get to be musician, you know, I shall have extra pay."

I did not know it, but I expressed due pleasure at the information, and wishing Krissman all manner of success in his dreams of ambition, or rather, I should say, of avarice, for the hopes of "extra pay" evidently preponderated over those of fame, I returned to my own quarters.

My husband, with his French tastes, was inclined to be somewhat disappointed when I told him of this little incident, and my refusal of Krissman's soup; but we were soon gratified by seeing his tall, awkward form bearing a kettle of the composition, which he set down before the two gentlemen, by whom, to his infinite satisfaction, it was pronounced excellent.

Everything being at length in readiness, the tents were struck and carried around the Portage, and my husband, the judge, and I followed at our leisure.

The woods were brilliant with wild flowers, although it was so late in the season that the glory of the summer was well-nigh past. But the lupin, the moss-pink, and the yellow wallflower, with all the varieties of the helianthus, the aster, and the solidago, spread their gay charms around. The gentlemen gathered clusters of the bittersweet (celastrus scandens) from the overhanging boughs to make a wreath for my hat, as we trod the tangled pathway, which, like that of Christabel, was

Now in glimmer and now in gloom,

....through the alternations of open glade and shady thicket. Soon, like the same lovely heroine,

We reached the place—right glad we were,

....and, without further delay, we were again on board our little boat and skimming over the now placid waters.

CHAPTER 5

Winnebago Lake—Miss Four-Legs

Our encampment this night was the most charming that can be imagined. Owing to the heavy service the men had gone through in the earlier part of the day, we took but a short stage for the afternoon, and, having pulled some seven or eight miles to a spot a short distance below the "little Butte," we drew in at a beautiful opening among the trees.

The soldiers now made a regular business of encamping, by cutting down a large tree for their fire and applying themselves to the preparing of a sufficient quantity of food for their next day's journey, a long stretch, namely, of twenty-one miles across Winnebago Lake. Our Frenchmen did the same. The fire caught in the light dry grass by which we were surrounded, and soon all was blaze and crackle.

Fortunately, the wind was sufficient to take the flames all in one direction, and, besides, there was not enough fuel to have made them a subject of any alarm. We hopped upon the fallen logs, and dignified the little circumscribed affair with the name of "a prairie on fire." The most serious inconvenience was its having consumed all the dry grass, some armfuls of which, spread under the bear-skin in my tent, I had found, the night before, a great improvement to my place of repose.

Our supper was truly delightful, at the pleasant sunset hour, under the tall trees beside the waters that ran murmuring by; and when the bright, broad moon arose, and shed her flood of light over the scene, so wild yet so beautiful in its vast solitude, I felt that I might well be an object of envy to the friends I had left behind.

But all things have an end, and so must at last my enthusiasm for the beauties around me, and, albeit unwillingly, I closed my tent and took my place within, so near the fall of canvas that I could raise it occasionally and peep forth upon the night.

In time all was quiet. The men had become silent, and appeared to have retired to rest, and we were just sinking to our slumbers, when a heavy tread and presently a bluff voice were heard outside.

"Mr. Kinzie! Mr. Kinzie!"

"Who is there? What is it?"

"I'm Krissman; didn't you mean, sir, that the men should have any liquor tonight?"

"Of course, I did. Has not Kilgour given out your rations?"

"No: he says you did not say anything particular about it, and he was not coming to ask you if you forgot it; but I thought I wouldn't be bashful—I'd just come and ask.'"

"That is right. Tell Kilgour I should like to have him serve out a ration apiece."

"Thank you, sir," in a most cheerful tone; "I'll tell him."

Krissman was getting to be quite a character with us.

A row of a few miles, on the following morning, brought us to Four-Legs' village, (site of the town of Nee-nah) at the entrance to Winnebago Lake, a picturesque cluster of Indian huts, spread around on a pretty green glade, and shaded by fine lofty trees.

We were now fairly in the Winnebago country, and I soon learned that the odd-sounding name of the place was derived from the principal chief of the nation, whose residence it was. The inhabitants were absent, having, in all probability, departed to their wintering grounds. We here took leave of our friend Wish-tay-yun, at the borders of whose country we had now arrived.

"*Bon-jour, Chon!*" (John:) "*bon-jour, maman.*" A hearty shake of the hand completed his *adieu*, as we pushed off into the lake, and left him smoking his *kin-nee-kin-nic*k (bark of the red willow, scraped fine, which is preferred by the Indians to tobacco), and waiting until the spirit should move him to take up his long *Indian trot* towards his home in the Menomonee country.

With him our sunshine seemed to have departed. The skies, hith-

FOUR LEGS VILLAGE. ENTRANCE TO WINNEBAGO LAKE. (The present town of Neenah.)

erto so bright and serene, became overcast, and, instead of the charming voyage we had anticipated over the silver waters of the lake, we were obliged to keep ourselves housed under our canvas shelter, only peeping out now and then to catch a glimpse of the surrounding prospect through the pouring rain.

It was what might have been expected on an autumnal day, but we were unreasonable enough to find it tedious; so, to beguile the time and lessen my disappointment, my husband related to me some incidents of his early history, *apropos* to the subject of "Four-Legs."

While he was living at Prairie du Chien, in the employ of the American Fur Company, the chiefs and other Indians from the Upper Mississippi used frequently to come to the place to sell their furs and peltries, and to purchase merchandise, ammunition, trinkets, etc.

As is usual with all who are not yet acclimated, he was seized with chills and fever. One day, while suffering with an unusually severe access of the latter, a chief of the Four-Legs family, a brother to the one before mentioned, came in to the Company's warehouse to trade. There is no ceremony or restraint among the Indians: so, hearing that Shaw-nee-aw-kee was sick, Four-Legs instantly made his way to him, to offer his sympathy and prescribe the proper remedies.

Everyone who has suffered from ague and the intense fever that succeeds it, knows how insupportable is the protracted conversation of an inconsiderate person, and will readily believe that the longer Four-Legs continued his pratings the higher mounted the fever of the patient, and the more intolerable became the pain of head, back, and limbs.

At length the old man arrived at the climax of what he had to say. "It was not good for a young man, suffering with sickness, and away from his family, to be without a home and a wife. He had a nice daughter at home, handsome and healthy, a capital nurse, the best hand in all the tribe at trapping beaver and musk-rats. He was coming down again in the spring, and he would bring her with him, and Shaw-nee-aw-kee should see that he had told no falsehood about her. Should he go now, and bring his daughter the next time he came?"

Stunned with his importunate babble, and anxious only for rest and quiet, poor Shaw-nee-aw-kee eagerly assented, and the chief took his departure.

So nearly had his disorder been aggravated to delirium, that the young man forgot entirely, for a time, the interview and the proposal which had been made him. But it was recalled to his memory some months after, when Four-Legs made his appearance, bringing with him a squaw of mature age, and a very *Hecate* for ugliness. She carried on her shoulders an immense pack of furs, which, approaching with her awkward *criss-cross* gait, she threw at his feet, thus marking, by an Indian custom, her sense of the relation that existed between them.

The conversation with her father now flashed across his mind, and he began to be sensible that he had got into a position that it would require some skill to extricate himself from.

He bade one of the young clerks take up the pack and carry it into the magazine where the furs were stored; then he coolly went on talking with the chief about indifferent matters.

Miss Four-Legs sat awhile with a sulky, discontented air; at length she broke out,—

"Humph! he seems to take no more notice of me than if I was nobody!"

He again turned to the clerk.—"Give her a calico shirt and half a dozen bread-tickets."

This did not dissipate the gloom on her countenance. Finding that he must commence the subject, the father says,—

"Well, I have brought you my daughter, according to our agreement. How do you like her?"

"Ah, yes—she is a very nice young woman, and would make a first-rate wife, I have no doubt. But do you know a very strange thing has happened since you were here? Our father, Governor Cass, (General Cass was then Governor of Michigan, and Superintendent of the Northwestern Indians), has sent for me to come to Detroit, that he may send me among the Wyandottes and other nations to learn their customs and manners. Now, if I go, as I shall be obliged to do, I shall be absent two or three years,—perhaps four. What then? Why, the people will say, Shaw-nee-aw-kee has married Four-Legs' daughter, and then has hated her and run away from her, and so everybody will laugh at her, and she will be ashamed. It will be better to take some good, valuable presents, blankets, guns, etc., and to marry her to one of her own people, who will always stay by her and take care of her."

The old man was shrewd enough to see that it was wisest to make the best bargain he could. I have no doubt it cost a round sum to settle the matter to the satisfaction of the injured damsel, though I have never been able to ascertain how much. This I know, that the young gentleman took care not to make his next bargain while in a fit of the ague. The lady up on the Mississippi is called, in derision, by his name to this day.

About midway of the lake, we passed Garlic Island—a lovely spot, deserving of a more attractive name. It belonged, together with the village on the opposite shore, to "Wild Cat," a fat, jolly, good-natured fellow, by no means the formidable animal his name would imply.

He and his band were absent, like their neighbours of Four-Legs' village, so there was nothing to vary the monotony of our sail. It was too wet to sing, and the men, although wrapped in their overcoats, looked like drowned chickens. They were obliged to ply their oars with unusual vigour to keep themselves warm and comfortable, and thus probably felt less than we, the dullness and listlessness of the cold, rainy, October day.

Towards evening the sun shone forth. We had passed into the Fox River, and were just entering that beautiful little expanse known as Butte des Morts Lake, at the farther extremity of which we were to encamp for the night.

The water along its shores was green with the fields of wild rice, the gathering of which, just at this season, is an important occupation of the Indian women. They push their canoes into the thick masses of the rice, bend it forward over the side with their paddles, and then beat the ripe husks off the stalks into a cloth spread in the canoe. After this, it is rubbed to separate the grain from the husk, and fanned in the open air. It is then put in their cordage bags and packed away for winter use. The grain is longer and more slender than the Carolina rice—it is of a greenish-olive colour, and, although it forms a pleasant article of food, it is far from being particularly nutritive. The Indians are fond of it in the form of soup, with the addition of birds or venison.

CHAPTER 6

Breakfast at Betty More's

The earth, the trees, and the shrubbery were all too much filled with the heavy rain which had fallen to allow us to think of encamping, so we made arrangements to bestow ourselves in our little saloon for the night. It was rather a difficult matter to light a fire, but among the underbrush, in a wild, undisturbed spot, there will always be found some fragments of dried branches, and tufts of grass which the rain has not reached, and by the assistance of the spunk, or light-wood, with which travellers always go well provided, a comforting fire was at length blazing brightly.

After our chilling, tedious day, it was pleasant to gather round it, to sit on the end of the blazing logs, and watch the Frenchmen preparing our supper—the kettle nestling in a little nook of bright glowing coals—the slices of ham browning and crisping on the forked sticks, or "*broches,*" which the *voyageurs* dexterously cut, and set around the burning brands—the savoury messes of "pork and onions" hissing in the frying-pan, always a tempting regale to the hungry Frenchmen. Truly, it needs a wet, chilly journey, taken nearly fasting, as ours had been, to enable one to enjoy to its full extent that social meal—a supper.

The bright sun, setting amid brilliant masses of clouds, such as are seen only in our Western skies, gave promise of a fine day on the morrow, with which comforting assurance we were glad to take our leave of him, and soon after of each other.

We had hardly roused up the following morning, in obedience to the call of the *bourgeois*, when our eyes were greeted with the sight of an addition to our company—a tall, stalwart, fine-looking young *mitiff*, or half-breed, accompanied by two or three Indians. Vociferous and joyous were the salutations of the latter to their "father" and their new "mother." They were the first Winnebagoes I had seen, and they were decidedly not the finest specimens of their tribe. The *mitiff*, a scion of the wide-spreading tree of the Grignons, was the bearer of an invitation to us from Judge Law, who, with one or two Green Bay friends, was encamped a few miles above, to come and breakfast with him in his tent. We had not dreamed of finding white neighbours here, but our vicinity could be no secret to them, as long as there was an Indian in the neighbourhood. So, delaying only for the soldiers to finish their breakfast, we pushed on for the "*Butte des Morts,*" or, as Mrs. A. always persisted in calling it, *Betty More's*.

The white tent of the judge gleamed in the morning sun as we approached the little rising ground on which it stood. The river was filled with canoes, paddled principally by squaws. Many Indians were to be seen on the banks, all with their guns and hunting accoutrements, for the air was filled in every direction with flocks of teal, which at this season are most abundant and delicious. The immense fields of wild rice abounding here and in the little lake below, make this vicinity their favourite place of resort in the autumn months. The effect of this nourishing food is to make the flesh of the birds so fat, so white, and so tender, that a caution is always given to a young sportsman to fire only at such as fly very low, for if shot high in the air they are bruised to pieces and rendered unfit for eating by their fall to the ground.

We were hemmed in by a little fleet of canoes which surrounded us, the women chattering, laughing, and eagerly putting forward their little wooden bowls of fresh cranberries as an offering of welcome to me.

I amused myself with tossing crackers to them, some of which would reach them, others would fall into the water, and then such a scrambling and shouting! Hands and paddles were in requisition, and loud was the triumph of her who was successful in reaching a floating one.

Among the Indians with whom Shaw-nee-aw-kee was now engaged in shaking hands, and who all seemed old friends, were many fine, straight, well-formed figures, all of them exhibiting frames capable of enduring fatigue and the hardships of their mode of life. One was describing with much gesticulation the abundance of the game in the neighbourhood, and he seemed greatly delighted at receiving a quantity of ammunition, with which he instantly departed to make good his boasts in the matter.

After walking a short distance, we reached the tent, where I was introduced to Judge Law and a pleasant little grey-haired French gentleman of the name of Porlier. Several *voyageurs* and half-breeds were near, the former busily at work, the latter lounging for the most part, and going through with what they had to do with a sort of listless indifference.

The contrast between the "all-alive" air of the one class and the apathetic manner of the other, was quite striking.

After a short conversation among the members of the party, breakfast was announced, and we entered the tent and took our seats on the ground around the Indian mat which supplied the place of a table.

The post of honour, namely, the *head* of the table, was of course given to me, so that I could not only look around upon the circle of the company, but also enjoy a fine view out of the open door of the tent, and take an observation of all that was going on at the *side-table* outside. Judge Doty sat opposite me, with his back to the opening of the tent, and the other gentlemen on either hand. We had for our waiter the tall *mitiff* who had been the messenger of the morning. He was still in the same garb—calico shirt, bright-coloured scarf around his waist, and on his head a straw hat encircled with a band of black ostrich feathers, the usual dress of his class.

The tin cups which were to hold our coffee were duly set around, then breakfast-plates of the same metal, with knives and forks; then followed the viands, among the most conspicuous of which was a large tin pan of boiled ducks.

The judge, wishing to show, probably, that, although we were in the vast wilderness, all fastidious nicety had not been left behind, took up the plate which had been set before him, and, seeing something adhering to it which did not exactly please him, handed it over his shoulder to Grignon, requesting him to wipe it carefully. Grignon complied by pulling a black silk barcelona handkerchief out of his bosom, where it had been snugly tucked away to answer any occasion that might present itself, and, giving the tin a furious polishing, handed it back again. The judge looked at it with a smile of approbation, and giving a glance around the table as much as to say, "You see how I choose to have things done," applied himself to his breakfast.

The trail for Fort Winnebago then led from the shore opposite Butte des Morts, through Ma-zhee-gaw-gaw swamp, and past Green Lake, and it was well for the judge that his horses stood waiting for him to "mount and away" as early as possible after breakfast, or I am afraid the story I should have been tempted to tell would have made his ride an uncomfortable one throughout the day.

We had hardly finished breakfast when our hunter, who had received the ammunition, returned, bringing with him about fifty fine ducks, which he had shot in little more than an hour. From that time until the close of our journey our supply of these delicate birds was never wanting.

Chapter 7

"Butte Des Morts"—Lake Puckaway

The Butte des Morts, or Hillock of the Dead, was the scene long since, (1714), of a most sanguinary battle between the French and the Mis-qua-kees, or Foxes. So great was the carnage in this engagement, that the memory of it has been perpetuated by the gloomy appellation given to the mound where the dead were buried. The Foxes up to this time had inhabited the shores of the river to which they had given their name, but, being completely overwhelmed and beaten in this conflict, they retired to the neighbourhood of the Mississippi, and sought an asylum among their allies, the Saukies, or, as they are now called, the Sauks, with whom they became gradually incorporated, until the combined tribes came to be known, as at present, by the name of "Sauks and Foxes."

Among the French inhabitants of the upper country, each tribe of Indians has a particular appellation, descriptive of some peculiarity of either their habits or their personal appearance. Thus, the Chippewas, from their agility, are denominated "*Sauteurs*," or Jumpers; the Ottawas, the "*Courtes-oreilles*," or Short-ears. The Menomonees, from the wild rice so abundant in their country, are called "*Folles Avoines;*"—the Winnebagoes, from their custom of wearing the fur of a polecat on their legs when equipped for war, are termed "*les Puans*,"—the Pottowattamies, from their uncleanly habits, "*les Poux*;"—the Foxes are "*les Renards*," etc. etc.

Hence you will never hear a French or half-breed resident of the country mention an Indian in any other style. "Such a person is a '*Court-oreille.*'" "Is that woman a 'Winnebago'?" "No, she is a '*Folle Avoine.*'" In this manner a stranger is somewhat puzzled at first to classify the acquaintances he forms.

All the native friends with whom we were here surrounded were "*les Puans*," or, to use their own euphonious appellation, the "*Hotshung-rahs*."

Having with great regret said *adieu* to our friend Judge Doty, whose society had contributed so much to the pleasure of our trip, and whose example, moreover, had given us a valuable lesson to take things as we find them, we bade goodbye at an early hour after breakfast to our kind hosts, and set forward on our journey.

From Butte des Morts to the Portage, the distance by land is about seventy miles; by water, it is not less than a hundred and thirty, so serpentine is the course of the river through the low swampy prairies which stretch over a great portion of this part of the country.

About six miles above the *butte*, a tolerably broad stream, called Wolf River, joins the Fox, and as it is much the more direct and promising of the two, strangers have sometimes mistaken it for the main stream, and journeyed up it a considerable distance before discovering, to their great chagrin, that they must retrace their steps.

Beyond this place, the river begins to play its pranks with the compass. As I was always looking out for pretty scenery to sketch, I was at one spot much attracted by a picturesque group on a bank quite close to the stream. There were broad overhanging trees, and two or three *wigwams* nestled under their shade. Bright-looking little children, quite unencumbered with clothing, were sporting about, and their two mothers were sitting on the ground, engaged in the manufacture of a mat for their lodge. It was a pretty scene, and I commenced a sketch. As usual, the whole party on the bank set up a shout when they recognised Shaw-nee-aw-kee,—

"*Ee-awn-chee-wee-rah, Hee-nee-kar-ray-kay-noo.*" (Father! How do you do?)

It was an occasion on which they became demonstrative. After a little time, we proceeded, and I went on to complete my drawing. The sun kept coming more and more into the wrong place. He had been just behind me, presently he was on my left hand, now he was straight ahead. I moved from time to time; at length the sun was decidedly on my right hand. What could be the matter? I looked up. "Oh, here is a pretty scene; I must have this too! But how surprisingly like the one I have just finished, only in a different direction." Again, we were greeted with shouts and laughter; it was the same spot which we had passed not an hour before, and, having taken a circuit of nearly four miles, we had returned to find that we had made an actual progress of only the width of the bank on which the trees and *wigwams* stood. Decidedly not very encouraging to an impatient traveller.

We reached Lake Puckaway late in the evening of our second day from Butte des Morts. Here lived a white man named Gleason, the same concerning whom, owing to his vast powers of exaggeration, poor Hooe was fond of uttering his little pun, "All is not gold that Gleasons." We did not seek shelter at his house, for, late as the season was, we found the shore so infested with mosquitoes that we were glad to choose a spot as far as possible from the bank, and make ourselves comfortable in our boat.

This lake has its name from the long flags or rushes which are found in its waters in great abundance, and of which the squaws manufacture the coarse matting used in covering their *wigwams*. Their mode of fabricating this is very primitive and simple. Seated on the ground, with the rushes laid side by side, and fastened at each extremity, they pass their shuttle, a long flat needle made of bone, to which is attached a piece of cordage formed of the bark of a tree, through each rush, thus confining it very closely, and making a fine substantial mat. These mats are seldom more than five or six feet in length, as a greater size would be inconvenient in adjusting and preparing the lodges.

It is a species of labour usually assigned to the elder women of the family. When they become broken down and worn out with exposure and hardship, so that they cannot cut down trees, hoe corn, or carry heavy burdens, they are set to weaving mats, taking care of the children, and disciplining the dogs, with which every Indian lodge abounds.

Lac de Boeuf, or Buffalo Lake, into which our course next brought us, is a lovely sheet of water. In some places its banks are exceedingly picturesque, with beautiful headlands jutting out into the clear depths, where they, and the magnificent groups of trees which crown them, lie reflected as in a mirror. Now and then we would catch a glimpse of deer darting across the glades which at intervals opened through the woodlands, or a pair of sand-hill cranes would rise, slowly flapping their wings, and seek a place of more undisturbed repose. The flocks of teal now skimming the surface of the water, now rising higher towards the shelter of the forests, tempted our sportsman sorely; but, as there was little prospect of finding his game when it was brought down, he did not give way to the wanton pleasure of shooting merely to destroy life.

In quitting this charming lake, and again entering the narrow, tortuous course of the river, we bade *adieu* to everything like scenery, until we should reach our journey's end.

We had now seventy miles to pass through a country perfectly monotonous and uninteresting, the distastefulness of which was aggravated by the knowledge that we could, had we been provided with horses or a carriage of any kind, have crossed over to the Portage from Gleason's, through a pleasant country, in little more than three hours. Even our great resource, the cheering, animating songs of our *voyageurs*, was out of the question; for the river, though deep, is so narrow that, in many places, there is no room for the regular play of the oars; and the voices of Frenchmen can never "keep tune" unless their oars can "keep time." Lapierre, one of our men, did his best with a paddle, or, as he called it, the "*little row*," but it was to no purpose—it *would not go.*

Besides this, the wild rice abounds to such an extent in many places, that it almost completely obstructs the progress of even a moderate-sized boat, so that a passage through its tangled masses is with difficulty forced by the oars. Tedious and monotonous as was the whole course of the two following days, the climax of impatience and discouragement was not reached until we arrived in sight of the white walls of Fort Winnebago, looking down from a rising ground upon the vast expanse of low land through which the river winds.

The Indians have a tradition that a vast serpent once lived in the

FORT WINNEBAGO IN 1831. (Portage City)

waters of the Mississippi, and that, taking a break to visit the Great Lakes, he left his trail through the prairies, which, collecting the waters from the meadows and the rains of heaven as they fell, at length became the Fox River.

The little lakes along its course were probably the spots where he flourished about in his uneasy slumbers at night. He must have played all the antics of a kitten in the neighbourhood of the Portage. When the fort was first pointed out to me, I exclaimed, with delight, "Oh, we shall be there in half an hour!"

"Not quite so soon," said my husband, smiling. "Wait and see." We sat and watched. We seemed approaching the very spot where we were to disembark. We could distinguish the officers and a lady on the bank waiting to receive us. Now we were turning our backs on them, and shooting out into the prairie again. *Anon* we approached another bank, on which was a range of comfortable-looking log houses. "That's the Agency," said my husband; "the largest house belongs to Paquette, the interpreter, and the others are the dwellings of our Frenchmen. The little building, just at the foot of the hill, is the blacksmith's shop, kept there by the government, that the Indians may have their guns and traps mended free of expense."

"But are we going to stop there?"

"No; do you not see we are going back to the fort?"

And, to be sure, our course had now turned, and we were setting in our first direction. In this manner, after tacking to the right and left and putting backwards and forwards during the greater part of two hours, we at length reached the little landing, on which the assembled party stood ready to greet us.

Chapter 8

Fort Winnebago

Major and Mrs. Twiggs, and a few of the younger officers (for nearly all of the older ones were absent), with our brother Robert, or, as he is called throughout all the Indian tribes, "Bob," gave us a cordial welcome—how cordial those alone can know who have come, like us, to a remote, isolated home in the wilderness. The major insisted on our taking possession at once of vacant quarters in the fort, instead of at "the Agency," as had been proposed.

"No—we must be under the same roof with them. Mrs. Twiggs had been without a companion of her own sex for more than four months, and would certainly not hear of a separation now. But we must be their guests until the arrival of the boats containing our furniture," which, under the care of our old acquaintance, Hamilton Arndt, was making its way slowly up from Green Bay.

A dinner had been prepared for us. This is one of the advantages of the zigzag approach by the Fox River—travellers never take their friends by surprise; and when the whole circle sat down to the hospitable board, we were indeed a merry company.

After dinner Mrs. Twiggs showed me the quarters assigned to us, on the opposite side of the spacious hall. They consisted of two large rooms on each of the three floors or stories of the building. On the ground-floor the front room was vacant. The one in the rear was to be the sleeping-apartment, as was evident from a huge, unwieldy bedstead, of proportions amply sufficient to have accommodated Og, the King of Bashan, with Mrs. Og and the children into the bargain. We could not repress our laughter; but the bedstead was nothing to another structure which occupied a second corner of the apartment.

This edifice had been built under the immediate superintendence of one of our young lieutenants, and it was plain to be seen that upon it both he and the soldiers who fabricated it had exhausted all their architectural skill. The timbers of which it was composed had been grooved and carved; the pillars that supported the front swelled in and out in a most fanciful manner; the doors were not only panelled, but radiated in a way to excite the admiration of all unsophisticated eyes. A similar piece of workmanship had been erected in each set of quarters, to supply the deficiency of closets, an inconvenience which had never occurred, until too late, to the bachelors who planned them.

The three apartments of which each structure was composed, were unquestionably designed for clothes-press, store-room, and china-closet; such, at least, were the uses to which Mrs. Twiggs had appropriated the one assigned to her. There was this slight difficulty, that in the latter the shelves were too close to admit of setting in even a gravy-boat, but they made up in number what was wanting in space. We christened the whole affair, in honour of its projector, a "Davis," thus placing the first laurel on the brow of one who was afterwards to signalise himself in Cabinet making of quite a different character.

The bold promontory on which Fort Winnebago was built looked down upon the extended prairie and the Fox River on one side, and on the other stretched away into the thickly-wooded ridge that led off to Belle Fontaine and Lake Puckaway.

In front lay an extent of meadow, across which was the Portage road, of about two miles in length, leading between the Fox and the Wisconsin Rivers. Teams of oxen and a driver were kept at the Agency by the government, to transport the canoes of the Indians across this place, which at many seasons was wet, miry, and almost impassable.

The woods were now brilliant with the many tints of autumn, and the scene around was further enlivened by groups of Indians, in all directions, and their lodges, which were scattered here and there, in the vicinity of the Agency buildings. On the low grounds might be seen the white tents of the traders, already prepared to furnish winter supplies to the Indians, in exchange for the annuity money they were about to receive.

A great concourse had been for many days assembling in anticipation of the payment, which was expected to take place as soon as Shaw-nee-aw-kee should arrive with the silver. Preparatory to this event, the great chief of the nation, Four-Legs, whose village we had passed at the entrance to Winnebago Lake, had thought proper to take a little carouse, as is too apt to be the custom when the savages come into the neighbourhood of a sutler's establishment. In the present instance, the facilities for a season of intoxication had been augmented by the presence on the ground of some traders, too regardless of the very stringent laws prohibiting the sale of liquor to the Indians.

Poor Four-Legs could not stand this full tide of prosperity. Unchecked by the presence of his Father, the agent, he carried his indulgence to such excess that he fell a victim in the course of a few days. His funeral had been celebrated with unusual pomp the day before our arrival, and great was my disappointment at finding myself too late to witness all the ceremonies.

His body, according to their custom, having been wrapped in a blanket, and placed in a rude coffin, along with his guns, tomahawk, pipes, and a quantity of tobacco, had been carried to the most elevated point of the hill opposite the fort, followed by an immense procession of his people, whooping, beating their drums, howling, and making altogether what is emphatically termed a "*pow-wow.*"

After the interment of the body, a stake was planted at its head, on which was painted in vermilion a series of hieroglyphics, descriptive of the great deeds and events of his life. The whole was then surrounded with pickets of the trunks of the tamarack-trees, and hither the friends would come for many successive days to renew the expression of their grief, and to throw over the grave tobacco and other offerings to the Great Spirit.

It was a consolation to find that, although delayed, we were yet in time to furnish a quantity of white cotton for a flag to wave over the grave, and also to pay a considerable bill at the sutler's for the different articles that had been found necessary for the funeral parade—it being a duty expected of their Father to bury the dead suitably.

The funeral observances in honour of the chief had not yet ceased. Throughout the day, and all that night, the sound of instruments, mingled with doleful lamentations, and with the discordant whoops and yells of those in a partial state of intoxication, filled the air, and disturbed our repose. To these were added occasionally the plaintive sounds of the Indian flute, upon which the young savage plays when he is in love. Grief and whiskey had made their hearts tender, and the woods resounded to their melancholy strains.

Early the following morning, before I left my room, I was startled by the sounds of lamentation and woe proceeding from the adjoining apartment. On entering it, I found several squaws seated on the floor, with downcast looks expressive of condolence and sympathy, while in their midst sat a little ugly woman, in tattered garments, with blackened face and dishevelled hair, sobbing and wailing bitterly.

Not doubting they were the family of the deceased chief, I was quite troubled at my inability to express, otherwise than by gestures, my participation in their sorrows.

Unacquainted as I was with their customs, I took it for granted from their wretched appearance that poverty and destitution formed one of the sources of their affliction. One of the party, at least, seemed in the very depths of misery. "Can it be possible," said I to myself, "that this poor creature has only these scanty rags to cover her?"

Stepping back to my own room, I brought out a pretty calico wrapper, which I presented to the little, dirty, blackened object. She took it, and commenced a fresh series of sobbing and sighing. I made signs to her to put it on, opening it and explaining to her how it was to be worn, and recommending to her, by gestures, to lose no time in making herself more comfortable.

At this, the other women burst into a laugh.

"Very *mal-à-propos*," thought I, "and somewhat unfeeling." At that moment my husband, entering, explained to me that the chief mourner was Madame Four-Legs, the widow; that she had undoubtedly a comfortable wardrobe at home, but that it was part of the etiquette of mourning to go for a season with neglected persons and blackened faces. All this was told me in the intervals of shaking hands, and offering and receiving condolences in the most uncouth, guttural language I had ever heard. Their father at length dismissed them, with a promise of some presents to help dry up their tears.

It must not be inferred that the grief of the poor little widow was not sincere. On the contrary, she was greatly attached to her husband, and had had great influence not only with him but with the nation at large. She was a Fox woman, and spoke the Chippewa, which is the court language among all the tribes, so that she was often called upon to act as interpreter, and had, in fact, been in the habit of accompanying her husband, and assisting him by her counsels upon all occasions. She was a person of great shrewdness and judgment, and, as I afterwards experienced, of strong and tenacious affections.

After breakfast I received a visit from the principal chiefs, who had put on their best of apparel and paint to receive their new mother.

There was Naw-kaw, or Kar-ray-mau-nee, "the Walking Turtle," now the principal chief of the nation, a stalwart Indian, with a broad, pleasant countenance, the great peculiarity of which was an immense under lip, hanging nearly to his chin. There was the old Day-kau-ray, the most noble, dignified, and venerable of his own, or indeed of any tribe. His fine Roman countenance, rendered still more striking by his bald head, with one solitary tuft of long silvery hair neatly tied and falling back on his shoulders; his perfectly neat, appropriate dress, almost without ornament, and his courteous demeanour, never laid aside under any circumstances, all combined to give him the highest place in the consideration of all who knew him. It will hereafter be seen that his traits of character were not less grand and striking than were his personal appearance and deportment.

There was Black-Wolf, whose lowering, surly face was well described by his name. The fierce expression of his countenance was greatly heightened by the masses of heavy black hair hanging round it, quite contrary to the usual fashion among the Winnebagoes. They, for the most part, remove a portion of their hair, the remainder of which is drawn to the back of the head, clubbed and ornamented with beads, ribbons, cock's feathers, or, if they are so entitled, an eagle's feather for every scalp taken from an enemy.

There was Talk-English, a remarkably handsome, powerful young Indian, who received his name in the following manner. He was one of a party of sixteen Winnebagoes who had, by invitation, accompanied their Agent and Major Forsyth (or the Chippewa, as he was called) on a visit to the President at Washington, the year previous.

On the journey, the question naturally addressed to them by people not familiar with Western Indians was,—

"Do you talk English?"

The young fellow, being very observant, came to his father. "What do they mean by this? Everybody says to me, *talk English!*"

The Agent interpreted the words to him. "Ah, very well."

The next place they arrived at was Lockport, in the State of New York. Jumping off the canal-boat upon the lock, he ran up to the first man he met, and, thrusting forward his face, cried out, "Talk Eengeesh?"

"Yes," said the man; "do you talk English?"

"Ya-as."

From that time forward he always bore the name of *Talk-English*, and was registered on the pay-rolls by a title of which he was not a little proud.

Hoo-wau-ne-kah, "the Little Elk," was another of the distinguished men of the tribe. He had likewise been at Washington. Henry Clay, when he visited them, after looking carefully at the countenances and bearing of all the members of the deputation, had indicated him as the one possessing the greatest talent; and he was greatly pleased when informed that he was the principal orator of the nation, and decidedly superior in abilities to any other individual of the tribe.

Wild-Cat, our Indian Falstaff in all save the cowardice and falsehood, I have already mentioned.

Then there was Kau-ray-kaw-saw-kaw, "the White Crow," a Rock River Indian, who afterwards distinguished himself as the friend of the whites during the Sauk war. He was called by the French "*le Borgne,*" from having lost an eye; and the black silk handkerchief which he wore drooping over the left side of his face to disguise the blemish, taken with his native costume, gave him a very singular appearance.

There was a nephew of the defunct chief Four-Legs, to whom with justice was given, by both whites and Indians, the appellation of "the Dandy." When out of mourning his dress was of the most studied and fanciful character. A shirt (when he condescended to wear any) of the brightest colours, ornamented with innumerable rows of silver brooches set thickly together; never less than two pairs of silver arm-bands; leggings and *moccasins* of the most elaborate embroidery in ribbons and porcupine-quills; everything that he could devise in the shape of ornament hanging to his club of hair behind; a feather fan in one hand, and in the other a mirror, in which he contemplated himself every five minutes; these, with the variety and brilliancy of the colours upon his face, the suitable choice and application of which occupied no small portion of the hours allotted to his toilet, made up the equipment of young Four-Legs.

This devotion to dress and appearance seemed not altogether out of place in a youthful dandy; but we had likewise an old one of the same stamp. Pawnee Blanc, or the White Pawnee, surpassed his younger competitor, if possible, in attention to his personal attractions. Upon the present occasion he appeared in all his finery, and went through the customary salutations with an air of solemn dignity, then walked, as did the others, into the parlour (for I had received them in the hall), where they all seated themselves upon the floor. Fortunately, the room was now bare of furniture, but "alas!" thought I, "for my pretty carpet, if this is to be the way they pay their respects to me!" I watched the falling of the ashes from their long pipes, and the other inconveniences of the use of tobacco, or *kin-nee-kin-nick*, with absolute dismay.

The visit of the chiefs was succeeded by one from the interpreter and his wife, with all the Canadian and half-breed women, whose husbands found employment at the Agency or at the American Fur Company's establishment.

By this time my piano had been taken from its case and set up in our quarters. To our great joy, we found it entirely uninjured. Thanks to the skill of Nunns and Clark, not a note was out of tune.

The women, to whom it was an entire novelty, were loud in their exclamations of wonder and delight.

"*Eh-h-h! regardez donc! Quelles inventions! Quelles merveilles!*" ("Only look! what inventions! what wonders!")

One, observing the play of my fingers reflected in the nameboard, called in great exultation to her companions. She had discovered, as she thought, the hidden machinery by which the sounds were produced, and was not a little mortified when she was undeceived.

CHAPTER 9

Housekeeping

As the boats might be expected in a few days, it was thought best to begin at once what preparations were in my power towards housekeeping. These were simply the fitting and sewing of my carpets, in which I was kindly assisted by Mrs. Twiggs; and, the wife of one of our

Frenchmen having come over from the Agency and made everything tidy and comfortable, the carpets were soon tacked down, and the rooms were ready for the reception of the rest of the furniture.

I had made many fruitless attempts, both in Detroit and Green Bay, to procure a servant-woman to accompany me to my new home. Sometimes one would present herself, but, before we could come to a final agreement, the thoughts of the distance, of the savages, the hardships of the journey, or, perhaps, the objections of friends, would interfere to break off the negotiation; so that I had at length been obliged to rest satisfied with the simple hope held out by my husband, that one of his French *employés*, with his wife, would be contented to take up their abode with us.

In this state of things, all difficulties seemed to be obviated by the proposal of Major Twiggs, that we should take into our service a young coloured girl whom he had brought from Buffalo, in the spring, to wait on Mrs. T. until her own servants should arrive from the South.

Louisa was accordingly sent for, an uncommonly handsome young negress, with an intelligent but very demure countenance, who called herself fifteen years of age, but who, from the progress in vice and iniquity I afterwards discovered her to have made, must have been at least several years older. Be that as it may, she now seemed to have no fault but carelessness and inexperience, both of which I had great hopes she would get the better of, under careful training.

My first week's visit with Mrs. Twiggs had just expired when word was given that the boats were in sight—the boats that contained our furniture—and the expected arrival of Louis Philippe to visit Queen Victoria could scarcely have created a more universal sensation, than did this announcement in our little community. Although we knew that some hours must yet elapse before they could reach the spot for disembarkation, we were constantly on the watch, and at length all the young officers, followed by as many of the soldiers as were off duty, accompanied Mr. Kinzie down the bank to the landing, to witness and, if necessary, to assist in helping everything safe to land.

Sad was the plight in which matters were found. The water poured out of the corners of the boxes as they were successively hoisted on shore. Too impatient to wait until they could be carried up to the fort, the gentlemen soon furnished themselves with, hammers and hatchets, and fell eagerly to work, opening the boxes to explore the extent of the damage. Alas for the mahogany! not a piece from which the edges and veneering were not starting. It had all the appearance of having lain under the Grande Chûte for days. Poor Hamilton was load in his protestations and excuses.

It was the fault of the men, of the weather, of the way the things were packed. "Confound it! he had taken the best care of the things he possibly could—better than he had ever taken before—it *would* get done!"

There was nothing but to be patient and make the best of it. And when the pretty sideboard and work-table had been thoroughly rubbed and set up, and all the little knick-knacks arranged on the mantel-piece—when the white curtains were hung at the windows, and the chairs and dining-table each in its proper place in relation to the piano, our parlour was pronounced "magnificent." At least so seemed to think Hamilton, who came to give one admiring look, and to hear the music of the piano, which was a perfect novelty to him. His description of it to the young officers, after his return to the Bay, was expressive of his admiration and wonder—"There it stood on its four legs! Anybody might go up and touch it!"

In due time the dinner- and tea-sets were carefully bestowed in the "Davis," together with sundry jars of sweetmeats that I had prepared in Detroit; the iron and tin utensils were placed in a neat cupboard in the kitchen, of which my piano-box supplied the frame; the barrel of eggs and tubs of butter, brought all the way from Ohio, were ranged in the store-room; a suitable quantity of salt pork and flour was purchased from the commissary; and, there being no lack of game of every description, the offering of our red children, we were ready to commence housekeeping.

The first dinner in her own home is an era in the life of a young housekeeper. I shall certainly never forget mine. While I was in the lower regions superintending my very inexpert little cook, my husband made his appearance, to say that, as the payment (then the all-absorbing topic of interest) would not commence until afternoon, he had invited M. Rolette, Mr. Hempstead, and four other gentlemen to dine with us.

"So unexpected—so unprepared for?"

"Never mind; give them anything you have. They have been living for some days in tents, and anything will taste well to them."

My dinner had been intended to consist chiefly of a venison pasty, and fortunately the only dish among my store was of very large proportions, so that there was already smoking in the oven a pie of a size nearly equal to the famous Norwich pudding; thus, with some trifling additions to the bill of fare, we made out very well, and the master of the house had the satisfaction of hearing the impromptu dinner very much commended by his six guests.

Chapter 10

Indian Payment—Mrs. Washington

There were two divisions of the Winnebago Indians, one of which was paid by the agent, at the Portage, the other at Prairie du Chien, by General Street. The first, between four and five thousand in number, received, according to treaty stipulations, fifteen thousand dollars annually, besides a considerable amount of presents, and a certain number of rations of bread and pork, to be issued in times of emergency throughout the year.

The principal villages of this division of the tribe were at Lake Winnebago, Green and Fox Lakes, the Barribault, Mud Lake, the Four Lakes, Kosh-ko-nong, and Turtle Creek. Messengers were dispatched, at or before the arrival of the annuity-money, to all the different villages, to notify the heads of families or lodges to assemble at "the Portage."

When arrived, the masters of families, under their different chiefs, give in their names, and the number in their lodges, to be registered. As, in paying, a certain sum of money is apportioned to each individual, it is, of course, an object to the head of a lodge to make the number registered as great as possible. Each one brings his little bundle of sticks, and presents it to the agent to register. Sometimes a dialogue like the following occurs:

"How many have you in your lodge?"

The Indian carefully, and with great ceremony, counts his bundle of sticks—"Fifteen"

"How many men?"

"Two." The agent lays aside two sticks

"How many women?"

"Three." Three more sticks are separated.

"How many children?"

"Eight" Eight sticks are added to the heap.

"What is the meaning of these two sticks that remain?"

The culprit, whose arithmetic has not served him to carry out his deception, disappears amid the shouts and jeers of his companions, who are always well pleased at the detection of any roguery in which they have had no share.

The young officers generally assisted in counting out and delivering the money at these payments, and it was no unusual thing, as the last band came up, for the chiefs to take a quantity of silver out of the box and request their father to pay his friends for their trouble, seeming really disturbed at his refusal. In this, as in almost every instance, we see the native courtesy and politeness, which are never lost sight of among them. If a party comes to their father to beg for provisions, and food is offered them, however hungry they may be, each waits patiently until one of the company makes an equal distribution of the whole, and then, taking his share, eats it quietly, with the greatest moderation. I never saw this rule violated, save in one instance.

Our friend, Pawnee Blanc, *the Old Dandy*, once came with a party of Indians, requesting permission to dance for us in the open space before the door. It was a warm, dusty afternoon, and as our friends grew heated and fatigued with the violent and long-continued exercise, a pitcher of raspberry *negus* was prepared and sent out to them. Pawnee received the pitcher and tumbler, and, pouring the latter about half full, gave it to the first of the circle, then filled the same for the next, and so on, until it suddenly occurred to him to look into the pitcher. What he saw there determined his course of action; so, setting the tumbler upon the ground, he raised the pitcher with both hands to his lips and gave a hearty pull, after which he went on, giving less and less, until he was called to have the pitcher replenished. All present agreed it was the only instance they had ever witnessed, of an Indian's appearing afraid of getting less of a thing than his share.

During the payment a good many kegs of whiskey find their way into the lodges of the Indians, notwithstanding the watchfulness of both officers and agent. Where there is a demand there will always be a supply, let the legal prohibitions be what they may. The last day of the payment is, invariably, one of general carousing.

When the men begin their *frolic*, the women carefully gather all the guns, knives, tomahawks, and weapons of every description, and secrete them, that as little mischief as possible may be done in the absence of all restraint and reason. I am sorry to record that our little friend, Pawnee Blanc, was greatly addicted to the pleasures of the bottle.

Among the presents for the chiefs, which Shaw-nee-aw-kee had brought from the East, was a trunk of blue cloth coats, trimmed with broad gold lace, and a box of round black hats, ornamented in a similar manner. All who are familiar with Indians, of whatever tribe, will have observed that their first step towards civilization, whether in man or woman, is mounting a man's hat, decorated with tinsel; ribbons, or feathers. Pawnee was among the happy number remembered in the distribution; so, donning at once his new costume, and tying a few additional bunches of gay-coloured ribbons to a long spear, that was always his baton of ceremony, he came at once, followed by an admiring train, chiefly of women, to pay me a visit of state.

The solemn gravity of his countenance, as he motioned away those who would approach too near and finger his newly-received finery—the dignity with which he strutted along, edging this way and that to avoid any possible contact from homely, every-day wardrobes—augured well for a continuance of propriety and self-respect, and a due consideration of the good opinion of all around. But, alas for Pawnee! late in the day we saw him assisted towards his lodge by two stout young Indians, who had pulled him out of a ditch, his fine coat covered with mud, his hat battered and bruised, his spear shorn of its gay streamers, and poor Pawnee himself weeping and uttering all the doleful lamentations of a tipsy Indian.

★★★★★★★★★★★★★★★★★

Among the women with whom I early made acquaintance was the wife of Wau-kaun-zee-kah, *the Yellow Thunder*. She had accompanied her husband, who was one of the deputation to visit the President, and from that time forth she had been known as "the Washington woman." She had a pleasant, old-acquaintance sort of air in greeting me, as much as to say, "You and I have seen something of the world." No expression of surprise or admiration escaped her lips, as her companions, with childlike, laughing simplicity, exclaimed and clapped their hands at the different wonderful objects I showed them. Her deportment said plainly, "Yes, yes, my children, I have seen all these things before." It was not until I put to her ear a tropical shell, of which I had a little cabinet, and she heard its murmuring sound, that she laid aside her apathy of manner. She poked her finger into the opening to get at the animal within, shook it violently, then raised it to her ear again, and finally burst into a hearty laugh, and laid it down, acknowledging, by her looks, that this was beyond her comprehension.

I had one shell of peculiar beauty—my favourite in the whole collection—a small conch, covered with rich, dark veins. Each of the visitors successively took up this shell, and by words and gestures expressed her admiration, evidently showing that she had an eye for beauty—this was on the occasion of the parting visit of my red daughters.

Shortly after the payment had been completed, and the Indians had left, I discovered that my valued shell was missing from the collection. Could it be that one of the squaws had stolen it? It was possible—they would occasionally, though rarely, do such things under the influence of strong temptation. I tried to recollect which, among the party, looked most likely to have been the culprit. It could not have been the Washington woman—she was partly civilized, and knew better.

A few weeks afterwards Mrs. Yellow Thunder again made her appearance, and carefully unfolding a gay-coloured chintz shawl, which she carried rolled up in her hand, she produced the shell, and laid it on the table before me. I did not know whether to show, by my countenance, displeasure at the trick she had played me, or joy at receiving my treasure back again, but at length decided that it was the best policy to manifest no emotion whatever.

She prolonged her visit until my husband's return, and he then questioned her about the matter.

"She had taken the shell to her village, to show to some of her people, who did not come to the payment."

"Why had she not asked her mother's leave before carrying it away?"

"Because she saw that her mother liked the shell, and she was afraid she would say, No."

This was not the first instance in which Madame Washington had displayed the shrewdness which was a predominant trait in her character. During the visit of the Indians to the Eastern cities, they were taken to various exhibitions, museums, menageries, theatres, etc. It did not escape their observation that some silver was always paid before entrance, and they inquired the reason. It was explained to them. The woman brightened up, as if struck with an idea.

"How much do you pay for each one?"

Her Father told her.

"How do you say that in English?"

"Two shillings."

"Two shinnin—*humph*" (good).

The next day, when, as usual, visitors began to flock to the rooms where the Indians were sojourning, the woman and a young Indian, her confederate, took their station by the door, which they kept closed. When any one knocked, the door was cautiously opened, and the woman, extending her hand, exclaimed—"*Two shinnin.*"

This was readily paid in each instance, and the game went on, until she had accumulated a considerable sum. But this did not satisfy her. At the first attempt of a visitor to leave the room, the door was held close, as before, the hand was extended, and "*Two shinnin*" again met his ear. He tried to explain that, having paid for his entrance, he must go out free. With an innocent shake of the head, "*Two shinnin,*" was all the English she could understand.

The Agent, who had entered a short time before, and who, overhearing the dialogue, sat laughing behind his newspaper, waiting to see how it would all end, now came forward and interfered, and the guests were permitted to go forth without a further contribution.

The good woman was moreover admonished that it was far from the custom of white people to tax their friends and visitors in this manner, and that the practice must be laid aside in future.

Another instance of the disposition of the Indians to avail themselves of all the goods that fortune throws in their way, was the following:

Upon the same trip, while passing through Ohio, one of the party inquired of the agent—

"Do you pay for all those provisions that are set before us at the hotels?"

"Yes. Why do you ask?"

"Nothing: I thought you perhaps paid for just what we ate of them."

At the next stopping-place a fine breakfast was set upon the table, of which, as usual, they partook plentifully. Just as they had finished, the horn sounded for all to take their places in the stage-coaches. Each sprang to his feet. One seized the plates of biscuits and poured them into the corner of his blanket; another the remains of a pair of chickens; a third emptied the sugar-bowls; each laid hold of what was nearest him, and in a trice, nothing was left upon the table but the empty plates and dishes. The landlord and waiters, meanwhile, stood laughing and enjoying the trick as much as any of the spectators.

Upon another occasion, their father had endeavoured to impress upon them the unseemliness of throwing their refuse pieces, bones, and fragments of food about on the table-cloth, pointing out to them the orderly manner of the whites at table, and the propriety of keeping everything neat and nice around them.

At their next meal, they were served first with a chicken-pie, of which they ate very heartily, and the accumulation of bones on their plates was very abundant. Presently another and more favourite dish appeared—a fine, large, roasted turkey. A gentleman sat near, and was evidently preparing to carve it. No time was to be lost. What was to be done with the bones? They looked around in some perplexity. A large apple-pie was standing near. The most eager drew it towards him, and quick as thought all the bones were deposited upon it, while, with a triumphant laugh at the happy idea, he coolly transferred the bird to his own dish, and proceeded to distribute it among his companions. The amazed stranger soon joined in the laugh at the unceremonious manner in which his share of the dinner had vanished.

CHAPTER 11

Louisa—Day-Kau-Ray on Education

The payment was now over, and the Indians had dispersed and gone to their wintering grounds. The traders, too, had departed, laden with a good share of the silver, in exchange for which each family had provided itself, as far as possible, with clothing, guns, traps, ammunition, and the other necessaries for their winter use. The Indians are good at a bargain. They are not easily overreached. On the contrary, they understand at once when a charge is exorbitant; and a trader who tries his shrewdness upon them is sure to receive an expressive sobriquet, which ever after clings to him.

For instance, M. Rolette was called by them "Ah-kay-zaup-ee-tah," *five more*—because, as they said, let them offer what number of skins they might, in bartering for an article, his terms were invariably "five more"

Upon one occasion a lady remarked to him, "Oh, M. Rolette, I would not be engaged in the Indian trade; it seems to me a system of cheating the poor Indians."

"Let me tell you, *madame*," replied he, with great *naïveté*, "it is not so easy a thing to cheat the Indians as you imagine. I have tried it these twenty years, and have never succeeded!"

****

We were now settled down to a quiet, domestic life. The military system under which everything was conducted—the bugle-call, followed by the music of a very good band, at reveille; the light, animated strains for "sick-call," and soon after for "breakfast;" the longer ceremony of "guard-mounting;" the "Old English Roast-Beef," to announce the dinner-hour; the sweet, plaintive strains of "Lochaber no more," followed most incongruously by "The Little Cock-Sparrow," at retreat; and, finally, the long, rolling "tattoo," late in the evening—made pleasant divisions of our time, which, by the aid of books, music, and drawing, in addition to household occupations, seemed to fly more swiftly than ever before.

It was on Sunday that I most missed my Eastern home. I had planned beforehand what we should do on the first recurrence of this sacred day, under our own roof. "We shall have at least," said I to myself, "the Sabbath's quiet and repose, and I can, among other things, benefit poor Louisa by giving her some additional lessons of a serious character."

So, while she was removing the breakfast-things, I said to her,—

"Now, Louisa, get your work all finished, and everything put neatly aside, and then come here to me again."

"Yes, ma'am."

We sat down to our books, and read and waited; we waited and read another hour—no Louisa.

There was music and the sound of voices on the parade in front of our windows, but that did not disturb us; it was what we were daily accustomed to.

I must go at length, and see what could be keeping my damsel so. I descended to the kitchen. The breakfast-things stood upon the table—the kettles and spider upon the hearth—the fire was out—the kitchen empty.

Passing back into the hall, which extended the whole length of the house and opened in front upon the parade, I perceived a group collected in the area, of all shades and colours, and in the midst, one round, woolly head which I could not mistake, bobbing up and down, now on this side, now on that, while peals of laughter were issuing from the whole group.

"Louisa," I called, "come here. What are you doing there?"

"Looking at inspection."

"But why are not your breakfast-things washed, and your kitchen swept? Did I not tell you I wished you to come up and learn your lessons?"

"Yes, ma'am; but I had to see inspection first. Everybody looks at inspection on Sunday."

I found it was in vain to expect to do more for Louisa than give her an afternoon's lesson, and with that I was obliged to content myself.

I felt that it would be very pleasant, and perhaps profitable, for all the inmates of the garrison to assemble on this day; one of our number might be found who would read a portion of the church-service, with a sermon from one of our different selections.

I approached the subject cautiously, with an inquiry to this effect: "Are there none among the officers who are religiously disposed?"

"Oh, yes," replied the one whom I addressed, "there is S——; when he is half tipsy, he takes his Bible and 'Newton's Works,' and goes to bed and cries over them; he thinks in this way he is excessively pious."

S—— was among the officers who had never called upon us; it was fair to infer that if his religious principles did not correct his own evil habits, they would not aid much in improving others; therefore, it seemed useless to call in his co-operation in any scheme for a better observance of the Lord's day.

We had to content ourselves with writing to our friends at the East to interest themselves in getting a missionary sent to us, who should officiate as chaplain in the garrison—a plan that seemed to find favour with the officers. The hope of any united religious services was, for the present, laid aside.

The post-surgeon having obtained a furlough, his place was supplied by Dr. Newhall, of Galena, and thus, by the addition of his gentle, quiet wife, our circle of ladies was now enlarged to three. Here we were, in a wilderness, but yet how contented and happy!

A gloom was soon to replace this envied tranquillity in our home. A Frenchman, named Letendre, one day suddenly presented himself. He had come from Chicago, with the distressing intelligence of the extreme—indeed, hopeless—illness of our dear relative, Dr. Wolcott. My husband immediately commenced his preparations for instant departure. I begged to be permitted to accompany him, but the rapidity with which he proposed to journey obliged him to refuse my entreaties. In a few hours his provisions, horses, and all other things necessary for the journey were in readiness, and he set off with Petaille Grignon, his usual attendant on such expeditions, leaving Letendre to follow as soon as recruited from his fatigue.

Sad and dreary were the hours of his absence, notwithstanding the kind efforts of our friends to cheer me. In a few days I received the news of the fatal termination of Dr. W.'s illness, brought by another messenger. That noble heart, so full of warm and kindly affections, had ceased to beat, and sad and desolate indeed were those who had so loved and honoured him.

As soon as he could possibly leave his family, my husband returned; and it was fortunate that he had delayed no longer, for the winter now began to set in, and with severity.

Our quarters were spacious, but having been constructed of the green trees of the forest, cut down and sawed into boards by the bands of the soldiers, they were considerably given to shrinking and warping, thus leaving many a yawning crevice. Stuffing the cracks with cotton batting, and pasting strips of paper over them, formed the employment of many a leisure hour.

Then the chimneys, spite of all the currents of air, which might have been expected to create a draught, had a sad habit of smoking. To remedy this, a couple of gun-barrels were, by order of the commanding officer, sawed off and inserted in the hearth, one on each side of the fire-place, in the hope that the air from the room below might help to carry the smoke into its proper place, the chimney.

The next morning after this had been done, Louisa was washing the hearth.

"Pray, ma'am," said she, "what are these things put in here for?"

I explained their use.

"Oh, I am so glad it is only that! Uncle Ephraim (Major Twiggs's servant) said they were to be filled with powder and fired off Christmas Day, and he was terribly afraid they would blow the house up, and we in it."

Ephraim, who was a most faithful and valuable servant, often amused himself with playing upon the credulity of the younger portions of the coloured fraternity.

"Is it true," asked Louisa, one day, "that Pillon and Plante were once prairie-wolves?"

"Prairie-wolves! what an idea! Why do you ask such a foolish question?"

"Because Uncle Ephraim says they, and all the Frenchmen about here, were once prairie-wolves, and that, living so near the white people, they grow, after a time, to be like them, and learn to talk and dress like them. And then, when they get to be old, they turn back into prairie-wolves again, and that all the wolves that the officers bait with their dogs used to be Frenchmen, once."

After a time, however, I ceased to straighten out these stories of Uncle Ephraim, for I was gradually arriving at the conviction that my little coloured damsel was by no means so simple and unsophisticated as she would have me believe, and that I was, after all, the one who was imposed upon.

The snow this winter was prodigious, and the cold intense. The water would freeze in our parlours at a very short distance from the fire, for, although the "fatigue-parties" kept the halls filled with wood, almost up to the ceiling, that did not counterbalance the inconvenience of having the wide doors thrown open to the outer air for a great portion of the day, to allow of their bringing it in. We Northerners should have had wood-houses specially for the purpose, and not only have kept our great hall-doors closed, but have likewise protected them with a "hurricane-house." But the Florida frontier was not a climate in which our Southern bachelors could have acquired the knowledge available when the thermometer was twenty-five degrees below zero—a point at which brandy congealed in the sideboard.

The arrival of Christmas and New-Year's brought us our Indian friends again. They had learned something of the observance of these holidays from their French neighbours, and I had been forewarned that I should see the squaws kissing every white man they met. Although not crediting this to its full extent, I could readily believe that they would each expect a present, as a "compliment of the season," so I duly prepared myself with a supply of beads, ribbons, combs, and other trinkets. Knowing them to be fond of dainties, I had also a quantity of crullers and doughnuts made ready the day before, as a treat to them.

To my great surprise and annoyance, only a moderate share of the cakes, the frying of which had been intrusted to Louisa, were brought up to be placed in the "Davis."

"Where are the rest of the cakes, Louisa?"

"That great fellow, Hancock, came in with the fatigue-party to fill the water-barrels, and while I had just stepped into the store-room to get some more flour, he carried off all I had got cooked."

And Louisa made a face and whined, as if she had not herself treated every soldier who had set his foot in the premises.

At an early hour the next morning I had quite a levee of the Hotshung-rah matrons. They seated themselves in a circle on the floor, and I was sorry to observe that the application of a little soap and water to their blankets had formed no part of their holiday preparations. There being no one to interpret, I thought I would begin the conversation in a way intelligible to themselves, so I brought out of the sideboard a china dish, filled with the nice brown crullers, over which I had grated, according to custom, a goodly quantity of white sugar. I handed it to the first of the circle.

She took the dish from my hand, and, deliberately pouring all the cakes into the corner of her blanket, returned it to me empty. "She must be a meat voracious person," thought I; "but I will manage better the next time."

I refilled the dish, and approached the next one, taking care to keep a fast hold of it as I offered the contents, of which I supposed she would modestly take one. Not so, however. She scooped out the whole with her two hands, and, like the former, bestowed them in her blanket. My sense of politeness revolted at handing them out one by one, as we do to children, so I sat down to deliberate what was to be done, for evidently the supply would not long answer such an ample demand, and there would be more visitors *anon*.

While I was thus perplexed, those who had received the cakes commenced a distribution, and the whole number was equitably divided among the company. But I observed they did not eat them. They passed their fingers over the grated sugar, looked in each other's faces, and muttered in low tones—there was evidently something they did not understand. Presently one more adventurous than the rest wet her fingers, and taking up a few grains of the sugar put it cautiously to her mouth.

"*Tah-nee-zhoo-rah!*" (Sugar!) was her delighted exclamation, and they all broke out into a hearty laugh. It is needless to say that the cakes disappeared with all the celerity they deemed compatible with good-breeding. Never having seen any sugar but the brown or yellow maple, they had supposed the white substance to be salt, and for that reason had hesitated to taste it.

Their visit was prolonged until Shaw-nee-aw-kee made his appearance, and then, having been made happy by their various gifts, they all took their departure.

About this time, Mr. Kinzie received a letter from Colonel Richard M. Johnson, of Kentucky. This gentleman had interested himself greatly in a school established in that State for the education of Indian youths and children.

The purport of his letter was to request the Agent to use every endeavour to induce the Winnebagoes not only to send their children to this institution for their education, but also (what was still more important) to set apart a portion of their annuity-money to assist in sustaining it.

There happened to be, at this holiday season, a number of the chiefs in the neighbourhood of the Portage, and a messenger was sent to convene them all at the house of Paquette, the interpreter, that their father might hold a talk with them.

On the day appointed they all assembled. The subject-matter of the letter was laid before them, and all the advantages of civilization and education duly set forth—the benefits which would arise to their nation, if even a small portion of the younger members could be well taught by the whites, and then return to their tribe, to instruct them in the learning, the arts, manufactures, and habits of civilized life. To each paragraph, as it was uttered to them, they responded with a unanimous "*Humph!*" (Good!)

When their father's address was ended, Day-kau-ray, the oldest and most venerable among the chiefs, rose and spoke as follows:

Father,—The Great Spirit made the white man and the Indian. He did not make them alike. He gave the white man a heart to love peace, and the arts of a quiet life. He taught him to live in towns, to build houses, to make books, to learn all things that would make him happy and prosperous in the way of life appointed him. To the red man the Great Spirit gave a different character. He gave him a love of the woods, of a free life, of hunting and fishing, of making war with his enemies and taking scalps. The white man does not live like the Indian—it is not his nature. Neither does the Indian love to live like the white man—the Great Spirit did not make him so.

Father,—We do not wish to do anything contrary to the will of the Great Spirit. If he had made us with white skins, and characters like the white men, then we would send our children to this school to be taught like the white children.

Father,—We think that if the Great Spirit had wished us to be like the whites, he would have made us so. As he has not seen fit to do so, we believe he would be displeased with us, to try and make ourselves different from what he thought good.

Father,—I have nothing more to say. This is what we think. If we change our minds, we will let you know.

It will be seen from these remarks of Day-kau-ray that the Indians entertain a conviction that the Great Spirit himself teaches the white man the arts and sciences, and since he has given the red man no instruction in these branches, it would be unbecoming in him to attempt to acquire them in an irregular manner.

With little incidents of this kind, and with an occasional dinner- or tea-party to the young officers, sometimes given at the major's quarters, sometimes at our own, our course of life passed pleasantly on. At times I would amuse myself by making something very nice, in the form of a fruit cake or pie, to send to the quarters of the young officers as a present, it being supposed that possibly, without a lady to preside over their mess, it might be sometimes deficient in these delicacies. Mrs. Twiggs was so fortunate as to have well-trained servants to do for her that which, thanks to my little dark handmaid, always fell to my share.

One day I had made some mince pies, which the major and my husband greatly approved, and I thought I would send one to each of the young officers.

It happened that my husband, that day, in returning from superintending his men on the other side of the river, had occasion to call on some errand at Captain Harney's quarters.

Dinner had just been placed upon the table, and the captain insisted on his visitor's sitting down and partaking with him and another gentleman who was present. The pork and beans were pronounced excellent, and being removed there followed a mince pie.

The captain cut it, and helped his guests, then taking a piece himself, he commenced tasting it.

Pushing back his plate with an exclamation and a sudden jerk, he called to his servant, a little thick-set *mulatto* who waited—"David, you yellow rascal, how dare you put such a pie on my table?" And, turning to the company apologetically, he said,—

"If there is anything on earth David does understand, it is how to make a mince pie, and here he has filled this with brandy, so we cannot eat a morsel of it!"

"Please, sir," said David, modestly, "I did not make the pie—it is one Mrs. Kinzie sent as a present."

The poor captain was now in a predicament. He raved at himself, at the same time conjuring my husband most earnestly not to tell me what a mistake he had made—an injunction that was lost sight of as soon as the latter returned to his home. As for the unlucky captain, he did not venture to call on me again until he felt sure I had forgotten the circumstance.

CHAPTER 12

Preparations for a Journey

Early in January the snow fell in great abundance. We had an unusual quantity at the Portage, but in "the diggings," as the lead-mining country was called, it was of an unheard-of depth—five or six feet upon a level.

An express had been dispatched to Chicago by the officers to take our letters, and bring back the mail from that place. A tough, hardy soldier, named Sulky, acted as messenger, and he had hitherto made light of his burden or the length of the way, notwithstanding that his task was performed on foot with his pack upon his shoulders. But now Sulky had been absent some weeks, and we had given him up entirely, persuaded that he must have perished with cold and starvation.

At length he appeared, nearly blind from travelling in the snow. He had lain by three weeks in an Indian lodge, the snow being too deep to permit him to journey. The account he gave put an end to the hopes I had begun to entertain of being able to visit our friends at Chicago in the course of this winter.

We had, before the last heavy fall of snow, been forming plans to that effect. Captain Harney had kindly commenced preparing some trains, or boxes placed on sledges, which it was thought would, when lined with buffalo-skins, furnish a very comfortable kind of vehicle for the journey; and I was still inclined to think a good, deep bed of snow over the whole country no great obstacle to a sleigh-ride. The whole matter was, however, cut short by the commanding officer, who from the first had violently opposed the scheme, declaring that he would order the sentinels to fire on us if we attempted to leave the fort. So, finding the majority against us, we were obliged to yield.

The arrival of sweet, lovely little Lizzie Twiggs, before January was quite past, was an event that shed light and joy in at least two dwellings. It seemed as if she belonged to all of us, and as she increased in size and beauty it was hard to say who, among us all, was most proud of her. If we had ever felt any languid hours before, we could have none now—she was the pet, the darling, the joint property of both households.

Whatever regret I might have had, previous to this event, at the idea of leaving my friend for the three weeks to which we proposed to limit our visit to Chicago, I felt now that she would scarcely miss me, and that we might hold ourselves in readiness to take advantage of the first improvement in the weather, to put this favourite project in execution.

During the latter part of February, the cold became less severe. The snows melted away, and by the beginning of March the weather was so warm and genial, that we were quite confident of being able to make the journey on horseback without any serious difficulty.

Our plans once settled upon, the first thing to be provided was warm and comfortable apparel. A riding-habit of stout broadcloth was pronounced indispensable to my equipment. But of such an article I was destitute. Nothing among my wedding travelling gear seemed in any way to offer a substitute. What was to be done? The requisite material was to be found in abundance at the sutler's store (*the shantee*, as it was technically termed), but how to get it manufactured into a suitable garment was the question.

The regimental tailor was summoned. He was cook to one of the companies, and there were at first some doubts whether he could be permitted to forsake the spit for the needle, during the time I should require his services. All his tailoring-work had, heretofore, been done at odd times on a bench in the company kitchen, and thither he now proposed to carry the riding-habit. I suggested that, in order to superintend the work, I should thus be driven to take up my abode for the time being in the barracks, which would be a decided inconvenience.

To remedy the difficulty, he was finally so happy as to find a soldier in "Company D," who consented to officiate in his place as cook until his term of service to me should expire.

Behold, then, a little, solemn-looking man in his stocking-feet, seated cross-legged on an Indian mat by my parlour window. He had made all his arrangements himself, and I deemed it wisest not to interfere with him. The cutting-out was the most difficult part, and, as he had never made a lady's riding-habit, that task fell to my share. I was as great a novice as himself, and I must admit that this, my first effort, was open to criticism. But the little tailor was of a different opinion. He was in an ecstasy with our joint performance.

"Upon my word, madam," he would exclaim, surveying it with admiring eyes, "we shall have a very respectable garment!" I do not know how many times he repeated this during the three days that the work was in progress.

I believe he had not perfect confidence in the culinary powers of his comrade of "Company D," for regularly a half-hour before beat of drum his work was folded and laid aside, his snips gathered up, and, all things being restored to order, he would slip out, resume his shoes, which, *Turk-like,* he had left outside the door, and speed over to the barrack-kitchen to see how matters were going on.

In the meantime, great preparations were making below, under the supervision of our tidy, active little French servant, Mrs. Pillon, the wife of one of the *engagés,* by whom the irregular and unmanageable Louisa had been replaced.

Biscuits were baked, a ham, some tongues, and sundry pieces of salt pork were boiled, coffee roasted and ground, sugar cracked, isinglass cut in pieces of the size requisite for a pot of coffee. For the reception of all these different articles cotton bags of different sizes had been previously prepared. Large sacks of skin, called by the Canadians *porches,* were also provided to hold the more bulky provisions, for our journey was to be a long one.

The distance from Fort Winnebago to Chicago was not very formidable, it is true, if the direct route were taken; but that we knew to be impossible at this season of the year. The route by Kosh-ko-nong was out of the question; all the Indians being absent from their villages in the winter, and the ice being now gone, we could have no means of crossing the Rock River at that place.

There remained therefore no alternative but to proceed south to Dixon, or, as it was then called, Ogie's Ferry, the only certain means of crossing this broad and rapid stream. This route being so much out of our direct course that we could not hope to accomplish it in less than six days, it was necessary to prepare accordingly.

While the wardrobe and provisions were thus in preparation, arrangements were also being made as to our retinue and mode of conveyance.

Mr. Kinzie decided to take with him but two men: Plante and Pierre Roy—the former to act as guide, on the assurance that he knew every mile of the way, from the Portage to Ogie's Ferry, and from Ogie's Ferry to Chicago.

The claims of the different saddle-horses were discussed, and the most eligible one was selected for my use. We hesitated for a time between "*Le Gris*" and "*Souris,*" two much-vaunted animals, belonging to Paquette, the interpreter. At length, being determined, like most of my sex, by a regard for exterior, I chose "*Le Gris,*" and "*Souris*" was assigned to young Roy; my own little stumpy pony, "*Brunet,*" being pronounced just the thing for a pack-saddle. My husband rode his own bay horse "Tom," while Plante, the gayest and proudest of the party, bestrode a fine, large animal called "Jerry," which had lately been purchased for my use; and thus was our *cortége* complete.

Chapter 13
Departure From Fort Winnebago

Having taken a tender leave of our friends, the morning of the 8th of March saw us mounted and equipped for our journey. The weather was fine—the streams, already fringed with green, were sparkling in the sun—everything gave promise of an early and genial season. In vain, when we reached the ferry at the foot of the hill on which the fort stood, did Major Twiggs repeat his endeavours to dissuade us from commencing a journey which he assured me would be perilous beyond what I could anticipate. I was resolute.

Our party was augmented by an escort of all the young officers, who politely insisted on accompanying us as far as Duck Creek, four miles distant. Indeed, there were some who would gladly have prosecuted the whole journey with us, and escaped the monotony of their solitary, uneventful life. In our rear followed an ox cart, on which was perched a canoe, destined to transport us over the creek, and also an extensive marsh beyond it, which was invariably, at this season, overflowed with water to a considerable depth. We had much amusement in watching the progress of this vehicle as it bumped and thumped over the road, unconscious hitherto of the dignity of a wheeled carriage.

Our little, shock-headed, sunburnt, thick-lipped Canadian (who happened most miraculously to be the husband of my pretty servant, Mrs. Pillon) shouted vociferously as the animals lagged in their pace, or jolted against a stump, "*Marchez, don-g,*" "*regardez,*" "*prenez garde,*" to our infinite diversion. I was in high spirits, foreseeing no hardships or dangers, but rather imagining myself embarked on a pleasure excursion across the prairies. It had not even suggested itself to me that a straw bonnet and kid gloves were no suitable equipment for such an expedition.

Never having travelled at so inclement a season, I was heedlessly ignorant of the mode of preparing against it, and had resisted or laughed at my husband's suggestions to provide myself with blanket socks, and a woollen *capuchon* for my head and shoulders. And now, although the wind occasionally lifted my head-gear with a rude puff, and my hands ere long became swollen and stiffened with the cold, I persuaded myself that these were trifling evils, to which I should soon get accustomed. I was too well pleased with the novelty of my outfit, with my hunting-knife in a gay scabbard hanging from my neck, and my tin cup at my saddle-bow, to regard minor inconveniences.

On reaching Duck Creek, we took leave of our young friends, who remained on the bank long enough to witness our passage across—ourselves in the canoe, and the poor horses swimming the stream, now filled with cakes of floating ice.

Beyond the rising ground which formed the opposite bank of the stream, extended a marsh of perhaps three hundred yards across. To this the men carried the canoe which was to bear us over. The water was not deep, so our attendants merely took off the pack from Brunet and my side-saddle from Le Gris, for fear of accidents, and then mounted their own steeds, leading the two extra ones. My husband placed the furniture of the pack-horse and my saddle in the centre of the canoe, which he was to paddle across.

"Now, wifie," said he, "jump in, and seat yourself flat in the bottom of the canoe."

"Oh, no," said I; "I will sit on the little trunk in the centre; I shall be so much more comfortable, and I can balance the canoe exactly."

"As you please; but I think you will find it is not the best way."

A vigorous push sent us a few feet from the bank. At that instant two favourite greyhounds whom we had brought with us, and who had stood whining upon the bank, reluctant to take to the water as they were ordered, gave a sudden bound, and alighted full upon me. The canoe balanced a moment—then yielded—and, quick as thought, dogs, furniture, and lady were in the deepest of the water.

My husband, who was just preparing to spring into the canoe when the dogs thus unceremoniously took precedence of him, was at my side in a moment, and, seizing me by the collar of my cloak, begged me not to be frightened. I was not, in the least, and only laughed as he raised and placed me again upon the bank.

The unfortunate saddle and little trunk were then rescued, but not until they had received a pretty thorough wetting. Our merriment was still further increased by the sight of the maladroit Pillon, who was attempting to ride my spirited Jerry across the marsh. He was clinging to the neck of the animal, with a countenance distorted with terror, as he shouted forth all manner of French objurgations. Jerry pranced and curveted, and finally shot forward his rider, or rather his *burden*, headforemost, a distance of several feet into the water.

A general outcry of mirth saluted the unfortunate Frenchman, which was redoubled as he raised himself puffing and snorting from his watery bed and waddled back to his starting-place, the horse, meanwhile, very sensibly making his way to join his companions, who had already reached the farther bank.

"Well, wifie," said Mr. Kinzie, "I cannot trust you in the canoe again. There is no way but to carry you across the marsh like a *papoose*. Will you take a ride on my shoulders?"

"With all my heart, if you will promise to take me safely." And I was soon mounted.

I must confess that the gentleman staggered now and then under his burden, which was no slight one, and I was sadly afraid, more than once, that I should meet a similar fate to old Pillon, but happily we reached the other side in safety.

There my husband insisted on my putting on dry shoes and stockings, and (must I confess it?) drinking a little brandy, to obviate the effects of my icy bath. He would fain have made a halt to kindle a fire and dry my apparel and wardrobe properly, but this I would not listen to. I endeavoured to prove to him that the delay would expose me to more cold than riding in my wet habit and cloak, and so indeed it might have been, but along with my convictions upon the subject there was mingled a spice of reluctance that our friends at the fort should have an opportunity, as they certainly would have done, of laughing at our inauspicious commencement.

Soon our horses were put in order, and our march recommenced. The day was fine for the season. I felt no inconvenience from my wet garments, the exercise of riding taking away all feeling of chilliness. It was to me a new mode of travelling, and I enjoyed it the more from having been secluded for more than five months within the walls of the fort, scarcely varying the tenor of our lives by an occasional walk of half a mile into the surrounding woods.

We had still another detention upon the road, from meeting Lapierre, the blacksmith, from Sugar Creek, who with one of his associates was going to the Portage for supplies, so that we had not travelled more than twenty-three miles when we came to our proposed encamping-ground. It was upon a beautiful stream, a tributary of one of the Four Lakes, (between two of these lakes is now situated the town of Madison—the capital of the State of Wisconsin), that chain whose banks are unrivalled for romantic loveliness.

I could not but admire the sagacity of the horses, who seemed, with human intelligence, to divine our approach to the spot where their toils were to cease. While still remote from the point of woods which foretold a halt, they pricked up their ears, accelerated their pace, and finally arrived at the spot on a full gallop.

We alighted at an open space, just within the verge of the wood, or, as it is called by Western travellers, "the timber." My husband recommended to me to walk about until a fire should be made, which was soon accomplished by our active and experienced woodsmen, to whom the felling of a large tree was the work of a very few minutes. The dry grass around furnished an excellent tinder, which, ignited by the sparks from the flint (there were no *loco-focos* in those days), and aided by the broken branches and bits of light-wood, soon produced a cheering flame.

"The *bourgeois*," in the meantime, busied himself in setting up the tent, taking care to place it opposite the fire, but in such a direction that the wind would carry the smoke and flame away from the opening or door. Within upon the ground were spread, first a bear-skin, then two or three blankets (of which each equestrian had carried two, one under the saddle and one above it), after which, the remainder of the luggage being brought in, I was able to divest myself of all my wet clothing and replace it with dry. Some idea of the state of the thermometer may be formed from the fact that my riding-habit, being placed over the end of the huge log against which our fire was made, was, in a very few minutes, frozen so stiff as to stand upright, giving the appearance of a dress out of which a lady had vanished in some unaccountable manner.

It would be but a repetition of our experience upon the Fox River to describe the ham broiled upon the "*broches*," the toasted bread, the steaming coffee, the primitive table-furniture. There is, however, this difference, that of the latter we carry with us in our journeys on horseback only a coffee-pot, a tea-kettle, and each rider his tin cup and hunting-knife. The deportment at table is marked by an absence of ceremony. The knife is drawn from the scabbard—those who remember to do so, vouchsafe it a wipe upon the napkin. Its first office is to stir the cup of coffee—next, to divide the piece of ham which is placed on the half of a travelling biscuit, held in the left hand, to fulfil the office of a plate. It is an art only to be acquired by long practice, to cut the meat so skilfully as not at the same time to destroy the dish.

We take our places around the mat to enjoy what, after our fatiguing ride, we find delicious food. The Frenchmen are seated at a little distance, receiving their supplies of coffee, meat, and bread, and occasionally passing jokes with the *bourgeois*, who is their *demi*-god, and for whom their respect and devotion are never lessened by his affability or condescension.

The meal being finished, the table-furniture is rinsed in hot water and set aside until morning. A wisp of dry prairie-grass is supposed in most cases to render the knife fit to be restored to the scabbard, and there being, at this season of the year, no amusement but that of watching the awkward movements of the spancelled horses in their progress from spot to spot in search of pasturage, we are usually soon disposed to arrange our blankets and retire to rest.

At break of day we are aroused by the shout of the *bourgeois*,—"*How! how! how!*"

All start from their slumbers. The fire, which has been occasionally replenished through the night, is soon kindled into a flame. The horses are caught and saddled, while a breakfast, similar in kind to the meal of the preceding evening, is preparing—the tent is struck—the pack-horse loaded—"*tout démanché*," as the Canadian says. The breakfast finished, we rinse our kettles and cups, tie them to our saddle-bows, and then mount and away, leaving our fire, or rather our smoke, to tell of our visit.

March 9th.—Our journey this day led us past the first of the Four Lakes. Scattered along its banks was an encampment of Winnebagoes. They greeted their father with vociferous joy—"*Bon-jour, bon-jour, Shaw-nee-aw-kee*," "*Hee-nee-kar-ray-kay-noo?*" (how do you do?)

To this succeeded the usual announcement, "*Wys-kap-rah tshoonsh-koo-nee-noh!*" (I have no bread.)

This is their form of begging; but we could not afford to be generous, for the uncertainty of obtaining a supply, should our own be exhausted, obliged us to observe the strictest economy.

How beautiful the entrapment looked in the morning sun! The matted lodges, with the blue smoke curling from their tops—the trees and bushes powdered with a light snow which had fallen through the night—the lake, shining and sparkling, almost at our feet—even the Indians, in their peculiar costume, adding to the picturesque!

I was sorry to leave it, as we were compelled to do, in all haste, Souris, the pack-horse, having taken it into his head to decamp while we were in conversation with our red friends. As he had, very sensibly, concluded to pursue his journey in the right direction, we had the good fortune to overtake him after a short race, and, having received much scolding and some blows from young Roy, whose charge he specially was, he was placed in the middle of the cavalcade, as a mark of disgrace for his breach of duty.

Our road, after leaving the lake, lay over a "rolling prairie," now bare and desolate enough. The hollows were filled with snow, which, being partly thawed, furnished an uncertain footing for the horses, and I could not but join in the ringing laughter of oar Frenchmen as occasionally Brunet and Souris, the two ponies, would flounder, almost imbedded, through the yielding mass. Even the vainglorious Plante, who piqued himself on his equestrian skill, was once or twice nearly unhorsed, from having chosen his road badly.

Sometimes the elevations were covered with a thicket or copse, in which our dogs would generally rouse up one or more deer. Their first bound, or "lope," was the signal for a chase. The horses seemed to enter into the spirit of it, as "halloo" answered "halloo;" but we were never so fortunate as to get a shot at one, for although the dogs once or twice caught they were not strong enough to hold them. It was about the middle of the afternoon when we reached the Blue Mound. I rejoiced much to have got so far, for I was sadly fatigued, and every mile now seemed like two to me. In fact, the miles are unconscionably long in this country. When I was told that we had still seven miles to go, to "Morrison's," where we proposed stopping for the night, I was almost in despair. It was my first journey on horseback, and I had not yet become inured to the exercise.

When we reached Morrison's, I was so much exhausted that, as my husband attempted to lift me from the saddle, I fell into his arms.

"This will never do," said he. "Tomorrow we must turn our faces towards Fort Winnebago again."

The door opened hospitably to receive us. We were welcomed by a lady with a most sweet, benignant countenance, and by her companion, some years younger. The first was Mrs. Morrison—the other, Miss Elizabeth Dodge, daughter of General Dodge.

My husband laid me upon a small bed, in the room where the ladies had been sitting at work. They took off my bonnet and riding-dress, chafed my hands, and prepared me some warm wine and water, by which I was soon revived. A half-hour's repose so refreshed me that I was able to converse with the ladies, and to relieve my husband's mind of all anxiety on my account. Tea was announced soon after, and we repaired to an adjoining building, for Morrison's, like the establishment of all settlers of that period, consisted of a group of detached log houses or *cabins*, each containing one or at most two apartments.

The table groaned with good cheer, and brought to mind some that I had seen among the old-fashioned Dutch residents on the banks of the Hudson.

I had recovered my spirits, and we were quite a cheerful party. Mrs. Morrison told us that during the first eighteen months she passed in this country she did not speak with a white woman, the only society she had being that of her husband and two black servant-women.

A Tennessee woman had called in with her little son just before tea, and we amused Mr. Kinzie with a description of the pair. The mother's visit was simply one of courtesy. She was a little, dumpy woman, with a complexion burned perfectly red by the sun, and hair of an exact tow-colour, braided up from her forehead in front and from her neck behind. These tails, meeting on the top of her head, were fastened with a small tin comb. Her dress was of checkered homespun, a "very tight fit," and, as she wore no ruff or handkerchief around her neck, she looked as if just prepared for execution.

She was evidently awestruck at the sight of visitors, and seemed inclined to take her departure at once; but the boy, not so easily intimidated, would not understand her signs and pinches until he had sidled up to Mrs. Morrison, and, drawing his old hat still farther over his eyes, begged for a *whang*, meaning a narrow strip of deer-skin. The lady very obligingly cut one from a large smoked skin, which she produced from its receptacle, and mother and son took their leave, with a smiling but rather a scared look.

After tea we returned to Mrs. Morrison's parlour, where she kindly insisted on my again reposing myself on the little bed, to recruit me, as she said, for the ensuing day's journey. My husband, in the meantime, went to look after the accommodation of his men and horses.

During the conversation that ensued, I learned that Mrs. Morrison had passed much time in the neighbourhood of my recent home in Oneida County, that many of the friends I had loved and valued were likewise her friends, and that she had even proposed to visit me at Fort Winnebago on hearing of my arrival there, in order to commence an acquaintance which had thus been brought about by other and unexpected means.

Long and pleasant was the discourse we held together until a late hour, and mutual was the satisfaction with which we passed old friends and by-gone events in review, much to the edification of Miss Dodge, and of the gentlemen when they once more joined us.

CHAPTER 14

William S. Hamilton—Kellogg's Grove

The next morning, after a cheerful breakfast, at which we were joined by the Rev. Mr. Kent, of Galena, we prepared for our journey. I had reconciled my husband to continuing our route towards Chicago, by assuring him that I felt as fresh and bright as when I first set out from home.

There seemed some apprehension, however, that we might have difficulty in "striking the trail" to Hamilton's *diggings*, our next point of destination.

The directions we received were certainly obscure. We were to pursue a given trail for a certain number of miles, when we should come to a crossing into which we were to turn, taking an easterly direction; after a time, this would bring us to a deep trail leading straight to Hamilton's. In this open country there are no landmarks. One elevation is so exactly like another, that if you lose your trail there is almost as little hope of regaining it as of finding a pathway in the midst of the ocean. (I speak, it will be understood, of things as they existed a quarter of a century ago.)

The trail, it must be remembered, is not a broad highway, but a narrow path, deeply indented by the hoofs of the horses on which the Indians travel in single file. So deeply is it sunk in the sod which covers the prairies, that it is difficult, sometimes, to distinguish it at a distance of a few rods.

It was new ground to Mr. Kinzie, whose journeys from the Portage to Chicago had hitherto been made in the direct route by Kosh-ko-nong. He therefore obliged Mr. Morrison to repeat the directions again and again, though Plante, our guide, swaggered and talked big, averring that "he knew every hill and stream and point of woods from that spot to Chicago."

We had not proceeded many miles on our journey, however, before we discovered that Monsieur Plante was profoundly ignorant of the country, so that Mr. Kinzie was obliged to take the lead himself, and make his way as he was best able, according to the directions he had received. Nothing, however, like the "cross trails" we had been promised met our view, and the path on which we had set out diverged so much from what we knew to be the right direction, that we were at length compelled to abandon it altogether.

We travelled the livelong day, barely making a halt at noon to bait our horses and refresh ourselves with a luncheon. The ride was as gloomy and desolate as could well be imagined. A rolling prairie, unvaried by forest or stream—hillock rising after hillock, at every ascent of which we vainly hoped to see a distant fringe of "*timber.*" But the same cheerless, unbounded prospect everywhere met the eye, diversified only here and there by the oblong openings, like gigantic graves, which marked an unsuccessful search for indications of a lead-mine.

So great was our anxiety to recover our trail, for the weather was growing more cold, and the wind more sharp and piercing, that we were not tempted to turn from our course even by the appearance, more than once, of a gaunt prairie-wolf, peering over the nearest rising-ground and seeming to dare us to an encounter. The Frenchmen, it is true, would instinctively give a shout and spur on their horses, while the hounds, Kelda and Cora, would rush to the chase; but the *bourgeois* soon called them back, with a warning that we must attend strictly to the prosecution of our journey. Just before sunset we crossed, with some difficulty, a muddy stream, which was bordered by a scanty belt of trees, making a tolerable encamping-ground; and of this we gladly availed ourselves, although we knew not whether it was near or remote from the place we were in search of.

We had ridden at least fifty miles since leaving Morrison's, yet I was sensible of very little fatigue; there was, however, a vague feeling of discomfort at the idea of being lost in this wild, cold region, altogether different from anything I had ever before experienced. The encouraging tones of my husband's voice, however, "Cheer up, wifie—we will find the trail tomorrow," served to dissipate all uneasiness.

The exertions of the men soon made our "camp" comfortable, notwithstanding the difficulty of driving the tent-pins into the frozen ground, and the want of trees sufficiently large to make a *rousing* fire. The place was a *stony side-hill,* as it would be called in New England, where such things abound; but we were not disposed to be fastidious, so we ate our salt ham and toasted our bread, and lent a pleased ear to the chatter of our Frenchmen, who could not sufficiently admire the heroism of "Madame John" amid the vicissitudes that befell her.

The wind, which at bed-time was sufficiently high to be uncomfortable, increased during the night. It snowed heavily, and we were every moment in dread that the tent would be carried away; but the matter was settled differently by the snapping of the poles, and the falling of the whole, with its superincumbent weight of snow, in a mass upon us.

Mr. Kinzie roused up his men, and at their head he sallied into the neighbouring wood to cut a new set of poles, leaving me to bear the burden of the whole upon my shoulders, my only safety from the storm being to keep snugly housed beneath the canvas.

With some difficulty a sort of support was at length adjusted for the tent-covering, which answered our purpose tolerably well until the break of day, when our damp and miserable condition made us very glad to rise and hang round the fire until breakfast was dispatched, and the horses once more saddled for our journey.

The prospect was not an encouraging one. Around us was an unbroken sheet of snow. We had no compass, and the air was so obscured by the driving sleet, that it was often impossible to tell in which direction the sun was. I tied my husband's silk pocket-handkerchief over my veil, to protect my face from the wind and icy particles with which the air was filled, and which cut like a razor; but, although shielded in every way that circumstances rendered possible, I suffered intensely from the cold.

We pursued our way, mile after mile, entering every point of woods, in hopes of meeting with, at least, some Indian *wigwam* at which we could gain intelligence. Every spot was solitary and deserted; not even the trace of a recent fire, to cheer us with the hope of human beings within miles of us.

Suddenly, a shout from the foremost of the party made each heart bound with joy.

"*Une clôture! une clôture!*" (A fence! a fence!)

It was almost like life to the dead.

We spurred on, and indeed perceived a few straggling rails crowning a rising ground at no great distance.

Never did music sound so sweet as the crowing of a cock which at this moment saluted our ears.

Following the course of the enclosure down the opposite slope, we came upon a group of log cabins, low, shabby, and unpromising in their appearance, but a most welcome shelter from the pelting storm.

"Whose cabins are these?" asked Mr. Kinzie, of a man who was cutting wood at the door of one.

"Hamilton's," was his reply; and he stepped forward at once to assist us to alight, hospitality being a matter of course in these wild regions.

We were shown into the most comfortable-looking of the buildings. A large fire was burning in the clay chimney, and the room was of a genial warmth, notwithstanding the apertures, many inches in width, beside the doors and windows. A woman in a tidy calico dress, and shabby black silk cap trimmed with still shabbier lace, rose from her seat beside a sort of bread-trough, which fulfilled the office of cradle to a fine, fat baby. She made room for us at the fire, but was either too timid or too ignorant to relieve me of wrappings and defences, now heavy with the snow.

I soon contrived, with my husband's aid, to disembarrass myself of them; and, having seen me comfortably disposed of, and in a fair way to be thawed after my freezing ride, he left me, to see after his men and horses.

He was a long time absent, and I expected he would return accompanied by our host; but when he reappeared it was to tell me, laughing, that Mr. Hamilton hesitated to present himself before me, being unwilling that one who had been acquainted with his family at the East should see him in his present mode of life. However, this feeling apparently wore off, for before dinner he came in and was introduced to me, and was as agreeable and polite as the son of Alexander Hamilton would naturally be.

The housekeeper, who was the wife of one of the miners, prepared us a plain, comfortable dinner, and a table as long as the dimensions of the cabin would admit was set out, the end nearest the fire being covered with somewhat nicer furniture and more delicate fare than the remaining portion.

The blowing of a horn was the signal for the entrance of ten or twelve miners, who took their places below us at the table. They were the roughest-looking set of men I ever beheld, and their language was as uncouth as their persons. They wore hunting-shirts, trowsers, and *moccasins* of deer-skin, the former being ornamented at the seams with a fringe of the same, while a coloured belt around the waist, in which was stuck a large hunting-knife, gave each the appearance of a brigand.

Mr. Hamilton, although so much their superior, was addressed by them uniformly as "Uncle Billy;" and I could not but fancy there was something desperate about them, that it was necessary to propitiate by this familiarity. This feeling was further confirmed by the remarks of one of the company who lingered behind after the rest of the gang had taken their departure. He had learned that we came from Fort Winnebago, and, having informed us that "he was a discharged soldier, and would like to make some inquiries about his old station and comrades," he unceremoniously seated himself and commenced questioning us.

The bitterness with which he spoke of his former officers made me quite sure he was a deserter, and I rather suspected he had made his escape from the service in consequence of some punishment. His countenance was fairly distorted as he spoke of Captain H., to whose company he had belonged. "There is a man in the mines," said he, "who has been in his hands, and if he ever gets a chance to come within shot of him, I guess the captain will remember it. He knows well enough he darsn't set his foot in the diggings. And there's T. is not much better. Everybody thought it a great pity that fellow's gun snapped when he so nearly *had* him at Green Bay."

Having delivered himself of these sentiments, he marched out, to my great relief.

Mr. Hamilton passed most of the afternoon with us; for the storm raged so without, that to proceed on our journey was out of the question. He gave us many pleasant anecdotes and reminiscences of his early life in New York, and of his adventures since he had come to the Western wilderness. When obliged to leave us for a while, he furnished us with some books to entertain us, the most interesting of which was the biography of his father.

Could this illustrious man have foreseen in what a scene—the dwelling of his son—this book was to be one day perused, what would have been his sensations?

The most amusing part of our experience was yet to come. I had been speculating, as evening approached, on our prospects for the night's accommodation. As our pale, melancholy-looking landlady and her fat baby were evidently the only specimens of the feminine gender about the establishment, it was hardly reasonable to suppose that any of the other cabins contained wherewithal to furnish us a comfortable lodging, and the one in which we were offered nothing of the sort to view, but two beds, uncurtained, extended against the farther wall. My doubts were after a time resolved, by observing the hostess stretch a cord between the two, on which she hung some petticoats and extra garments, by way of a partition, after which she invited us to occupy one of them.

My only preparation was, to wrap my cloak around me and lie down with my face to the wall; but the good people were less ceremonious, for at the distance of scarcely two feet, we could not be mistaken in the sound of their garments being, not "laid aside," but whipped over the partition-wall between us.

Our waking thoughts, however, were only those of thankfulness for so comfortable a lodging after the trials and fatigues we had undergone; and even these were of short duration, for our eyes were soon closed in slumber.

The next day's sun rose clear and bright. Refreshed and invigorated, we looked forward with pleasure to a recommencement of our journey, confident of meeting no more mishaps by the way. Mr. Hamilton kindly offered to accompany us to his next neighbour's, the trifling distance of twenty-five miles. From Kellogg's to Ogie's Ferry, on the Rock River, the road being much travelled, we should be in no danger, Mr. H. said, of again losing our way.

The miner who owned the wife and baby, and who, consequently, was somewhat more humanized than his comrades, in taking leave of us "wished us well out of the country, and that we might never have occasion to return to it!"

"I pity a body," said he, "when I see them making such an awful mistake as to come out this way; for comfort *never touched* this Western country."

We found Mr. Hamilton as agreeable a companion as on the preceding day, but a most desperate rider. He galloped on at such a rate that, had I not exchanged my pony for the fine, noble Jerry, I should have been in danger of being left behind.

Well mounted as we all were, he sometimes nearly distanced us. We were now among the branches of the Pickatonick, and the country had lost its prairie character and become rough and broken. We went dashing on, sometimes down ravines, sometimes through narrow passes, where, as I followed, I left fragments of my veil upon the projecting and interwoven branches. Once my hat became entangled, and, had not my husband sprung to my rescue, I must have shared the fate of Absalom, Jerry's ambition to keep his place in the race making it probable he would do as did the mule who was under the unfortunate prince.

There was no halting upon the route, and, as we kept the same pace until three o'clock in the afternoon, it was beyond a question that when we reached "Kellogg's" we had travelled at least thirty miles. One of my greatest annoyances during the ride had been the behaviour of the little beast Brunet. He had been hitherto used as a saddle-horse, and had been accustomed to a station in the file near the guide or leader. He did not relish being put in the background as a pack-horse, and accordingly, whenever we approached a stream, where the file broke up to permit each horseman to choose his own place of fording, it was, invariably the case that just as I was reining Jerry into the water, Brunet would come rushing past and throw himself into our very footsteps.

Plunging, snorting, and splashing me with water, and sometimes even starting Jerry into a leap aside, he more than once brought me into imminent danger of being tossed into the stream. It was in vain that, after one or two such adventures, I learned to hold back and give the vexatious little animal the precedence. His passion seemed to be to go into the water precisely at the moment Jerry did; and I was obliged at last to make a bargain with young Roy to dismount and hold him at every stream until I had got safely across.

"Kellogg's" (it was at this spot that the unfortunate St. Vrain lost his life, during the Sauk war, in 1832), was a comfortable mansion, just within the verge of a pleasant "grove of timber," as a small forest is called by Western travellers. We found Mrs. Kellogg a very respectable-looking matron, who soon informed us she was from the city of New York. She appeared proud and delighted to entertain Mr. Hamilton, for whose family, she took occasion to tell us, she had, in former days, been in the habit of doing needlework.

The worthy woman provided us an excellent dinner, and afterwards installed me in a rocking-chair beside a large fire, with the *Life of Mrs. Fletcher* to entertain me, while the gentlemen explored the premises, visited Mr. Kellogg's stock, and took a careful look at their own. We had intended to go to Dixon's the same afternoon, but the snow, beginning again to fall, obliged us to content ourselves where we were.

In the meantime, finding we were journeying to Chicago, Mr. Kellogg came to the determination to accompany us, having, as he said, some business to accomplish at that place: so Mrs. Kellogg busied herself in preparing him to set off with us the following morning. I pleaded hard to remain yet another day, as the following was Sunday, on which I objected to travel; but in view of the necessities of the case, the uncertainty of the weather, and the importance of getting as quickly as possible through this wild country, my objections were overruled, and I could only obtain a delay in starting until so late in the afternoon as would give us just time to ride the sixteen miles to "Dixon's" before sunset.

No great time was required for Mr. Kellogg's preparations. He would take, he said, only two days' provisions, for at his brother-in-law Dixon's we should get our supper and breakfast, and the route from there to Chicago could, he well knew, be accomplished in a day and a half.

Although, according to this calculation, we had sufficient remaining of our stores to carry us to the end of our journey, yet my husband took the precaution of begging Mrs. Kellogg to bake us another bag of biscuits, in case of accidents, and he likewise suggested to Mr. Kellogg the prudence of furnishing himself with something more than his limited allowance; but the good man objected that he was unwilling to burden his horse more than was absolutely necessary, seeing that, at this season of the year, we were obliged to carry fodder for the animals, in addition to the rest of their load. It will be seen that we had reason to rejoice in our own foresight.

My experience of the previous night had rendered me somewhat less fastidious than when I commenced my journey, so that, when introduced to our sleeping-apartment, which I found we were to share with six men, travellers like ourselves, my only feeling was one of thankfulness that each bed was furnished with a full suit of blue checked curtains, which formed a very tolerable substitute for a dressing-room.

CHAPTER 15

Rock River—Hours of Trouble

It was late on the following day (March 13th) when we took leave of our kind hostess. She loaded us with cakes, good wishes, and messages to her sister Dixon and the children. We journeyed pleasantly along through a country beautiful in spite of its wintry appearance.

There was a house at Buffalo Grove, at which we stopped for half an hour, and where a nice-looking young girl presented us with some maple-sugar of her own making. She entertained us with the history of a contest between two rival claimants for the patronage of the stage-wagon, the proprietors of which had not decided whether to send it by Buffalo Grove or by another route, which she pointed out to us, at no great distance. The *driver*, she took care to inform us, was in favour of the former; and the blush with which she replied in the affirmative to our inquiry, "Is he a young man?" explained the whole matter satisfactorily.

At length, just at sunset, we reached the dark, rapid waters of the Rock River. The ferry which we had travelled so far out of our way to take advantage of, proved to be merely a small boat or skiff, the larger one having been swept off into the stream, and carried down in the breaking-up of the ice, the week previous.

My husband's first care was to get me across. He placed me with the saddles, packs, etc. in the boat, and as, at that late hour, no time was to be lost, he ventured, at the same time, to hold the bridles of the two most docile horses, to guide them in swimming the river.

When we had proceeded a few rods from the shore, we were startled by a loud puffing and blowing near us, and looking around, to our great surprise, discovered little Brunet just upon our "weather-bow." Determined not to be outdone by his model, Jerry, he had taken to the water on his own responsibility, and arrived at the opposite shore as soon as any of the party.

All being safely landed, a short walk brought us to the house of Mr. Dixon. Although so recently come into the country, he had contrived to make everything comfortable around him; and when he ushered us into Mrs. Dixon's sitting-room, and seated us by a glowing wood fire, while Mrs. Dixon busied herself in preparing us a nice supper, I felt that the comfort overbalanced the inconvenience of such a journey.

Mrs. Dixon was surrounded by several children. One leaning against the chimney-piece was dressed in the full Indian costume—calico shirt, blanket, and leggings. His dark complexion, and full, melancholy eyes, which he kept fixed upon the ashes in which he was making marks with a stick, rarely raising them to gaze on us, as children are wont to do, interested me exceedingly, and I inquired of an intelligent little girl, evidently a daughter of our host,—

"Who is that boy?"

"Oh, that is John Ogie," answered she.

"What is the matter with him? he looks very sad."

"Oh, he is fretting after his mother."

"Is she dead, then?"

"Some say she is dead, and some say she is gone away. I guess she is dead, and buried up in one of those graves yonder"—pointing to two or three little picketed enclosures upon a rising ground opposite the window.

I felt a strong sympathy with the child, which was increased when the little spokeswoman, in answer to my inquiry, "Has he no father?" replied,—

"Oh, yes, but he goes away, and drinks, and don't care for his children."

"And what becomes of John then?"

"He stays here with us, and we teach him to read, and he learns *dreadful* fast."

When the boy at length turned his large dark eyes upon me, it went to my heart. It was such a *motherless* look. And it was explained when, long afterwards, I learned his further history. His mother was still living, and he knew it, although, with the reserve peculiar to his people, he never spoke of her to his young companions. Unable to endure the continued ill treatment of her husband, a surly, intemperate Canadian, she had left him, and returned to her own family among the Pottowattamies. Years after, this boy and a brother who had also been left behind with their father found their way to the Upper Missouri, to join their mother, who, with the others of her tribe, had been removed by the government from the shores of Lake Michigan.

A most savoury supper of ducks and venison, with their accompaniments, soon smoked upon the board, and we did ample justice to it. Travelling is a great sharpener of the appetite, and so is cheerfulness; and the latter was increased by the encouraging account Mr. Dixon gave us of the remainder of the route yet before us.

"There is no difficulty," said he, "if you keep a little to the north, and strike the great *Sauk trail*. If you get too far to the south, you will come upon the Winnebago Swamp, and, once in that, there is no telling when you will ever get out again. As for the distance, it is nothing at all to speak of. Two young men came out here from Chicago, on foot, last fall. They got here the evening of the second day; and, even with a lady in your party, you could go on horseback in less time than that. The only thing is to be sure and get on the great track that the Sauks have made, in going every year from the Mississippi to Canada, to receive their presents from the British Indian Agent."

The following morning, which was a bright and lovely one for that season of the year, we took leave of Mr. and Mrs. Dixon, in high spirits. We travelled for the first few miles along the beautiful, undulating banks of the Rock River, always in an easterly direction, keeping the beaten path, or rather road, which led to Fort Clark, or Peoria. The Sauk trail, we had been told, would cross this road at the distance of about six miles.

After having travelled, as we judged, fully that distance, we came upon a trail bearing northeast, and a consultation was held as to the probability of its being the one we were in search of.

Mr. Kinzie was of opinion that it tended too much to the north, and was, moreover, too faint and obscure for a trail so much used, and by so large a body of Indians in their annual journeys.

Plante was positive as to its being the very spot where he and "Piché" in their journey to Fort Winnebago, the year before, struck into the great road. "On that very rising-ground at the point of woods, he remembered perfectly well stopping to shoot ducks, which they ate for their supper."

Mr. Kellogg was non-committal, but sided alternately with each speaker.

As Plante was "the guide," and withal so confident of being right, it was decided to follow him, not without some demurring, however, on the part of the *bourgeois*, who every now and then called to halt, to discuss the state of affairs.

"Now, Plante," he would say, "I am sure you are leading us too far north. Why, man, if we keep on in this direction, following the course of the river, we shall bring up at Kosh-ko-nong, instead of Chicago."

"Ah! *mon bourgeois,*" would the light-hearted Canadian reply, "would I tell you this is the road if I were not quite certain? Only one year ago I travelled it, and can I forget so soon? Oh, no—I remember every foot of it."

But Monsieur Plante was convinced of his mistake when the trail brought us to the great bend of the river with its bold rocky bluffs.

"Are you satisfied now, Plante?" asked Mr. Kinzie. "By your leave, I will now play pilot myself." And he struck off from the trail, in a direction as nearly east as possible.

The weather had changed and become intensely cold, and we felt that the detention we had met with, even should we now be in the right road, was no trifling matter. We had not added to our stock of provisions at Dixon's, wishing to carry as much forage as we were able for our horses, for whom the scanty picking around our encamping-grounds afforded an insufficient meal. But we were buoyed up by the hope that we were in the right path at last, and we journeyed on until night, when we reached a comfortable "encampment," in the edge of a grove near a small stream.

Oh, how bitterly cold that night was! The salted provisions, to which I was accustomed, occasioned me an intolerable thirst, and my husband was in the habit of placing the little tin coffee-pot filled with water at my bed's head when we went to rest, but this night it was frozen solid long before midnight. We were so well wrapped up in blankets that we did not suffer from cold while within the tent, but the open air was severe in the extreme.

March 15th.—We were roused by the *bourgeois* at peep of day to make preparations for starting. We must find the Sauk trail this day at all hazards. What would become of us should we fail to do so? It was a question no one liked to ask, and certainly one that none could have answered.

On leaving our encampment, we found ourselves entering a marshy tract of country. Myriads of wild geese, brant, and ducks rose up screaming at our approach. The more distant lakes and ponds were black with them, but the shallow water through which we attempted to make our way was frozen, by the severity of the night, to a thickness not quite sufficient to bear the horses, but just such as to cut their feet and ankles at every step as they broke through it. Sometimes the difficulty of going forward was so great that we were obliged to retrace our steps and make our way round the head of the marsh, thus adding to the discomforts of our situation by the conviction that, while journeying diligently, we were, in fact, making very little progress.

This swampy region at length passed, we came upon more solid ground, chiefly the open prairie. But now a new trouble assailed us. The weather had moderated, and a blinding snow-storm came on. Without a trail that we could rely upon, and destitute of a compass, our only dependence had been the sun to point out our direction; but the atmosphere was now so obscure that it was impossible to tell in what quarter of the heavens he was.

We pursued our way, however, and a devious one it must have been. After travelling in this way many miles, we came upon an Indian trail, deeply indented, running at right angles with the course we were pursuing. The snow had ceased, and, the clouds becoming thinner, we were able to observe the direction of the sun, and to perceive that the trail ran north and south. What should we do? Was it safest to pursue our easterly course, or was it probable that by following this new path we should fall into the direct one we had been so long seeking? If we decided to take the trail, should we go north or south? Mr. Kinzie was for the latter. He was of opinion we were still too far north—somewhere about the Grand Marais, or Kish-wau-kee. Mr. Kellogg and Plante were for taking the northerly direction.

The latter was positive his *bourgeois* had already gone too far south—in fact, that we must now be in the neighbourhood of the Illinois River. Finding himself in the minority, my husband yielded, and we turned our horses' heads north, much against his will. After proceeding a few miles, however, he took a sudden determination. "You may go north, if you please," said he, "but I am convinced that the other course is right, and I shall face about—follow who will."

So, we wheeled round and rode south again, and many a long and weary mile did we travel, the monotony of our ride broken only by the querulous remarks of poor Mr. Kellogg. "I am really afraid we are wrong, Mr. Kinzie. I feel pretty sure that the young man is right. It looks most natural to me that we should take a northerly course, and not be stretching away so far to the south."

To all this, Mr. Kinzie turned a deaf ear. The Frenchmen rode in silence. They would as soon have thought of cutting off their right hand as showing opposition to the *bourgeois* when he had once expressed his decision. They would never have dreamed of offering an opinion or remark unless called upon to do so.

The road, which had continued many miles through the prairie, at length, in winding round a point of woods, brought us suddenly upon an Indian village. A shout of joy broke from the whole party, but no answering shout was returned—not even a bark of friendly welcome—as we galloped up to the *wigwams*. All was silent as the grave. We rode round and round, then dismounted and looked into several of the spacious huts. They had evidently been long deserted. Nothing remained but the bare walls of bark, from which everything in the shape of furniture had been stripped by the owners and carried with them to their wintering-grounds, to be brought back in the spring, when they returned to make their cornfields and occupy their summer cabins.

Our disappointment may be better imagined than described. With heavy hearts, we mounted and once more pursued our way, the snow again falling and adding to the discomforts of our position. At length we halted for the night. We had long been aware that our stock of provisions was insufficient for another day, and here we were—nobody knew where—in the midst of woods and prairies—certainly far from any human habitation, with barely enough food for a slender evening's meal.

The poor dogs came whining round us to beg their usual portion, but they were obliged to content themselves with a bare bone, and we retired to rest with the feeling that if not actually hungry then, we should certainly be so tomorrow.

The morrow came. Plante and Roy had a bright fire and a nice pot of coffee for us. It was our only breakfast, for, on shaking the bag and turning it inside out, we could make no more of our stock of bread than three crackers, which the rest of the party insisted I should put in my pocket for my dinner. I was much touched by the kindness of Mr. Kellogg, who drew from his wallet a piece of tongue and a slice of fruitcake, which he said "he had been saving for the lady since the day before, for he saw how matters were a going."

Poor man! it would have been well if he had listened to Mr. Kinzie and provided himself at the outset with a larger store of provisions. As it was, those he brought with him were exhausted early in the second day, and he had been *boarding* with us for the last two meals.

We still had the trail to guide us, and we continued to follow it until about nine o'clock, when, in emerging from a wood, we came upon a broad and rapid river. A collection of Indian *wigwams* stood upon the opposite bank, and, as the trail led directly to the water, it was fair to infer that the stream was fordable. We had no opportunity of testing it, however, for the banks were so lined with ice, which was piled up tier upon tier by the breaking-up of the previous week, that we tried in vain to find a path by which we could descend the bank to the water.

The men shouted again and again, in hopes some straggling inhabitant of the village might be at hand with his canoe. No answer was returned, save by the echoes. What was to be done? I looked at my husband and saw that care was on his brow, although he still continued to speak cheerfully. "We will follow this cross-trail down the bank of the river," said he. "There must be Indians wintering near, in some of these points of wood."

I must confess that I felt somewhat dismayed at our prospects, but I kept up a show of courage, and did not allow my despondency to be seen. All the party were dull and gloomy enough.

We kept along the bank, which was considerably elevated above the water, and bordered at a little distance with a thick wood. All at once my horse, who was mortally afraid of Indians, began to jump and prance, snorting and pricking up his ears as if an enemy were at hand. I screamed with delight to my husband, who was at the head of the file, "Oh, John! John! there are Indians near—look at Jerry!"

At this instant a little Indian dog ran out from under the bushes by the roadside, and began barking at us. Never were sounds more welcome. We rode directly into the thicket, and, descending into a little hollow, found two squaws crouching behind the bushes, trying to conceal themselves from our sight.

They appeared greatly relieved when Mr. Kinzie addressed them in the Pottowattamie language,—

"What are you doing here?"

"Digging Indian potatoes"—(a species of artichoke.)

"Where is your lodge?"

"On the other side of the river."

"Good—then you have a canoe here. Can you take us across?"

"Yes—the canoe is very small."

They conducted us down the bank to the water's edge where the canoe was. It was indeed *very small*. My husband explained to them that they must take me across first, and then return for the others of the party.

"Will you trust yourself alone over the river?" inquired he. "You see that but one can cross at a time."

"Oh, yes"—and I was soon placed in the bottom of the canoe, lying flat and looking up at the sky, while the older squaw took the paddle in her hand, and placed herself on her knees at my head, and the younger, a girl of fourteen or fifteen, stationed herself at my feet. There was just room enough for me to lie in this position, each of the others kneeling in the opposite ends of the canoe.

While these preparations were making, Mr. Kinzie questioned the women as to our whereabout. They knew no name for the river but "Saumanong." This was not definite, it being the generic term for any large stream. But he gathered that the village we had passed higher up, on the opposite side of the stream, was Wau-ban-see's, and then he knew that we were on the Fox River, and probably about fifty miles from Chicago.

The squaw, in answer to his inquiries, assured him that Chicago was "close by."

"That means," said he, "that it is not so far off as Canada. We must not be too sanguine."

The men set about unpacking the horses, and I in the meantime was paddled across the river. The old woman immediately returned, leaving the younger one with me for company. I seated myself on the fallen trunk of a tree, in the midst of the snow, and looked across the dark waters. I am not ashamed to confess my weakness—for the first time on my journey I shed tears. It was neither hunger, nor fear, nor cold, which extorted them from me. It was the utter desolation of spirit, the sickness of heart which "hope deferred" ever occasions, and which of all evils is the hardest to bear.

The poor little squaw looked into my face with a wondering and sympathizing expression. Probably she was speculating in her own mind what a person who rode so fine a horse, and wore so comfortable a broadcloth dress, could have to cry about. I pointed to a seat beside me on the log, but she preferred standing and gazing at me, with the same pitying expression. Presently she was joined by a young companion, and, after a short chattering, of which I was evidently the subject, they both trotted off into the woods, and left me to my own solitary reflections.

"What would my friends at the East think," said I to myself, "if they could see me now? What would poor old Mrs. Welsh say? She who warned me that *if I came away so far to the West, I should break my heart?* Would she not rejoice to find how likely her prediction was to be fulfilled?"

These thoughts roused me. I dried up my tears, and by the time my husband with his party and all his horses and luggage were across, I had recovered my cheerfulness, and was ready for fresh adventures.

CHAPTER 16

Relief

We followed the old squaw to her lodge, which was at no great distance in the woods. I had never before been in an Indian lodge, although I had occasionally peeped into one of the many always clustered round the house of the interpreter at the Portage.

This one was very nicely arranged. Four sticks of wood placed to form a square in the centre, answered the purpose of a hearth, within which the fire was built, the smoke escaping through an opening in the top. The mats of which the lodge was constructed were very neat and new, and against the sides, depending from the poles or framework, hung various bags of Indian manufacture, containing their dried food and other household treasures.

Sundry ladles, small kettles, and wooden bowls also hung from the cross-poles; and dangling from the centre, by an iron chain, was a large kettle in which some dark, suspicious-looking substance was seething over the scanty fire. On the floor of the lodge, between the fire and the outer wall, were spread mats, upon which my husband invited me to be seated and make myself comfortable.

The first demand of an Indian on meeting a white man is for *bread*, of which they are exceedingly fond, and I knew enough of the Pottowattamie language to comprehend the timid *"pe-qua-zhe-gun choh-kay-go"* (I have no bread) with which the squaw commenced our conversation after my husband had left the lodge.

I shook my head, and endeavoured to convey to her that, so far from being able to give, I had had no breakfast myself. She understood me, and instantly produced a bowl, into which she ladled a quantity of Indian potatoes from the kettle over the fire, and set them before me. I was too hungry to be fastidious, and, owing partly, no doubt, to the sharpness of my appetite, I really found them delicious.

Two little girls, inmates of the lodge, sat gazing at me with evident admiration and astonishment, which were increased when I took my little Prayer book from my pocket and began to read. They had, undoubtedly, never seen a book before, and I was amused at the care with which they looked away from me, while they questioned their mother about my strange employment and listened to her replies.

While thus occupied, I was startled by a sudden sound of *"hogh!"* and the mat which hung over the entrance of the lodge was raised, and an Indian entered with that graceful bound which is peculiar to themselves. It was the master of the lodge, who had been out to shoot ducks, and was just returned. He was a tall, finely-formed man, with a cheerful, open countenance, and he listened to what his wife in a quiet tone related to him, while he divested himself of his accoutrements, in the most unembarrassed, well-bred manner imaginable.

Soon my husband joined us. He had been engaged in attending to the comfort of his horses, and assisting his men in making their fire, and pitching their tent, which the rising storm made a matter of some difficulty.

From the Indian he learned that we were in what was called the Big Woods, (probably at what is now Oswego, the name of a portion of the wood is since corrupted into *Specie's Grove*), or "Piché's Grove," from a Frenchman of that name living not far from the spot—that the river we had crossed was the Fox River—that he could guide us to Piché's, from which the road was perfectly plain, or even into Chicago if we preferred—but that we had better remain encamped for that day, as there was a storm coming on, and in the meantime he would go and shoot some ducks for our dinner and supper. He was accordingly furnished with powder and shot, and set off again for game without delay.

I had put into my pocket, on leaving home, a roll of scarlet ribbon, in case a stout string should be wanted, and I now drew it forth, and with the knife which hung around my neck I cut off a couple of yards for each of the little girls. They received it with great delight, and their mother, dividing each portion into two, tied a piece to each of the little clubs into which their hair was knotted on the temples. They laughed, and exclaimed "*Saum!*" as they gazed at each other, and their mother joined in their mirth, although, as I thought, a little unwilling to display her maternal exultation before a stranger.

The tent being all in order, my husband came for me, and we took leave of our friends in the *wigwam*, with grateful hearts.

The storm was raging without. The trees were bending and cracking around us, and the air was completely filled with the wild-fowl screaming and *quacking* as they made their way southward before the blast. Our tent was among the trees not far from the river. My husband took me to the bank to look for a moment at what we had escaped. The wind was sweeping down from the north in a perfect hurricane. The water was filled with masses of snow and ice, dancing along upon the torrent, over which were hurrying thousands of wild-fowl, making the woods resound to their deafening clamour.

Had we been one hour later, we could not possibly have crossed the stream, and there would have been nothing for us but to have remained and starved in the wilderness. Could we be sufficiently grateful to that kind Providence that had brought us safely through such dangers?

The men had cut down an immense tree, and built a fire against it, but the wind shifted so continually that every five minutes the tent would become completely filled with smoke, so that I was driven into the open air for breath. Then I would seat myself on one end of the huge log, as near the fire as possible, for it was dismally cold, but the wind seemed actuated by a kind of caprice, for in whatever direction I took my seat, just that way came the smoke and hot ashes, puffing in my face until I was nearly blinded. Neither veil nor silk handkerchief afforded an effectual protection, and I was glad when the arrival of our huntsmen, with a quantity of ducks, gave me an opportunity of diverting my thoughts from my own sufferings, by aiding the men to pick them and get them ready for our meal.

We borrowed a kettle from our Indian friends. It was not remarkably clean; but we heated a little water in it, and *prairie-hay'd* it out, before consigning our birds to it, and with a bowl of Indian potatoes, a present from our kind neighbours, we soon had an excellent soup.

What with the cold, the smoke, and the driving ashes and cinders, this was the most uncomfortable afternoon I had yet passed, and I was glad when night came, and I could creep into the tent and cover myself up in the blankets, out of the way of all three of these evils.

The storm raged with tenfold violence during the night. We were continually startled by the crashing of the falling trees around us, and who could tell but that the next would be upon us? Spite of our fatigue, we passed an almost sleepless night. When we arose in the morning, we were made fully alive to the perils by which we had been surrounded. At least fifty trees, the giants of the forest, lay prostrate within view of the tent.

When we had taken our scanty breakfast, and were mounted and ready for departure, it was with difficulty we could thread our way, so completely was it obstructed by the fallen trunks.

Our Indian guide had joined us at an early hour, and after conducting us carefully out of the wood, and pointing out to us numerous bee-trees, for which he said that grove was famous, he set off at a long trot, and about nine o'clock brought us to Piché's, a log cabin on a rising ground, looking off over the broad prairie to the east. (The honey-bee is not known in the perfectly wild countries of North America. It is ever the pioneer of civilization, and the Indians call it "*the white man's bird.*") We had hoped to get some refreshment here, Piché being an old acquaintance of some of the party; but, alas! the master was from home. We found his cabin occupied by Indians and travellers—the latter few, the former numerous.

There was no temptation to a halt, except that of warming ourselves at a bright fire that was burning in the clay chimney. A man in Quaker costume stepped forward to answer our inquiries, and offered to become our escort to Chicago, to which place he was bound—so we dismissed our Indian friend, with a satisfactory remuneration for all the trouble he had so kindly taken for us.

A long reach of prairie extended from Piché's to the Du Page, between the two forks of which, Mr. Dogherty, our new acquaintance, told us, we should find the dwelling of a Mr. Hawley, who would give us a comfortable dinner.

The weather was intensely cold; the wind, sweeping over the wide prairie with nothing to break its force, chilled our very hearts. I beat my feet against the saddle to restore the circulation, when they became benumbed with the cold, until they were so bruised, I could beat them no longer. Not a house or *wigwam*, not even a clump of trees as a shelter, offered itself for many a weary mile. At length we reached the west fork of the Du Page. It was frozen, but not sufficiently so to bear the horses. Our only resource was to cut a way for them through the ice. It was a work of time, for the ice had frozen to several inches in thickness during the last bitter night. Plante went first with an axe, and cut as far as he could reach, then mounted one of the hardy little ponies, and with some difficulty broke the ice before him, until he had opened a passage to the opposite shore.

How the poor animals shivered as they were reined in among the floating ice! And we, who sat waiting in the piercing wind, were not much better off. Probably Brunet was of the same opinion; for, with his usual perversity, he plunged in immediately after Plante, and stood shaking and quaking behind him, every now and then looking around him, as much as to say, "I've got ahead of you, this time!" We were all across at last, and spurred on our horses, until we reached Hawley's—a large, commodious dwelling, near the east fork of the river. (It was near this spot that the brother of Mr. Hawley, a Methodist preacher, was killed by the Sauks, in 1832, after having been tortured by them with the most wanton barbarity.)

The good woman welcomed us kindly, and soon made us warm and comfortable. We felt as if we were in a civilized land once more. She proceeded immediately to prepare dinner for us; and we watched her with eager eyes, as she took down a huge ham from the rafters, out of which she cut innumerable slices, then broke a dozen or more of fine fresh eggs into a pan, in readiness for frying—then mixed a *johnny-cake*, and placed it against a board in front of the fire to bake. It seemed to me that even with the aid of this fine, bright fire, the dinner took an unconscionable time to cook; but cooked it was, at last, and truly might the good woman stare at the travellers' appetites we had brought with us. She did not know what short commons we had been on for the last two days.

We found, upon inquiry, that we could, by pushing on, reach Lawton's, on the Aux Plaines, that night—we should then be within twelve miles of Chicago. Of course, we made no unnecessary delay, but set off as soon after dinner as possible.

The crossing of the east fork of the Du Page was more perilous than the former one had been. The ice had become broken, either by the force of the current, or by some equestrians having preceded us and cut through it, so that when we reached the bank, the ice was floating down in large cakes. The horses had to make a rapid dart through the water, which was so high, and rushing in such a torrent, that if I had not been mounted on Jerry, the tallest horse in the cavalcade, I must have got a terrible splashing.

As it was, I was well frightened, and grasped both bridle and mane with the utmost tenacity. After this we travelled on as rapidly as possible, in order to reach our place of destination before dark.

Mr. Dogherty, a tall, bolt-upright man, half Quaker, half Methodist, did his best to entertain me, by giving me a thorough schedule of his religious opinions, with the reasons from Scripture upon which they were based. He was a good deal of a perfectionist, and evidently looked upon himself with no small satisfaction, as a living illustration of his favourite doctrine.

"St. John says," this was the style of his discourse, "St. John says, 'He that is born of God, doth not commit sin' Now, *if* I am born of God, I do not commit sin."

I was too cold and too weary to argue the point, so I let him have it all his own way. I believe he must have thought me rather a dull companion; but at least he gave me the credit of being a good listener.

It was almost dark when we reached Lawton's. The Aux Plaines was frozen, and the house was on the other side. (Rivière Aux Plaines was the original French designation, now changed to *Desplaines*, pronounced as in English.) By loud shouting, we brought out a man from the building, and he succeeded in cutting the ice, and bringing a canoe over to us; but not until it had become difficult to distinguish objects in the darkness.

A very comfortable house was Lawton's, after we did reach it—carpeted, and with a warm stove—in fact, quite in civilized style, Mr. Weeks, the man who brought us across, was the *major-domo*, during the temporary absence of Mr. Lawton.

Mrs. Lawton was a young woman, and not ill-looking. She complained bitterly of the loneliness of her condition, and having been "brought out there into the woods; which was a thing she had not expected, when she came from the East." We did not ask her with what expectations she had come to a wild, unsettled country; but we tried to comfort her with the assurance that things would grow better in a few years. She said, "She did not mean to wait for that. She should go back to her family in the East, if Mr. Lawton did not invite some of her young friends to come and stay with her, and make it agreeable."

We could hardly realise, on rising the following morning, that only twelve miles of prairie intervened between us and *Chicago le Désiré*, as I could not but name it.

We could look across the extended plain, and on its farthest verge were visible two tall trees, which my husband pointed out to me as the planting of his own hand, when a boy. Already they had become so lofty as to serve as landmarks, and they were constantly in view as we travelled the beaten road. I was continually repeating to myself, "There live the friends I am so longing to see! There will terminate all our trials and hardships!"

A Mr. Wentworth joined us on the road, and of him we inquired after the welfare of the family, from whom we had, for a long time, received no intelligence. When we reached Chicago, he took us to a little tavern at the forks of the river. This portion of the place was then called *Wolf Point,* from its having been the residence of an Indian named "*Moaway,*" or "the Wolf."

"Dear me," said the old landlady, at the little tavern, "what dreadful cold weather you must have had to travel in! Why, two days ago the river was all open here, and now it's frozen hard enough for folks to cross a-horseback!"

Notwithstanding this assurance, my husband did not like to venture, so he determined to leave his horses and proceed on foot to the residence of his mother and sister, a distance of about half a mile.

We set out on our walk, which was first across the ice, then down the northern bank of the river. As we approached the house we were espied by Genevieve, a half-breed servant of the family. She did not wait to salute us, but flew into the house, crying,—

"Oh! Madame Kinzie, who do you think has come? Monsieur John and Madame John, all the way from Fort Winnebago on foot!"

Soon we were in the arms of our dear, kind friends. A messenger was dispatched to "the garrison" for the remaining members of the family, and for that day, at least, I was the wonder and admiration of the whole circle, "for the dangers I had seen."

CHAPTER 17

Chicago in 1831

Fort Dearborn at that day consisted of the same buildings as at present, (1855). They were, of course, in a better state of preservation, though still considerably dilapidated. They had been erected in 1816, under the supervision of Captain Hezekiah Bradley, and there was a story current that, such was his patriotic regard for the interests of the Government, he obliged the soldiers to fashion wooden pins, instead of spikes and nails, to fasten the timbers of the buildings, and that he

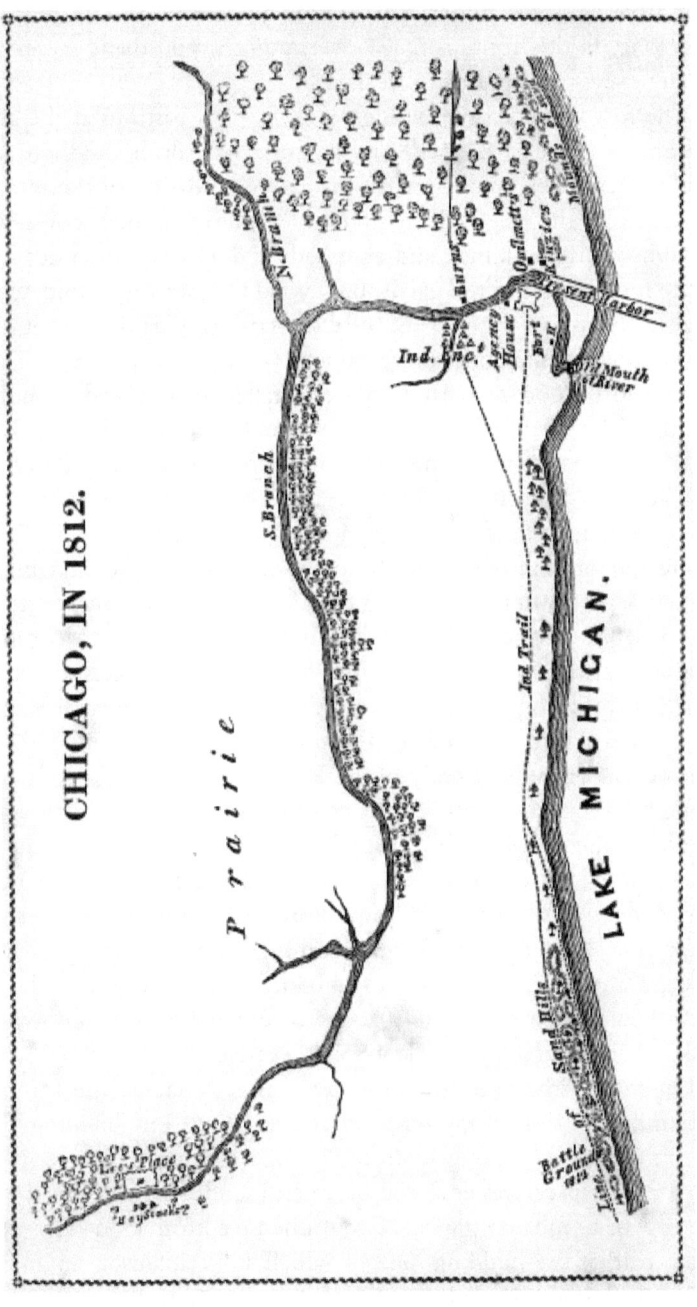

even called on the junior officers to aid in their construction along with the soldiers, whose business it was. If this were true, the captain must have laboured under the delusion (excusable in one who had lived long on the frontier) that Government would thank its servants for any excess of economical zeal.

The fort was enclosed by high pickets, with bastions at the alternate angles. Large gates opened to the north and south, and there were small posterns here and there for the accommodation of the inmates. The bank of the river which stretches to the west, now covered by the light-house buildings, and enclosed by docks, was then occupied by the root-houses of the garrison. Beyond the parade-ground, which extended south of the pickets, were the company gardens, well filled with currant-bushes and young fruit-trees.

The fort stood at what might naturally be supposed to be the mouth of the river. It was not so, however, for in those days the latter took a turn, sweeping round the promontory on which the fort was built, towards the south, and joining the lake about half a mile below. These buildings stood on the right bank of the river, the left being a long spit of land extending from the northern shore, of which it formed a part. After the cutting through of this portion of the left bank in 1833 by the United States Engineers employed to construct a harbour at this point, and the throwing out of the piers, the water overflowed this long tongue of land, and, continually encroaching on the southern bank, robbed it of many valuable acres; while, by the same action of the vast body of the lake, an accretion was constantly taking place on the north of the harbour.

The residence of Jean Baptiste Beaubien stood at this period between the gardens and the river-bank, and still farther south was a rickety tenement, built many years before by Mr. John Dean, the sutler of the post. A short time after the commencement of the growth of Chicago, the foundations of this building were undermined by the gradual encroachment of the lake, and it tumbled backward down the bank, where it long lay, a melancholy spectacle.

On the northern bank of the river, directly facing the fort, was the family mansion of my husband. It was a long, low building, with a *piazza* extending along its front, a range of four or five rooms. A broad green space was enclosed between it and the river, and shaded by a row of Lombardy poplars. Two immense cottonwood-trees stood in the rear of the building, one of which still remains as an ancient landmark. A fine, well-cultivated garden extended to the north of the

dwelling, and surrounding it were various buildings appertaining to the establishment—dairy, bake-house, lodging-house for the Frenchmen, and stables.

A vast range of sand-hills, covered with stunted cedars, pines, and dwarf-willow-trees, intervened between the house and the lake, which was, at this time, not more than thirty rods distant.

Proceeding from this point along the northern bank of the river, we came first to the Agency House, "Cobweb Castle," as it had been denominated while long the residence of a bachelor, and the *sobriquet* adhered to it ever after. It stood at what is now the southwest corner of Wolcott (since called N. State Street—1870), and N. Water Streets. Many will still remember it, a substantial, compact little building of logs hewed and squared, with a centre, two wings, and, strictly speaking, two tails, since, when there was found no more room for additions at the sides, they were placed in the rear, whereon a vacant spot could be found.

These appendages did not mar the symmetry of the whole, as viewed from the front, but when, in the process of the town's improvement, a street was maliciously opened directly in the rear of the building, the whole establishment, with its comical little adjuncts, was a constant source of amusement to the passers-by. No matter. There were pleasant, happy hours passed under its odd-shaped roof, as many of Chicago's early settlers can testify.

Around the Agency House were grouped a collection of log buildings, the residences of the different persons in the employ of Government, appertaining to that establishment—blacksmith, striker, and laborers. These were for the most part Canadians or half-breeds, with occasionally a stray Yankee, to set all things going by his activity and enterprise.

There was still another house on the north side of the river, built by a former resident by the name of Miller, but he had removed to "*Rivière du Chemin,*" or Trail Creek, which about this time began to be called "Michigan City." This house, which stood near the forks of the river, was at this time vacant.

★★★★★★★★★★

I can recall a petition that was circulated at the garrison about this period, for "building a brigg over Michigan City." By altering the orthography, it was found to mean, not the stupendous undertaking it would seem to imply, but simply "building a bridge" over at Michigan City—an accommodation much needed by travellers at that day.

****

There was no house on the southern bank of the river, between the fort and "The Point," as the forks of the river were then called. The land was a low wet prairie, scarcely affording good walking in the driest summer weather, while at other seasons it was absolutely impassable. A muddy streamlet, or, as it is called in this country, a *slew*, (proper orthography of this word is *slough*, as it invariably indicates something like that which Christian fell into in flying from the City of Destruction, I spell it, however, as it is pronounced), after winding around from about the present site of the Tremont House, fell into the river at the foot of State Street. (A gentleman who visited Chicago at that day, thus speaks of it: "I passed over the ground from the fort to the point, on horseback. I was up to my stirrups in water the whole distance. I would not have given sixpence an acre for the whole of it.")

At the point, on the south side, stood a house just completed by Mark Beaubien. It was a pretentious white two-storey building, with bright-blue wooden shutters, the admiration of all the little circle at Wolf Point. Here a canoe ferry was kept to transport people across the south branch of the river.

Facing down the river from the west was, first a small tavern kept by Mr. Wentworth, familiarly known as "Old Geese," not from any want of shrewdness on his part, but in compliment to one of his own cant expressions. Near him were two or three log cabins occupied by Robinson, the Pottowattamie chief, and some of his wife's connexions. Billy Caldwell, the Sau-ga-nash, too, resided here occasionally, with his wife, who was a daughter of Nee-scot-nee-meg, one of the most famous chiefs of the nation. A little remote from these residences was a small square log building, originally designed for a schoolhouse, but occasionally used as a place of worship whenever any itinerant minister presented himself.

The family of Clybourn had, previous to this time, established themselves near their present residence on the North Branch—they called their place *New Virginia*. Four miles up the South Branch was an old building which was at one time an object of great interest as having been the theatre of some stirring events during the troubles of 1812. (See the narrative of the massacre in chapter 18). It was denominated Lee's Place, or Hardscrabble. Here lived, at this time, a settler named Heacock.

Owing to the badness of the roads a greater part of the year, the usual mode of communication between the fort and the Point was by a boat rowed up the river, or by a canoe paddled by some skilful hand. By the latter means, too, an intercourse was kept up between the residents of the fort and the Agency House.

There were, at this time, two companies of soldiers in the garrison, but of the officers one, Lieutenant Furman, had died the autumn previous, and several of the others were away on furlough. In the absence of Major Fowle and Captain Scott, the command devolved on Lieutenant Hunter. Besides him, there were Lieutenants Engle and Foster—the latter unmarried. Dr. Finley, the post surgeon, was also absent, and his place was supplied by Dr. Harmon, a gentleman from Vermont.

My husband's mother, two sisters, and brother resided at the Agency House—the family residence near the lake being occupied by J.N. Bailey, the postmaster.

In the Dean House lived a Mr. and Mrs. Forbes, who kept a school. Gholson Kercheval had a small trading establishment in one of the log buildings at Wolf Point, and John S.C. Hogan superintended the sutler's store in the garrison.

There was also a Mr. See lately come into the country, living at the Point, who sometimes held forth in the little school-house on a Sunday, less to the edification of his hearers than to the unmerciful slaughter of the "King's English."

I think this enumeration comprises all the white inhabitants of Chicago at a period less than half a century ago. To many who may read these pages the foregoing particulars will, doubtless, appear uninteresting. But to those who visit Chicago, and still more to those who come to make it their home, it may be not without interest to look back to its first beginnings; to contemplate the almost magical change which a few years have wrought; and from the past to augur the marvellous prosperity of the future.

The origin of the name Chicago is a subject of discussion, some of the Indians deriving it from the fitch or polecat, others from the wild onion with which the woods formerly abounded; but all agree that the place received its name from an old chief who was drowned in the stream in former times. That this event, although so carefully preserved by tradition, must have occurred in a very remote period, is evident from an old French manuscript brought by General Cass from France.

In this paper, which purports to be a letter from M. de Ligney, at Green Bay, to M. de Siette, among the Illinois, dated as early as

1726, the place is designated as "Chica-goux." This orthography is also found in old family letters of the beginning of the present century.

★★★★★★★★★★★★★★★★★★

In giving the early history of Chicago, the Indians say, with great simplicity, "the first white man who settled here was a negro."

This was Jean Baptiste Point-au-Sable, a native of St. Domingo, who, about the year 1796, found his way to this remote region, and commenced a life among the Indians. There is usually a strong affection between these two races, and Jean Baptiste imposed upon his new friends by making them believe that he had been a "great chief" among the whites. Perhaps he was disgusted at not being elected to a similar dignity by the Pottowattamies, for he quitted this vicinity, and finally terminated his days at Peoria, under the roof of his friend Glamorgan, another St. Domingo negro, who had obtained large Spanish grants in St. Louis and its environs, and who, at one time, was in the enjoyment of an extensive landed estate.

Point-au-Sable had made some improvements at Chicago, which were taken possession of by a Frenchman named Le Mai, who commenced trading with the Indians. After a few years Le Mai's establishment was purchased by John Kinzie, Esq., who at that time resided at Bertrand, or *Parc aux Vaches,* as it was then called, near Niles, in Michigan. As this gentleman was for nearly twenty years, with the exception of the military, the only white inhabitant of Northern Illinois, some particulars of his early life may not be uninteresting.

He was born in Quebec in 1163. His mother had been previously married to a gentleman of the name of Haliburton. The only daughter of this marriage was the mother of General Fleming, Nicholas Low, Esq., and Mrs. Charles King, of New York. She is described as a lady of remarkable beauty and accomplishments. Mr. Kinzie was the only child of the second marriage. His father died in his infancy, and his mother married a third time a Mr. Forsyth, after which they removed to the city of New York.

At the age of ten or eleven years he was placed at school with two of his half-brothers at Williamsburg, L.I. A negro servant was sent from the city every Saturday, to bring the children home, to remain until the following Monday morning. Upon one occasion, when the messenger arrived at the school, he found all things in commotion. Johnny Kinzie was missing! Search was made in all directions; every place was ransacked. It was all in vain; no Johnny Kinzie could be found.

The heavy tidings were carried home to his mother. By some it was supposed the lad was drowned; by others that he had strayed away, and would return. Weeks passed by, and months, and he was at length given up and mourned as lost. In the meantime, the boy was fulfilling a determination he had long formed, to visit his native city of Quebec, and make his way in life for himself.

He had by some means succeeded in crossing from Williamsburg to the city of New York, and finding at one of the docks on the North River a sloop bound for Albany, he took passage on board of her. While on his way up the river, he was noticed by a gentleman, who, taking an interest in the little lonely passenger, questioned him about his business.

"He was going to Quebec, where he had some friends."

"Had he the means to carry him there?"

"Not much, but he thought he could get along."

It happened, fortunately, that the gentleman himself was going to Quebec. He took the boy under his care, paid his expenses the whole distance, and finally parted with him in the streets of the city, where he was, in truth, a stranger.

He wandered about for a time, looking into various "stores" and workshops. At length, on entering the shop of a silversmith, he was satisfied with the expression he read in the countenance of the master, and he inquired if he wanted an apprentice.

"What, you, my little fellow! What can you do?"

"Anything you can teach me."

"Well, we will make a trial and see."

The trial was satisfactory. He remained in the family of his kind friend for more than three years, when his parents, who, in removing to Detroit, had necessarily returned to Canada, discovered his place of abode, and he was restored to them.

There were five younger half-brothers, of the name of Forsyth. In the old family Bible, we find the following touching record of an event that occurred after the family had removed to Detroit:—

> George Forsyth was lost in the woods 6th August, 1775, when Henry Hays and Mark Stirling ran away and left him. The remains of George Forsyth were found by an Indian the 2nd of October, 1776, close by the Prairie Ronde.

It seems a singular fatality that the unhappy mother should have been twice called to suffer a similar affliction—the loss of a child in a manner worse than death, inasmuch as it left room for all the horrors that imagination can suggest. The particulars of the loss of this little brother were these. As he came from school one evening, he met the coloured servant-boy on horseback, going to the common for the cows. The schoolhouse stood quite near the old fort, and all beyond that, towards the west, was a wild, uncultivated tract called "the Common." The child begged of the servant to take him up and give him a ride, but the other refused, bidding him return home at once. He was accompanied by two other boys, somewhat older, and together they followed the negro for some distance, hoping to prevail upon him to give them a ride.

As it grew dark, the two older boys turned back, but the other kept on. When the negro returned, he had not again seen the child, nor were any tidings ever received of him, notwithstanding the diligent search made by the whole little community, until, as related in the record, his remains were found the following year by an Indian. There was nothing to identify them, except the auburn curls of his hair, and the little boots he had worn. He must have perished very shortly after having lost his way, for the Prairie Ronde was too near the settlement to have prevented his bearing the calls and sounding horns of those in search of him, had he been living.

Mr. Kinzie's enterprising and adventurous disposition led him, as he grew older, to live much on the frontier. He early entered into the Indian trade, and had establishments at Sandusky and Maumee. About the year 1800 he pushed farther west, to St. Joseph's, Michigan. In this year he married Mrs. McKillip, the widow of a British officer, and in 1804 came to make his home at Chicago. It was in this year that the first fort was built by Major John Whistler.

By degrees more remote trading-posts were established by him, all contributing to the parent one at Chicago; at Milwaukie with the Menomonees; at Rock River with the Winnebagoes and the Pottowattamies; on the Illinois River and Kankakee with the Pottowattamies of the Prairies, and with the Kickapoos in what was called "*Le Large*," being the widely extended district afterwards erected into Sangamon County.

Each trading-post had its superintendent, and its complement of *engagés*—its train of pack-horses and its equipment of boats and canoes. From most of the stations the furs and peltries were brought to Chicago on packhorses, and the goods necessary for the trade were transported in return by the same method.

The vessels which came in the spring and fall (seldom more than two or three annually), to bring the supplies and goods for the trade, took the furs that were already collected to Mackinac, the depot of the Southwest and American Fur Companies. At other seasons they were sent to that place in boats, coasting around the lake.

★★★★★★★★★★★★★★★

Of the Canadian *voyageurs* or *engagés*, a race that has now so nearly passed away, some notice may very properly here be given.

They were unlike any other class of men. Like the poet, they seemed born to their vocation. Sturdy, enduring, ingenious, and light-hearted, they possessed a spirit capable of adapting itself to any emergency. No difficulties baffled, no hardships discouraged them; while their affectionate nature led them to form attachments of the warmest character to their "*bourgeois*," or master, as well as to the native inhabitants, among whom their engagements carried them.

Montreal, or, according to their own pronunciation, *Marrialle*, was their depot. It was at that place that the agents commissioned to make up the quota for the different companies and traders found the material for their selections.

The terms of engagement were usually from four to six hundred *livres* (ancient Quebec currency) *per annum* as wages, with rations of one quart of lyed corn, and two ounces of tallow *per diem*, or "its equivalent in whatever sort of food is to be found in the Indian country." Instances have been known of their submitting cheerfully to fare upon fresh fish and maple-sugar for a whole winter, when cut off from other supplies.

It was a common saying, "Keep an *engagé* to his corn and tallow, he will serve you well—give him pork and bread, and he soon gets beyond your management." They regard the terms of their engagement as binding to the letter. An old trader, M. Berthelet, engaged a crew at Montreal. The terms of agreement were, that they should eat when their *bourgeois* did, and what he did. It was a piece of fun on the part of the old gentleman, but the simple Canadians believed it to be a signal instance of good luck that had provided them such luxurious prospects. The *bourgeois* stuffed his pockets with crackers, and, when sure of being quite unobserved, would slily eat one. Pipe after pipe passed—the men grew hungry, but, observing that there were no preparations of a meal for the *bourgeois*, they bore their fast without complaining.

At length the matter became too serious—they could stand it no longer. In their distress they begged off from the bargain, and gladly compounded to take the customary rations, instead of the dainty fare they had been promising themselves with their master.

On arriving at Mackinac, which was the *entrepôt* of the fur trade, a small proportion of the *voyageur's* wages was advanced him, to furnish his winter's outfit, his pipes and tobacco, his needles and thread, some pieces of bright-coloured ribbons, and red and yellow gartering (quality binding), with which to purchase their little necessaries from the Indians. To these, if his destination were Lake Superior, or a post far to the north where such articles could not be readily obtained, were added one or two smoked deer-skins for *moccasins*.

Thus equipped, he entered upon his three years' service, to toil by day, and laugh, joke, sing, and tell stories when the evening hour brought rest and liberty.

There was not wanting here and there an instance of obstinate adherence to the exact letter of the agreement in regard to the nature of employment, although, as a general thing, the *engagé* held himself ready to fulfil the behests of his *bourgeois*, as faithfully as ever did vassal those of his chief.

A story is told of M. St. Jean, a trader on the Upper Mississippi, who upon a certain occasion ordered one of his Frenchmen to accompany a party to the forest to chop wood. The man refused. "He was not hired," he said, "to chop wood."

"Ah! for what, then, were you hired?"

"To steer a boat."

"Very well; steer a boat, then, since you prefer it."

It was mid-winter. The recusant was marched to the river-side, and placed in the stern of the boat, which lay fastened in the ice.

After serving a couple of hours at his legitimate employment, with the thermometer below zero, he was quite content to take his place with the chopping-party, and never again thought it good policy to choose work for himself.

There is an aristocracy in the *voyageur* service which is quite amusing. The engagement is usually made for three years. The *engagé* of the first year, who is called a "*mangeur-de-lard*," or pork-eater, is looked down upon with the most sovereign contempt by an "*hivernant*," or one who has already passed a winter in the country. He will not only not associate with him, but if invited by him to join him in a friendly glass, he will make some excuse for declining. The most inveterate drunkard, while tortured by a longing to partake his favourite indulgence, will yet never suffer himself to be enticed into an infringement of this custom.

After the first winter, the *mangeur-de-lard* rises from his freshman class, and takes his place where he can in turn lord it over all newcomers.

Another peculiarity of the *voyageurs* is their fancy for transforming the names of their *bourgeois* into something funny, which resembles it in sound. Thus, Kinzie would be called by one "*Quinze nez*" (fifteen noses), by another "*Singé*" (monkeyfied). Mr. Kercheval was denominated Mons. *Court-cheval* (short horse), the Judge of Probate, "*le Juge Trop-bête*" (too foolish), etc. The following is an instance in point.

Mr. Shaw, one of the agents of the Northwest Fur Company, had passed many years on the frontier, and was by the *voyageurs* called *Monsieur Le Chat*. (Mr. Cat).

On quitting the Indian country, he married a Canadian lady and became the father of several children. Some years after his return to Canada, his old foreman, named Louis la Liberté, went to Montreal to spend the winter. He had heard of his old *bourgeois*' marriage, and was anxious to see him.

Mr. Shaw was walking in the Champ de Mars with a couple of officers, when La Liberté espied him. He immediately ran up, and, seizing him by both hands, accosted him,—

"*Ah! mon cher Monsieur le Chat: comment vous portez-vous?*" (My dear Mr. Cat, how do you do?)

"*Très-bien, Louizon.*"

"*Et comment se porte Madame la Chatte?*" (How is the mother cat?)

"*Bien, bien, Louizon; elle est très-bien*" (She is very well.)

"*Et tous les petits Chatons?*" (And all the kittens?)

This was too much for Mr. Shaw. He answered shortly that the kittens were all well, and turned away with his military friends, leaving poor Louizon quite astonished at the abruptness of his departure.

Cut off, in the manner described, from the world at large, with no society but the military, thus lived the family of Mr. Kinzie, in great contentment, and in the enjoyment of all the comforts, together with most of the luxuries, of life.

The Indians reciprocated the friendship that was shown them, and formed for them an attachment of no ordinary strength, as was manifested during the scenes of the year 1812, eight years after Mr. Kinzie first came to live among them.

Some of the most prominent events of that year are recorded in the following *Narrative*.

CHAPTER 18

Massacre at Chicago

(This *Narrative*, first published in pamphlet form in 1836, was transferred, with little variation, to Brown's *History of Illinois*, and to a work called *Western Annals*. It was likewise made, by Major Richardson, the basis of his two tales, Hardscrabble, and *Wau-nan-gee*.)

It was the evening of the 7th of April, 1812. The children of Mr. Kinzie were dancing before the fire to the music of their father's violin. The tea-table was spread, and they were awaiting the return of their mother, who had gone to visit a sick neighbour about a quarter of a mile up the river.

Suddenly their sports were interrupted. The door was thrown open, and Mrs. Kinzie rushed in, pale with terror, and scarcely able to articulate, "The Indians! the Indians!"

"The Indians? What? Where?" eagerly demanded they all.

"Up at Lee's Place, killing and scalping!"

With difficulty Mrs. Kinzie composed herself sufficiently to give the information, "That, while she was up at Burns's, a man and a boy were seen running down with all speed on the opposite side of the river; that they had called across to give notice to Burns's family to save themselves, for *the Indians* were at Lee's Place, from which they had just made their escape. Having given this terrifying news, they had made all speed for the fort, which was on the same side of the river that they then were."

All was now consternation and dismay. The family were hurried into two old *pirogues*, that lay moored near the house, and paddled with all possible haste across the river to take refuge in the fort.

All that the man and boy who had made their escape were able to tell, was soon known; but, in order to render their story more intelligible, it is necessary to describe the scene of action.

Lee's Place, since known by the name of Hardscrabble, was a farm intersected by the Chicago River, about four miles from its mouth. The farmhouse stood on the western bank of the south branch of this river. On the north side of the main stream, but quite near its junction with Lake Michigan, stood (as has already been described) the dwelling-house and trading-establishment of Mr. Kinzie.

The fort was situated on the southern bank, directly opposite this mansion—the river, and a few rods of sloping green turf on either side, being all that intervened between them.

The fort was differently constructed from the one erected on the same site in 1816. It had two block-houses on the southern side, and on the northern a sally-port, or subterranean passage from the parade-ground to the river. This was designed either to facilitate escape in case of an emergency, or as a means of supplying the garrison with water during a siege.

The officers in the fort at this period were Captain Heald, the commanding officer, Lieutenant Helm, the son-in-law of Mr. Kinzie, and Ensign Ronan—the two last were very young men—and the surgeon, Dr. Van Voorhees.

The command numbered about seventy-five men; very few of whom were effective.

A constant and friendly intercourse had been maintained between these troops and the Indians. It is true that the principal men of the Pottowattamie nation, like those of most other tribes, went yearly to Fort Malden, in Canada, to receive a large amount of presents, with which the British Government had, for many years, been in the habit of purchasing their alliance; and it was well known that many of the Pottowattamies, as well as Winnebagoes, had been engaged with the Ottawas and Shawnees at the Battle of Tippecanoe, the preceding autumn; yet, as the principal chiefs of all the bands in the neighbourhood appeared to be on the most amicable terms with the Americans, no interruption of their harmony was at any time anticipated.

After the 15th of August, however, many circumstances were recollected that might have opened the eyes of the whites, had they not been lulled in a fatal security. One instance in particular may be mentioned.

In the spring preceding the destruction of the fort, two Indians of the Calumet band came to the fort on a visit to the commanding officer. As they passed through the quarters, they saw Mrs. Heald and Mrs. Helm playing at battledore.

Turning to the interpreter, one of them, Nau-non-gee, remarked, "The white chiefs' wives are amusing themselves very much; it will not be long before they are hoeing in our cornfields!"

This was considered at the time an idle threat, or, at most, an ebullition of jealous feeling at the contrast between the situation of their own women and that of the "white chiefs' wives." Some months after, how bitterly was it remembered!

★★★★★★★★★★★★★★★★★★

The farm at Lee's Place was occupied by a Mr. White and three persons employed by him in the care of the farm.

In the afternoon of the day on which our narrative commences, a party of ten or twelve Indians, dressed and painted, arrived at the house, and, according to the custom among savages, entered and seated themselves without ceremony.

Something in their appearance and manner excited the suspicions of one of the family, a Frenchman, who remarked, "I do not like the appearance of these Indians—they are none of our folks. I know by their dress and paint that they are not Pottowattamies."

Another of the family, a discharged soldier, then said to the boy who was present, "If that is the case, we had better get away from them if we can. Say nothing; but do as you see me do."

As the afternoon was far advanced, the soldier walked leisurely towards the canoes, of which there were two tied near the bank. Some of the Indians inquired where he was going. He pointed to the cattle which were standing among the haystacks on the opposite bank, and made signs that they must go and fodder them, and then they should return and get their supper.

He got into one canoe, and the boy into the other. The stream was narrow, and they were soon across. When they had gained the opposite side, they pulled some hay for the cattle—made a show of collecting them—and when they had gradually made a circuit, so that their movements were concealed by the haystacks, they took to the woods, which were close at hand, and made for the fort.

They had run about a quarter of a mile, when they heard the discharge of two guns successively, which they supposed to have been levelled at the companions they had left behind.

They stopped not nor stayed until they arrived opposite Burns's, where, as before related, they called across to advertise the family of their danger, and then hastened on to the fort. (Burns's house stood near the spot where the Agency Building, or "Cobweb Castle," was afterwards erected, at the foot of N. State Street.)

It now occurred to those who had secured their own safety, that the family of Burns was at this moment exposed to the most imminent peril. The question was, who would hazard his own life to bring them to a place of safety? A gallant young officer, Ensign Ronan, volunteered, with a party of five or six soldiers, to go to their rescue.

They ascended the river in a scow, and took the mother, with her infant of scarcely a day old, upon her bed to the boat, in which they carefully conveyed her and the other members of the family to the fort.

A party of soldiers, consisting of a corporal and six men, had that afternoon obtained leave to go up the river to fish.

They had not returned when the fugitives from Lee's Place arrived at the fort, and, fearing that they might encounter the Indians, the commanding officer ordered a cannon to be fired, to warn them of danger.

They were at the time about two miles above Lee's Place. Hearing the signal, they took the hint, put out their torches (for it was now night), and dropped down the river towards the garrison, as silently as possible. It will be remembered that the unsettled state of the country since the battle of Tippecanoe, the preceding November, had rendered every man vigilant, and the slightest alarm was an admonition to "beware of the Indians."

When the fishing-party reached Lee's Place, it was proposed to stop and warn the inmates to be upon their guard, as the signal from the fort indicated danger of some kind. All was still as death around the house. They groped their way along, and as the corporal jumped over the small enclosure, he placed his hand upon the dead body of a man. By the sense of touch, he soon ascertained that the head was without a scalp, and otherwise mutilated. The faithful dog of the murdered man stood guarding the lifeless remains of his master.

The tale was now told. The men retreated to their canoes, and reached the fort unmolested about eleven o'clock at night. The next morning a party of the citizens and soldiers volunteered to go to Lee's Place, to learn further the fate of its occupants. The body of Mr. White was found pierced by two balls, and with eleven stabs in the breast. The Frenchman, as already described, lay dead, with his dog still beside him. Their bodies were brought to the fort and buried in its immediate vicinity.

It was subsequently ascertained, from traders out in the Indian country, that the perpetrators of this bloody deed were a party of Winnebagoes, who had come into this neighbourhood to "take some white scalps." Their plan had been, to proceed down the river from Lee's Place, and kill every white man without the walls of the fort. Hearing, however, the report of the cannon, and not knowing what it portended, they thought it best to remain satisfied with this one exploit, and forthwith retreated to their homes on Rock River.

The inhabitants outside the fort, consisting of a few discharged soldiers and some families of half-breeds, now intrenched themselves in the Agency House. This stood west of the fort, between the pickets and the river, and distant about twenty rods from the former.

It was an old-fashioned log building, with a hall running through the centre, and one large room on each side. *Piazzas* extended the whole length of the building in front and rear. These were planked up, for greater security, port-holes were cut, and sentinels posted at night.

As the enemy were believed to be lurking still in the neighbourhood, or, emboldened by former success, likely to return at any moment, an order was issued prohibiting any soldier or citizen from leaving the vicinity of the garrison without a guard.

One night a sergeant and private, who were out on a patrol, came suddenly upon a party of Indians in the pasture adjoining the esplanade. The sergeant fired his piece, and both retreated towards the fort. Before they could reach it, an Indian threw his tomahawk, which missed the sergeant and struck a wagon standing near. The sentinel from the blockhouse immediately fired, and with effect, while the men got safely in. The next morning it was ascertained, from traces of blood to a considerable distance into the prairie, and from the appearance of a body having been laid among the long grass, that some execution had been done.

On another occasion the enemy entered the esplanade to steal horses. Not finding them in the stable, as they had expected, they made themselves amends for their disappointment by stabbing all the sheep in the stable and then letting them loose. The poor animals flocked towards the fort. This gave the alarm—the garrison was aroused—parties were sent out, but the marauders escaped unmolested.

★★★★★★★★★★★★★★★★

The inmates of the fort experienced no farther alarm for many weeks.

On the afternoon of the 7th of August, Winnemeg, or *Catfish*, a Pottowattamie chief, arrived at the post, bringing despatches from General Hull. These announced the declaration of war between the United States and Great Britain, and that General Hull, at the head of the Northwestern Army, had arrived at Detroit; also, that the island of Mackinac had fallen into the hands of the British.

The orders to Captain Heald were:

"To evacuate the fort, if practicable, and, in that event, to distribute all the United States' property contained in the fort, and in the United

States' factory or agency, among the Indians in the neighbourhood."

After having delivered his despatches, Winnemeg requested a private interview with Mr. Kinzie, who had taken up his residence in the fort. He stated to Mr. K. that he was acquainted with the purport of the communications he had brought, and begged him to ascertain if it were the intention of Captain Heald to evacuate the post. He advised strongly against such a step, inasmuch as the garrison was well supplied with ammunition, and with provisions for six months. It would, therefore, be far better, he thought, to remain until a reinforcement could be sent to their assistance. If, however, Captain Heald should decide upon leaving the post, it should by all means be done immediately. The Pottowattamies, through whose country they must pass, being ignorant of the object of Winnemeg's mission, a forced march might be made, before those who were hostile in their feelings were prepared to interrupt them.

Of this advice, so earnestly given, Captain Heald was immediately informed. He replied that it was his intention to evacuate the post, but that, inasmuch as he had received orders to distribute the United States' property, he should not feel justified in leaving it until he had collected the Indians of the neighbourhood and made an equitable division among them.

Winnemeg then suggested the expediency of marching out, and leaving all things standing—possibly while the Indians were engaged in the partition of the spoils, the troops might effect their retreat unmolested. This advice was strongly seconded by Mr. Kinzie, but did not meet the approbation of the commanding officer.

The order for evacuating the post was read next morning upon parade. It is difficult to understand why Captain Heald, in such an emergency, omitted the usual form of calling a council of war with his officers. It can only be accounted for by the fact of a want of harmonious feeling between himself and one of his junior officers—Ensign Ronan, a high-spirited and somewhat overbearing, but brave and generous young man.

In the course of the day, finding that no council was called, the officers waited on Captain Heald to be informed what course he intended to pursue. When they learned his intentions, they remonstrated with him, on the following grounds:

First—It was highly improbable that the command would be permitted to pass through the country in safety to Fort Wayne. For although it had been said that some of the chiefs had opposed an attack upon the fort, planned the preceding autumn, yet it was well known that they had been actuated in that matter by motives of private regard to one family, that of Mr. Kinzie, and not to any general friendly feeling towards the Americans; and that, at any rate, it was hardly to be expected that these few individuals would be able to control the whole tribe, who were thirsting for blood.

In the next place—Their march must necessarily be slow, as their movements must be accommodated to the helplessness of the women and children, of whom there were a number with the detachment. That of their small force, some of the soldiers were superannuated, others invalid; therefore, since the course to be pursued was left discretional, their unanimous advice was, to remain where they were, and fortify themselves as strongly as possible. Succours from the other side of the peninsula might arrive before they could be attacked by the British from Mackinac; and even should they not, it were far better to fall into the hands of the latter than to become the victims of the savages.

Captain Heald argued in reply, that a special order had been issued by the War Department, that no post should be surrendered without battle having been given, and his force was totally inadequate to an engagement with the Indians; that he should unquestionably be censured for remaining, when there appeared a prospect of a safe march through; and that, upon the whole, he deemed it expedient to assemble the Indians, distribute the property among them, and then ask of them an escort to Fort Wayne, with the promise of a considerable reward upon their safe arrival—adding, that he had full confidence in the friendly professions of the Indians, from whom, as well as from the soldiers, the capture of Mackinac had been kept a profound secret.

From this time the officers held themselves aloof, and spoke but little upon the subject, though they considered the project of Captain Heald little short of madness. The dissatisfaction among the soldiers hourly increased, until it reached a high pitch of insubordination.

Upon one occasion, as Captain Heald was conversing with Mr. Kinzie upon the parade, he remarked, "I could not remain, even if I thought it best, for I have but a small store of provisions."

"Why, captain," said a soldier who stood near, forgetting all etiquette in the excitement of the moment, "you have cattle enough to last the troops six months."

"But," replied Captain Heald, "I have no salt to preserve it with."

"Then jerk it," said the man, "as the Indians do their venison."

(This is done by cutting the meat in thin slices, placing it upon a scaffold, and making a fire under it, which dries it and smokes it at the same time.)

The Indians now became daily more unruly. Entering the fort in defiance of the sentinels, they made their way without ceremony into the officers' quarters. On one occasion an Indian took up a rifle and fired it in the parlour of the commanding officer, as an expression of defiance. Some were of opinion that this was intended among the young men as a signal for an attack. The old chiefs passed backwards and forwards among the assembled groups, with the appearance of the most lively agitation, while the squaws rushed to and fro, in great excitement, and evidently prepared for some fearful scene.

Any further manifestation of ill feeling was, however, suppressed for the present, and Captain Heald, strange as it may seem, continued to entertain a conviction of having created so amicable a disposition among the Indians as would ensure the safety of the command on their march to Fort Wayne.

Thus passed the time until the 12th of August. The feelings of the inmates of the fort during this time may be better imagined than described. Each morning that dawned seemed to bring them nearer to that most appalling fate—butchery by a savage foe—and at night they scarcely dared yield to slumber, lest they should be aroused by the war-whoop and tomahawk. Gloom and mistrust prevailed, and the want of unanimity among the officers debarred them the consolation they might have found in mutual sympathy and encouragement.

The Indians being assembled from the neighbouring villages, a council was held with them on the afternoon of the 12th. Captain Heald alone attended on the part of the military. He requested his officers to accompany him, but they declined. They had been secretly informed that it was the intention of the young chiefs to fall upon the officers and massacre them while in council, but they could not persuade Captain Heald of the truth of their information.

They waited therefore only until he had left the garrison, accompanied by Mr. Kinzie, when they took command of the blockhouses which overlooked the esplanade on which the council was held, opened the portholes, and pointed the cannon so as to command the whole assembly. By this means, probably, the lives of the whites who were present in council were preserved.

In council, the commanding officer informed the Indians that it was his intention to distribute among them, the next day, not only the goods lodged in the United States' factory, but also the ammunition and provisions, with which the garrison was well supplied. He then requested of the Pottowattamies an escort to Fort Wayne, promising them a liberal reward on arriving there, in addition to the presents they were now about to receive. With many professions of friendship and good will, the savages assented to all be proposed, and promised all he required.

After the council, Mr. Kinzie, who understood well, not only the Indian character, but the present tone of feeling among them, had a long interview with Captain Heald, in hopes of opening his eyes to the present posture of affairs.

He reminded him that since the troubles with the Indians upon the Wabash and its vicinity, there had appeared a settled plan of hostilities towards the whites, in consequence of which it had been the policy of the Americans to withhold from them whatever would enable them to carry on their warfare upon the defenceless inhabitants of the frontier.

Mr. Kinzie also recalled to Captain Heald how that, having left home for Detroit, the preceding autumn, on receiving, when he had proceeded as far as De Charme's, (trading-establishment—now Ypsilanti), the intelligence of the Battle of Tippecanoe, he had immediately returned to Chicago, that he might dispatch orders to his traders to furnish no ammunition to the Indians; in consequence of which all they had on hand was secreted, and such of the traders as had not already started for their wintering-grounds, took neither powder nor shot with them.

Captain Heald was struck with the impolicy of furnishing the enemy (for such they must now consider their old neighbours) with arms against himself, and determined to destroy all the ammunition except what should be necessary for the use of his own troops.

On the 13th, the goods, consisting of blankets, broadcloths, calicoes, paints, etc., were distributed, as stipulated. The same evening the ammunition and liquor were carried, part into the sally-port, and thrown into a well which had been dug there to supply the garrison with water in case of emergency; the remainder was transported as secretly as possible through the northern gate, the heads of the barrels knocked in, and the contents poured into the river.

The same fate was shared by a large quantity of alcohol belonging to Mr. Kinzie, which had been deposited in a warehouse near his residence opposite the fort.

The Indians suspected what was going on, and crept, serpent-like, as near the scene of action as possible, but a vigilant watch was kept up, and no one was suffered to approach but those engaged in the affair. All the muskets not necessary for the command on the march were broken up and thrown into the well, together with the bags of shot, flints, gun-screws, and, in short, everything relating to weapons of offence.

Some relief to the general feeling of despondency was afforded, by the arrival, on the 14th of August, of Captain Wells with fifteen friendly Miamis.

****

Captain Wells, when a boy, was stolen, by the Miami Indians, from the family of Hon. Nathaniel Pope, in Kentucky. Although recovered by them, he preferred to return and live among his new friends. He married a Miami woman, and became a chief of the nation. He was the father of the late Mrs. Judge Wolcott, of Maumee, Ohio.

****

Of this brave man, who forms so conspicuous a figure in our frontier annals, it is unnecessary here to say more than that he had been residing from his boyhood among the Indians, and consequently possessed a perfect knowledge of their character and habits.

He had heard, at Fort Wayne, of the order for evacuating the fort at Chicago, and, knowing the hostile determination of the Pottowattamies, he had made a rapid march across the country, to prevent the exposure of his relative, Captain Heald, and his troops, to certain destruction.

But he came "all too late." When he reached the post, he found that the ammunition had been destroyed, and the provisions given to the Indians. There was, therefore, now no alternative, and every preparation was made for the march of the troops on the following morning.

On the afternoon of the same day, a second council was held with the Indians. They expressed great indignation at the destruction of the ammunition and liquor.

Notwithstanding the precautions that had been taken to preserve secrecy, the noise of knocking in the heads of the barrels had betrayed the operations of the preceding night; indeed, so great was the quantity of liquor thrown into the river, that the taste of the water the next morning was, as one expressed it, "strong grog."

Murmurs and threats were everywhere heard among the savages.

It was evident that the first moment of exposure would subject the troops to some manifestation of their disappointment and resentment.

Among the chiefs were several who, although they shared the general hostile feeling of their tribe towards the Americans, yet retained a personal regard for the troops at this post, and for the few white citizens of the place. These chiefs exerted their utmost influence to allay the revengeful feelings of the young men, and to avert their sanguinary designs, but without effect.

On the evening succeeding the council, Black Partridge, a conspicuous chief, entered the quarters of the commanding officer. He said:

"Father, I come to deliver up to you the medal I wear. It was given me by the Americans, and I have long worn it in token of our mutual friendship. But our young men are resolved to imbrue their hands in the blood of the whites. I cannot restrain them, and I will not wear a token of peace while I am compelled to act as an enemy."

Had further evidence been wanting, this circumstance would have sufficiently proved to the devoted band the justice of their melancholy anticipations. Nevertheless, they went steadily on with the necessary preparations; and, amid the horrors of their situation, there were not wanting gallant hearts, who strove to encourage, in their desponding companions, the hopes of escape they were far from indulging themselves.

Of the ammunition there had been reserved but twenty-five rounds, besides one box of cartridges, contained in the baggage-wagons. This must, under any circumstances of danger, have proved an inadequate supply; but the prospect of a fatiguing march, in their present ineffective state, forbade the troops embarrassing themselves with a larger quantity.

Chapter 19

Narrative of the Massacre, Continued

The morning of the 15th arrived. All things were in readiness, and nine o'clock was the hour named for starting.

Mr. Kinzie, having volunteered to accompany the troops in their march, had intrusted his family to the care of some friendly Indians, who promised to convey them in a boat around the head of Lake Michigan to a point on the St. Joseph's River, there to be joined by the troops, should the prosecution of their march be permitted them.

(The spot now called Bertrand, then known as *Parc aux Vaches*, from its having been a favourite "stamping-ground" of the buffalo which then abounded in the country.)

Early in the morning Mr. Kinzie received a message from To-pee-nee-bee, a chief of the St. Joseph's band, informing him that mischief was intended by the Pottowattamies who had engaged to escort the detachment, and urging him to relinquish his design of accompanying the troops by land, promising him that the boat containing himself and family should be permitted to pass in safety to St. Joseph's.

Mr. Kinzie declined acceding to this proposal, as he believed that his presence might operate as a restraint upon the fury of the savages, so warmly were the greater part of them attached to himself and his family.

The party in the boat consisted of Mrs. Kinzie and her four younger children, their nurse Josette, a clerk of Mr. Kinzie's, two servants and the boatmen, besides the two Indians who acted as their protectors. The boat started, but had scarcely reached the mouth of the river, which, it will be recollected, was here half a mile below the fort, when another messenger from To-pee-nee-bee arrived to detain them where they were. There was no mistaking the reason of this detention.

In breathless anxiety sat the wife and mother. She was a woman of uncommon energy and strength of character, yet her heart died within her as she folded her arms around her helpless infants, and gazed upon the march of her husband and eldest child to certain destruction.

As the troops left the fort, the band struck up the Dead March. On they came, in military array, but with solemn mien. Captain Wells took the lead at the head of his little band of Miamis. He had blackened his face before leaving the garrison, in token of his impending fate. They took their route along the lake shore. When they reached the point where commenced a range of sand-hills intervening between the prairie and the beach, the escort of Pottowattamies, in number about five hundred, kept the level of the prairie, instead of continuing along the beach with the Americans and Miamis.

They had marched perhaps a mile and a half, when Captain Wells, who had kept somewhat in advance with his Miamis, came riding furiously back.

"They are about to attack us," shouted he; "form instantly, and charge upon them."

Scarcely were the words uttered, when a volley was showered from among the sand-hills. The troops were hastily brought into line, and charged up the bank. One man, a veteran of seventy winters, fell as they ascended. The remainder of the scene is best described in the words of an eye-witness and participator in the tragedy, Mrs. Helm, the wife of Captain (then Lieutenant) Helm, and stepdaughter of Mr. Kinzie. (Mrs. Helm is represented by the female figure in the bronze group erected by M. Pulman, at the foot of 18th Street, to commemorate the massacre which took place at that spot.)

★★★★★★★★★★★★★★★★

"After we had left the bank, the firing became general. The Miamis fled at the outset. Their chief rode up to the Pottowattamies, and said:

"'You have deceived the Americans and us. You have done a bad action, and (brandishing his tomahawk) I will be the first to head a party of Americans to return and punish your treachery.' So saying, he galloped after his companions, who were now scouring across the prairies.

"The troops behaved most gallantly. They were but a handful, but they seemed resolved to sell their lives as dearly as possible. Our horses pranced and bounded, and could hardly be restrained as the balls whistled among them. I drew off a little, and gazed upon my husband and father, who were yet unharmed. I felt that my hour was come, and endeavoured to forget those I loved, and prepare myself for my approaching fate.

"While I was thus engaged, the surgeon, Dr. Van Voorhees, came up. He was badly wounded. His horse had been shot under him, and he had received a ball in his leg. Every muscle of his face was quivering with the agony of terror. He said to me, 'Do you think they will take our lives? I am badly wounded, but I think not mortally. Perhaps we might purchase our lives by promising them a large reward. Do you think there is any chance?'

"'Dr. Van Voorhees,' said I, 'do not let us waste the few moments that yet remain to us in such vain hopes. Our fate is inevitable. In a few moments we must appear before the bar of God. Let us make what preparation is yet in our power.'

"'Oh, I cannot die!' exclaimed he, 'I am not fit to die—if I had but a short time to prepare—death is awful!'

"I pointed to Ensign Ronan, who, though mortally wounded and nearly down, was still fighting with desperation on one knee. (The exact spot of this encounter was about where 21st Street crosses Indiana Avenue.)

"'Look at that man!' said I. 'At least he dies like a soldier.'

"'Yes,' replied the unfortunate man, with a convulsive gasp, 'but he has no terrors of the future—he is an unbeliever!'

"At this moment a young Indian raised his tomahawk at me. By springing aside, I partially avoided the blow, which was intended for my skull, but which alighted on my shoulder. I seized him around the neck, and while exerting my utmost efforts to get possession of his scalping-knife, which hung in a scabbard over his breast, I was dragged from his grasp by another and older Indian.

"The latter bore me struggling and resisting towards the lake. Notwithstanding the rapidity with which I was harried along, I recognised, as I passed them, the lifeless remains of the unfortunate surgeon. Some murderous tomahawk had stretched him upon the very spot where I had last seen him.

"I was immediately plunged into the water and held there with a forcible hand, notwithstanding my resistance. I soon perceived, however, that the object of my captor was not to drown me, for he held me firmly in such a position as to place my head above water. This reassured me, and, regarding him attentively, I soon recognised, in spite of the paint with which he was disguised, The Black Partridge.

"When the firing had nearly subsided, my preserver bore me from the water and conducted me up the sand-banks. It was a burning August morning, and walking through the sand in my drenched condition was inexpressibly painful and fatiguing. I stooped and took off my shoes to free them from the sand with which they were nearly filled, when a squaw seized and carried them off, and I was obliged to proceed without them.

"When we had gained the prairie, I was met by my father, who told me that my husband was safe and but slightly wounded. They led me gently back towards the Chicago River, along the southern bank of which was the Pottowattamie encampment. At one time I was placed upon a horse without a saddle, but, finding the motion insupportable, I sprang off. Supported partly by my kind conductor, Black Partridge, and partly by another Indian, Pee-so-tum, who held dangling in his hand a scalp, which by the black ribbon around the queue I recognised as that of Captain Wells, I dragged my fainting steps to one of the *wigwams*.

"The wife of Wau-bee-nee-mah, a chief from the Illinois River, was standing near, and, seeing my exhausted condition, she seized a kettle, dipped up some water from a stream that flowed near, (along the present State Street), threw into it some maple-sugar, and, stirring it up with her hand, gave it me to drink. This act of kindness, in the midst of so many horrors, touched me most sensibly; but my attention was soon diverted to other objects.

"The fort had become a scene of plunder to such as remained after the troops marched out. The cattle had been shot down as they ran at large, and lay dead or dying around. This work of butchery had commenced just as we were leaving the fort. I well remembered a remark of Ensign Ronan, as the firing went on. 'Such,' turning to me, 'is to be our fate—to be shot down like brutes!'

"'Well, sir,' said the commanding officer, who overheard him, 'are you afraid?'

"'No,' replied the high-spirited young man, 'I can march up to the enemy where you dare not show your face.' And his subsequent gallant behaviour showed this to be no idle boast.

"As the noise of the firing grew gradually less and the stragglers from the victorious party came dropping in, I received confirmation of what my father had hurriedly communicated in our rencontre on the lake shore; namely, that the whites had surrendered, after the loss of about two-thirds of their number. They had stipulated, through the interpreter, Peresh Leclerc, for the preservation of their lives, and those of the remaining women and children, and for their delivery at some of the British posts, unless ransomed by traders in the Indian country. It appears that the wounded prisoners were not considered as included in the stipulation, and a horrid scene ensued upon their being brought into camp.

"An old squaw, infuriated by the loss of friends, or excited by the sanguinary scenes around her, seemed possessed by a demoniac ferocity. She seized a stable-fork and assaulted one miserable victim, who lay groaning and writhing in the agony of his wounds, aggravated by the scorching beams of the sun. With a delicacy of feeling scarcely to have been expected under such circumstances, Wau-bee-nee-mah stretched a mat across two poles, between me and this dreadful scene. I was thus spared in some degree a view of its horrors, although I could not entirely close my ears to the cries of the sufferer The following night five more of the wounded prisoners were tomahawked."

★★★★★★★★★★★★★★★★★

The Americans, it appears, after their first attack by the Indians, charged upon those who had concealed themselves in a sort of ravine, intervening between the sand-banks and the prairie. The latter gathered themselves into a body, and after some hard fighting, in which the number of whites had become reduced to twenty-eight, this little band succeeded in breaking through the enemy, and gaining a rising ground, not far from the Oak Woods. Further contest now seeming hopeless, Lieutenant Helm sent Peresh Leclerc, a half-breed boy in the service of Mr. Kinzie, who had accompanied the detachment and fought manfully on their side, to propose terms of capitulation. It was stipulated that the lives of all the survivors should be spared, and a ransom permitted as soon as practicable.

But in the meantime, a horrible scene had been enacted. One young savage, climbing into the baggage-wagon containing the children of the white families, twelve in number, tomahawked the entire group. This was during the engagement near the sand-hills. When Captain Wells, who was fighting near, beheld it, he exclaimed,—

"Is that their game, butchering the women and children? Then I will kill, too!"

So saying, he turned his horse's head, and started for the Indian camp, near the fort, where had been left their squaws and children.

Several Indians pursued him as he galloped along. He laid himself flat on the neck of his horse, loading and firing in that position, as he would occasionally turn on his pursuers. At length their balls took effect, killing his horse, and severely wounding himself. At this moment he was met by Winnemeg and Wau-ban-see, who endeavoured to save him from the savages who had now overtaken him. As they supported him along, after having disengaged him from his horse, he received his death-blow from another Indian, Pee-so-tum, who stabbed him in the back.

The heroic resolution of one of the soldiers' wives deserves to be recorded. She was a Mrs. Corbin, and had, from the first, expressed the determination never to fall into the hands of the savages, believing that their prisoners were always subjected to tortures worse than death.

When, therefore, a party came upon her, to make her a prisoner, she fought with desperation, refusing to surrender, although assured, by signs, of safety and kind treatment, and literally suffered herself to be cut to pieces, rather than become their captive.

There was a Sergeant Holt, who, early in the engagement, received a ball in the neck. Finding himself badly wounded, he gave his sword to his wife, who was on horseback near him, telling her to defend herself; he then made for the lake, to keep out of the way of the balls. Mrs.

Holt rode a very fine horse, which the Indians were desirous of possessing, and they therefore attacked her, in hopes of dismounting her.

They fought only with the butt-ends of their guns, for their object was not to kill her. She hacked and hewed at their pieces as they were thrust against her, now on this side, now that. Finally, she broke loose from them, and dashed out into the prairie. The Indians pursued her, shouting and laughing, and now and then calling out,—

"The brave woman! do not hurt her!"

At length they overtook her again, and, while she was engaged with two or three in front, one succeeded in seizing her by the neck behind, and dragging her, although a large and powerful woman, from her horse. Notwithstanding that their guns had been so hacked and injured, and even themselves cut severely, they seemed to regard her only with admiration. They took her to a trader on the Illinois River, by whom she was restored to her friends, after having received every kindness during her captivity. (At time of publication, Mrs. Holt is believed to be still living, in the State of Ohio.)

Those of the family of Mr. Kinzie who had remained in the boat, near the mouth of the river, were carefully guarded by Kee-po-tah and another Indian. They had seen the smoke—then the blaze—and immediately after, the report of the first tremendous discharge sounded in their ears. Then all was confusion They realised nothing until they saw an Indian come towards them from the battle-ground, leading a horse on which sat a lady, apparently wounded.

"That is Mrs. Heald," cried Mrs. Kinzie. "That Indian will kill her. Run, Chandonnai," to one of Mr. Kinzie's clerks, "take the mule that is tied there, and offer it to him to release her."

Her captor, by this time, was in the act of disengaging her bonnet from her head, in order to scalp her. Chandonnai ran up, and offered the mule as a ransom, with the promise of ten bottles of whiskey as soon as they should reach his village. The latter was a strong temptation.

"But," said the Indian, "she is badly wounded—she will die. Will you give me the whiskey at all events?"

Chandonnai promised that he would, and the bargain was concluded. The savage placed the lady's bonnet on his own head, and, after an ineffectual effort on the part of some squaws to rob her of her shoes and stockings, she was brought on board the boat, where she lay moaning with pain from the many bullet-wounds she had received in both arms.

The horse Mrs. Heald had ridden was a fine, spirited animal, and, being desirous of possessing themselves of it uninjured, the Indians had aimed their shots so as to disable the rider, without injuring her steed.

She had not lain long in the boat, when a young Indian of savage aspect was seen approaching. A buffalo robe was hastily drawn over her, and she was admonished to suppress all sound of complaint, as she valued her life.

The heroic woman remained perfectly silent, while the savage drew near. He had a pistol in his hand, which he rested on the side of the boat, while, with a fearful scowl, he looked pryingly around. Black Jim, one of the servants, who stood in the bow of the boat, seized an axe that lay near, and signed to him that if he shot, he would cleave his skull; telling him that the boat contained only the family of Shawnee-aw-kee. Upon this, the Indian retired. It afterwards appeared that the object of his search was Mr. Burnett, a trader from St. Joseph's, with whom he had some account to settle.

When the boat was at length permitted to return to the mansion of Mr. Kinzie, and Mrs. Heald was removed to the house, it became necessary to dress her wounds.

Mr. K. applied to an old chief who stood by, and who, like most of his tribe, possessed some skill in surgery, to extract a ball from the arm of the sufferer.

"No, father," replied he. "I cannot do it—it makes me sick here"— (placing his hand on his heart.)

Mr. Kinzie then performed the operation himself, with his penknife.

At their own mansion the family of Mr. Kinzie were closely guarded by their Indian friends, whose intention it was to carry them to Detroit for security. The rest of the prisoners remained at the *wigwams* of their captors.

The following morning, the work of plunder being completed, the Indians set fire to the fort. A very equitable distribution of the finery appeared to have been made, and shawls, ribbons, and feathers fluttered about in all directions. The ludicrous appearance of one young fellow, who had arrayed himself in a muslin gown and the bonnet of one of the ladies, would, under other circumstances, have afforded matter of amusement.

Black Partridge, Wau-ban-see, and Kee-po-tah, with two other Indians, having established themselves in the porch of the building as sentinels, to protect the family from any evil that the young men might be excited to commit, all remained tranquil for a short space after the conflagration.

Very soon, however, a party of Indians from the Wabash made their appearance. These were, decidedly, the most hostile and implacable of all the tribes of the Pottowattamies.

Being more remote, they had shared less than some of their brethren in the kindness of Mr. Kinzie and his family, and consequently their sentiments of regard for them were less powerful.

Runners had been sent to the villages to apprise them of the intended evacuation of the post, as well as of the plan of the Indians assembled to attack the troops.

Thirsting to participate in such a scene, they hurried on; and great was their mortification, on arriving at the river Aux Plaines, to meet with a party of their friends having with them their chief Nee-scot-nee-meg, badly wounded, and to learn that the battle was over, the spoils divided, and the scalps all taken.

On arriving at Chicago, they blackened their faces, and proceeded towards the dwelling of Mr. Kinzie.

From his station on the *piazza* Black Partridge had watched their approach, and his fears were particularly awakened for the safety of Mrs. Helm (Mr. Kinzie's stepdaughter), who had recently come to the post, and was personally unknown to the more remote Indians. By his advice she was made to assume the ordinary dress of a Frenchwoman of the country; namely, a short gown and petticoat, with a blue cotton handkerchief wrapped around her head. In this disguise she was conducted by Black Partridge himself to the house of Ouilmette, a Frenchman with a half-breed wife, who formed a part of the establishment of Mr. Kinzie and whose dwelling was close at hand.

It so happened that the Indians came first to this house, in their search for prisoners. As they approached, the inmates, fearful that the fair complexion and general appearance of Mrs. Helm might betray her for an American, raised a large feather bed and placed her under the edge of it, upon the bedstead, with her face to the wall. Mrs. Bisson, a half-breed, the sister of Ouilmette's wife, then seated herself with her sewing upon the front of the bed.

It was a hot day in August, and the feverish excitement of fear and agitation, together with her position, which was nearly suffocating, became so intolerable, that Mrs. Helm at length entreated to be released and given up to the Indians.

"I can but die," said she; "let them put an end to my misery at once."

Mrs. Bisson replied, "Your death would be the destruction of us all, for Black Partridge has resolved that if one drop of the blood of your family is spilled, he will take the lives of all concerned in it, even his nearest friends; and if once the work of murder commences, there will be no end of it, so long as there remains one white person or half-breed in the country."

This expostulation nerved Mrs. Helm with fresh resolution.

The Indians entered, and she could occasionally see them from her hiding-place, gliding about, and stealthily inspecting every part of the room, though without making any ostensible search, until, apparently satisfied that there was no one concealed, they left the house.

All this time Mrs. Bisson had kept her seat upon the side of the bed, calmly sorting and arranging the patchwork of the quilt on which she was engaged, and preserving an appearance of the utmost tranquillity, although she knew not but that the next moment, she might receive a tomahawk in her brain. Her self-command unquestionably saved the lives of all present.

From Ouilmette's house the party of Indians proceeded to the dwelling of Mr. Kinzie. They entered the parlour in which the family were assembled with their faithful protectors, and seated themselves upon the floor in silence. Black Partridge perceived from their moody and revengeful looks what was passing in their minds, but he dared not remonstrate with them. He only observed in a low tone to Wau-ban-see,—

"We have endeavoured to save our friends, but it is in vain—nothing will save them now."

At this moment a friendly whoop was heard from a party of new-comers on the opposite bank of the river. Black Partridge sprang to meet their leader, as the canoes in which they had hastily embarked touched the bank near the house.

"Who are you?" demanded he.

"A man. Who are *you?*"

"A man like yourself. But tell me *who* you are,"—meaning, Tell me your disposition, and which side you are for.

"I am a *Sau-ga-nash!*"

"Then make all speed to the house—your friend is in danger, and you alone can save him."

Billy Caldwell for it was he, entered the parlour with a calm step, and without a trace of agitation in his manner. He deliberately took off his accoutrements and placed them with his rifle behind the door, then saluted the hostile savages.

****

Billy Caldwell was a half-breed, and a chief of the nation. In his reply, "*I am a Sau-ga-nash,*" or Englishman, he designed to convey, "I am a white man." Had he said, "*I am a Pottowattamie,*" it would have been interpreted to mean, "I belong to my nation, and am prepared to go all lengths with them."

****

"How now, my friends! A good-day to you. I was told there were enemies here, but I am glad to find only friends. Why have you blackened your faces? Is it that you are mourning for the friends you have lost in battle?" (Purposely misunderstanding this token of evil designs.)

"Or is it that you are fasting? If so, ask our friend, here, and he will give you to eat. He is the Indian's friend, and never yet refused them what they had need of."

Thus, taken by surprise, the savages were ashamed to acknowledge their bloody purpose. They, therefore, said modestly that they came to beg of their friends some white cotton in which to wrap their dead before interring them. This was given to them, with some other presents, and they took their departure peaceably from the premises.

Along with Mr. Kinzie's party was a non-commissioned officer who had made his escape in a singular manner. As the troops were about leaving the fort, it was found that the baggage-horses of the surgeon had strayed off. The quartermaster-sergeant, Griffith, was sent to collect them and bring them on, it being absolutely necessary to recover them, since their packs contained part of the surgeon's apparatus, and the medicines for the march.

This man had been for a long time on the sick report and for this reason was given the charge of the baggage, instead of being placed with the troops. His efforts to recover the horses being unsuccessful, he was hastening to rejoin his party, alarmed at some appearances of disorder and hostile indications among the Indians, when he was met and made prisoner by To-pee-nee-bee.

Having taken from him his arms and accoutrements, the chief put him into a canoe and paddled him across the river, bidding him make for the woods and secrete himself. This he did; and the following day, in the afternoon, seeing from his lurking-place that all appeared quiet, he ventured to steal cautiously into the garden of Ouilmette, where he concealed himself for a time behind some currant-bushes.

At length he determined to enter the house, and accordingly climbed up through a small back window into the room where the family were. This was just as the Wabash Indians had left the house of Ouilmette for that of Mr. Kinzie. The danger of the sergeant was now imminent. The family stripped him of his uniform and arrayed him in a suit of deer-skin, with belt, *moccasins*, and pipe, like a French *engagé*. His dark complexion and large black whiskers favoured the disguise. The family were all ordered to address him in French, and, although utterly ignorant of the language, he continued to pass for a *Weemtee-gosh*, (Frenchman), and as such to accompany Mr. Kinzie and his family, undetected by his enemies, until they reached a place of safety.

On the third day after the battle, the family of Mr. Kinzie, with the clerks of the establishment, were put into a boat, under the care of François, a half-breed interpreter, and conveyed to St. Joseph's, where they remained until the following November, under the protection of To-pee-nee-bee's band. They were then conducted to Detroit, under the escort of Chandonnai and their trusty Indian friend, Kee-po-tah, and delivered up, as prisoners of war, to Colonel McKee, the British Indian Agent.

Mr. Kinzie was not allowed to leave St. Joseph's with his family, his Indian friends insisting on his remaining and endeavouring to secure some remnant of his scattered property. During his excursions with them for that purpose, he wore the costume and paint of the tribe, in order to escape capture and perhaps death at the hands of those who were still thirsting for blood. In time, however, his anxiety for his family induced him to follow them to Detroit, where, in the month of January, he was received and paroled by General Proctor.

Captain and Mrs. Heald were sent across the lake to St. Joseph the day after the battle. The former had received two wounds, the latter seven, in the engagement.

Lieutenant Helm, who was likewise wounded, was carried by some friendly Indians to their village on the Au Sable, and thence to Peoria, where he was liberated by the intervention of Mr. Thomas Forsyth, the half-brother of Mr. Kinzie. Mrs. Helm accompanied her parents to St. Joseph, where they resided in the family of Alexander Robinson, (the Pottowattamie chief, so well known to many of the citizens of Chicago, now—1870—residing at the Aux Plaines), receiving from them all possible kindness and hospitality for several months.

After their arrival in Detroit, Mrs. Helm was joined by her husband, when they were both arrested by order of the British commander, and sent on horseback, in the dead of winter, through Canada to Fort George, on the Niagara frontier. When they arrived at that post, there had been no official appointed to receive them, and, notwithstanding their long and fatiguing journey in weather the most cold and inclement, Mrs. Helm, a delicate woman of seventeen years, was permitted to sit waiting in her saddle, outside the gate, for more than an hour, before the refreshment of fire or food, or even the shelter of a roof, was offered them.

When Colonel Sheaffe, who had been absent at the time, was informed of this brutal inhospitality, he expressed the greatest indignation. He waited on Mrs. Helm immediately, apologized in the most courteous manner, and treated both her and Lieutenant Helm with the most considerate kindness, until, by an exchange of prisoners, they were liberated, and found means to reach their friends in Steuben County, N.Y.

Captain Heald had been taken prisoner by an Indian from the Kankakee, who had a strong personal regard for him, and who, when he saw the wounded and enfeebled state of Mrs. Heald, released her husband that he might accompany his wife to St. Joseph. To the latter place they were accordingly carried, as has been related, by Chandonnai and his party. In the meantime, the Indian who had so nobly released his prisoner returned to his village on the Kankakee, where he had the mortification of finding that his conduct had excited great dissatisfaction among his band. So great was the displeasure manifested, that he resolved to make a journey to St. Joseph and reclaim his prisoner.

News of his intention being brought to To-pee-nee-bee and Kee-po-tah, under whose care the prisoners were, they held a private council with Chandonnai, Mr. Kinzie, and the principal men of the village, the result of which was a determination to send Captain and Mrs. Heald to the island of Mackinac, and deliver them up to the British.

They were accordingly put in a bark canoe, and paddled by Robinson and his wife a distance of three hundred miles along the coast of Michigan, and surrendered as prisoners of war to the commanding officer at Mackinac.

As an instance of the procrastinating spirit of Captain Heald, it may be mentioned that, even after he had received certain intelligence that his Indian captor was on his way from the Kankakee to St. Joseph to retake him, he would still have delayed another day at that place, to make preparation for a more comfortable journey to Mackinac.

The soldiers, with their wives and surviving children, were dispersed among the different villages of the Pottowattamies upon the Illinois, Wabash, Rock River, and at Milwaukie, until the following spring, when they were, for the most part, carried to Detroit and ransomed.

Mrs. Burns, with her infant, became the prisoner of a chief, who carried her to his village and treated her with great kindness. His wife, from jealousy of the favour shown to "the white woman" and her child, always treated them with great hostility. On one occasion she struck the infant with a tomahawk, and narrowly missed her aim of putting an end to it altogether.

****

> Twenty-two years after this, as I was on a journey to Chicago in the steamer *Uncle Sam*, a young woman, hearing my name, introduced herself to me, and, raising the hair from her forehead, showed me the mark of the tomahawk which had so nearly been fatal to her.

****

They were not left long in the power of the old hag after this demonstration, but on the first opportunity were carried to a place of safety.

The family of Mr. Lee had resided in a house on the Lake shore, not far from the fort. Mr. Lee was the owner of Lee's Place, which he cultivated as a farm. It was his son who ran down with the discharged soldier to give the alarm of "Indians," at the fort, on the afternoon of the 7th of April. The father, the son, and all the other members of the family had fallen victims on the 15th of August, except Mrs. Lee and her young infant. These were claimed by Black Partridge, and carried to his village on the Au Sable. He had been particularly attached to a little girl of Mrs. Lee's, about twelve years of age. This child had been placed on horseback for the march; and, as she was unaccustomed to the exercise, she was tied fast to the saddle, lest by any accident she should slip off or be thrown.

She was within reach of the balls at the commencement of the engagement, and was severely wounded. The horse set off on a full gallop, which partly threw her, but she was held fast by the bands which confined her, and hung dangling as the animal ran violently about. In this state she was met by Black Partridge, who caught the horse and disengaged her from the saddle. Finding her so much wounded that she could not recover, and that she was suffering great agony, he put the finishing stroke to her at once with his tomahawk. He afterwards said that this was the hardest thing he ever tried to do, but he did it because he could not bear to see her suffer.

He took the mother and her infant to his village, where he became warmly attached to the former—so much so, that he wished to marry her; but, as she very naturally objected, he treated her with the greatest respect and consideration. He was in no hurry to release her, for he was in hopes of prevailing on her to become his wife. In the course of the winter her child fell ill. Finding that none of the remedies within their reach were effectual, Black Partridge proposed to take the little one to Chicago, where there was now a French trader living in the mansion of Mr. Kinzie, and procure some medical aid from him. Wrapping up his charge with the greatest care, he set out on his journey.

When he arrived at the residence of M. Du Pin, he entered the room where he was, and carefully placed his burden on the floor.

"What have you there?" asked M. Du Pin.

"A young raccoon, which I have brought you as a present," was the reply; and, opening the pack, he showed the little sick infant.

When the trader had prescribed for its complaint, and Black Partridge was about to return to his home, he told his friend of the proposal he had made to Mrs. Lee to become his wife, and the manner in which it had been received.

M. Du Pin, entertaining some fears that the chief's honourable resolution to leave it to the lady herself whether to accept his addresses or not, might not hold out, entered at once into a negotiation for her ransom, and so effectually wrought upon the good feelings of Black Partridge that he consented to bring his fair prisoner at once to Chicago, that she might be restored to her friends.

Whether the kind trader had at the outset any other feeling in the matter than sympathy and brotherly kindness, we cannot say; we only know that in process of time Mrs. Lee became Madame Du Pin, and that the worthy couple lived together in great happiness for many years after.

The fate of Nau-non-gee, one of the chiefs of the Calumet village, and who is mentioned in the early part of the narrative, deserves to be recorded.

Daring the battle of the 15th of August, the chief object of his attack was one Sergeant Hays, a man from whom he had received many acts of kindness.

After Hays had received a ball through the body, this Indian ran up to him to tomahawk him, when the sergeant, collecting his remaining strength, pierced him through the body with his bayonet. They fell together. Other Indians running up soon dispatched Hays, and it was not until then that his bayonet was extracted from the body of his adversary.

The wounded chief was carried after the battle to his village on the Calumet, where he survived for several days. Finding his end approaching, he called together his young men, and enjoined them, in the most solemn manner, to regard the safety of their prisoners after his death, and to take the lives of none of them from respect to his memory, as he deserved his fate from the hands of those whose kindness, he had so ill requited.

CHAPTER 20
Captivity of J. Kinzie, Sen.—An Amusing Mistake

It had been a stipulation of General Hull at the surrender of Detroit, which took place the day after the massacre at Chicago, that the inhabitants should be permitted to remain undisturbed in their homes. Accordingly, the family of Mr. Kinzie took up their quarters with their friends in the old mansion, which many will still recollect as standing on the northwest corner of Jefferson Avenue and Wayne Street.

The feelings of indignation and sympathy were constantly aroused in the hearts of the citizens during the winter that ensued. They were almost daily called upon to witness the cruelties practised upon the American prisoners brought in by their Indian captors. Those who could scarcely drag their wounded, bleeding feet over the frozen ground, were compelled to dance for the amusement of the savages; and these exhibitions sometimes took place before the Government House, the residence of Colonel McKee. Some of the British officers looked on from their windows at these heart-rending performances; for the honour of humanity, we will hope such instances were rare.

Everything that could be made available among the effects of the citizens was offered, to ransom their countrymen from the hands of these inhuman beings. The prisoners brought in from the River Raisin—those unfortunate men who were permitted, after their surrender to General Proctor, to be tortured and murdered by inches by his savage allies—excited the sympathies and called for the action of the whole community. Private houses were turned into hospitals, and everyone was forward to get possession of as many as possible of the survivors. To effect this, even the articles of their apparel were bartered by the ladies of Detroit, as they watched from their doors or windows the miserable victims carried about for sale.

In the dwelling of Mr. Kinzie one large room was devoted to the reception of the sufferers. Few of them survived. Among those spoken of as objects of the deepest interest were two young gentlemen of Kentucky, brothers, both severely wounded, and their wounds aggravated to a mortal degree by subsequent ill usage and hardships. Their solicitude for each other, and their exhibition in various ways of the most tender fraternal affection, created an impression never to be forgotten.

The last bargain made was by Black Jim, and one of the children, who had permission to redeem a negro servant of the gallant Colonel Allen, with an old white horse, the only available article that remained among their possessions.

A brother of Colonel Allen afterwards came to Detroit, and the negro preferred returning to servitude rather than remaining a stranger in a strange land.

Mr. Kinzie, as has been related, joined his family at Detroit in the month of January. A short time after, suspicions arose in the mind of General Proctor that he was in correspondence with General Harrison, who was now at Fort Meigs, and who was believed to be meditating an advance upon Detroit. Lieutenant Watson, of the British Army, waited upon Mr. Kinzie one day with an invitation to the quarters of General Proctor on the opposite side of the river, saying he wished to speak with him, on business.

Quite unsuspicious, he complied with the invitation, when to his surprise he was ordered into confinement, and strictly guarded in the house of his former partner, Mr. Patterson, of Sandwich. Finding that he did not return to his home, Mrs. Kinzie informed some of the Indian chiefs, his particular friends, who immediately repaired to the headquarters of the commanding officer, demanded "their friend's" release, and brought him back to his home. After waiting a time until a favourable opportunity presented itself, the general sent a detachment of dragoons to arrest Mr. Kinzie. They had succeeded in carrying him away, and crossing the river with him. Just at this moment a party of friendly Indians made their appearance.

"Where is the Shaw-nee-aw-kee?" was the first question.

"There," replied his wife, pointing across the river, "in the hands of the red-coats, who are taking him away again."

The Indians ran to the river, seized some canoes that they found there, and, crossing over to Sandwich, compelled General Proctor a second time to forego his intentions.

A third time this officer made the attempt, and succeeded in arresting Mr. Kinzie and conveying him heavily ironed to Fort Malden, in Canada, at the mouth of the Detroit River. Here he was at first treated with great severity, but after a time the rigor of his confinement was somewhat relaxed, and he was permitted to walk on the bank of the river for air and exercise.

On the 10th of September, as he was taking his promenade under the close supervision of a guard of soldiers, the whole party were startled by the sound of guns upon Lake Erie, at no great distance below. What could it mean? It must be Commodore Barclay firing into some of the Yankees. The firing continued. The time allotted the prisoner for his daily walk expired, but neither he nor his guard observed the lapse of time, so anxiously were they listening to what they now felt sure was an engagement between ships of war. At length Mr. Kinzie was reminded that the hour for his return to confinement had arrived. He petitioned for another half-hour.

"Let me stay," said he, "till we can learn how the battle has gone."

Very soon a sloop appeared under press of sail, rounding the point, and presently two gun-boats in chase of her.

"She is running—she bears the British colours," cried he—"yes, yes, they are lowering—she is striking her flag! Now," turning to the soldiers, "I will go back to prison contented—I know how the battle has gone."

The sloop was the *Little Belt*, the last of the squadron captured by the gallant Perry on that memorable occasion which he announced in the immortal words:

"We have met the enemy, and they are ours!"

Matters were growing critical, and it was necessary to transfer all prisoners to a place of greater security than the frontier was now likely to be. It was resolved therefore to send Mr. Kinzie to the mother-country. Nothing has ever appeared which would explain the course of General Proctor in regard to this gentleman. He had been taken from the bosom of his family, where he was living quietly under the parole which he had received, and protected by the stipulations of the surrender. He was kept for months in confinement. Now he was placed on horseback under a strong guard, who announced that they had orders to shoot him through the head if he offered to speak to a person upon the road. He was tied upon the saddle to prevent his escape, and thus they set out for Quebec. A little incident occurred, which will help to illustrate the course invariably pursued towards our citizens, at this period, by the British Army on the Northwestern frontier.

The saddle on which Mr. Kinzie rode had not been properly fastened, and, owing to the rough motion of the animal on which it was, it turned, so as to bring the rider into a most awkward and painful position. His limbs being fastened, he could not disengage himself, and in this manner, he was compelled by those who had charge of him to ride until he was nearly exhausted, before they had the humanity to release him.

Arrived at Quebec, he was put on board a small vessel to be sent to England. The vessel when a few days out at sea was chased by an American frigate and driven into Halifax. A second time she set sail, when she sprung a leak and was compelled to put back.

The attempt to send him across the ocean was now abandoned, and he was returned to Quebec. Another step, equally inexplicable with his arrest, was soon after taken. This was, his release and that of Mr. Macomb, of Detroit, who was also in confinement in Quebec, and the permission given them to return to their friends and families, although the war was not yet ended. It may possibly be imagined that in the treatment these gentlemen received, the British commander-in-chief sheltered himself under the plea of their being "native-born British subjects," and perhaps when it was ascertained that Mr. Kinzie was indeed a citizen of the United States it was thought safest to release him.

In the meantime, General Harrison at the head of his troops had reached Detroit. He landed on the 29th of September. All the citizens went forth to meet him—Mrs. Kinzie, leading her children by the hand, was of the number. The general accompanied her to her home, and took up his abode there. On his arrival he was introduced to Kee-po-tah, who happened to be on a visit to the family at that time. The general had seen the chief the preceding year, at the Council at Vincennes, and the meeting was one of great cordiality and interest.

★★★★★★★★★★★★★★★★★

In 1816, Mr. Kinzie and his family again returned to Chicago. The fort was rebuilt on a somewhat larger scale than the former one. It was not until the return of the troops that the bones of the unfortunate Americans who had been massacred four years before, were collected and buried.

An Indian Agency, under the charge of Charles Jewett, Esq., of Kentucky, was established. He was succeeded in 1820 by Dr. Alexander Wolcott, of Connecticut, who occupied that position until his death in 1830.

The troops were removed from the garrison in 1823, but restored in 1828, after the Winnebago war. This was a disturbance between the Winnebagoes and white settlers on and near the Mississippi. After some murders had been committed, the young chief, Red Bird, was taken and imprisoned at Prairie du Chien to await his trial, where he committed suicide in consequence of chagrin and the irksomeness of confinement. It was feared that the Pottowattamies would make common cause with the Winnebagoes, and commence a general system of havoc and bloodshed on the frontier. They were deterred from such a step, probably, by the exertions of Billy Caldwell, Robinson, and Shaw-bee-nay, who made an expedition among the Rock River bands, to argue and persuade them into remaining tranquil.

The few citizens of Chicago in those days, lived for the most part a very quiet, unvaried life. The great abundance of game, and the immense fertility of the lands they cultivated, furnished them with a superabundance of all the luxuries of garden, cornfield, and dairy. The question was once asked by a friend in the "East Countrie,"

"How do you dispose of all the good things you raise? You have no market?" "No." "And you cannot consume them all yourselves?" "No." "What then do you do with them?"

"Why, we manage, when a vessel arrives, to persuade the captain to accept a few kegs of butter, and stores of corn and vegetables, as a present, and that helps us to get rid of some of our overplus."

The mails arrived, as may be supposed, at very rare intervals. They were brought occasionally from Fort Clark (Peoria), but more frequently from Fort Wayne, or across the peninsula of Michigan, which was still a wilderness peopled with savages. The hardy adventurer who acted as express was, not unfrequently, obliged to imitate the birds of heaven and "lodge among the branches," in order to ensure the safety of himself and his charge.

Visitors were very rare, unless it was a friend who came to sojourn for several months and share a life in the wilderness. A traveller, however, occasionally found his way to the spot, in passing to or from "parts unknown," and such a one was sure of a hospitable and hearty welcome.

A gentleman journeying from the southern settlements once arrived late in the evening at Wolf Point, where was then the small trading-establishment of George Hunt and a Mr. Wallace. He stopped and inquired if he could have accommodation for the night for himself and his horse. The answer was, that they were ill provided to entertain a stranger—the house was small, and they were keeping "bachelor's hall."

"Is there no place," inquired the traveller, "where I can obtain a lodging?"

"Oh, yes—you will find a very comfortable house, Mr. Kinzie's, about half a mile below, near the mouth of the river."

The stranger turned his horse's head and took the road indicated.

Arrived at the spot, his first inquiry was,—

"Is this the residence of Mr. Kinzie?"

"Yes, sir."

"I should be glad to get accommodation for myself and horse."

"Certainly, sir—walk in."

The horse was taken to the stable, while the gentleman was ushered into a parlour where were two ladies. The usual preliminary questions and answers were gone through, for in a new country people soon become acquainted, and the gentleman ere long found himself seated at a comfortable hot supper—we will venture to say a fine supper, since the table in this domestic establishment has always been somewhat famous.

Apparently, the gentleman enjoyed it, for he made himself quite at home. He even called for a boot-jack after tea, and drew off his boots. The ladies were a little surprised, but they had lived a good while out of the world, and they did not know what changes in etiquette might have taken place during their retirement.

Before taking his leave for the night, the traveller signified what it would please him to have for breakfast, which was duly prepared. The next day proved stormy. The gentleman was satisfied with his quarters, and, having taken care to ascertain that there was no neglect or deficiency of accommodation so far as his horse was concerned, he got through the day very comfortably.

Now and then, when he was tired of reading, he would converse with the family, and seemed, upon the whole, by no means disposed to hold himself aloof, but to indulge in a little becoming sociability, seeing they were all there away in the woods.

The second day the weather brightened. The traveller signified his intention to depart. He ordered his horse to the door—then he called for his bill.

"My house is not a tavern, sir," was the astounding reply.

"Not a tavern! Good heavens! have I been making myself at home in this manner in a private family?"

He was profuse in his apologies, which, however, were quite unnecessary, for the family had perceived from the first the mistake he had fallen into, and they had amused themselves during his whole visit in anticipating the consternation of their guest when he should be undeceived.

★★★★★★★★★★★★★★★★★

It was in the year 1816 (the year of the rebuilding of the fort, after its destruction by the Indians) that the tract of land on which Chicago stands, together with the surrounding country, was ceded to the United States by the Pottowattamies. They remained the peaceful occupants of it, however, for twenty years longer. It was not until 1836 that they were removed by government to lands appropriated for their use on the Upper Missouri.

In the year 1830 the town of Chicago was laid out into lots by commissioners appointed by the State. At this time the prices of these lots ranged from ten to sixty dollars.

★★★★★★★★★★★★★★★★★

Mr. Kinzie, who, from the geographical position of this place, and the vast fertility of the surrounding country, had always foretold its eventual prosperity and importance, was not permitted to witness the realisation of his predictions. He closed his useful and energetic life on the 6th of January, 1828, having just completed his sixty-fifth year.

CHAPTER 21

A Sermon

Chicago was not, at the period of my first visit, the cheerful, happy place it had once been. The death of Dr. Wolcott, of Lieutenant Furman, and of a promising young son of Mr. Beaubien, all within a few weeks of each other, had thrown a gloom over the different branches of the social circle.

The weather, too, was inclement and stormy beyond anything that had been known before. Only twice, during a period of two months, did the sun shine out through the entire day. So late as the second week in April, when my husband had left to return to Fort Winnebago, the storms were so severe that he and his men were obliged to lie by two or three days in an Indian lodge.

Robert Kinzie, Medard Beaubien, and Billy Caldwell had gone at the same time to the Calumet to hunt, and, as they did not make their appearance for many days, we were persuaded they had perished with cold. They returned at length, however, to our infinite joy, having only escaped freezing by the forethought of Robert and Caldwell in carrying each two blankets instead of one.

Our only recreation was an occasional ride on horseback, when the weather would permit, through the woods on the north side of the river, or across the prairie, along the lake shore on the south.

When we went in the former direction, a little bridle-path took us along what is now Rush Street. The thick boughs of the trees arched over our heads, and we were often compelled, as we rode, to break away the projecting branches of the shrubs which impeded our path. The little prairie west of Wright's Woods was the usual termination of our ride in this direction.

When we chose the path across the prairie towards the south, we generally passed a newcomer, Dr. Harmon, superintending the construction of a *sod fence*, at a spot he had chosen, near the shore of the lake. In this enclosure he occupied himself, as the season advanced, in planting fruit-stones of all descriptions, to make ready a garden and orchard for future enjoyment.

We usually stopped to have a little chat. The two favourite themes of the doctor were horticulture, and the certain future importance of Chicago. That it was destined to be a great city, was his unalterable conviction; and in deed, by this time, all forest and prairie as it was, we half began to believe it ourselves.

On the pleasant afternoons which we occasionally enjoyed as the season advanced, we found no small amusement in practising pistol-firing. The place appropriated to this sport was outside the pickets, the mark being placed on a panel in one of the bastions. The gentlemen must not be offended if I record that, in process of time, the ladies acquired a degree of skill that enabled them, as a general thing, to come off triumphant. One of the ladies, Mrs. Hunter, was a great shot, having brought down her grouse on the wing, to the no small delight of one of the officers, Captain Martin Scott, of raccoon celebrity.

Now and then, there was a little excitement within the fort, aroused by the discovery that a settler had been engaged in selling milk-punch, instead of milk, to the soldiers, thereby interfering in no small degree with the regularity and perfect discipline of the service. The first step was to "drum out" the offender with all the honours of war—that is, with a party-coloured dress, and the Rogue's March played behind him. The next, to place all the victims of this piece of deception in the guard-house, where the commanding officer's lady supplied them bountifully with coffee and hot cakes, by way of opening their eyes to the enormity of their offence.

It is not to be wondered at that the officers sometimes complained of its being more of a strife with the soldiers who should get into the guard-house, than who should keep out of it. The poor fellows knew when they were well off.

Once, upon a Sunday, we were rowed up to Wolf Point to attend a religious service, conducted by Father See, as he was called.

We saw a tall, slender man, dressed in a green frock-coat, from the sleeves of which dangled a pair of hands giving abundant evidence, together with the rest of his dress, that he placed small faith in the axiom—*"cleanliness is a part of holiness."*

He stepped briskly upon a little platform behind a table, and commenced his discourse. His subject was, "The fear of God."

"There was a kind of fear," he told us, "that was very nearly alee-a-nated to love: so nearly, that it was not worthwhile splitting hairs for the difference." He then went on to describe this kind of fear. He grew more and more involved as he proceeded with his description until at length, quite bewildered, he paused, and exclaimed, "Come, let's stop a little while, and clear away the brush." He unravelled, as well as he was able, the tangled thread of his ideas, and went on with his subject.

But soon, again losing his way, he came to a second halt. "Now," said he, wiping the perspiration from his forehead with a red cotton handkerchief many degrees from clean, "now, suppose we drive back a little piece." Thus, he recapitulated what he wished to impress upon us, of the necessity of cherishing a fear that maketh wise unto salvation, "which fear," said he, "may we all enjoy, that together we may soar away, on the rolling clouds of aether, to a boundless and happy eternity, which is the wish of your humble servant." And, flourishing abroad his hands, with the best of dancing-school bows, he took his seat.

It will be readily imagined that we felt our own religious exercises at home to be more edifying than such as this, and that we confined ourselves to them for the future.

The return of our brother, Robert Kinzie, from Palestine (not the Holy Land, but the seat of the Land Office), with the certificate of the title of the family to that portion of Chicago since known as "Kinzie's Addition," was looked upon as establishing a home for us at some future day, if the glorious dreams of good Dr. Harmon, and a few others, should come to be realised. One little incident will show how moderate were the anticipations of most persons at that period.

The certificate, which was issued in Robert's name (he representing the family in making the application), described only a fractional quarter-section of one hundred and two acres, instead of one hundred and sixty acres, the river and Lake Michigan cutting off fifty-eight acres on the southern and eastern lines of the quarter. The applicants had liberty to select their complement of fifty-eight acres out of any unappropriated land that suited them.

"Now, my son," said his mother to Robert, "lay your claim on the cornfield at Wolf Point. It is fine land, and will always be valuable for cultivation; besides, as it faces down the main river, the situation will always be a convenient one."

The answer was a hearty laugh. "Hear mother!" said Robert. "We have just got a hundred and two acres—more than we shall ever want, or know what to do with, and now she would have me go and claim fifty-eight acres more!"

"Take my advice, my boy," repeated his mother, "or you may live one day to regret it."

"Well, I cannot see how I can ever regret not getting more than we can possibly make use of." And so, the matter ended. The fifty-eight acres were never claimed, and there was, I think, a very general impression that asking for our just rights in the case would have a very grasping, covetous look. How much wiser five-and-twenty years have made us!

****

During my sojourn of two months at Chicago, our mother often entertained me with stories of her early life and adventures. The following is her history of her captivity among the Senecas, which I have put in the form of a tale, although without the slightest variation from the facts as I received them from her lips, and those of her sister, Mrs. William Forsyth, of Sandwich (C.W.), the little Maggie of the story.

CHAPTER 22

The Captives

It is well known that previous to the war of the Revolution the whole of the western portion of Pennsylvania was inhabited by different Indian tribes. Of these, the Delawares were the friends of the whites, and, after the commencement of the great struggle, took part with the United States. The Iroquois, on the contrary, were the friends and allies of the mother-country.

Very few white settlers had ventured beyond the Susquehanna. The numerous roving bands of Shawanoes, Nanticokes, etc., although at times professing friendship with the Americans and acting in concert with the Delawares or Lenape as allies, at others suffered themselves to be seduced by their neighbours, the Iroquois, to show a most sanguinary spirit of hostility.

For this reason, the life of the inhabitants of the frontier was one of constant peril and alarm. Many a scene of dismal barbarity was enacted, as the history of the times testifies, and even those who felt themselves in some measure protected by their immediate neighbours, the Delawares, never lost sight of the caution required by their exposed situation.

The vicinity of the military garrison at Pittsburg—or Fort Pitt, as it was then called—gave additional security to those who had pushed farther west, among the fertile valleys of the Alleghany and Monongahela. Among these were the family of Mr. Lytle, who, some years previous to the opening of our story, had removed from Baltimore to Path Valley, near Carlisle, and subsequently settled himself on the banks of Plum River, a tributary of the Alleghany. Here, with his wife and five children, he had continued to live in comfort and security, undisturbed by any hostile visit, and only annoyed by occasional false alarms from his more timorous neighbours, who, having had more experience in frontier life, were prone to anticipate evil, as well as to magnify every appearance of danger.

★★★★★★★★★★★★★★★★★

On a bright afternoon in the autumn of 1779, two children of Mr. Lytle, a girl of nine, and her brother, two years younger, were playing in a little dingle or hollow in the rear of their father's house. Some large trees, which had been recently felled, were lying here and there, still untrimmed of their branches, and many logs, prepared for fuel, were scattered around. Upon one of these the children, wearied with their sports, seated themselves, and to beguile the time they fell into conversation upon a subject that greatly perplexed them.

While playing in the same place a few hours previous, they had imagined they saw an Indian lurking behind one of the fallen trees. The Indians of the neighbourhood were in the habit of making occasional visits to the family, and they had become familiar and even affectionate with many of them, but this seemed a stranger, and after the first hasty glance they fled in alarm to the house.

Their mother chid them for the report they brought, which she endeavoured to convince them was without foundation. "You know," said she, "you are always alarming us unnecessarily: the neighbours' children have frightened you to death. Go back to your play, and learn to be more courageous."

So, the children returned to their sports, hardly persuaded by their mother's arguments. While they were thus seated upon the trunk of the tree, their discourse was interrupted by the note, apparently, of a quail not far off.

"Listen," said the boy, as a second note answered the first; "do you hear that?"

"Yes," was the reply, and, after a few moments' silence, "do you not hear a rustling among the branches of the tree yonder?"

"Perhaps it is a squirrel—but look! what is that? Surely, I saw something red among the branches. It looked like a fawn popping up its head."

At this moment, the children, who had been gazing so intently in the direction of the fallen tree that all other objects were forgotten, felt themselves seized from behind and pinioned in an iron grasp. What were their horror and dismay to find themselves in the arms of savages, whose terrific countenances and gestures plainly showed them to be enemies!

They made signs to the children to be silent, on pain of death, and hurried them off, half dead with terror, in a direction leading from their father's habitation. After travelling some distance in profound silence, the severity of their captors somewhat relaxed, and as night approached the party halted, after adopting the usual precautions to secure themselves against a surprise.

In an agony of uncertainty and terror, torn from their beloved home and parents, and anticipating all the horrors with which the rumours of the times had invested a captivity among the Indians— perhaps even a torturing death—the poor children could no longer restrain their grief, but gave vent to sobs and lamentations.

Their distress appeared to excite the compassion of one of the party, a man of mild aspect, who approached and endeavoured to soothe them. He spread them a couch of the long grass which grew near the encamping-place, offered them a portion of his own stock of dried meat and parched corn, and gave them to understand by signs that no farther evil was intended them.

These kindly demonstrations were interrupted by the arrival of another party of the enemy, bringing with them the mother of the little prisoners, with her youngest child, an infant of three months old.

It had so happened that the father of the family, with his serving-men, had gone early in the day to a *raising* at a few miles' distance, and the house had thus been left without a defender. The long period of tranquillity which they had enjoyed, free from all molestation or alarm from the savages, had thrown the settlers quite off their guard, and they had recently laid aside some of the caution they had formerly deemed necessary.

These Indians, by lying in wait, had found the favourable moment for seizing the defenceless family and making them prisoners. Judging from their paint, and other marks by which the early settlers learned to distinguish the various tribes, Mrs. Lytle conjectured that those into whose hands she and her children had fallen were Senecas. Nor was she mistaken. It was a party of that tribe who had descended from their village with the intention of falling upon some isolated band of their enemies, the Delawares, but failing in this, had made themselves amends by capturing a few white settlers.

It is to be attributed to the generally mild disposition of this tribe, together with the magnanimous character of the chief who accompanied the party, that their prisoners in the present instance escaped the fate of most of the Americans who were so unhappy as to fall into the hands of the Iroquois.

The children learned from their mother that she was profoundly ignorant of the fate of their remaining brother and sister, a boy of six and a little girl of four years of age, but she was in hopes they had made good their escape with the servant-girl, who had likewise disappeared from the commencement.

After remaining a few hours to recruit the exhausted frames of the prisoners, the savages again started on their march, one of the older Indians offering to relieve the mother from the burden of her infant, which she had hitherto carried in her arms. Pleased with the unexpected kindness, she resigned to him her tender charge.

Thus, they pursued their way, the savage who carried the infant lingering somewhat behind the rest of the party, until, finding a spot convenient for his purpose, he grasped his innocent victim by the feet, and, with one whirl, to add strength to the blow, dashed out its brains against a tree. Leaving the body upon the spot, he rejoined the party.

The mother, unsuspicious of what had passed, regarded him earnestly as he reappeared without the child—then gazed wildly around on the rest of the group. Her beloved little one was not there. Its absence spoke its fate; but, suppressing the shriek of agony, for she knew that the lives of the remaining ones depended upon her firmness in that trying hour, she drew them yet closer to her and pursued her melancholy way without a word spoken or a question asked.

From the depths of her heart, she cried unto Him who is able to save, and He comforted her with hopes of deliverance for the surviving ones, for she saw that if blood had been their sole object the scalps of herself and her children would have been taken upon the spot where they were made prisoners.

She read too in the eyes of one who was evidently the commander of the party an expression more merciful than she had even dared to hope. Particularly had she observed his soothing manner and manifest partiality towards her eldest child, the little girl of whom we have spoken, and she built many a bright hope of escape or ransom upon these slender foundations.

After a toilsome and painful march of many days, the party reached the Seneca village, upon the headwaters of the Alleghany, near what is now called Olean Point. On their arrival the chief, their conductor, who was distinguished by the name of the *Big White Man* led his prisoners to the principal lodge. (Although this is the name our mother preserved of her benefactor, it seems evident that this chief was in fact *Corn-Planter*, a personage well known in the history of the times. There could hardly have been two such prominent chiefs in the same village.) This was occupied by his mother, the widow of the head-chief of that band, and who was called by them the *Old Queen*.

On entering her presence, her son presented her the little girl, saying,—

"My mother, I bring you a child to supply the place of my brother, who was killed by the Lenape six moons ago. She shall dwell in my lodge, and be to me a sister. Take the white woman and her children and treat them kindly—our father will give us many horses and guns to buy them back again."

He referred to the British Indian Agent of his tribe, Colonel Johnson, an excellent and benevolent gentleman, who resided at Fort Niagara, on the British side of the river of that name.

The Old Queen fulfilled the injunctions of her son. She received the prisoners, and every comfort was provided them that her simple and primitive mode of life rendered possible.

★★★★★★★★★★★★★★★★

We must now return to the place and period at which our story commences.

Late in the evening of that day the father returned to his dwelling. All within and around was silent and desolate. No trace of a living creature was to be found throughout the house or grounds. His nearest neighbours lived at a considerable distance, but to them he hastened, frantically demanding tidings of his family.

As he aroused them from their slumbers, one and another joined him in the search, and at length, at the house of one of them, was found the servant-maid who had effected her escape. Her first place of refuge, she said, had been a large brewing-tub in an outer kitchen, under which she had, at the first alarm, secreted herself until the departure of the Indians, who were evidently in haste, gave her an opportunity of fleeing to a place of safety. She could give no tidings of her mistress and the children, except that they had not been murdered in her sight or hearing.

At length, having scoured the neighbourhood without success, Mr. Lytle remembered an old settler who lived alone, far up the valley. Thither he and his friends immediately repaired, and from him they learned that, being at work in his field just before sunset, he had seen a party of strange Indians passing at a short distance from his cabin. As they wound along the brow of the hill, he could perceive that they had prisoners with them—a woman and a child. The woman he knew to be a white, as she carried her infant in her arms, instead of upon her back, after the manner of the savages.

Day had now begun to break, for the night had been passed in fruitless searches, and the agonised father, after a consultation with his kind friends and neighbours, accepted their offer to accompany him to Fort Pitt to ask advice and assistance of the *commandant* and Indian Agent at that place.

Proceeding down the valley, as they approached a hut which the night before they had found apparently deserted, they were startled by observing two children standing upon the high bank in front of it. The delighted father recognised two of his missing flock, but no tidings could they give him of their mother and the other lost ones. Their story was simple and touching.

They were playing in the garden, when they were alarmed by seeing the Indians enter the yard near the house. Unperceived by them, the brother, who was but six years of age, helped his little sister over the fence into a field overrun with bushes of the blackberry and wild raspberry. They concealed themselves among these for a while, and then, finding all quiet, they attempted to force their way to the side of the field farthest from the house. Unfortunately, the little girl in her play in the garden had pulled off her shoes and stockings, and the briers tearing and wounding her tender feet, she with difficulty could refrain from crying out. Her brother took off his stockings and put them on her feet.

He attempted, too, to protect them with his shoes, but they were too large, and kept slipping off, so that she could not wear them. For a time, they persevered in making what they considered their escape from certain death, for, as I have said, the children had been taught, by the tales they had heard, to regard all strange Indians as ministers of torture, and of horrors worse than death. Exhausted with pain and fatigue, the poor little girl at length declared she could go no farther.

"Then, Maggie," said her brother, "I must kill you, for I cannot let you be killed by the Indians."

"Oh, no, Thomas!" pleaded she, "do not, pray do not kill me! I do not think the Indians will find us."

"Oh, yes, they will, Maggie, and I could kill you so much easier than they would.'"

For a long time, he endeavoured to persuade her, and even looked about for a stick sufficiently large for his purpose; but despair gave the little creature strength, and she promised her brother that she would neither complain nor falter, if he would assist her in making her way out of the field.

The idea of the little boy that he could save his sister from savage barbarity by taking her life himself, shows what tales of horror the children of the early settlers were familiar with.

After a few more efforts, they made their way out of the field, into an unenclosed pasture-ground, where, to their great delight, they saw some cows feeding. They recognised them as belonging to Granny Myers, an old woman who lived at some little distance, but in what direction from the place they then were, they were utterly ignorant.

With a sagacity beyond his years, the boy said,—

"Let us hide ourselves till sunset, when the cows will go home, and we will follow them."

They did so, but, to their dismay, when they reached Granny Myers's they found the house deserted. The old woman had been called by some business down the valley, and did not return that night.

Tired and hungry, they could go no farther, but, after an almost fruitless endeavour to get some milk from the cows, they laid themselves down to sleep under an old bedstead that stood behind the house. Their father and his party had caused them additional terror in the night. The shouts and calls which had been designed to arouse the inmates of the house, they had mistaken for the whoop of the Indians, and, not being able to distinguish friends from foes, they had crept close to one another, as far out of sight as possible. When found the following morning, they were debating what course to take next, for safety.

The *commandant* at Fort Pitt entered warmly into the affairs of Mr. Lytle, and readily furnished him with a detachment of soldiers, to aid him and his friends in the pursuit of the marauders. Some circumstances having occurred to throw suspicion upon the Senecas, the party soon directed their search among the villages of that tribe.

Their inquiries were prosecuted in various directions, and always with great caution, for all the tribes of the Iroquois, or, as they pompously called themselves, the Five Nations, being allies of Great Britain, were inveterate in their hostility to the Americans. Thus, some time elapsed before the father with his attendants reached the village of the Big White Man.

A treaty was immediately entered into for the ransom of the captives, which was easily accomplished in regard to Mrs. Lytle and the younger child. But no offers, no entreaties, no promises, could procure the release of the little Eleanor, the adopted child of the tribe. "No," the chief said, "she was his sister; he had taken her to supply the place of his brother who was killed by the enemy—she was dear to him, and he would not part with her."

Finding every effort unavailing to shake this resolution, the father was compelled to take his sorrowful departure with such of his beloved ones as he had had the good fortune to recover.

We will not attempt to depict the grief of parents compelled thus to give up a darling child, and to leave her in the hands of savages, whom until now they had too much reason to regard as merciless. But there was no alternative. Commending her to the care of their heavenly Father, and cheered by the manifest tenderness with which she had thus far been treated, they set out on their melancholy journey homeward, trusting that some future effort would be more effectual for the recovery of their little girl.

Having placed his family in safety at Pittsburg, Mr. Lytle, still assisted by the *commandant* and the Indian Agent, undertook an expedition to the frontier to the residence of the British Agent, Colonel Johnson. His representation of the case warmly interested the feelings of that benevolent officer, who promised him to spare no exertions in his behalf. This promise he religiously performed. He went in person to the village of the Big White Man, as soon as the opening of the spring permitted, and offered him many splendid presents of guns and horses, but the chief was inexorable.

Time rolled on, and every year the hope of recovering the little captive became more faint. She, in the meantime, continued to wind herself more and more closely around the heart of her Indian brother. Nothing could exceed the consideration and affection with which she was treated, not only by himself, but by his mother, the Old Queen. All their stock of brooches and *wampum* was employed in the decoration of her person. The principal seat and the most delicate viands were invariably reserved for her, and no efforts were spared to promote her happiness, and to render her forgetful of her former home and kindred.

Thus, though she had beheld, with a feeling almost amounting to despair, the departure of her parents and dear little brother, and had for a long time resisted every attempt at consolation, preferring even death to a life of separation from all she loved, yet time, as it ever does, brought its soothing balm, and she at length grew contented and happy.

From her activity and the energy of her character, qualities for which she was remarkable to the latest period of her life, the name was given her of *The Ship under full sail.*

✶✶✶✶✶✶✶✶✶✶✶✶✶✶✶✶✶

The only drawback to the happiness of the little prisoner, aside from her longings after her own dear home, was the enmity she encountered from the wife of the Big White Man. This woman, from the day of her arrival at the village, and adoption into the family as a sister, had conceived for her the greatest animosity, which, at first, she had the prudence to conceal from the observation of her husband.

It was perhaps natural that a wife should give way to some feelings of jealousy at seeing her own place in the heart of her husband usurped by the child of their enemy, the American. But these feelings were aggravated by a bad and vindictive temper, and by the indifference with which her husband listened to her complaints and murmurings.

As she had no children of her own to engage her attention, her mind was the more engrossed and inflamed with her fancied wrongs, and with devising means for their redress. An opportunity of attempting the latter was not long wanting.

During the absence of the Big White Man upon some war-party or hunting-excursion, his little sister was taken ill with fever and ague. She was nursed with the utmost tenderness by the Old Queen; and the wife of the chief, to lull suspicion, and thereby accomplish her purpose, was likewise unwearied in her assiduities to the little favourite.

One afternoon, during the temporary absence of the Old Queen, her daughter-in-law entered the lodge with a bowl of something she had prepared, and, stooping down to the mat on which the child lay, said, in an affectionate accent,—

"Drink, my sister, I have brought you that which will drive this fever far from you."

On raising her head to reply, the little girl perceived a pair of eyes peeping through a crevice in the lodge, and fixed upon her with a very peculiar and significant expression. With the quick perception acquired partly from nature and partly from her intercourse with this people, she replied, faintly,—

"Set it down, my sister. When this fit of the fever has passed, I will drink your medicine."

The squaw, too cautious to use importunity, busied herself about in the lodge for a short time, then withdrew to another, near at hand. Meantime, the bright eyes continued peering through the opening, until they had watched their object fairly out of sight; then a low voice, the voice of a young friend and playfellow, spoke:

"Do not drink that which your brother's wife has brought you. She hates you, and is only waiting an opportunity to rid herself of you. I have watched her all the morning, and have seen her gathering the most deadly roots and herbs. I knew for whom they were intended, and came hither to warn you."

"Take the bowl," said the little invalid, "and carry it to my mother's lodge."

This was accordingly done. The contents of the bowl were found to consist principally of a decoction of the root of the May-apple, the most deadly poison known among the Indians.

It is not in the power of language to describe the indignation that pervaded the little community when this discovery was made known. The squaws ran to and fro, as is their custom when excited, each vying with the other in heaping invectives upon the culprit. No further punishment was, however, for the present inflicted upon her, but, the first burst of rage over, she was treated with silent abhorrence.

The little patient was removed to the lodge of the Old Queen, and strictly guarded, while her enemy was left to wander in silence and solitude about the fields and woods, until the return of her husband should determine her punishment.

In a few days, the excursion being over, the Big White Man and his party returned to the village. Contrary to the usual custom of savages, he did not, in his first transport at learning the attempt on the life of his little sister, take summary vengeance on the offender. He contented himself with banishing her from his lodge, never to return, and condemning her to hoe corn in a distant part of the large field or enclosure which served the whole community for a garden.

Although she would still show her vindictive disposition whenever, by chance, the little girl with her companions wandered into that vicinity, by striking at her with her hoe, or by some other spiteful manifestation, yet she was either too well watched, or stood too much in awe of her former husband, to repeat the attempt upon his sister's life.

****

Four years had now elapsed since the capture of little Nelly. Her heart was by nature warm and affectionate, so that the unbounded tenderness of those she dwelt among had called forth a corresponding feeling in her heart. She regarded the chief and his mother with love and reverence, and had so completely learned their language and customs as almost to have forgotten her own.

So identified had she become with the tribe, that the remembrance of her home and family had nearly faded from her memory; all but her mother—her mother, whom she had loved with a strength of affection natural to her warm and ardent character, and to whom her heart still clung with a fondness that no time or change could destroy.

The peace of 1783 between Great Britain and the United States now took place. A general pacification of the Indian tribes was the consequence, and fresh hopes were renewed in the bosoms of Mr. and Mrs. Lytle.

They removed with their family to Fort Niagara, near which, on the American side, was the Great Council-Fire of the Senecas. Colonel Johnson readily undertook a fresh negotiation with the chief, but in order to make sure every chance of success, he again proceeded in person to the village of the Big White Man.

His visit was most opportune. It was the "Feast of the Green Corn," when he arrived among them. This observance, which corresponds so strikingly with the Jewish Feast of Tabernacles that, together with other customs, it has led many to believe the Indian nations the descendants of the lost ten tribes of Israel, made it a season of general joy and festivity. All other occupations were suspended to give place to social enjoyment in the open air or in arbours formed of the green branches of the trees. Everyone appeared in his gala-dress.

That of the little adopted child consisted of a petticoat of blue broadcloth, bordered with gay-coloured ribbons; a sack or upper garment of black silk, ornamented with three rows of silver brooches, the centre ones from the throat to the hem being of large size, and those from the shoulders down being no larger than a shilling-piece, and set as closely as possible. Around her neck were innumerable strings of white and purple *wampum*—an Indian ornament manufactured from the inner surface of the muscle-shell. Her hair was clubbed behind and loaded with beads of various colours. Leggings of scarlet cloth, and *moccasins* of deer-skin embroidered with porcupine-quills, completed her costume.

Colonel Johnson was received with all the consideration due to his position, and to the long friendship that had subsisted between him and the tribe.

Observing that the hilarity of the festival had warmed and opened all hearts, he took occasion in an interview with the chief to expatiate upon the parental affection which had led the father and mother of his little sister to give up their friends and home, and come hundreds of miles away, in the single hope of sometimes looking upon and embracing her. The heart of the chief softened as he listened to this representation, and he was induced to promise that at the Grand Council soon to be held at Fort Niagara, on the British side of the river, he would attend, bringing his little sister with him.

He exacted a promise, however, from Colonel Johnson, that not only no effort should be made to reclaim the child, but that even no proposition to part with her should be offered him.

The time at length arrived when, her heart bounding with joy, little Nelly was placed on horseback to accompany her Indian brother to the Great Council of the Senecas. She had promised him that she would never leave him without his permission, and he relied confidently on her word thus given.

As the chiefs and warriors arrived in successive bands to meet their father, the agent, at the council-fire, how did the anxious hearts of the parents beat with alternate hope and fear! The officers of the fort had kindly given them quarters for the time being, and the ladies, whose sympathies were strongly excited, had accompanied the mother to the place of council, and joined in her longing watch for the first appearance of the band from the Alleghany River.

At length they were discerned, emerging from the forest on the opposite or American side. Boats were sent across by the commanding officer, to bring the chief and his party. The father and mother, attended by all the officers and ladies, stood upon the grassy bank awaiting their approach. They had seen at a glance that the *little captive* was with them.

When about to enter the boat, the chief said to some of his young men, "Stand here with the horses, and wait until I return."

He was told that the horses should be ferried across and taken care of.

"No," said he; "let them wait."

He held his darling by the hand until the river was passed—until the boat touched the bank—until the child sprang forward into the arms of the mother from whom she had been so long separated.

When the chief witnessed that outburst of affection, he could withstand no longer.

"She shall go," said he. "The mother must have her child again. I will go back alone."

With one silent gesture of farewell, he turned and stepped on board the boat. No arguments or entreaties could induce him to remain at the council, but, having gained the other side of the Niagara, he mounted his horse, and with his young men was soon lost in the depths of the forest.

After a sojourn of a few weeks at Niagara, Mr. Lytle, dreading lest the resolution of the Big White Man should give way, and measures be taken to deprive him once more of his child, came to the determination of again changing his place of abode. He therefore took the first opportunity of crossing Lake Erie with his family, and settled himself in the neighbourhood of Detroit, where he continued afterwards to reside.

Little Nelly saw her friend the chief no more, but she never forgot him. To the day of her death, she remembered with tenderness and gratitude her brother the Big White Man, and her friends and playfellows among the Senecas.

CHAPTER 23

Second-Sight—Hickory Creek

At the age of fourteen the heroine of the foregoing story married Colonel McKillip, a British officer. This gentleman was killed near Fort Defiance, as it was afterwards called, at the Miami Rapids, in 1794. A detachment of British troops had been sent down from Detroit to take possession of this post. General Wayne was then on a campaign against the Indians, and the British Government thought proper to make a few demonstrations in behalf of their allies. Having gone out with a party to reconnoitre, Colonel McKillip was returning to his post after dark, when he was fired upon and killed by one of his own sentinels. Mrs. Helm was the daughter of this marriage.

During the widowhood of Mrs. McKillip, she resided with her parents, at Grosse Pointe, eight miles above Detroit, and it was during this period that an event occurred which, from the melancholy and mysterious circumstances attending it, was always dwelt upon by her with peculiar interest.

Her second brother, Thomas Lytle, was, from his amiable and affectionate character, the most dearly beloved by her of all the numerous family circle. He was paying his addresses to a young lady who resided at the River Trench, (from the French—*Tranche*, a deep cut), as it was then called, now the River Thames, a stream emptying into Lake St. Clair about twenty miles above Detroit. In visiting this young lady, it was his custom to cross the Detroit River by the ferry with his horse, and then proceed by land to the River Trench, which was, at some seasons of the year, a fordable stream.

On a fine forenoon, late in the spring, he had taken leave of his mother and sister for one of these periodical visits, which were usually of two or three days' duration.

After dinner, as his sister was sitting at work by an open window which looked upon a little side enclosure filled with fruit-trees, she was startled by observing some object opposite the window, between her and the light. She raised her eyes and saw her brother Thomas. He was without his horse, and carried his saddle upon his shoulders.

Surprised that she had not heard the gate opening for his entrance, and also at his singular appearance, laden in that manner, she addressed him, and inquired what had happened, and why he had returned so soon. He made her no reply, but looked earnestly in her face, as he moved slowly along the paved walk that led to the stables.

She waited a few moments, expecting he would reappear to give an account of himself and his adventures, but at length, growing impatient at his delay, she put down her work and went towards the rear of the house to find him.

The first person she met was her mother. "Have you seen Thomas?" she inquired.

"Thomas! He has gone to the River Trench."

"No, he has returned—I saw him pass the window not fifteen minutes since."

"Then he will be in presently."

His sister, however, could not wait. She proceeded to the stables, she searched in all directions. No Thomas—no horse—no saddle. She made inquiry of the domestics. No one had seen him. She then returned and told her mother what had happened.

"You must have fallen asleep and dreamed it," said her mother.

"No, indeed! I was wide awake—I spoke to him, and he gave me no answer, but such a look!"

All the afternoon she felt an uneasiness she could not reason herself out of.

The next morning came a messenger from the River Trench with dismal tidings.

The bodies of the young man and his horse had been found drowned a short distance below the ford of the river.

It appeared that, on arriving at the bank of the river, he found it swollen beyond its usual depth by the recent rains. It being necessary to swim the stream with his horse, he had taken off his clothes and made them into a packet which he fastened upon his shoulders. It was supposed that the strength of the rapid torrent displaced the bundle, which thus served to draw his head under water and keep it there, without the power of raising it. All this was gathered from the position and appearance of the bodies when found.

From the time at which he had been seen passing a house which stood near the stream, on his way to the ford, it was evident that he must have met his fate at the very moment his sister saw, or thought she saw him, passing before her.

I could not but suggest the inquiry, when these sad particulars were narrated to me,—

"Mother, is it not possible this might have been a dream?"

"A dream? No, indeed, my child. I was perfectly wide awake—as much so as I am at this moment. I am not superstitious. I have never believed in ghosts or witches, but nothing can ever persuade me that this was not a warning sent from God, to prepare me for my brother's death."

And those who knew her rational good sense—her freedom from fancies or fears, and the calm self-possession that never deserted her under the most trying circumstances—would almost be won to view the matter in the light she did.

★★★★★★★★★★★★★★★★

The order for the evacuation of Fort Dearborn, and the removal of the troops to Fort Howard (Green Bay), had now been received. The family circle was to be broken up. Our mother, our sister Mrs. Helm, and her little son, were to return with us to Fort Winnebago; the other members of the family, except Robert, were to move with the command to Green Bay.

The schooner *Napoleon* was to be sent from Detroit to convey the troops with their goods and chattels to their destined post. Our immediate party was to make the journey by land—we were to choose, however, a shorter and pleasanter route than the one we had taken in coming hither. My husband, with his Frenchmen, Petaille Grignon and Simon Lecuyer, had arrived, and all hands were now busily occupied with the necessary preparations for breaking up and removal.

I should be doing injustice to the hospitable settlers of Hickory Creek were I to pass by without notice an entertainment with which they honoured our Chicago *beaux* about this time. The merry-making was to be a ball, and the five single gentlemen of Chicago were invited. Mr. Dole, who was a newcomer, declined; Lieutenant Foster was on duty, but he did what was still better than accepting the invitation, he loaned his beautiful horse to Medard Beaubien, who with Robert Kinzie and Gholson Kercheval promised himself much fun in eclipsing the *beaux* and creating a sensation among the *belles* of Hickory Creek.

Chicago was then, as now, looked upon as the City *par excellence*. Its few inhabitants were supposed to have seen something of the world, and it is to be inferred that the arrival of the smart and dashing young men was an event looked forward to with more satisfaction by the fair of the little settlement than by the swains whose rivals they might become.

The day arrived, and the gentlemen set off in high spirits. They took care to be in good season, for the dancing was to commence at two o'clock in the afternoon. They were well mounted, each priding himself upon the animal he rode, and they wore their best suits, as became city gallants who were bent on cutting out their less fashionable neighbours and breaking the hearts of the admiring country damsels.

When they arrived at the place appointed, they were received with great politeness—their steeds were taken care of, and a dinner was provided them, after which they were ushered into the dancing-hall.

All the beauty of the neighbouring precincts was assembled. The ladies were for the most part white, or what passed for such, with an occasional dash of copper colour. There was no lack of bombazet gowns and large white pocket-handkerchiefs, perfumed with oil of cinnamon; and as they took their places in long rows on the puncheon floor, they were a merry and a happy company.

But the city gentlemen grew more and more gallant—the girls more and more delighted with their attentions—the country swains, alas! more and more scowling and jealous. In vain they pigeon-winged and double-shuffled—in vain they nearly dislocated hips and shoulders at "hoe corn and dig potatoes"—they had the mortification to perceive that the smart young sprigs from Chicago had their "pick and choose" among their very sweethearts, and that they themselves were fairly danced off the ground.

The revelry lasted until daylight, and it was now time to think of returning. There was no one ready with obliging politeness to bring them their horses from the stable.

"Poor fellows!" said one of the party, with a compassionate sort of laugh, "they could not stand it. They have gone home to bed!"

"Serves them right," said another; "they'd better not ask us down among their girls again!"

They groped their way to the stable and went in. There were some animals standing at the manger, but evidently not their horses. What could they be? Had the rogues been trying to cheat them, by putting these strange nondescripts into their place?

They led them forth into the grey of the morning, and then—such a trio as met their gaze!

There were the original bodies, it is true, but where were their manes and tails? A scrubby, pickety ridge along the neck, and a bare stump projecting behind, were all that remained of the flowing honours with which they had come gallivanting down to "bear away the bell" at Hickory Creek, or, in the emphatic language of the country, "to take the rag off the bush."

Gholson sat down on a log and cried outright. Medard took the matter more philosophically—the horse was none of his—it was Lieutenant Foster's.

Robert characteristically looked around to see whom he could knock down on the occasion; but there was no one visible on whom to wreak their vengeance.

The bumpkins had stolen away, and, in some safe, quiet nook, were snugly enjoying their triumph, and doubtless the deceitful fair ones were by this time at their sides, sharing their mirth and exultation.

The unlucky gallants mounted their steeds, and set their faces homeward. Never was there a more crestfallen and sorry-looking cavalcade. The poor horses seemed to realise that they had met the same treatment as the messengers of King David at the hands of the evil-disposed Hanun. They hung their heads, and evidently wished that they could have "tarried at Jericho" for a season. Unfortunately, there was in those days no back way by which they could steal in, unobserved. Across the prairie, in view of the whole community, must their approach be made; and to add to their confusion, in the rarity of stirring events, it was the custom of the whole settlement to turn out and welcome the arrival of any newcomer.

As hasty a retreat as possible was beaten, amid the shouts, the jeers, and the condolences of their acquaintances; and it is on record that these three young gentlemen were in no hurry to accept, at any future time, an invitation to partake of the festivities of Hickory Creek.

★★★★★★★★★★★★★★★★

In due time the *Napoleon* made her appearance. (Alas that this great name should be used in the feminine gender!) As there was at this period no harbour, vessels anchored outside the bar, or tongue of land which formed the left bank of the river, and the lading and unlading were carried on by boats, pulling in and out, through the mouth of the river, some distance below.

Of course, it always was a matter of great importance to get a vessel loaded as quickly as possible, that she might be ready to take advantage of the first fair wind, and be off from such an exposed and hazardous anchoring-ground.

For this reason, we had lived packed up for many days, intending only to see our friends safe on board, and then commence our own journey back to Fort Winnebago.

Our heavy articles of furniture, trunks, etc. had been sent on board the *Napoleon*, to be brought round to us by way of Fox River. We had retained only such few necessaries as could be conveniently carried on a pack-horse, and in a light Dearborn wagon lately brought by Mr. Kercheval from Detroit (the first luxury of the kind ever seen on the prairies), and which my husband had purchased as an agreeable mode of conveyance for his mother and little nephew.

It was a matter requiring no small amount of time and labour to transport, in the slow method described, the effects of so many families of officers and soldiers, with the various *etceteras* incident to a total change and removal. It was all, however, happily accomplished—everything, even to the last article, sent on board—nothing remaining on shore but the passengers, whose turn it would be next.

It was a moment of great relief; for Captain Hinckley had been in a fever and a fuss many hours, predicting a change of weather, and murmuring at what he thought the unnecessary amount of boat-loads to be taken on board.

Those who had leisure to be looking out towards the schooner, which had continued anchored about half a mile out in the lake, had, at this crisis, the satisfaction to see her hoist sail and leave her station for the open lake; those who were a little later could just discern her bearing away to a distance, as if she had got all on board that she had any idea of taking. Here we were, and here we might remain a week or more, if it so pleased Captain Hinckley and the schooner *Napoleon*, and the good east wind which was blowing with all its might.

There was plenty of provisions to be obtained, so the fear of starvation was not the trouble; but how were the cooking and the table to be provided for? Various expedients were resorted to. Mrs. Engle, in her quarters above-stairs, ate her breakfast off a shingle with her husband's jack-knife, and when she had finished, sent them down to Lieutenant Foster for his accommodation.

We were at the old mansion on the north side, and the news soon flew up the river that the *Napoleon* had gone off with "the plunder" and left the people behind. It was not long before we were supplied by

Mrs. Portier (our kind Victoire) with dishes, knives, forks, and all the other conveniences which our mess-basket failed to supply.

This state of things lasted a couple of days, and then, early one fine morning, the gratifying intelligence spread like wild-fire that the *Napoleon* was at anchor out beyond the bar.

There was no unnecessary delay this time, and at an early hour in the afternoon we had taken leave of our dear friends, and they were sailing away from Chicago.

★★★★★★★★★★

It is a singular fact that all the martins, of which there were great numbers occupying the little houses constructed for them by the soldiers, were observed to have disappeared from their homes on the morning following the embarkation of the troops. After an absence of five days, they returned. They had perhaps taken a fancy to accompany their old friends, but finding they were not Mother Carey's chickens, deemed it most prudent to return and reoccupy their old dwellings.

★★★★★★★★★★

Chapter 24

Return to Fort Winnebago

A great part of the command, with the cattle belonging to the officers and soldiers, had, a day or two previous to the time of our departure, set out on their march by land to Green Bay, via Fort Winnebago. Lieutenant Foster, under whose charge they were, had lingered behind that he might have the pleasure of joining our party, and we, in turn, had delayed in order to see the other members of our family safely on board the *Napoleon*. But now, all things being ready, we set our faces once more homeward.

We took with us a little *bound-girl,* Josette, a bright, pretty child of ten years of age, a daughter of Ouilmette, a Frenchman who had lived here at the time of the Massacre, and of a Pottowattamie mother. She had been at the St. Joseph's mission-school, under Mr. McCoy, and she was now full of delight at the prospect of a journey all the way to the Portage with Monsieur and Madame John.

We had also a negro boy, Harry, brought a year before from Kentucky, by Mr. Kercheval. In the transfer at that time from a slave State to a free one, Harry's position became somewhat changed—he could be no more than an indentured servant. He was about to become a member of Dr. Wolcott's household, and it was necessary for him to choose a guardian. All this was explained to him on his being brought into the parlour, where the family were assembled. My husband was then a young man, on a visit to his home. "Now, Harry," it was said to him, "you must choose your guardian;" and the natural expectation was that Harry would select the person of his acquaintance of the greatest age and dignity. But, rolling round his great eyes, and hanging his head on one side, he said,—

"I'll have Master John for my guardian."

From that day forward Harry felt as if he belonged, in a measure, to Master John, and at the breaking-up of the family in Chicago he was, naturally, transferred to our establishment.

There were three ladies of our travelling party—our mother, our sister Mrs. Helm, and myself. To guard against the burning effect of the sun and the prairie winds upon our faces, I had, during some of the last days of my visit, prepared for each of us a mask of brown linen, with the eyes, nose, and mouth fitted to our features; and, to enhance their hideousness, I had worked eyebrows, eyelashes, and a circle around the opening for the mouth, in black silk. Gathered in plaits under the chin, and with strings to confine them above and below, they furnished a complete protection against the sun and wind, though nothing can be imagined more frightful than the appearance we presented when fully equipped. It was who should be called the ugliest.

We left amid the good wishes and laughter of our few remaining acquaintances. Our wagon had been provided with a pair of excellent travelling horses, and, sister Margaret and myself being accommodated with the best pacers the country could afford, we set off in high spirits towards the Aux Plaines—our old friend, Billy Caldwell (the Sau-ga-nash), with our brother Robert, and Gholson Kercheval, accompanying us to that point of our journey.

There was no one at Barney Lawton's when we reached there, save a Frenchman and a small number of Indians. My sister and I dismounted, and entered the dwelling, the door of which stood open. Two Indians were seated on the floor, smoking. They raised their eyes as we appeared, and never shall I forget the expression of wonder and horror depicted on the countenances of both. Their lips relaxed until the pipe of one fell upon the floor. Their eyes seemed starting from their heads, and raising their outspread hands, as if to wave us from them, they slowly ejaculated, "*Manitou!*" (a spirit.)

As we raised our masks, and, smiling, came forward to shake hands with them, they sprang to their feet and fairly uttered a cry of delight at the sight of our familiar faces.

"*Bonjour, bonjour, Maman!*" was their salutation, and they instantly plunged out of doors to relate to their companions what had happened.

Our afternoon's ride was over a prairie stretching away to the northeast No living creature was to be seen upon its broad expanse, but flying and circling over our heads were innumerable flocks of curlews—

Screaming their wild notes to the listening waste.

Their peculiar, shrill cry of "*crack, crack, crack—rackety, rackety, rackety,*" repeated from the throats of dozens, as they sometimes stooped quite close to our ears, became at length almost unbearable. It seemed as if they had lost their senses in the excitement of so unusual and splendid a *cortége* in their hitherto desolate domain.

The accelerated pace of our horses, as we approached a beautiful, wooded knoll, warned us that this was to be our place of repose for the night. These animals seem to know by instinct a favourable encamping-ground, and this was one of the most lovely imaginable.

The trees, which near the lake had, owing to the coldness and tardiness of the season, presented the pale-yellow appearance of unfledged goslings, were here bursting into full leaf. The ground around was carpeted with flowers—we could not bear to have them crushed by the felling of a tree and the pitching of our tent among them. The birds sent forth their sweetest notes in the warm, lingering sunlight, and the opening buds of the young hickory and *sassafras* filled the air with perfume.

Nothing could be more perfect than our enjoyment of this sylvan and beautiful retreat, (now known as Dunkley's Grove), after our ride in the glowing sun. The children were in ecstasies. They delighted to find ways of making themselves useful—to pile up the saddles—to break boughs for the fire—to fill the little kettles with water for Petaille and Lecuyer, the Frenchmen, who were preparing our supper.

Their amusement at the awkward movements of the horses after they were spancelled knew no bounds. To our little nephew Edwin everything was new, and Josette, who had already made more than one horseback journey to St. Joseph, manifested all the pride of an old traveller in explaining to him whatever was novel or unaccountable.

They were not the last to spring up at the call "*how! how!*" on the following morning.

The fire was replenished, the preparations for breakfast commenced, and the Frenchmen dispatched to bring up the horses in readiness for an early start.

Harry and Josette played their parts, under our direction, in preparing the simple meal, and we soon seated ourselves, each with cup and knife, around the table-mat. The meal was over, but no men, no horses appeared. When another half-hour had passed, my husband took Harry and commenced exploring in search of the missing ones.

The day wore on, and first one and then another would make his appearance to report progress. Petaille and Lecuyer at length brought two of the horses, but the others could nowhere be found. In time, Mr. Kinzie and Harry returned, wet to their knees by the dew upon the long prairie-grass, but with no tidings. Again, the men were dispatched after having broken their fast, but returned unsuccessful as before.

The morning had been passed by our party at the encampment in speculating upon the missing animals. Could they have been stolen by the Indians? Hardly: these people seldom committed robberies in time of peace—never upon our family, whom they regarded as their best friends. The horses would doubtless be found. They had probably been carelessly fastened the preceding evening, and had therefore been able to stray farther than was their wont.

A council was held, at which it was decided to send Grignon back to Chicago to get some fresh horses from Gholson Kercheval, and return as speedily as possible. If on his return our encampment were deserted, he might conclude we had found the horses and proceeded to Fox River, where he would doubtless overtake us.

He had not been gone more than an hour before, slowly hopping out of a point of woods to the north of us (a spot which each of the seekers averred he had explored over and over again), and making directly for the place where we were, appeared the vexatious animals. They came up as demurely as if nothing had happened, and seemed rather surprised to be received with a hearty scolding, instead of being patted and caressed as usual.

It was the work of a very short half-hour to strike and pack the tent, stow away the mats and kettles, saddle the horses, and mount for our journey.

"Whoever pleases may take my place in the carriage," said our mother. "I have travelled so many years on horseback, that I find any other mode of conveyance too fatiguing."

So, spite of her sixty years, she mounted sister Margaret's pacer with the activity of a girl of sixteen.

Lieutenant Foster had left us early in the morning, feeling it necessary to rejoin his command, and now, having seen us ready to set off, with a serene sky above us, and all things "right and tight" for the journey, our friend the Sau-ga-nash took leave of us, and retraced his steps towards Chicago.

We pursued our way through a lovely country of alternate glade and forest, until we reached the Fox River. The current ran clear and rippling along, and, as we descended the steep bank to the water, the question, so natural to a traveller in an unknown region, presented itself, "Is it fordable?"

Petaille, to whom the ground was familiar, had not yet made his appearance Lecuyer was quite ignorant upon the subject. The troops had evidently preceded us by this very trail. True, but they were on horseback—the difficulty was, could we get the carriage through? It must be remembered that the doubt was not about the depth of the water, but about the hardness of the bottom of the stream.

It was agreed that two or three of the equestrians should make the trial first. My mother, Lecuyer, and myself advanced cautiously across to the opposite bank, each choosing a different point for leaving the water, in order to find the firmest spot. The bottom was hard and firm until we came near the shore; then it yielded a little. With one step, however, we were each on dry ground.

"*Est-il beau?*" called my husband, who was driving.

"*Oui, monsieur.*"

"Yes, John, come just here, it is perfectly good."

"No, no—go a little farther down. See the white gravel just there—it will be firmer still, there."

Such were the contradictory directions given. He chose the latter, and when it wanted but one step more to the bank, down sunk both horses, until little more than their backs were visible.

The white gravel proved to be a bed of treacherous yellow clay, which, gleaming through the water, had caused so unfortunate a deception.

With frantic struggles, for they were nearly suffocated with mud and water, the horses made desperate efforts to free themselves from the harness. My husband sprang out upon the pole. "Someone give me a knife," he cried. I was back in the water in a moment, and, approaching as near as I dared, handed him mine from the scabbard around my neck.

"Whatever you do, do not cut the traces," cried his mother.

He severed some of the side-straps, when, just as he had reached the extremity of the pole, and was stretching forward to separate the head-couplings, one of the horses gave a furious plunge, which caused his fellow to rear, and throw himself nearly backwards. My husband was between them. For a moment we thought he was gone—trampled down by the excited animals; but he presently showed himself, nearly obscured by the mud and water. With the agility of a cat, Harry, who was near him, now sprang forward on the pole, and in an instant, with his sharp jack-knife which he had ready, divided the straps that confined their heads.

The horses were at this moment lying floating on the water—one apparently dead, the other as if gasping out his last breath. But hardly did they become sensible of the release of their heads from bondage, than they made, simultaneously, another furious effort to free themselves from the pole, to which they were still attached by the neck-strap.

Failing in this, they tried another expedient, and, by a few judicious twists and turns, succeeded in wrenching the pole asunder, and finally carried it off in triumph across the river again, and up the bank, where they stood waiting to decide what were the next steps to be taken.

Here was a predicament! A few hours before, we had thought ourselves uncomfortable enough, because some of our horses were missing. Now, a greater evil had befallen us. The wagon was in the river, the harness cut to pieces, and, what was worse, carried off in the most independent manner, by Tom and his companion; the pole was twisted to fragments, and there was not so much as a stick on our side of the river with which to replace it.

At this moment, a whoop from the opposite bank, echoed by two or three hearty ones from our party, announced the reappearance of Petaille Grignon. He dismounted and took charge of the horses, who were resting themselves after their fatigues under a shady tree, and by this time Lecuyer had crossed the river, and now joined him in bringing back the delinquents.

In the meantime, we had been doing our best to minister to our sister Margaret. She, with her little son Edwin, had been in the wagon at the time of the accident, and it had been a work of some difficulty to get them out and bring them on horseback to shore. The effect of the agitation and excitement was to throw her into a fit of the ague, and she now lay blue and trembling among the long grass of the little prairie which extended along the bank.

The tent, which had been packed in the rear of the wagon, was too much saturated with mud and water to admit of its being used as a shelter; it could only be stretched in the sun to dry. We opened an umbrella over our poor sister's head, and now began a discussion of ways and means to repair damages. The first thing was to cut a new pole for the wagon, and for this, the master and men must recross the river and choose an *iron-tree* out of the forest.

Then, for the harness. With provident care, a little box had been placed under the seat of the wagon, containing an awl, waxed ends, and various other little conveniences exactly suited to an emergency like the present.

It was question and answer, like Cock Robin:

"Who can mend the harness?"

"I can, for I learned when I was a young girl to make shoes as an accomplishment, and I can surely now, as a matter of usefulness and duty, put all those wet, dirty pieces of leather together."

So, we all seated ourselves on the grass, under the shade of the only two umbrellas we could muster.

I stitched away diligently, blistering my hands, I must own, in no small degree.

A suitable young tree had been brought, and the hatchets, without which one never travels in the woods, were busy fashioning it into shape, when a peculiar hissing noise was heard, and instantly the cry,—

"*Un serpent sonnette!* A rattlesnake!"

All sprang to their feet, even the poor, shaking invalid, just in time to see the reptile glide past within three inches of my mother's feet, while the men assailed the spot it had left with whips, missiles, and whatever would help along the commotion.

This little incident proved an excellent remedy for the ague. One excitement drives away another, and by means of this (upon the homoeopathic principle) sister Margaret was so much improved that by the time all the mischiefs were repaired, she was ready to take her place in the cavalcade, as bright and cheerful as the rest of us.

So great had been the delay occasioned by all these untoward circumstances, that our afternoon's ride was but a short one, bringing us no farther than the shores of a beautiful sheet of water, now known as Crystal Lake. Its clear surface was covered with loons, and *Poules d'Eau*, a species of rail; with which, at certain seasons, this region abounds.

The Indians have the genius of Aesop for depicting animal life and character, and there is among them a fable or legend illustrative of every peculiarity in the personal appearance, habits, or dispositions of each variety of the animal creation.

The back of the little rail is very concave, or hollow. The Indians tell us that it became so in the following manner:—

Story of the Little Rail, or *Poule d'Eau*

There is supposed, by most of the Northwestern tribes, to exist an invisible being, corresponding to the "*Genie*" of Oriental story. Without being exactly the father of evil, *Nan-nee-bo-zho* is a spirit whose office it is to punish what is amiss. He is represented, too, as constantly occupied in entrapping and making examples of all the animals that come in his way.

One pleasant evening, as he walked along the banks of a lake, he saw a flock of ducks, sailing and enjoying themselves on the blue waters. He called to them:

"Ho! come with me into my lodge, and I will teach you to dance!" Some of the ducks said among themselves, "It is Nan-nee-bo-zho; let us not go." Others were of a contrary opinion, and, his words being fair, and his voice insinuating, a few turned their faces towards the land—all the rest soon followed, and, with many pleasant quackings, trooped after him, and entered his lodge.

When there, he first took an Indian sack, with a wide mouth, which he tied by the strings around his neck, so that it would hang over his shoulders, leaving the mouth unclosed. Then, placing himself in the centre of the lodge, he ranged the ducks in a circle around him.

"Now," said he, "you must all shut your eyes *tight*; whoever opens his eyes at all, something dreadful will happen to him. I will take my Indian flute and play upon it, and you will, at the word I shall give, open your eyes, and commence dancing, as you see me do."

The ducks obeyed, shutting their eyes *tight*, and keeping time to the music by stepping from one foot to the other, all impatient for the dancing to begin.

Presently a sound was heard like a smothered "quack," but the ducks did not dare to open their eyes.

Again, and again, the sound of the flute would be interrupted, and a gurgling cry of "qu-a-a-ck" be heard. There was one little duck, much smaller than the rest, who, at this juncture, could not resist the temptation to open one eye, cautiously. She saw Nan-nee-bo-zho, as he played his flute, holding it with one hand, stoop a little at intervals and seize the duck nearest him, which he throttled and stuffed into the bag on his shoulders. So, edging a little out of the circle, and getting nearer the door, which had been left partly open, to admit the light, she cried out,—

"Open your eyes—Nan-nee-bo-zho is choking you all and putting you into his bag!"

With that she flew, but Nan-nee-bo-zho pounced upon her. His hand grasped her back, yet, with desperate force, she released herself and gained the open air. Her companions flew, quacking and screaming, after her. Some escaped, and some fell victims to the sprite.

The little duck had saved her life, but she had lost her beauty. She ever after retained the attitude she had been forced into in her moment of danger—her back pressed down in the centre, and her head and neck unnaturally stretched forward into the air.

CHAPTER 25

Return Journey, Continued

The third day of our journey rose brilliantly clear, like the two preceding ones, and we shaped our course more to the north than we had hitherto done, in the direction of Big-Foot Lake, now known by the somewhat hackneyed appellation, Lake of Geneva.

Our journey this day was without mishaps or disasters of any kind. The air was balmy, the foliage of the forests fresh and fragrant, the little brooks clear and sparkling—everything in nature spoke the praises of the beneficent Creator.

It is in scenes like this, far removed from the bustle, the strife, and the sin of civilized life, that we most fully realise the presence of the great Author of the Universe. Here can the mind most fully adore his majesty and goodness, for here only is the command obeyed, "Let all the earth keep silence before Him!"

It cannot escape observation that the deepest and most solemn devotion is in the hearts of those who, shut out from the worship of God in temples made with hands, are led to commune with him amid the boundless magnificence that his own power has framed.

This day was not wholly without incident. As we stopped for our noon-tide refreshment, and dismounting threw ourselves on the fresh herbage just at the verge of a pleasant thicket, we were startled by a tender bleating near us, and presently, breaking its way through the low branches, there came upon us a sweet little dappled fawn, evidently in search of its mother. It did not seem in the least frightened at the sight of us. As poor Selkirk might have been parodied,—

It was so unacquainted with man,
Its tameness was charming to us.

But the vociferous delight of the children soon drove it bounding again into the woods, and all hopes of catching it for a pet were at once at an end.

We had travelled well this day, and were beginning to feel somewhat fatigued, when, just before sunset, we came upon a ridge, overlooking one of the loveliest little dells imaginable. It was an oak opening, and browsing under the shade of the tall trees which were scattered around were the cattle and horses of the soldiers, who had got thus far on their journey. Two or three white tents were pitched in the bottom of the valley, beside a clear stream. The camp-fires were already lighted, and the men, singly or in groups, were busied in their various preparations for their own comfort, or that of their animals.

Lieutenant Foster came forward with great delight to welcome our arrival, and accepted without hesitation an invitation to join our mess again, as long as we should be together.

We soon found a pleasant encamping-ground, far enough removed from the other party to secure us against all inconvenience, and our supper having received the addition of a kettle of fine fresh milk, kindly brought us by Mrs. Gardiner, the hospital matron, who with her little covered cart formed no unimportant feature in the military group, we partook of our evening meal with much hilarity and enjoyment.

If people are ever companionable, it is when thrown together under circumstances like the present. There has always been sufficient incident through the day to furnish themes for discourse, and subjects of merriment, as long as the company feel disposed for conversation, which is, truth to tell, not an unconscionable length of time after their supper is over.

The poor lieutenant looked grave enough when we set out in advance of him the next morning. None of his party were acquainted with the road; but, after giving him directions both general and particular, Mr. Kinzie promised to *blaze* a tree, or *set up a chip* for a guide, at every place which appeared more than usually doubtful.

We now found ourselves in a much more diversified country than any we had hitherto travelled. Gently swelling hills, lovely valleys, and

BIG-FOOT VILLAGE AND LAKE. (Geneva Lake.)

bright sparkling streams were the features of the landscape. But there was little animate life. Now and then a shout from the leader of the party (for, according to custom, we travelled Indian file) would call our attention to a herd of deer "loping," as the Westerners say, through the forest; or an additional spur would be given to the horses on the appearance of some small dark object, far distant on the trail before us. But the game invariably contrived to disappear before we could reach it, and it was out of the question to leave the beaten track for a regular hunt.

Soon after mid-day, we descended a long, sloping knoll, and by a sudden turn came full in view of the beautiful sheet of water denominated *Gros-pied* by the French, *Maunk-suck* by the natives, and by ourselves Big-foot, from the chief whose village overlooked its waters. Bold, swelling hills jutted forward into the clear blue expanse, or retreated slightly to afford a green, level nook, as a resting-place for the dwelling of man. On the nearer shore stretched a bright, gravelly beach, across which coursed here and there a pure, sparkling rivulet to join the larger sheet of water.

On a rising ground at the foot of one of the bold bluffs in the middle distance, a collection of neat *wigwams* formed, with their surrounding gardens, no unpleasant feature in the picture.

A shout of delight burst involuntarily from the whole party, as this charming landscape met our view. "It was like the Hudson, only less bold—no, it was like the lake of the Forest Cantons, in the picture of the Chapel of William Tell! What could be imagined more enchanting? Oh! if our friends at the East could but enjoy it with us!"

We paused long to admire, and then spurred on, skirting the head of the lake, and were soon ascending the broad platform on which stood the village of Maunk-suck, or Big-foot.

The inhabitants, who had witnessed our approach from a distance, were all assembled in front of their *wigwams* to greet us, if friends—if otherwise, whatever the occasion should demand. It was the first time such a spectacle had ever presented itself to their wondering eyes. Their salutations were not less cordial than we expected. "Shaw-nee-aw-kee" and his mother, who was known throughout the tribe by the touching appellation "Our friend's wife," were welcomed most kindly, and an animated conversation commenced, which I could understand only so far as it was conveyed by gestures; so, I amused myself by taking a minute survey of all that met my view.

The chief was a large, raw-boned, ugly Indian, with a countenance bloated by intemperance, and with a sinister, unpleasant expression. He had a gay-coloured handkerchief upon his head, and was otherwise attired in his best, in compliment to the strangers.

It was to this chief that Chambly, or, as he is now called, Shaw-beenay, Billy Caldwell, and Robinson were dispatched, by Dr. Wolcott, their Agent, during the Winnebago war, in 1821, to use their earnest endeavours to prevent this chief and his band from joining the hostile Indians. With some difficulty they succeeded, and were thus the means, doubtless, of saving the lives of all the settlers who lived exposed upon the frontier.

Among the various groups of his people, there was none attracted my attention so forcibly as a young man of handsome face, and a figure that was striking even where all were fine and symmetrical. He too had a gay handkerchief on his head, a shirt of the brightest lemon-coloured calico, an abundance of silver ornaments, and, what gave his dress a most fanciful appearance, one legging of blue and the other of bright scarlet. I was not ignorant that this peculiar feature in his toilet indicated a heart suffering from the tender passion. The flute, which he carried in his hand, added confirmation to the fact, while the joyous, animated expression of his countenance showed with equal plainness that he was not a despairing lover.

I could have imagined him to have recently returned from the chase, laden with booty, with which he had, as is the custom, entered the lodge of the fair one, and thrown his burden at the feet of her parents, with an indifferent, superb sort of air, as much as to say, "Here is some meat—it is a mere trifle, but it will show you what you might expect with me for a son-in-law." I could not doubt that the damsel had stepped forward and gathered it up, in token that she accepted the offering, and the donor along with it. There was nothing in the appearance or manner of any of the maidens by whom we were surrounded, to denote which was the happy fair, neither, although I peered anxiously into all their countenances, could I there detect any blush of consciousness; so, I was obliged to content myself with selecting the youngest and prettiest of the group, and go on weaving my romance to my own satisfaction.

The village stood encircled by an amphitheatre of hills, so precipitous, and with gorges so steep and narrow, that it seemed almost impossible to scale them, even on horseback; how, then, could we hope to accomplish the ascent of the four-wheeled carriage? This was the point now under discussion between my husband and the Pottowattamies. There was no alternative but to make the effort, selecting the pass that the inhabitants pointed out as the most practicable. Petaille went first, and I followed on my favourite Jerry. It was such a scramble as is not often taken—almost perpendicularly, through what seemed the dry bed of a torrent, now filled with loose stones, and scarcely affording one secure foothold from the bottom to the summit! I clang fast to the mane, literally at times clasping Jerry around his neck, and, amid the encouraging shouts and cheers of those below, we at length arrived safely, though nearly breathless, on the pinnacle, and sat looking down, to view the success of the next party.

The horses had been taken from the carriage, the luggage it contained being placed upon the shoulders of some of the young Indians, to be *toted* up the steep. Ropes were now attached to its sides, and a regular bevy of our red friends, headed by our two Frenchmen, placed to man them. Two or three more took their places in the rear, to hold the vehicle and keep it from slipping backwards—then the labour commenced. Such a pulling! such a shouting! such a clapping of hands by the spectators of both sexes! such a stentorian word of command or encouragement from the *bourgeois!* Now and then, there would be a slight halt, a wavering, as if carriage and men were about to tumble backwards into the plain below; but no—they would recover themselves, and after incredible efforts they too safely gained the table-land above. In process of time all were landed there, and, having remunerated our friends to their satisfaction, the goods and chattels were collected, the wagon repacked, and we set off for our encampment at Turtle Creek.

The exertions and excitement of our laborious ascent, together with the increasing heat of the sun, made this afternoon's ride more uncomfortable than anything we had previously felt. We were truly rejoiced when the whoop of our guide, and the sight of a few scattered lodges, gave notice that we had reached our encamping-ground. We chose a beautiful sequestered spot by the side of a clear, sparkling stream, and, having dismounted and seen that our horses were made comfortable, my husband, after giving his directions to his men, led me to a retired spot where I could lay aside my hat and mask and bathe my flushed face and aching head in the cool, refreshing waters. Never had I felt anything so grateful, so delicious. I sat down, and leaned my head against one of the tall, overshadowing trees, and was almost dreaming, when summoned to partake of our evening meal.

The Indians had brought us, as a present, some fine brook trout, which our Frenchmen had prepared in the most tempting fashion, and before the bright moon rose and we were ready for our rest, all headache and fatigue had alike disappeared.

✶✶✶✶✶✶✶✶✶✶✶✶✶✶✶✶

One of the most charming features of this mode of travelling is the joyous, vocal life of the forest at early dawn, when all the feathered tribe come forth to pay their cheerful salutations to the opening day.

The rapid, chattering flourish of the bob-o'-link, the soft whistle of the thrush, the tender coo of the wood-dove, the deep, warbling bass of the grouse, the drumming of the partridge, the melodious trill of the lark, the gay carol of the robin, the friendly, familiar call of the duck and the teal, resound from tree and knoll and lowland, prompting the expressive exclamation of the simple half-breed,—

"*Voilà la forêt qui parle!*" (How the woods talk!)

It seems as if man must involuntarily raise his voice, to take part in the general chorus—the mating song of praise.

Birds and flowers, and the soft balmy airs of morning! Must it not have been in a scene like this that Milton's Adam poured out his beautiful hymn of adoration,—

"*These are thy glorious works, Parent of Good*"?

This day we were journeying in hopes to reach, at an early hour, that broad expanse of the Rock River which here forms the Kosh-ko-nong. The appellation of this water, rendered doubly affecting by the subsequent fate of its people, imports "*the lake we live on.*"

Our road for the early part of the day led through forests so thick and tangled that Grignon and Lecuyer were often obliged to go in advance as pioneers with their axes, to cut away the obstructing shrubs and branches. It was slow work, and at times quite discouraging, but we were through with it at last, and then we came into a country of altogether a different description—low prairies, intersected with deep, narrow streams like canals, the passage of which, either by horses or carriages, was often a matter of delay and even difficulty.

Several times in the course of the forenoon the horses were to be taken from the carriage and the latter pulled and pushed across the deep narrow channels as best it might.

The wooded banks of the Kosh-ko-nong were never welcomed with greater delight than by us when they at length broke upon our sight. A ride of five or six miles through the beautiful oak openings brought us to *Man-Eater's* village, a collection of neat bark *wigwams*, with extensive fields on each side of corn, beans, and squashes, recently planted, but already giving promise of a fine crop. In front was the broad blue lake, the shores of which, to the south, were open and marshy, but near the village, and stretching far away to the north, were bordered by fine lofty trees. The village was built but a short distance below the point where the Rock River opens into the lake, and during a conversation between our party and the Indians at the village, an arrangement was made with them to take us across at a spot about half a mile above.

After a short halt, we again took up our line of march through the woods, along the bank of the river.

A number of the Winnebagoes (for we had been among our own people since leaving Gros-pied Lake) set out for the appointed place by water, paddling their canoes, of which they had selected the largest and strongest.

Arrived at the spot indicated, we dismounted, and the men commenced the task of unsaddling and unloading. We were soon placed in the canoes, and paddled across to the opposite bank. Next, the horses were swum across—after them was to come the carriage. Two long wooden canoes were securely lashed together side by side, and being of sufficient width to admit of the carriage standing within them, the passage was commenced. Again, and again the tottering barks would sway from side to side, and a cry or a shout would arise from our party on shore, as the whole mass seemed about to plunge sideways into the water, but it would presently recover itself, and at length, after various deviations from the perpendicular, it reached the shore in safety.

We now hoped that our troubles were at an end, and that we had nothing to do but to mount and trot on as fast as possible to Fort Winnebago. But no. Half a mile farther on was a formidable swamp, of no great width it is true, but with a depth of from two to three feet of mud and water. It was a question whether, with the carriage, we could get through it at all. Several of the Indians accompanied us to this place, partly to give us their aid and counsel, and partly to enjoy the fun of the spectacle.

On reaching the swamp, we were disposed to laugh at the formidable representations which had been made to us. We saw only a strip of what seemed rather low land, covered with tall, dry rushes.

It is true the ground looked a little wet, but there seemed nothing to justify all the apprehensions that had been excited. Great was my surprise, then, to see my husband, who had been a few minutes absent, return to our circle attired in his duck trousers, and without shoes or stockings.

"What are you going to do?" inquired I.

"Carry you through the swamp on my shoulders. Come, Petaille, you are the strongest—you are to carry Madame Kinzie, and To-shunnuck there (pointing to a tall, stout Winnebago), he will take Madame Helm."

"Wait a moment," said I, and, seating myself on the grass, I deliberately took off my own boots and stockings.

"What is that for?" they all asked.

"Because I do not wish to ride with wet feet all the rest of the day."

"No danger of that," said they, and no one followed my example.

By the time they were in the midst of the swamp, however, they found my precaution had been by no means useless. The water through which our bearers had to pass was of such a depth that no efforts of the ladies were sufficient to keep their feet above the surface; and I had the satisfaction of feeling that my burden upon my husband's shoulders was much less, from my being able to keep my first position instead of changing constantly to avoid a contact with the water.

The laugh was quite on my side when I resumed my equipment and mounted, *dry-shod*, into my saddle.

It will be perceived that journeying in the woods is, in some degree, a deranger of ceremony and formality; that it necessarily restricts us somewhat in our conventionalities. The only remedy is, to make ourselves amends by a double share when we return to the civilized walks of life.

By dint of much pulling, shouting, encouraging, and threatening, the horses at length dragged the carriage through the difficult pass, and our red friends were left to return to their village, with, doubtless, a very exaggerated and amusing account of all that they had seen and assisted in.

We had not forgotten our promise to Lieutenant Foster to put up a "guide-board" of some sort, for his accommodation in following us. We therefore, upon several occasions, carried with us from the woods a few pieces, of three or four feet in length, which we planted at certain points, with a transverse stick through a cleft in the top, thus marking the direction he and his party were to take.

We therefore felt sure that, although a few days later, he would find our trail, and avail himself of the same assistance as we had, in getting through the difficulties of the way.

Our encamping-ground, this night, was to be not far distant from the Four Lakes. We were greatly fatigued with the heat and exercise of the day, and most anxiously did we look out for the clumps of willows and alders which were to mark the spot where water would be found. We felt hardly equal to pushing on quite to the bank of the nearest lake. Indeed, it would have taken us too much off our direct course.

When we, at a late hour, came upon a spot fit for our purpose, we exchanged mutual congratulations that this was to be our last night upon the road. The next day we should be at Winnebago!

Our journey had been most delightful—a continued scene of exhilaration and enjoyment; for the various mishaps, although for the moment they had perplexed, yet, in the end, had but added to our amusement. Still, with the inconstancy of human nature, we were pleased to exchange its excitement for the quiet repose of home.

Our next morning's ride was of a more tranquil character than any that had preceded it; for at an early hour, we entered upon what was known as the "Twenty-mile Prairie,"—and I may be permitted to observe that the miles are wonderfully long on the prairies. Our passage over this was, except the absence of the sand, like crossing the desert. Mile after mile of unbroken expanse—not a tree—not a living object except ourselves.

The sun, as if to make himself amends for his two months' seclusion, shone forth with redoubled brilliancy. There is no such thing as carrying an umbrella on horseback, though those in the wagon were able to avail themselves of such a shelter.

Our mother's energies had sustained her in the saddle until this day, but she was now fairly obliged to give in, and yield her place on little Brunet to sister Margaret.

Thus, we went on, one little knoll rising beyond another, from the summit of each of which, in succession, we hoped to descry the distant woods, which were to us as the promised land.

"Take courage," were the cheering words, often repeated; "very soon you will begin to see the timber."

Another hour would pass heavily by.

"Now, when we reach the rising ground just ahead, look *sharp*."

We would look sharp—nothing but the same unvarying landscape.

There were not even streams to allay the feverish thirst occasioned by fatigue and impatience.

At length a whoop from Shaw-nee-aw-kee broke the silence in which we were pursuing our way.

"*Le voilà!*" (There it is!)

Our less practised eye could not at first discern the faint blue strip edging the horizon, but it grew and grew upon our vision, and fatigue and all discomfort proportionably disappeared.

We were in fine spirits by the time we reached "Hastings's Woods," a noble forest, watered by a clear, sparkling stream.

Grateful as was the refreshment of the green foliage and the cooling waters, we did not allow ourselves to forget that the day was wearing on, and that we must, if possible, complete our journey before sunset; so, we soon braced up our minds to continue our route, although we would gladly have lingered another hour.

The marsh of Duck Creek was, thanks to the heat of the past week, in a very different state from what it had been a few months previous, when I had been so unfortunately submerged in its icy waters.

We passed it without difficulty, and soon found ourselves upon the banks of the creek.

The stream, at this point, was supposed to be always fordable; and even were it not so, that to the majority of our party would have been a matter of little moment. To the ladies, however, the subject seemed to demand consideration.

"This water looks very deep—are you sure we can cross it on horseback?"

"Oh, yes! Petaille, go before, and let us see how the water is."

Petaille obeyed. He was mounted on a horse like a giraffe, and, extending his feet horizontally, he certainly managed to pass through the stream without much of a wetting.

It seemed certain that the water would come into the wagon, but that was of the less consequence as, in case of the worst, the passengers could mount upon the seats.

My horse, Jerry, was above the medium height, so that I soon passed over, with no inconvenience but that of being obliged to disengage my feet from the stirrups and tuck them up snugly against the mane of the horse.

Sister Margaret was still upon Brunet. She was advised to change him for one of the taller horses, but while the matter was under debate, it was settled by the perverse little wretch taking to the water most unceremoniously, in obedience to the example of the other animals.

He was soon beyond his depth, and we were at once alarmed and diverted at seeing his rider, with surprising adroitness, draw her feet from the stirrups and perch herself upon the top of the saddle, where she held her position, and navigated her little refractory steed safely to land.

This was the last of our adventures. A pleasant ride of four miles brought us to the Fort, just as the sun was throwing his last beams over the glowing landscape; and on reaching the ferry we were at once conducted, by the friends who were awaiting us, to the hospitable roof of Major Twiggs.

Chapter 26

Four-Legs, the Dandy

The companies of the First Infantry, which had hitherto been stationed at Fort Winnebago, had before our arrival received orders to move on to the Mississippi as soon as relieved by a portion of the Fifth, now at Fort Howard.

As many of the officers of the latter regiment were married, we had reason to expect that all the quarters at the post would be put in requisition. For this reason, although strongly pressed by Major Twiggs to take up our residence again in the Fort until he should go on furlough, we thought it best to establish ourselves at once at "the Agency."

It seemed laughable to give so grand a name to so very insignificant a concern. We had been promised, by the heads of department at Washington, a comfortable dwelling so soon as there should be an appropriation by Congress sufficient to cover any extra expense in the Indian Department. It was evident that Congress had a great spite at us, for it had delayed for two sessions attending to our accommodation. There was nothing to be done, therefore, but to make ourselves comfortable with the best means in our power.

The old log barracks, which had been built for the officers and soldiers on the first establishment of the post, two years previous, had been removed by our French *engagés* and put up again upon the little hill opposite the fort. To these some additions were now made in the shape of dairy, stables, smoke-house, etc., constructed of tamarack logs brought from the neighbouring swamp. The whole presented a very rough and primitive appearance.

The main building consisted of a range of four rooms, no two of which communicated with each other, but each opened by a door into the outward air. A small window cut through the logs in front and rear, gave light to the apartment. An immense clay chimney for every two rooms, occupied one side of each, and the ceiling overhead was composed of a few rough boards laid upon the transverse logs that supported the roof.

It was surprising how soon a comfortable, homelike air was given to the old dilapidated rooms, by a few Indian mats spread upon the floor, the piano and other furniture ranged in their appropriate places, and even a few pictures hung against the logs. The latter, alas! had soon to be displaced, for with the first heavy shower the rain found entrance through sundry crevices, and we saw ourselves obliged to put aside, carefully, everything that could be injured by the moisture.

We made light of these evils, however—packed away our carpets and superfluous furniture upon the boards above, which we dignified with the name of attic, and contentedly resolved to await the time when government should condescend to remember us. The greatest inconvenience I experienced, was from the necessity of wearing my straw bonnet throughout the day, as I journeyed from bedroom to parlour, and from parlour to kitchen. I became so accustomed to it that I even sometimes forgot to remove it when I sat down to table, or to my quiet occupations with my mother and sister.

Permission was, however, in time, received to build a house for the blacksmith—that is, the person kept in pay by the government at this station to mend the guns, traps, etc. of the Indians.

It happened most fortunately for us that Monsieur Isidore Morrin was a bachelor, and quite satisfied to continue boarding with his friend Louis Frum, *dit* Manaigre, so that when the new house was fairly commenced, we planned it and hurried it forward entirely on our own account.

It was not very magnificent, it is true, consisting of but a parlour and two bedrooms on the ground-floor, and two low chambers under the roof, with a kitchen in the rear; but compared with the rambling old stable-like building we now inhabited, it seemed quite a palace.

Before it was completed, Mr. Kinzie was notified that the money for the annual Indian payment was awaiting his arrival in Detroit to take it in charge and superintend its transportation to the Portage; and he was obliged to set off at once to fulfil this part of his duty.

The workmen who had been brought from the Mississippi to erect the main building, were fully competent to carry on their work without an overseer; but the kitchen was to be the task of the Frenchmen, and the question was, how could it be executed in the absence of the *bourgeois?*

"You will have to content yourselves in the old quarters until my return," said my husband, "and then we will soon have things in order." His journey was to be a long and tedious one, for the operations of Government were not carried on by railroad and telegraph in those days.

After his departure I said to the men, "Come, you have all your logs cut and hauled—the squaws have brought the bark for the roof—what is to prevent our finishing the house and getting all moved and settled to surprise Monsieur John on his return?"

"Ah! to be sure, Madame John," said Plante, who was always the spokesman, "provided the one who plants a green bough on the chimney-top is to have a treat."

"Certainly. All hands fall to work, and see who will win the treat."

Upon the strength of such an inducement to the one who should put the finishing stroke to the building, Plante, Pillon, and Manaigre, whom the waggish Plante persisted in calling *"mon nègre,"* whenever he felt himself out of the reach of the other's arm, all went vigorously to work.

Building a log house is a somewhat curious process. First, as will be conceived, the logs are laid one upon another and jointed at the corners, until the walls have reached the required height. The chimney is formed by four poles of the proper length, interlaced with a wicker-work of small branches. A hole or pit is dug, near at hand, and, with a mixture of clay and water, a sort of mortar is formed. Large wisps of hay are filled with this thick substance, and fashioned with the hands into what are technically called *"clay cats,"* and these are filled in among the frame-work of the chimney until not a chink is left. The whole is then covered with a smooth coating of the wet clay, which is denominated "plastering."

Between the logs which compose the walls of the building, small bits of wood are driven, quite near together; this is called "chinking," and after it is done, clay cats are introduced, and smoothed over with the plaster. When all is dry, both walls and chimney are whitewashed, and present a comfortable and tidy appearance.

The roof is formed by laying upon the transverse logs thick sheets of bark. Around the chimney, for greater security against the rain, we took care to have placed a few layers of the palisades that had been left when Mr. Peach, an odd little itinerant genius, had fenced in our garden, the pride and wonder of the surrounding settlement and *wigwams*.

While all these matters were in progress, we received frequent visits from our Indian friends. First and foremost, among them was "the young Dandy," Four-Legs.

One fine morning he made his appearance, accompanied by two squaws, whom he introduced as his wives. He could speak a little Chippewa, and by this means he and our mother contrived to keep up something of a conversation. He was dressed in all his finery, brooches, *wampum*, fan, looking-glass and all. The paint upon his face and chest showed that he had devoted no small time to the labours of his toilet.

He took a chair, as he had seen done at Washington, and made signs to his women to sit down upon the floor.

The custom of taking two wives is not very general among the Indians. They seem to have the sagacity to perceive that the fewer they have to manage, the more complete is the peace and quiet of the *wigwam*.

Nevertheless, it sometimes happens that a husband takes a foolish fancy for a second squaw, and in that case, he uses all his cunning and eloquence to reconcile the first to receiving a new inmate in the lodge. Of course, it is a matter that must be managed adroitly, in order that harmony may be preserved.

"My dear, your health is not very good; it is time you should have some rest. You have worked very hard, and it grieves me that you should have to labour any longer. Let me get you some nice young squaw to wait upon you, that you may live at ease all the rest of your life."

The first wife consents; indeed, she has no option. If she is of a jealous, vindictive disposition, what a life the newcomer leads! The old one maintains all her rights of dowager and *duenna*, and the husband's tenderness is hardly a compensation for all the evils the young rival is made to suffer.

It was on Sunday morning that this visit of the Dandy was made to us. We were all seated quietly, engaged in reading. Four-Legs inquired of my mother, why we were so occupied, and why everything around us was so still.

My mother explained to him our observance of the day of rest— that we devoted it to worshipping and serving the Great Spirit, as he had commanded in his Holy Word.

Four-Legs gave a nod of approbation. That was very right, he said—he was glad to see us doing our duty—he was very religious himself, and he liked to see others so. He always took care that his squaws attended to their duties—not reading, perhaps, but such as the

Great Spirit liked, and such as he thought proper and becoming.

He seemed to have no fancy for listening to any explanation of our points of difference. The impression among the Winnebagoes "that if the Great Spirit had wished them different from what they are, he would have made them so," seems too strong to yield to either argument or persuasion.

Sometimes those who are desirous of appearing somewhat civilized will listen quietly to all that is advanced on the subject of Christianity, then, coolly saying, "Yes, we believe that too," will change the conversation to other subjects.

As a general thing, they do not appear to perceive that there is anything to be gained by adopting the religion and the customs of the whites. "Look at them," they say, "always toiling and striving—always wearing a brow of care—shut up in houses—afraid of the wind and the rain—suffering when they are deprived of the comforts of life! We, on the contrary, live a life of freedom and happiness. We hunt and fish, and pass our time pleasantly in the open woods and prairies. If we are hungry, we take some game; or, if we do not find that, we can go without. If our enemies trouble us, we can kill them, and there is no more said about it. What should we gain by changing ourselves into white men?" (It will be remembered that these were the arguments used at a period when the Indians possessed most of the broad lands on the Upper Mississippi and its tributaries—when they were still allowed some share of the blessings of life.)

Christian missionaries, with all their efforts to convert them, had at this day made little progress in enlightening their minds upon the doctrines of the Gospel. Mr. Mazzuchelli, a Roman Catholic priest, accompanied by Miss Elizabeth Grignon as interpreter, made a missionary visit to the Portage during our residence there, and, after some instruction from him, about forty consented to be baptised. Christian names were given to them, with which they seemed much pleased; and not less so with the little plated crucifixes which each received, and which the women wore about their necks.

These they seemed to regard with a devotional feeling; but I was not sufficiently acquainted with their language to gather from them whether they understood the doctrine the symbol was designed to convey. Certain it is, they expressed no wish to learn our language, in order that they might gain a fuller knowledge of the Saviour, nor any solicitude to be taught more about him than they had received during the missionary's short visit.

One woman, to whom the name of Charlotte had been given, signified a desire to learn the domestic ways of the whites, and asked of me as a favour through Madame Paquette that she might be permitted to come on "washing-day," and learn of my servants our way of managing the business. A tub was given her, and my woman instructed her, by signs and example, how she was to manage. As I was not a little curious to observe how things went on, I proceeded after a time to the kitchen where they all were. Charlotte was at her tub, scouring and rubbing with all her might at her little crucifix. Two other squaws sat upon the floor near her, watching the operation.

"That is the work she has been at for the last half-hour," said Josette, in a tone of great impatience. "*She'll* never learn to wash."

Charlotte, however, soon fell diligently to work, and really seemed as if she would tear her arms off, with her violent exertions.

After a time, supposing that she must feel a good deal fatigued and exhausted with the unaccustomed labour, I did what it was at that day very much the fashion to do—what, at home, I had always seen done on washing-day,—what, in short, I imagine was then a general custom among housekeepers. I went to the dining-room closet, intending to give Charlotte a glass of wine or brandy and water. My "cupboard" proved to be in the state of the luckless "Mother Hubbard's"—nothing of the kind could I find but a bottle of orange shrub.

Of this I poured out a wineglassful, and, carrying it out, offered it to the woman. She took it with an expression of great pleasure; but, in carrying it to her lips, she stopped short, and exclaiming, "Whiskey!" immediately returned it to me. I would still have pressed it upon her; for, in my inexperience, I really believed it was a cordial she needed; but, pointing to her crucifix, she shook her head and returned to her work. I received this as a lesson more powerful than twenty sermons. It was the first time in my life that I had ever seen spirituous liquors rejected upon a religious principle, and it made an impression upon me that I never forgot.

CHAPTER 27

The Cut-Nose

Among the women of the tribe with whom we early became acquainted, our greatest favourite was a daughter of one of the Day-kau-rays. This family, as I have elsewhere said, boasted in some remote generation a cross of the French blood, and this fact might account for the fair complexion and soft curling hair which distinguished our friend. She had a noble forehead, full, expressive eyes, and fine teeth. Unlike the women of her people, she had not grown brown and haggard with advancing years. Indeed, with the exception of one feature, she might be called beautiful.

She had many years before married a Mus-qua-kee, or Fox Indian, and, according to the custom among all the tribes, the husband came home to the wife's family, and lived among the Winnebagoes.

It is this custom, so exactly the reverse of civilized ways, that makes the birth of a daughter a subject of peculiar rejoicing in an Indian family. "She will bring another hunter to our lodge," is the style of mutual congratulation.

The Mus-qua-kee continued, for some few years, to live among his wife's relations; but, as no children blessed their union, he at length became tired of his new friends, and longed to return to his own people. He tried, for a time, to persuade his wife to leave her home, and accompany him to the Mississippi, on the banks of which the Sauks and Foxes lived, but in vain. She could not resolve to make the sacrifice.

One day, after many fruitless efforts to persuade her, he flew into a violent passion.

"Then, if you will not go with me," said he, "I will leave you; but you shall never be the wife of any other man—I will mark you!"

Saying this, he flew upon her, and bit off the end of her nose. This, the usual punishment for conjugal infidelity, is the greatest disgrace a woman can receive—it bars her forever from again entering the pale of matrimony. The wretch fled to his own people; but his revenge fell short of its aim. Day-kau-ray was too well known and too universally respected to suffer opprobrium in any member of his family. This bright, loving creature in particular, won all hearts upon a first acquaintance—she certainly did ours, from the outset.

She suffered much from rheumatism, and a remedy we gave her soon afforded her almost entire relief. Her gratitude knew no bounds. Notwithstanding that from long suffering she had become partially crippled, she would walk all the way from the Barribault, a distance of ten miles, as often as once in two or three weeks, to visit us. Then, to sit and gaze at us, to laugh with childish glee at everything new or strange that we employed ourselves about—to pat and stroke us every time we came near her—sometimes to raise our hand or arm and kiss it—these were her demonstrations of affection. And we loved her in return. It was always a joyful announcement when, looking out over the Portage road, somebody called out, "The *Cut-Nose* is coming!" In time, however, we learned to call her by her baptismal name of Elizabeth, for she, too, was one of Mr. Mazzuchelli's converts.

She came one day, accompanied by a half-grown boy, carrying a young fawn she had brought me as a present. I was delighted with the pretty creature—with its soft eyes and dappled coat; but having often heard the simile, "as wild as a fawn," I did not anticipate much success in taming it. To my great surprise, it soon learned to follow me like a dog. Wherever I went, there Fan was sure to be. At breakfast, she would lie down at my feet, under the table. One of her first tokens of affection was to gnaw off all the trimming from my black silk apron, as she lay pretending to caress and fondle me. Nor was this her only style of mischief.

One day we heard a great rattling among the crockery in the kitchen. We ran to see what was the matter, and found that Miss Fan had made her way to a shelf of the dresser, about two feet from the ground, and was endeavouring to find a comfortable place to lie down, among the plates and dishes. I soon observed that it was the shelter of the shelf above her head that was the great attraction, and that she was in the habit of seeking out a place of repose under a chair, or something approaching to an "umbrageous bower." So, after this I took care, as the hour for her morning nap approached, to open a large green parasol, and set it on the matting in the corner—then when I called "Fan, Fan," she would come and nestle under it, and soon fall fast asleep.

One morning Fan was missing. In vain we called and sought her in the garden—in the enclosure for the cattle—at the houses of the Frenchmen—along the hill towards Paquette's—no Fan was to be found. We thought she had asserted her own wild nature and sped away to the woods.

It was a hot forenoon, and the doors were all open. About dinner-time, in rushed Fan, panting violently, and threw herself upon her side, where she lay with her feet outstretched, her mouth foaming, and exhibiting all the signs of mortal agony. We tried to give her water, to soothe her, if perhaps it might be fright that so affected her; but in a few minutes, with a gasp and a spasm, she breathed her last. Whether she had been chased by the greyhounds, or whether she had eaten some poisonous weed, which, occasioning her suffering, had driven her to her best friends for aid, we never knew; but we lost our pretty pet, and many were the tears shed for her.

★★★★★★★★★★★★★★★

Very shortly after the departure of my husband, we received a visit from "the White Crow," the "Little Priest," and several others of the principal chiefs of the Rock River Indians. They seemed greatly disappointed at learning that their father was from home, even though his errand was to get "the silver." We sent for Paquette, who interpreted for us the object of their visit.

They had come to inform us that the Sauk chief Black Hawk and his band, who, in compliance with a former treaty, had removed some time previous to the west of the Mississippi, had now returned to their old homes and hunting-grounds, and expressed a determination not to relinquish them, but to drive off the white settlers who had begun to occupy them.

The latter, in fact, the chief had already done, and having, as it was said, induced some of the Pottowattamies to join him, there was reason to fear that he might persuade some of the Winnebagoes to follow their example.

These chiefs had come to counsel with their father, and to assure him that they should do all in their power to keep their young men quiet. They had heard that troops were being raised down among the whites in Illinois, and they had hopes that their people would be wise enough to keep out of difficulty. Furthermore, they begged that their father, on his return, would see that the soldiers did not meddle with them, so long as they remained quiet and behaved in a friendly manner.

White Crow seemed particularly anxious to impress it upon me, that if any danger should arise in Shaw-nee-aw-kee's absence, he should come with his people to protect me and my family. I relied upon his assurances, for he had ever shown himself an upright and honourable Indian.

Notwithstanding this, the thoughts of Indian troubles so near us, in the absence of our guardian and protector, occasioned us many an anxious moment, and it was not until we learned of the peaceable retreat of the Sauks and Foxes west of the Mississippi, that we were able wholly to lay aside our fears.

We were now called to part with our friends, Major Twiggs and his family, which we did with heartfelt regret. He gave me a few parting words about our old acquaintance, Krissman.

"When I went into the barracks the other day," said he, "about the time the men were taking their dinner, I noticed a great six-foot soldier standing against the window-frame, crying and blubbering.

'Halloo,' said I, 'what on earth does this mean?'

"'Why, that fellow there,' said Krissman (for it was he), 'has scrouged me out of my place!' A pretty soldier your *protége* will make, madam!" added the major.

I never heard more of my hero. Whether he went to exhibit his prowess against the Seminoles and Mexicans, or whether he returned to till the fertile soil of his native German Flats and blow his favourite boatman's horn, must be left for some future historian to tell.

There is one more character to be disposed of—Louisa. An opportunity offering in the spring, the major placed her under the charge of a person going to Buffalo, that she might be returned to her parents. In compliment to the new acquaintances she had formed, she shortened her skirts, mounted a pair of scarlet leggings embroidered with porcupine-quills, and took her leave of military life, having deposited with the gentleman who took charge of her sixty dollars, for safe keeping, which she remarked "she had *saved up*, out of her wages at a dollar a week, through the winter."

★★★★★★★★★★★★★★★★

A very short time after we were settled in our new home at the Agency, we attempted the commencement of a little Sunday-school. Edwin, Harry and Josette were our most reliable scholars, but besides them there were the two little Manaigres, Thérèse Paquette, and her mother's half-sister, Florence Courville, a pretty young girl of fifteen. None of these girls had even learned their letters. They spoke only French, or rather the Canadian *patois*, and it was exceedingly difficult to give them at once the sound of the words, and their signification, which they were careful to inquire. Besides this, there was the task of correcting the false ideas, and remedying the ignorance and superstition which presented so formidable an obstacle to rational improvement. We did our best, however, and had the satisfaction of seeing them, after a time, making really respectable progress with their spelling-book, and, what was still more encouraging, acquiring a degree of light and knowledge in regard to better things.

In process of time, however, Florence was often absent from her class. "Her sister," she said, "could not always spare her. She wanted her to keep house while she herself went over on Sunday to visit her friends the Roys, who lived on the Wisconsin."

We reasoned with Madame Paquette on the subject. "Could she not spare Florence on some hour of the day? We would gladly teach her on a week-day, for she seemed anxious to learn, but we had always been told that for that there was no time."

"Well—she would see. Madame Alum (Helm) and Madame John were so kind!"

There was no improvement, however, in regularity. After a time Manaigre was induced to send his children to Mr. Cadle's mission-school at Green Bay. Thérèse accompanied them, and very soon Florence discontinued her attendance altogether.

We were obliged, from that time forward, to confine our instructions to our own domestic circle.

CHAPTER 28

Indian Customs and Dances

Before we had any right to look for my husband's return, I one day received a message inviting me to come up to the new house. We all went in a body, for we had purposely stayed away a few days, expecting this summons, of which we anticipated the meaning.

Plante, in full glee, was seated astride of a small keg on the roof, close beside the kitchen chimney, on the very summit of which he had planted a green bough. To this he held fast with one hand, while he exultingly waved the other and called out,—

"*Eh ban, Madame John! à cette heure, pour le régal!*"

"Yes, Plante, you are entitled to a treat, and I hope you will not enjoy it the less that Pillon and Manaigre are to share it with you."

A suitable gratification made them quite contented with their "*bourgeoise*," against whom Plante had sometimes been inclined to grumble, "because," as he said, "she had him called up too early in the morning." He might have added, because, too, she could not understand the philosophy of his coming in to work in his own garden, under the plea that it was too rainy to work in Monsieur John's.

It was with no ordinary feelings of satisfaction that we quitted the old log tenement and took possession of our new dwelling, small and insignificant though it was.

I was only too happy to enjoy the luxury of a real bedchamber, in place of the parlour floor which I had occupied as such for more than two months. It is true that our culinary arrangements were still upon no greatly improved plan. The clay chimney was not of sufficient strength to hold the trammel and pot-hooks, which at that day had not been superseded by the cooking-stove and kitchen-range. Our fire was made as in the olden time, with vast logs behind, and smaller sticks in front, laid across upon the andirons or *dogs*.

Upon these sticks were placed such of the cooking-utensils as could not be accommodated on the hearth; but woe to the dinner or the supper, if through a little want of care or scrutiny one treacherous piece was suffered to burn away. Down would come the whole arrangement—kettles, saucepans, burning brands, and cinders, in one almost inextricable mass. How often this happened under the supervision of Harry or little Josette, while the mistress was playing lady to some visitor in the parlour, "'twere vain to tell."

Then, spite of Monsieur Plante's palisades round the chimney, in a hard shower the rain would come pelting down, and, the hearth unfortunately sloping a little the wrong way, the fire would become extinguished; while, the bark on the roof failing to do its duty, we were now and then so completely deluged, that there was no resource but to catch up the breakfast or dinner and tuck it under the table until better times—that is, till fair weather came again. In spite of all these little adverse occurrences, however, we enjoyed our new quarters exceedingly.

Our garden was well furnished with vegetables, and even the currant-bushes which we had brought from Chicago with us, tied in a bundle at the back of the carriage, had produced us some fruit.

The Indian women were very constant in their visits and their presents. Sometimes it was venison—sometimes ducks or pigeons—whortleberries, wild plums, or cranberries, according to the season—neat pretty mats for the floor or the table—wooden bowls or ladles, fancy work of deer-skin or porcupine-quills. These they would bring in and throw at my feet. If through inattention I failed to appear pleased, to raise the articles from the floor and lay them carefully aside, a look of mortification and the observation, "Our mother hates our gifts," showed how much their feelings were wounded. It was always expected that a present would be received graciously, and returned with something twice its value.

Meantime, week after week wore on, and still was the return of "the master" delayed.

The rare arrival of a schooner at Green Bay, in which to take passage for Detroit, made it always a matter of uncertainty what length of time would be necessary for a journey across the lakes and back—so that it was not until the last of August that he again reached his home. Great was his surprise to find us so nicely moved and settled; and under his active supervision the evils of which we had had to complain were soon remedied.

My husband had met at Fort Gratiot, and brought with him, my young brother Julian, whom my parents were sending, at our request, to reside with us. Edwin was overjoyed to have a companion once more, for he had hitherto been very solitary. The boys soon had enough to occupy their attention, as, in obedience to a summons sent to the different villages, the Indians very shortly came flocking in to the payment.

There was among their number, this year, one whom I had never before seen—the mother of the elder Day-kau-ray. No one could tell her age, but all agreed that she must have seen upwards of a hundred winters. Her eyes dimmed, and almost white with age—her face dark and withered, like a baked apple—her voice tremulous and feeble, except when raised in fury to reprove her graceless grandsons, who were fond of playing her all sorts of mischievous tricks, indicated the very great age she must have attained.

She usually went upon all-fours, not having strength to hold herself erect. On the day of the payment, having received her portion, which she carefully hid in the corner of her blanket, she came crawling along and seated herself on the doorstep, to count her treasure.

My sister and I were watching her movements from the open window.

Presently, just as she had, unobserved, as she thought, spread out her silver before her, two of her descendants came suddenly upon her. At first, they seemed begging for a share, but she repulsed them with angry gestures, when one of them made a sudden swoop, and possessed himself of a handful.

She tried to rise, to pursue him, but was unable to do more than clutch the remainder and utter the most unearthly screams of rage. At this instant the boys raised their eyes and perceived us regarding them. They burst into a laugh, and with a sort of mocking gesture they threw her the half-dollars, and ran back to the pay-ground.

In spite of their vexatious tricks, she seemed very fond of them, and never failed to beg something of her father, that she might bestow upon them.

She crept into the parlour one morning, then straightening herself up, and supporting herself by the frame of the door, she cried, in a most piteous tone—"*Shaw-nee-aw-kee! Wau-tshob-ee-rah Thsoonsh-koo-nee-noh!*" (Silver-man, I have no looking-glass.) My husband, smiling and taking up the same little tone, cried, in return,—

"Do you wish to look at yourself, mother?"

The idea seemed to her so irresistibly comic that she laughed until she was fairly obliged to seat herself upon the floor and give way to her enjoyment. She then owned that it was for one of the boys that she wanted the little mirror. When her father had given it to her, she found that she had "no comb," then that she had "no knife," then that she had "no calico shawl," until it ended, as it generally did, by Shaw-nee-aw-kee paying pretty dearly for his joke.

★★★★★★★★★★★★★★★★★

When the Indians arrived and when they departed, my sense of "woman's rights" was often greatly outraged. The master of the family, as a general thing, came leisurely bearing his gun and perhaps a lance in his hand; the woman, with the mats and poles of her lodge upon her shoulders, her *papoose*, if she had one, her kettles, sacks of corn, and wild rice, and, not unfrequently, the household dog perched on the top of all. If there is a horse or pony in the list of family possessions, the man rides, the squaw trudges after.

This unequal division of labour is the result of no want of kind, affectionate feeling on the part of the husband. It is rather the instinct of the sex to assert their superiority of position and importance, when a proper occasion offers. When out of the reach of observation, and in no danger of compromising his own dignity, the husband is willing enough to relieve his spouse from the burden that custom imposes on her, by sharing her labours and hardships.

The payment had not passed without its appropriate number of complimentary and medicine dances. The latter take place only at rare intervals—the former whenever an occasion demanding a manifestation of respect and courtesy presents itself.

It is the custom to ask permission of the person to be complimented, to dance for him. This granted, preparation is made by painting the face elaborately, and marking the person, which is usually bare about the chest and shoulders, after the most approved pattern. All the ornaments that can be mustered are added to the hair, or headdress. Happy is he who, in virtue of having taken one or more scalps, is entitled to proclaim it by a corresponding number of eagle's feathers.

The less fortunate make a substitute of the feathers of the wild turkey, or, better still, of the first unlucky "rooster" that falls in their way. My poor fowls, during the time of payment, were always thoroughly plucked.

When their preparations are completed, the dancers assemble at some convenient place, whence they come marching to the spot appointed, accompanied by the music of the Indian drum and *shee-sheequa* or rattle. They range themselves in a circle and dance with violent contortions and gesticulations, some of them graceful, others only energetic, the squaws, who stand a little apart and mingle their discordant voices with the music of the instruments, rarely participating in the dance. Occasionally, however, when excited by the general gaiety, a few of them will form a circle outside and perform a sort of ungraceful, up-and-down movement, which has no merit, save the perfect time which is kept, and for which the Indians seem, without exception, to possess a natural ear. The dance finished, which is only when the strength of the dancers is quite exhausted, a quantity of presents are brought and placed in the middle of the circle, by order of the party complimented. An equitable distribution is made by one of their number; and, the object of all this display having been accomplished, they retire.

The medicine dance is carried on chiefly to celebrate the skill of the "Medicine-man" in curing diseases. This functionary belongs to a fraternity who are supposed to add to their other powers some skill in interpreting the will of the Great Spirit in regard to the conduct of his people. He occasionally makes offerings and sacrifices which are regarded as propitiatory. In this sense, the term "priest" may be deemed applicable to him. He is also a "prophet" in so far as he is, in a limited degree, an instructor; but he does not claim to possess the gift of foretelling future events.

A person is selected to join the fraternity of the "Medicine-man" by those already initiated, chiefly on account of some skill or sagacity that has been observed in him. Sometimes it happens that a person who has had a severe illness which has yielded to the prescriptions of one of the members, is considered a proper object of choice from a sort of claim thus established.

When he is about to be initiated, a great feast is made, of course at the expense of the candidate, for in simple as in civilized life the same principle of politics holds good, "honours must be paid for." An animal is killed and dressed, of which the people at large partake—there are dances and songs and speeches in abundance. Then the chief Medicine-man takes the candidate and privately instructs him in all the ceremonies and knowledge necessary to make him an accomplished member of the fraternity. Sometimes the new member selected is still a child. In that case he is taken by the Medicine-man so soon as he reaches a proper age, and qualified by instruction and example to become a creditable member of the fraternity.

Among the Winnebagoes there seems a considerable belief in magic. Each Medicine-man has a bag or sack, in which is supposed to be enclosed some animal, to whom, in the course of their *pow-wows*, he addresses himself, crying to him in the note common to his imagined species. And the people seem to be persuaded that the answers which are announced are really communications, in this form, from the Great Spirit.

The Indians appear to have no idea of a retribution beyond this life. They have a strong appreciation of the great fundamental virtues of natural religion—the worship of the Great Spirit, brotherly love, parental affection, honesty, temperance, and chastity. Any infringement of the laws of the Great Spirit, by a departure from these virtues, they believe will excite his anger and draw down punishment. These are their principles. That their practice evinces more and more a departure from them, under the debasing influences of a proximity to the whites, is a melancholy truth, which no one will admit with so much sorrow as those who lived among them, and esteemed them, before this signal change had taken place.

★★★★★★★★★★★★★★★★

One of the first improvements that suggested itself about our new dwelling, was the removal of some very unsightly pickets surrounding two or three Indian graves, on the esplanade in front of the house. Such, however, is the reverence in which these burial-places are held, that we felt we must approach the subject with great delicacy and consideration.

My husband at length ventured to propose to Mrs. "Pawnee Blanc," the nearest surviving relative of the person interred, to replace the pickets with a neat wooden platform.

The idea pleased her much, for, through her intimacy in Paquette's family, she had acquired something of a taste for civilization. Accordingly, a little platform about a foot in height, properly finished with a moulding around the edge, was substituted for the worn and blackened pickets; and it was touching to witness the mournful satisfaction with which two or three old crones would come regularly every evening at sunset, to sit and gossip over the ashes of their departed relatives.

On the fine moonlight nights, too, there might often be seen a group sitting there, and enjoying what is to them a solemn hour, for they entertain the poetic belief that "the moon was made to give light to the dead."

The reverence of the Indians for the memory of their departed friends, and their dutiful attention in visiting and making offerings to the Great Spirit, over their last resting-places, is an example worthy of imitation among their more enlightened brethren. Not so, however, with some of their customs in relation to the dead.

The news of the decease of one of their number is a signal for a general mourning and lamentation; it is also in some instances, I am sorry to say, when the means and appliances can be found, the apology for a general carouse.

The relatives weep and howl for grief—the friends and acquaintance bear them company through sympathy. A few of their number are deputed to wait upon their father, to inform him of the event, and to beg some presents "to help them," as they express it, "dry up their tears."

We received such a visit one morning, not long after the payment was concluded.

A drunken little Indian, named, by the French people around, "Old Boilvin," from his resemblance to an Indian Agent of that name at Prairie du Chien, was the person on account of whose death the application was made. "He had been fishing," they said, "on the shores of one of the little lakes near the Portage, and, having taken a little too much '*whiskee*,' had fallen into the water and been drowned." Nothing of him had been found but his blanket on the bank, so there could be no funeral ceremonies, but his friends were prepared to make a great lamentation about him.

Their Father presented them with tobacco, knives, calico, and looking-glasses, in proportion to what he thought might be their reasonable grief at the loss of such a worthless vagabond, and they departed.

There was no difficulty, notwithstanding the stringent prohibitions on the subject, in procuring a keg of whiskey from some of the traders who yet remained. Armed with that and their other treasures, they assembled at an appointed spot, not far from the scene of the catastrophe, and, sitting down with the keg in their midst, they commenced their affliction. The more they drank, the more clamorous became their grief, and the faster flowed their tears.

In the midst of these demonstrations, a little figure, bent and staggering, covered with mud and all in disorder, with a countenance full of wonder and sympathy, approached them, and began,—

"Why? what? what? Who's dead?"

"Who's dead?" repeated they, looking up in astonishment. "Why, you're dead! you were drowned in Swan Lake! Did not we find your blanket there? Come, sit down and help us mourn."

The old man did not wait for a second invitation. He took his seat and cried and drank with the rest, weeping and lamenting as bitterly as any of them, and the strange scene was continued as long as they had power to articulate, or any portion of the whiskey was left.

Chapter 29

Story of the Red Fox

The Indians, of whatever tribe, are exceedingly fond of narrating or listening to tales and stories, whether historical or fictitious. They have their professed storytellers, like the Oriental nations, and these go about, from village to village, collecting an admiring and attentive audience, however oft-told and familiar the matter they recite.

It is in this way that their traditions are preserved and handed down unimpaired from generation to generation. Their knowledge of the geography of their country is wonderfully exact. I have seen an Indian sit in his lodge, and draw a map, in the ashes, of the Northwestern States, not of their statistical but their geographical features, lakes, rivers, and mountains, with the greatest accuracy, giving their relative distances, by days' journeys, without hesitation, and even extending his drawings and explanations as far as Kentucky and Tennessee.

Of biography they preserve not only the leading events in the life of the person, but his features, appearance, and bearing, his manners, and whatever little trait or peculiarity characterized him.

The women are more fond of fiction, and some of their stories have a strange mingling of humour and pathos. I give the two which follow as specimens. The Indian names contained in them are in the Ottawa or "*Courte-Oreilles*" language, but the same tales are current in all the different tongues and dialects.

★★★★★★★★★★★★★★★★

Story of the Red Fox

This is an animal to which many peculiarities are attributed. He is said to resemble the jackal in his habit of molesting the graves of the dead, and the Indians have a superstitious dread of hearing his bark at night, believing that it forebodes calamity and death. They say, too, that he was originally of one uniform reddish-brown colour, but that his legs became black in the manner related in the story.

There was a chief of a certain village who had a beautiful daughter. He resolved upon one occasion to make a feast and invite all the animals. When the invitation was brought to the red fox, he inquired, "What are you going to have for supper?"

"*Mee-dau-mee-nau-bo*," was the reply. (This is a porridge made of parched corn, slightly cracked.)

The fox turned up his little sharp nose. "No, I thank you," said he; "I can get plenty of that at home."

The messenger returned to the chief, and reported the contemptuous refusal of the fox.

"Go back to him," said the chief, "and tell him we are going to have a nice fresh body, and we will have it cooked in the most delicate manner possible." (The Indians, in relating a story like this, apologise for alluding to a revolting subject. "You will think this *unpleasant*," they say.)

Pleased with the prospect of such a treat, the fox gave a very hearty assent to the second invitation.

The hour arrived, and he set off for the lodge of the chief to attend the feast. The company were all prepared for him, for they made common cause with their friend who had been insulted. As the fox entered, the guest next the door, with great courtesy, rose from his place, and begged the new-comer to be seated. Immediately the person next him also rose, and insisted that the fox should occupy his place, as it was still nearer the fire—the post of honour. Then the third, with many expressions of civility, pressed him to exchange with him; and thus, with many ceremonious flourishes, he was passed along the circle, always approaching the fire, where a huge cauldron stood, in which the good cheer was still cooking. The fox was by no means unwilling to occupy the highest place in the assembly, and, besides, he was anxious to take a peep into the kettle, for he had his suspicions that he might be disappointed of the delicacies he had been expecting.

So, by degrees, he was ushered nearer and nearer the great blazing fire, until by a dexterous push and shove he was hoisted into the seething kettle.

His feet were dreadfully scalded, but he leaped out, and ran home to his lodge, howling and crying with pain. His grandmother, with whom, according to the custom of animals, he lived, demanded of him an account of the affair. When he had faithfully related all the circumstances (for, unlike the civilized animals, he did not think of telling his grandmother a story), she reproved him very strongly.

"You have committed two great faults," said she. "In the first place, you were very rude to the chief who was so kind as to invite you, and by returning insult for civility you made yourself enemies who were determined to punish you. In the next place, it was very unbecoming in you to be so forward to take the place of honour. Had you been contented modestly to keep your seat near the door, you would have escaped the misfortune that has befallen you."

All this was not very consolatory to the poor fox, who continued to whine and cry most piteously, while his grandmother, having finished her lecture, proceeded to bind up his wounds. Great virtue is supposed to be added to all medical prescriptions and applications by a little dancing; so, the dressing having been applied, the grandmother fell to dancing with all her might, round and round in the lodge.

When she was nearly exhausted, the fox said, "Grandmother, take off the bandages and see if my legs are healed."

She did as he requested, but no—the burns were still fresh. She danced and danced again. Now and then, as he grew impatient, she would remove the coverings to observe the effect of the remedies. At length, towards morning, she looked, and, to be sure, the burns were quite healed. "But, oh!" cried she, "your legs are as black as a coal! They were so badly burned that they will never return to their colour!"

The poor fox, who, like many another brave, was vain of his legs, fell into a transport of lamentation.

"Oh! my legs! My pretty red legs! What shall I do? The young girls will all despise me. I shall never dare to show myself among them again!"

He cried and sobbed until his grandmother, fatigued with her exercise, fell asleep. By this time, he had decided upon his plan of revenge.

He rose and stole softly out of his lodge, and, pursuing his way rapidly towards the village of the chief, he turned his face in the direction of the principal lodge and barked. When the inhabitants heard this sound in the stillness of the night, their hearts trembled. They knew that it foreboded sorrow and trouble to some one of their number.

A very short time elapsed before the beautiful daughter of the chief fell sick, and she grew rapidly worse and worse, spite of medicines, charms, and dances. At length she died. The fox had not intended to bring misfortune on the village in this shape, for he loved the beautiful daughter of the chief, so he kept in his lodge and mourned and fretted for her death.

Preparations were made for a magnificent funeral, but the friends of the deceased were in great perplexity. "If we bury her in the earth," said they, "the fox will come and disturb her remains. He has barked her to death, and he will be glad to come and finish his work of revenge."

They took counsel together, and determined to hang her body high in a tree as a place of sepulture. They thought the fox would go groping about in the earth, and not lift up his eyes to the branches above his head.

But the grandmother had been at the funeral, and she returned and told the fox all that had been done.

"Now, my son," said she, "listen to me. Do not meddle with the remains of the chief's daughter. You have done mischief enough already. Leave her in peace."

As soon as the grandmother was asleep at night, the fox rambled forth. He soon found the place he sought, and came and sat under the tree where the young girl had been placed. He gazed and gazed at her all the livelong night, and she appeared as beautiful as when in life. But when the day dawned, and the light enabled him to see more clearly, then he observed that decay was doing its work—that instead of a beautiful she presented only a loathsome appearance.

He went home sad and afflicted, and passed all the day mourning in his lodge.

"Have you disturbed the remains of the chief's beautiful daughter?" was his parent's anxious question.

"No, grandmother,"—and he uttered not another word.

Thus, it went on for many days and nights. The fox always took care to quit his watch at the early dawn of day, for he knew that her friends would suspect him, and come betimes to see if all was right.

At length he perceived that, gradually, the young girl looked less and less hideous in the morning light, and that she by degrees resumed the appearance she had presented in life, so that in process of time her beauty and look of health quite returned to her.

One day he said, "Grandmother, give me my pipe, that I may take a smoke."

"Ah!" cried she, "you begin to be comforted. You have never smoked since the death of the chief's beautiful daughter. Have you heard some good news?"

"Never you mind," said he; "bring the pipe."

He sat down and smoked, and smoked. After a time, he said, "Grandmother, sweep your lodge and put it all in order, for this day you will receive a visit from your daughter-in-law."

The grandmother did as she was desired. She swept her lodge, and arranged it with all the taste she possessed, and then both sat down to await the visit.

"When you hear a sound at the door," said the fox, "you must give the salutation, and say, Come in."

When they had been thus seated for a time, the grandmother heard a faint, rustling sound. She looked towards the door. To her surprise, the mat which usually hung as a curtain was rolled up, and the door was open.

"*Peen-tee-geen n'dau-nis!*" (Come in, my daughter!) cried she.

Something like a faint, faint shadow appeared to glide in. It took gradually a more distinct outline. As she looked and looked, she began to discern the form and features of the chief's beautiful daughter, but it was long before she appeared like a reality, and took her place in the lodge like a thing of flesh and blood.

They kept the matter hid very close, for they would not for the world that the father or friends of the bride should know what had happened. Soon, however, it began to be rumoured about that the chief's beautiful daughter had returned to life, and was living in the Red Fox's lodge. How it ever became known was a mystery, for, of course, the grandmother never spoke of it.

Be that as it may, the news created great excitement in the village. "This must never be," said they all. "He barked her to death once, and who knows what he may do next time?"

The father took at once a decided part. "The Red Fox is not worthy of my daughter," he said. "I had promised her to the Hart, the finest and most elegant among the animals. Now that she has returned to life, I shall keep my word."

So, the friends all went in a body to the lodge of the Red Fox. The bridegroom, the bride, and the grandmother made all the resistance possible, but they were overpowered by numbers, and, the Hart having remained conveniently waiting on the outside where there was no danger, the beautiful daughter of the chief was placed upon his back, and he coursed away through the forest to carry her to his own home. When he arrived at the door of his lodge, however, he turned his head, but no bride was in the place where he expected to see her. He had thought his burden very light from the beginning, but that he supposed was natural to spirits returned from the dead. He never imagined she had at the outset glided from her seat, and in the midst of the tumult slipped back, unobserved, to her chosen husband.

One or two attempts were made by the friends, after this, to repossess themselves of the young creature, but all without success. Then they said, "Let her remain where she is. It is true the Red Fox occasioned her death, but by his watchfulness and care he caressed her into life again; therefore, she rightfully belongs to him." So, the Red Fox and his beautiful bride lived long together in great peace and happiness.

CHAPTER 30

Story of Shee-Shee-Banze

There was a young man named Shee-shee-banze (the Little Duck) paddling his canoe along the shore of the lake.

Two girls came down to the edge of the water, and, seeing him, the elder said to the younger, "Let us call to him to take us a sail."

It must be remarked that in all Indian stories where two or more sisters are the *dramatis personae*, the elder is invariably represented as silly, ridiculous, and disgusting—the younger, as wise and beautiful.

In the present case the younger remonstrated. "Oh, no," said she, "let us not do such a thing. What will he think of us?"

But the other persevered, and called to him, "*Ho!* come and take us into your canoe." The young man obeyed, and, approaching the shore, he took them with him into the canoe.

"Who are you?" asked the elder sister.

"I am *Way-gee-mar-kin*," replied he, "the great chief."

This Way-gee-mar-kin was something of a fairy, for when surrounded by his followers, and wishing to confer favours on them, he had a habit of coughing slightly, when there would fly forth from his mouth quantities of silver brooches, ear-bobs, and other ornaments, for which it was the custom of his people to scramble, each striving, as in more civilized life, to get more than his share.

Accordingly, the elder sister said, "If you are Way-gee-mar-kin, let us see you cough."

Shee-shee-banze had a few of these silver ornaments which he had got by scrambling, and which he kept stowed away in the sides of his mouth in case of emergency. So, he gave some spasmodic coughs and brought forth a few, which the girl eagerly seized.

After a time, as they paddled along, a fine noble elk came forth from the forest, and approached the water to drink.

"What is that?" asked the spokeswoman; for the younger sister sat silent and modest all the time.

"It is my dog that I hunt with."

"Call him to us, that I may see him."

Shee-shee-banze called, but the elk turned and fled into the woods.

"He does not seem to obey you, however."

"No; it is because you inspire him with disgust, and therefore he flies from you."

Soon a bear made his appearance by the water's edge.

"What is that?"

"One of my servants."

Again, he was requested to call him, and, as the call was disregarded, the same reason as before was assigned.

Their excursion was at length ended. There had been a little magic in it, for although the young girls had supposed themselves to be in a canoe, there was, in reality, no canoe at all. They only imagined it to have been so.

Now, Shee-shee-banze lived with his grandmother, and to her lodge he conducted his young friends.

They stood outside while he went in.

"Grandmother," said he, "I have brought you two young girls, who will be your daughters-in-law. Invite them into your lodge."

Upon this, the old woman called, "Ho! come in," and they entered. They were made welcome and treated to the best of everything.

In the meantime, the real Way-gee-mar-kin, the great chief, made preparations for a grand feast. When he was sending his messenger out with the invitations, he said to him, "Be very particular to bid Shee-shee-banze to the feast, for, as he is the smallest and meanest person in the tribe, you must use double ceremony with him, or he will be apt to think himself slighted."

Shee-shee-banze was sitting in his lodge with his new friends, when the messenger arrived.

"Ho! Shee-shee-banze," cried he, "you are invited to a great feast that Way-gee-mar-kin is to give tonight, to all his subjects."

But Shee-shee-banze took no notice of the invitation. He only whistled, and pretended not to hear. The messenger repeated his words, then, finding that no attention was paid to them, he went his way.

The young girls looked at each other, during the scene, greatly astonished. At length the elder spoke.

"What does this mean?" said she. "Why does he call you Shee-shee-banze, and invite you to visit Way-gee-mar-kin?"

"Oh," said Shee-shee-banze, "it is one of my followers that always likes to be a little impudent. I am obliged to put up with it sometimes, but you observed that I treated him with silent contempt."

The messenger returned to the chief, and reported the manner in which the invitation had been received.

"Oh," said the good-natured chief, "it is because he feels that he is poor and insignificant. Go back again—call him by my name, and make a flourishing speech to him."

The messenger fulfilled his mission as he was bid.

"Way-gee-mar-kin," said he, pompously, "a great feast is to be given tonight, and I am sent most respectfully to solicit the honour of your company!"

"Did I not tell you?" said Shee-shee-banze to the maidens Then, nodding with careless condescension, he added, "Tell them I'll come."

At night, Shee-shee-banze dressed himself in his very best paint, feathers, and ornaments—but before his departure he took his grandmother aside.

"Be sure," said he, "that you watch these young people closely until I come back. Shut up your lodge tight, tight. Let no one come in or go out, and, above all things, do not go to sleep."

These orders given, he went his way.

The grandmother tried her best to keep awake, but finding herself growing more and more sleepy, as the night wore on, she took a strong cord and laced across the mat which hung before the entrance to the lodge, as the Indians lace up the mouths of their bags, then, having seen all things secure and the girls quiet in bed, she lay down and soon fell into a comfortable sleep.

The young girls, in the meanwhile, were dying with curiosity to know what had become of Shee-shee-banze, and as soon as they were sure the old lady was asleep, they prepared to follow him and see what was going on. Fearing, however, that the grandmother might awake and discover their absence, they took two logs of wood, and, putting them under the blanket, so disposed them as to present the appearance of persons sleeping quietly. They then cut the cords that fastened the door, and, guided by the sounds of the music, the dancing, and the merry-making, they soon found their way to the dwelling of Way-gee-mar-kin.

When they entered, they saw the chief seated on a throne, surrounded by light and splendour. Everything was joy and amusement. Crowds of courtiers were in the apartment, all dressed in the most brilliant array. The strangers looked around for their friend Shee-shee-banze, but he was nowhere to be seen.

Now and then the chief would cough, when a shower of silver ornaments and precious things would fly in all directions, and instantly a scramble would commence among the company, to gather them up and appropriate them.

As they thus rushed forward, the brides-elect saw their poor little friend crowded up into a corner, where nobody took any notice of him, except to push him aside, or step on him whenever he was in the way. He uttered piteous little squeaks as one and another would thus maltreat him, but he was too busy taking care of himself to perceive that those whom he had left snug at home in the lodge were witnesses of all that was going on.

At length the signal was given for the company to retire, all but the two young damsels, upon whom Way-gee-mar-kin had set his eye, and to whom he had sent, by one of his assistants, great offers to induce them to remain with him and become his wives.

Poor Shee-shee-banze returned to his lodge, but what was his consternation to find the door open!

"*Ho!* grandmother," cried he, "is this the way you keep watch?"

The old woman started up. "There are my daughters-in-law," said she, pointing to the two logs of wood. Shee-shee-banze threw himself on the ground between them. His back was broken by coming so violently in contact with them, but that he did not mind—he thought only of revenge, and the recovery of his sweethearts.

He waited but to get some powerful poison and prepare it, and then he stole softly back to the *wigwam* of Way-gee-mar-kin. All was silent, and he crept in without making the slightest noise. There lay the chief, with a young girl on each side of him.

They were all sound asleep, the chief lying on his back, with his mouth wide open. Before he was aware of it, the poison was down his throat, and Shee-shee-banze had retreated quietly to his own lodge.

The next morning the cry went through the village that Way-gee-mar-kin had been found dead in his bed. Of course, it was attributed to over-indulgence at the feast. All was grief and lamentation. "Let us go and tell poor Shee-shee-banze," said one, "he was so fond of Way-gee-mar-kin."

They found him sitting on a bank, fishing. He had been up at peep of day, to make preparation for receiving the intelligence.

He had caught two or three fish, and, extracting their bladders, had filled them with blood, and tied them under his arm. When the friends of Way-gee-mar-kin saw him, they called out to him,—

"Oh! Shee-shee-banze—your friend, Way-gee-mar-kin, is dead!"

With a gesture of despair, Shee-shee-banze drew his knife and plunged it—not into his heart, but into the bladders filled with blood that he had prepared. As he fell, apparently lifeless, to the ground, the messengers began to reproach themselves: "Oh! why did we tell him so suddenly? We might have known he would not survive it. Poor Shee-shee-banze! he loved Way-gee-mar-kin so."

To their great surprise, the day after the funeral, Shee-shee-banze came walking towards the *wigwam* of the dead chief. As he walked, he sang, or rather chaunted to a monotonous strain, (Indians sing these words to an air peculiar to themselves), the following:—

"*Way-gee-mar-kin is dead, is dead,*
I know who killed him.
I guess it was I—I guess it was I."

All the village was aroused. Everybody flew in pursuit of the murderer, but he evaded them, and escaped to a place of safety.

Soon after, he again made his appearance, mincing as he walked, and singing to the same strain as before,—

"*If you wish to take and punish me,*
Let the widows come and catch me."

It seemed a good idea, and the young women were recommended to go and entice the culprit into the village, so that the friends of the deceased could lay hold of him.

They went forth on their errand. Shee-shee-banze would suffer them to approach, then he would dance off a little—now he would allow them to come quite near; *anon* he would retreat a little before them, all the time singing,

"*Come, pretty widows, come and catch me.*"

Thus, he decoyed them on, occasionally using honeyed words and flattering speeches, until he had gained their consent to return with him to his lodge, and take up their abode with him.

The friends of the murdered chief were scandalized at such inconstancy, and resolved to punish all three, as soon as they could catch them.

They surrounded his lodge with cries and threatenings, but Shee-shee-banze and his two brides had contrived to elude their vigilance and gain his canoe, which lay in the river, close at hand.

Hardly were they on board when their escape was discovered. The whole troop flew after them. Some plunged into the stream, and seized the canoe. In the struggle it was upset, but immediately on touching the water, whether from the magical properties of the canoe, or the necromantic skill of the grandmother, they were transformed into ducks, and flew quacking away.

Since that time the water-fowl of this species are always found in companies of three—two females and a male.

★★★★★★★★★★★★★★★★

The *Canard de France,* or Mallard, and the *Brancheuse,* or Wood Duck, are of different habits from the foregoing, flying in pairs. Indeed, the constancy of the latter is said to be so great that if he loses his mate, he never takes another partner, but goes mourning to the end of his days.

Chapter 31

A Visit to Green Bay—Ma-Zhee-Gaw-Gaw Swamp

The payment over, and the Indians dispersed, we prepared ourselves to settle down quietly in our little home. But now a new source of disturbance arose.

My husband's accounts of disbursements as Agent of the Winnebagoes, which he had forwarded to the Department at Washington, had failed to reach there, of which he received due notice—that is to say, such a notice as could reach us by the circuitous and uncertain mode of conveyance by which intercourse with the Eastern world was then kept up. If the vouchers for the former expenditures, together with the recent payment of $15,000 annuity money, should not be forthcoming, it might place him in a very awkward position; he therefore decided to go at once to Washington, and be the bearer himself of his duplicate accounts.

"Should you like to go and see your father and mother," said he to me, one morning, "and show them how the West agrees with you?"

It was a most joyful suggestion after a year's separation, and in a few days all things were in readiness for our departure.

There was visiting us, at that time, Miss Brush, of Detroit, who had come from Green Bay with Mr. and Mrs. Whitney and Miss Frances Henshaw, on an excursion to the Mississippi. Our little India-rubber house had contrived to expand itself for the accommodation of the whole party during the very pleasant visit they made us.

The arrival of two young ladies had been, as may be imagined, quite a godsend to the unmarried lieutenants, and when, tired of the journey, or intimidated by the snow, which fell eight inches on the 4th of October, Miss Brush determined to give up the remainder of her excursion, and accept our pressing invitation to remain with us until the return of her friends, we were looked upon as public benefactors. She was now to accompany us to Green Bay, and possibly to Detroit.

Our voyage down the river was without incident, and we reached Green Bay just as all the place was astir in the expectation of the arrival of one of Mr. Newbery's schooners. This important event was the subject of interest to the whole community, from Fort Howard to "Dickenson's." To some its arrival would bring friends, to some supplies—to the ladies, the fashions, to the gentlemen, the news, for it was the happy bearer of the mails, not for that place alone, but for all the "upper country."

In a few days the vessel arrived. She brought a mail for Fort Winnebago, it being only in the winter season that letters were carried by land to that place, *via Niles's Settlement* and Chicago.

In virtue of his office as Postmaster, my husband opened the mail-bag, and took possession of his own letters. One informed him of the satisfactory appearance at the Department of the missing accounts, but oh! sad disappointment, another brought the news that my parents had gone to Kentucky for the winter—not to any city or accessible place, but "up the Sandy," and over among the mountains of Virginia, hunting up old land-claims belonging to my grandfather's estate.

It was vain to hope to follow them. We might hardly expect to find them during the short period we could be absent from home—not even were we to receive the lucid directions once given my father by an old settler during his explorations through that wild region.

"You must go up *Tug*," said the man, "and down *Troublesome*, and fall over on to *Kingdom-come*." (Three streams or water courses of that region.)

We did not think it advisable to undertake such an expedition, and therefore made up our minds to retrace our steps to Fort Winnebago.

No boats were in readiness to ascend the river. Our old friend Hamilton promised to have one in preparation at once, but time passed by, and no boat was made ready.

It was now the beginning of November. We were passing our time very pleasantly with the Irwins and Whitneys, and at the residence of Colonel Stambaugh, the Indian Agent, but still this delay was inconvenient and vexatious.

I suggested undertaking the journey on horseback. "No, indeed," was the answer I invariably received. "No mortal woman has ever gone that road, unless it was some native on foot, nor ever could."

"But suppose we set out in the boat and get frozen in on the way. We can neither pass the winter there, nor possibly find our way to a human habitation. We have had one similar experience already. Is it not better to take it for granted that I can do what you and others of your sex have done?"

Dr. Finley, the post-surgeon at Fort Howard, on hearing the matter debated, offered me immediately his favourite horse Charlie. "He is very sure-footed," the doctor alleged, "and capital in a marsh or troublesome stream."

By land, then, it was decided to go; and as soon as our old Menomonee friend "Wish-tay-yun," who was as good a guide by land as by water, could be summoned, we set off, leaving our trunks to be forwarded by Hamilton whenever it should please him to carry out his intention of sending up his boat.

We waited until a late hour on the morning of our departure for our fellow-travellers, Mr. Wing, of Monroe, and Dr. Philleo, of Galena; but, finding they did not join us, we resolved to lose no time, confident that we should all meet at the *Kakalin* in the course of the evening.

After crossing the river at what is now Depere, and entering the wild, unsettled country on the west of the river, we found a succession of wooded hills, separated by ravines so narrow and steep that it seemed impossible that any animals but mules or goats could make their way among them.

Wish-tay-yun took the lead. The horse he rode was accustomed to the country, and well trained to this style of road. As for Charlie, he was perfectly admirable. When he came to a precipitous descent, he would set forward his forefeet, and slide down on his haunches in the most scientific manner, while my only mode of preserving my balance was to hold fast by the bridle and lay myself braced almost flat against his back. Then our position would suddenly change, and we would be scaling the opposite bank, at the imminent risk of falling backward into the ravine below.

It was amusing to see Wish-tay-yun, as he scrambled on ahead, now and then turning partly round to see how I fared. And when, panting and laughing, I at length reached the summit, he would throw up his hands, and shout, with the utmost glee, "*Mamma Manitou!*" (My mother is a spirit.)

Our old acquaintances, the Grignons, seemed much surprised that I should have ventured on such a journey. They had never undertaken it, although they had lived so long at the *Kakalin*; but then there was no reason why they should have done so. They could always command a canoe or a boat when they wished to visit "the Bay."

As we had anticipated, our gentlemen joined us at supper. "They had delayed to take dinner with Colonel Stambaugh—had had a delightful gallop up from the bay—had seen no ravines, nor anything but fine smooth roads—might have been asleep, but, if so, were not conscious of it." This was the account they gave of themselves, to our no small amusement.

From the *Kakalin* to the Butte des Morts, where lived a man named Knaggs, was our next day's stage. The country was rough and wild, much like that we had passed through the spring before, in going from Hamilton's diggings to Kellogg's Grove, but we were fortunate in having Wish-tay-yun, rather than "Uncle Billy," for our guide, so that we could make our way with some degree of moderation.

We had travelled but forty miles when we reached Knaggs's, yet I was both cold and fatigued, so that the cosy little room in which we found Mrs. Knaggs, and the bright fire, were most cheering objects; and, as we had only broken our fast since morning with a few crackers we carried in our pockets, I must own we did ample justice to her nice coffee and cakes, not to mention venison-steaks and bear's meat, the latter of which I had never before tasted.

Our supper over, we looked about for a place of repose. The room in which we had taken our meal was of small dimensions, just sufficient to accommodate a bed, a table placed against the wall, and the few chairs on which we sat. There was no room for any kind of a "shakedown."

"Where can you put us for the night?" inquired my husband of Mr. Knaggs, when he made his appearance.

"Why, there is no place that I know of, unless you can camp down in the old building outside."

We went to look at it. It consisted of one room, bare and dirty. A huge chimney, in which a few brands were burning, occupied nearly one side of the apartment. Against another was built a rickety sort of bunk. This was the only vestige of furniture to be seen. The floor was thickly covered with mud and dirt, in the midst of which, near the fire, was seated an old Indian with a pan of boiled corn on his lap, which he was scooping up with both hands and devouring with the utmost voracity.

We soon discovered that he was blind. On hearing footsteps and voices, he instinctively gathered his dish of food close to him, and began some morose grumblings; but when he was told that it was "Shaw-nee-aw-kee" who was addressing him, his features relaxed into a more agreeable expression, and he even held forth his dish and invited us to share its contents.

"But are we to stay here?" I asked. "Can we not sleep out-of-doors?"

"We have no tent," replied my husband, "and the weather is too cold to risk the exposure without one."

"I could sit in a chair all night, by the fire."

"Then you would not be able to ride to Bellefontaine tomorrow."

There was no alternative. The only thing Mr. Knaggs could furnish in the shape of bedding was a small bear-skin. The bunk was a trifle less filthy than the floor; so, upon its boards we spread first the skin, then our saddle-blankets, and, with a pair of saddle-bags for a bolster, I wrapped myself in my cloak, and resigned myself to my distasteful accommodations.

The change of position from that I had occupied through the day, probably brought some rest, but sleep I could not. Even on a softer and more agreeable couch, the snoring of the old Indian and two or three companions who had joined him, and his frequent querulous exclamations as he felt himself encroached upon in the darkness, would have effectually banished slumber from my eyes.

It was a relief to rise with early morning and prepare for the journey of the day. Where our fellow-travellers had bestowed themselves, I knew not, but they evidently had fared no better than we. They were in fine spirits, however, and we cheerfully took our breakfast and were ferried over the river to continue on the trail from that point to Bellefontaine, twelve miles distant from Fort Winnebago.

The great "bug-bear" of this road, Ma-zhee-gaw-gaw Swamp, was the next thing to be encountered. We reached it about nine o'clock. It spread before us, a vast expanse of morass, about half a mile in width, and of length interminable, partly covered with water, with black knobs rising here and there above the surface, affording a precarious foothold for the animals in crossing it. Where the water was not, there lay in place of it a bed of black oozy mud, which looked as if it might give way under the foot, and let it, at each step, sink to an unknown depth.

This we were now to traverse. All three of the gentlemen went in advance of me, each hoping, as he said, to select the surest and firmest path for me to follow. One and another would call, "Here, madam, come this way!" "This is the best path, wifie; follow me," but often Charlie knew better than either, and selected a path according to his own judgment, which proved the best of the whole.

On he went, picking his way so slowly and cautiously, now pausing on one little hillock, now on another, and *anon* turning aside to avoid a patch of mud which seemed more than usually suspicious, that all the company had got some little distance ahead of me. On raising my eyes, which had been kept pretty closely on my horse's footsteps, I saw my husband on foot, striving to lead his horse by the bridle from a difficult position into which he had got, Mr. Wing and his great white floundering animal lying sideways in the mud, the rider using all his efforts to extricate himself from the stirrups, and Dr. Philleo standing at a little distance from his steed, who was doing his best to rise up from a deep bog into which he had pitched himself. It was a formidable sight! They all called out with one accord,—

"Oh, do not come this way!"

"Indeed," cried I, "I have no thought of it. Charlie and I know better." And, trusting to the sagacious creature, he picked his way carefully along, and carried me safely past the dismounted company. I could not refrain from a little triumphant flourish with my whip, as I looked back upon them and watched their progress to their saddles once more.

Three hours had we been thus unpleasantly engaged, and yet we were not over the "Slough of Despond." At length we drew near its farthest verge. Here ran a deep stream some five or six feet in width. The gentlemen, as they reached it, dismounted, and began debating what was to be done.

"Jump off, jump off, madam," cried Mr. Wing, and "Jump off, jump off," echoed Dr. Philleo; "we are just consulting how we are to get you across."

"What do you think about it?" asked my husband.

"Charlie will show you," replied I. "Come, Charlie." And as I raised his bridle quickly, with a pat on his neck and an encouraging chirp, he bounded over the stream as lightly as a deer, and landed me safe on *terra firma*.

Poor Mr. Wing had fared the worst of the company; the clumsy animal he rode seeming to be of opinion when he got into a difficulty that he had nothing to do but to lie down and resign himself to his fate; while his rider, not being particularly light and agile, was generally undermost, and half imbedded in the mire before he had quite made up his mind as to his course of action.

It was therefore a wise movement in him, when he reached the little stream, to plunge into it and wade across, thus washing out, as much as possible, the traces of the morning's adventures from himself and his steed; and the other gentlemen, having no alternative, concluded to follow his example.

We did not halt long on the rising ground beyond the morass, for we had a long stretch before us to Bellefontaine, forty-five miles, and those none of the shortest.

Our horses travelled admirably the whole afternoon, Charlie keeping a canter all the way; but it was growing dark, and there were no signs of the landmarks which were to indicate our near approach to the desired haven.

"Can we not stop and rest for a few moments under one of the trees?" inquired I, for I was almost exhausted with fatigue, and, to add to our discomfort, a cold, November rain was pouring upon us.

"If it were possible, we would," was the reply; "but see how dark it is growing. If we should lose our way, it would be worse than being wet and tired."

So, we kept on. Just at dark we crossed a clear stream. "That," said my husband, "is, I think, two miles from Bellefontaine. Cheer up—we shall soon be there." Quite encouraged, we pursued our way more cheerfully. Mile after mile we passed, but still no light gleamed friendly through the trees.

"We have certainly travelled more than six miles now," said I.

"Yes—that could not have been the two-mile creek."

It was eight o'clock when we reached Bellefontaine. We were ushered into a large room made cheerful by a huge blazing fire. Mr. Wing and Dr. Philleo had arrived before us, and there were other travellers, on their way from the Mississippi. I was received with great kindness and volubility by the immense hostess, "la grosse Américaine," as she was called, and she soon installed me in the armchair, in the warmest corner, and in due time set an excellent supper before us.

But her hospitality did not extend to giving up her only bed for my accommodation. She spread all the things she could muster on the hard floor before the fire, and did what she could to make me comfortable; then, observing my husband's solicitude lest I might feel ill from the effects of the fatigue and rain, she remarked, in tones of admiring sympathy, "How kind your *companion* is to you!"—an expression which, as it was then new to us, amused us not a little.

Our travelling companions started early in the morning for the Fort, which was but twelve miles distant, and they were so kind as to take charge of a note to our friends at home, requesting them to send Plante with the carriage to take us the rest of the distance.

We reached the Portage in safety; and thus ended the first journey by land that any white woman had made from Green Bay to Fort Winnebago. I felt not a little raised in my own esteem when my husband informed me that the distance, I had the previous day travelled, from Knaggs's to Bellefontaine, was sixty-two miles!

CHAPTER 32

Commencement of the Sauk War

A few weeks after our return, my husband took his mother to Prairie du Chien for the benefit of medical advice from Dr. Beaumont, of the U.S. Army. The journey was made in a large open boat down the Wisconsin River, and it was proposed to take this opportunity to bring back a good supply of corn for the winter's use of both men and cattle.

The ice formed in the river, however, so early, that after starting with his load he was obliged to return with it to the Prairie, and wait until the thick winter's ice enabled him to make a second journey and bring it up in sleighs—with so great an expense of time, labour, and exposure were the necessaries of life conveyed from one point to another through that wild and desolate region!

****

The arrival of my brother Arthur from Kentucky, by way of the Mississippi, in the latter part of April, brought us the uncomfortable intelligence of new troubles with the Sauks and Foxes. Black Hawk had, with the flower of his nation, recrossed the Mississippi, once more to take possession of their old homes and cornfields. (See Appendix)

It was not long before our own Indians came flocking in, to confirm the tidings, and to assure us of their intention to remain faithful friends to the Americans. We soon heard of the arrival of the Illinois Rangers in the Rock River country, also of the progress of the regular force under General Atkinson, in pursuit of the hostile Indians, who, by the reports, were always able to elude their vigilance. It not being their custom to stop and give battle, the Sauks soon scattered themselves through the country, trusting to some lucky accident (and such arrived, alas! only too often) to enable them to fall upon their enemies unexpectedly.

The experience of the pursuing army was, for the most part, to make their way, by toilsome and fatiguing marches, to the spot where they imagined the Sauks would be waiting to receive them, and then to discover that the rogues had scampered off to quite a different part of the country.

Wherever these latter went, their course was marked by the most atrocious barbarities, though the worst had not, at this time, reached our ears. We were only assured that they were down in the neighbourhood of the Rock River and Kishwaukee, and that they lost no opportunity of falling upon the defenceless inhabitants and cruelly murdering them.

As soon as it became certain that the Sauks and Foxes would not pursue the same course they had on the previous year, that is, retreat peaceably across the Mississippi, Mr. Kinzie resolved to hold a council with all the principal chiefs of the Winnebagoes who were accessible at this time. He knew that the Sauks would use every effort to induce their neighbours to join them, and that there existed in the breasts of too many of the young savages a desire to distinguish themselves by "taking some white scalps." They did not love the Americans—why should they? By them they had been gradually dispossessed of the broad and beautiful domains of their forefathers, and hunted from place to place, and the only equivalent they had received in exchange had been a few thousands annually in silver and presents, together with the pernicious example, the debasing influence, and the positive ill treatment of too many of the new settlers upon their lands.

With all these facts in view, therefore, their father felt that the utmost watchfulness was necessary, and that the strongest arguments must be brought forward, to preserve the young men of the Winnebagoes in their allegiance to the Americans. Of the older members he felt quite sure. About fifty lodges had come at the commencement of the disturbances and encamped around our dwelling, saying that if the Sauks attacked us it must be after killing them; and, knowing them well, we had perfect confidence in their assurances.

But their vicinity, while it gave us a feeling of protection, likewise furnished us with a channel of the most exciting and agitating daily communications. As the theatre of operations approached nearer and nearer, intelligence was brought in by their runners—now, that "Captain Barney's head had been recognised in the Sauk camp, where it had been brought the day previous," next, that "the Sauks were carrying Lieutenant Beall's head on a pole in front of them as they marched to meet the whites." Sometimes it was a story which we afterwards found to be unhappily true, as that of the murder of their Agent, M. St Vrain, at Kellogg's Grove, by the Sauks themselves, who ought to have protected him.

It was after the news of this last occurrence that the appointed council with the Winnebagoes was to be held at the Four Lakes, thirty-five miles distant from Fort Winnebago.

In vain we pleaded and remonstrated against such an exposure. "It was his duty to assemble his people and talk to them," my husband said, "and he must run the risk, if there were any. He had perfect confidence in the Winnebagoes. The enemy, by all he could learn, were now far distant from the Four Lakes—probably at Kosh-ko-nong. He would set off early in the morning with Paquette, bold his council, and return to us the same evening."

It were useless to attempt to describe our feelings during that long and dreary day. When night arrived, the cry of a drunken Indian, or even the barking of a dog, would fill our hearts with terror.

As we sat, at a late hour, at the open window, listening to every sound, with what joy did we at length distinguish the tramp of horses! We knew it to be Griffin and Jerry ascending the hill, and a cheerful shout soon announced that all was well. My husband and his interpreter had ridden seventy miles that day, besides holding a long "talk" with the Indians.

The Winnebagoes in council had promised to use their utmost endeavours to preserve peace and good order among their young men. They informed their Father that the bands on the Rock River, with the exception of Win-no-sheek's, were all determined to remain friendly and keep aloof from the Sauks. To that end, they were abandoning their villages and cornfields and moving north, that their Great Father, the President, might not feel dissatisfied with them. With regard to Win-no-sheek and his people, they professed themselves unable to answer.

Time went on, and brought with it, stories of fresh outrages. Among these were the murders of Auberry, Green, and Force, at Blue Mound, and the attack on Apple Fort. The tidings of the latter were brought by old Crély, the father of Mrs. Paquette, who rode express from Galena, and who averred that he once passed a bush behind which the Sauks were hiding, but that his horse smelt the sweet-scented grass with which they always adorn their persons when on a war-party, and set out on such a gallop that he never stopped until he arrived at the Portage. (As "the venerable Joseph Crély" has become historic from his claim to have reached the age of one hundred and thirty-nine years, I will state that at this period, 1832, he was a hale, hearty man of sixty years or less).

Another bearer of news was a young gentleman named Follett, whose eyes had become so protruded and set from keeping an anxious look-out for the enemy, that it was many days after his arrival at a place of safety before they resumed their accustomed limits and expression.

Among other rumours which at this time reached us, was one that an attack upon Fort Winnebago was in contemplation among the Sauks. That this was in no state of defence the Indians very well knew. All the effective men had been withdrawn, upon a requisition from General Atkinson, to join him at his newly-built fort at Kosh-ko-nong.

Fort Winnebago was not picketed in; there were no defences to the barracks or officers' quarters, except slight panelled doors and Venetian blinds—nothing that would long resist the blows of clubs or hatchets. There was no artillery, and the Commissary's store was without the bounds of the Fort, under the hill.

Mr. Kinzie had, from the first, called the attention of the officers to the insecurity of their position in case of danger, but he generally received a scoffing answer.

"Never fear," they would say; "the Sauks are not coming here to attack us."

One afternoon we were over on a visit to some ladies in the garrison, and, several officers being present, the conversation, as usual, turned upon the present position of affairs.

"Do you not think it wiser," inquired I of a blustering young officer, "to be prepared against possible danger?"

"Not against these fellows," replied he, contemptuously. "I do not think I would even take the trouble to fasten the blinds to my quarters."

"At least," said I, "if you some night find a tomahawk raised to cleave your skull, you will have the consolation of remembering that you have not been one of those foolish fellows who keep on the safe side."

He seemed a little nettled at this, and still more so when sister Margaret observed,—

"For my part, I am of Governor Cass's opinion. He was at Chicago during the Winnebago war. We were all preparing to move into the fort on the first alarm. Some were for being brave and delaying, like our friends here. 'Come, come,' said the governor, 'hurry into the fort as fast as possible—there is no merit in being brave with the Indians. It is the height of folly to stay and meet danger which you may by prudence avoid.'"

In a few days our friends waked up to the conviction that something must be done at once. The first step was to forbid any Winnebago coming within the garrison, lest they should find out what they had known as well as ourselves for three months past—namely, the feebleness of the means of resistance. The next was to send fatigue-parties into the woods, under the protection of a guard, to cut pickets for inclosing the garrison.

There was every reason to believe that the enemy were not very far distant, and that their object in coming north was to break a way into the Chippewa country, where they would find a place of security among their friends and allies. The story that our Indian runners brought in most frequently was, that the Sauks were determined to fall upon the whites at the Portage and Fort, and massacre all, except the families of the Agent and Interpreter.

Plante and Pillon with their families had departed at the first word of danger. There only remained with us Manaigre, whose wife was a half-Winnebago, Isidore Morrin, and the blacksmiths from Sugar Creek—Mâtâ and Turcotte.

At night we were all regularly armed and our posts assigned us. After every means had been taken to make the house secure, the orders were given. Sister Margaret and I, in case of attack, were to mount with the children to the rooms above, while my husband and his men were to make good their defence as long as possible against the enemy. Since I had shown my sportsmanship by bringing down accidentally a blackbird on the wing, I felt as if I could do some execution with my little pistols, which were regularly placed beside my pillow at night; and I was fully resolved to use them, if necessity required. I do not remember to have felt the slightest compunction at the idea of taking the lives of two Sauks, as I had no doubt I should do; and this explains to me what I had before often wondered at, the indifference, namely, of the soldier on the field of battle to the destruction of human life Had I been called upon, however, to use my weapons effectually, I should no doubt have looked back upon it with horror.

Surrounded as we were by Indian lodges, which seldom became perfectly quiet, and excited as our nerves had become by all that we were daily in the habit of hearing, we rarely slept very soundly. One night, after we had as much as possible composed ourselves, we were startled at a late hour by a tap upon the window at the head of our bed, and a call of "*Chon! Chon!*" (John! John!) (The Indians who had "been at Washington" were very fond of calling their father thus. Black Wolf's son would go further, and vociferate "K'hizzie," to show his familiarity.)

"*Tshah-ko-zhah?*" (What is it?)

It was Hoo-wau-ne-kah, the Little Elk. He spoke rapidly, and in a tone of great agitation. I could not understand him, and I lay trembling, and dreading to hear his errand interpreted. Now and then I could distinguish the words Sau-kee (Sauks) and Shoonk-hat-tay-rah (horse), and they were not very reassuring.

The trouble, I soon learned, was this. A fresh trail had been observed near the Petit Rocher, on the Wisconsin, and the people at the villages on the Barribault were in a state of great alarm, fearing it might be the Sauks. There was the appearance of a hundred or more horses having passed by this trail. Hoo-wau-ne-kah had been dispatched at once to tell their father, and to ask his advice.

After listening to all he had to communicate, his father told him the trail was undoubtedly that of General Henry's troops, who were said to have come north, looking for the enemy; that as the marks of the horses' hoofs showed them, by this report, to have been shod, that was sufficient proof that it was not the trail of the Sauks. He thought that the people at the villages need not feel any uneasiness.

"Very well, father," replied Hoo-wau-ne-kah; "I will go back and tell my people what you say. They will believe you, for you always tell them the truth. You are not like us Indians, who sometimes deceive each other." So, saying, he returned to his friends, much comforted.

The completion of the picketing and other defences, together with the arrival of a detachment of troops from Fort Howard under Lieutenant Hunter, at our fort, now seemed to render the latter the place of greatest safety. We therefore regularly, every evening immediately before dusk, took up our line of march for the opposite side of the river, and repaired to quarters that had been assigned us within the garrison, leaving our own house and chattels to the care of the Frenchmen and our friends the Winnebagoes.

It was on one of these days that we were sitting at the windows which looked out over the Portage—indeed, we seldom sat anywhere else, our almost sole occupation being to look abroad and see what was coming next—when a loud, long, shrill whoop from a distance gave notice of something to be heard. "The news-halloo! what could it portend? What were we about to hear?" By gazing intently towards the farthest extremity of the road, we could perceive a moving body of horsemen, which, as they approached, we saw to be Indians. They were in full costume. Scarlet streamers fluttered at the ends of their lances—their arms glittered in the sun.

Presently, as they drew nearer, their paint and feathers and brooches became visible. There were fifty or more warriors. They passed the road which turns to the Fort, and rode directly up the hill leading to the Agency. Shaw-nee-aw-kee was absent. The Interpreter had been sent for on the first distant appearance of the strangers, but had not yet arrived. The party, having ascended the hill, halted near the blacksmith's shop, but did not dismount.

Our hearts trembled—it must surely be the enemy. At this moment my husband appeared from the direction of the Interpreter's house. We called to entreat him to stop, but he walked along towards the newcomers.

To our infinite joy, we saw the chief of the party dismount, and all the others following his example and approaching to shake hands.

A space was soon cleared around the leader and my husband, when the former commenced an oration, flourishing his sword and using much violent gesticulation. It was the first time I had seen an Indian armed with that weapon, and I dreaded to perceive it in such hands. Sometimes he appeared as if he were about to take off the head of his auditor at a blow; and our hearts sank as we remembered the stratagems at Mackinac and Detroit in former days. At length the speech was concluded, another shaking of hands took place, and we saw my husband leading the way to his storehouse, from which some of his men presently brought tobacco and pipes and laid them at the feet of the chief.

Our suspense was soon relieved by being informed that the strangers were Man-Eater, the principal chief of the Rock River Indians, who had come with his band to "hold a talk" and bring information.

These Indians were under the special care of Mr. Henry Gratiot, and his efforts had been most judicious and unremitting in preserving the good feeling of this the most dangerous portion of the Winnebagoes.

The intelligence that Man-Eater, who was a most noble Indian in appearance and character, brought us, confirmed that already received, namely, that the Sauks were gradually drawing north, towards the Portage, although he evidently did not know exactly their whereabouts.

There was, soon after they had taken leave, an arrival of another party of Winnebagoes, and these requested permission to dance for their father.

The compliment having been accepted, they assembled, as usual, on the esplanade in front of the house. My sister, the children, and myself stationed ourselves at the open windows, according to custom, and my husband sat on the broad step before the door, which opened from the outer air directly into the parlour where we were.

The performance commenced, and as the dancers proceeded, following each other round and round in the progress of the dance, my sister, Mrs. Helm, remarked to me, "Look at that small, dark Indian, with the green boughs on his person—that is a *Sauk!* They always mark themselves in this manner with white clay, and ornament themselves with leaves when they dance!" In truth, I had never seen this costume among our own Indians, and as I gazed at this one with green chaplets round his head and his legs, and even his gun wreathed in the same manner, while his body displayed no paint except the white transverse streaks with which it was covered, I saw that he was, indeed, a stranger. Without owing anything to the exaggeration of fear, his countenance was truly ferocious.

He held his gun in his hand, and every time the course of the dance brought him directly in front of where we sat, he would turn his gaze full upon us, and club his weapon before him with what we interpreted into an air of defiance. We sat as still as death, for we knew it would not be wise to exhibit any appearance of fear; but my sister remarked, in a low tone, "I have always thought that I was to lose my life by the hands of the Indians. This is the third Indian war I have gone through, and now, I suppose, it will be the last."

It was the only time I ever saw her lose her self-possession. She was always remarkably calm and resolute, but now I could see that she trembled. Still, we sat there—there was a sort of fascination as our imaginations became more and more excited. Presently some rain-drops began to fall. The Indians continued their dance for a few minutes longer, then, with whoopings and shoutings, they rushed simultaneously towards the house. We fled into my apartment and closed the door, which my sister at first held fast, but she presently came and seated herself by me on the bed, for she saw that I could not compose myself. Of all forms of death, that by the hands of savages is the most difficult to face calmly; and I fully believed that our hour was come.

There was no interruption to the dance, which the Indians carried on in the parlour, leaping and yelling as if they would bring down the roof over our heads. In vain we tried to persuade my husband and the children, through a crevice of the door, to come and join us. The latter, feeling no danger, were too much delighted with the exhibition to leave it, and the former only came for a moment to reassure me, and then judged it wisest to return, and manifest his satisfaction at the compliment by his presence. He made light of our fears, and would not admit that the object of our suspicions was in fact a Sauk, but only some young Winnebago, who had, as is sometimes the custom, imitated them in costume and appearance.

It may have been "good fun" to him to return to his village and tell how he frightened "the white squaws." Such a trick would not be unnatural in a white youth, and perhaps, since human nature is everywhere the same, it might not be out of the way in an Indian.

Chapter 33

Fleeing From the Indians

The danger had now become so imminent that my husband determined to send his family to Fort Howard, a point which was believed to be far out of the range of the enemy. It was in vain that I pleaded to be permitted to remain; he was firm.

"I must not leave my post," said he, "while there is any danger. My departure would perhaps be the signal for an immediate alliance of the Winnebagoes with the Sauks. I am certain that as long as I am here my presence will act as a restraint upon them. You wish to remain and share my dangers! Your doing so would expose us both to certain destruction in case of attack. By the aid of my friends in both tribes, I could hope to preserve my own life if I were alone; but surrounded by my family, that would be impossible—we should all fall victims together. My duty plainly is, to send you to a place of safety."

An opportunity for doing this soon occurred. Paquette, the Interpreter, who was likewise an agent of the American Fur Company, had occasion to send a boat-load of furs to Green Bay, on their way to Mackinac. Mr. Kinzie, having seen it as comfortably fitted up as an open boat of that description could be, with a tent-cloth fastened on a frame-work of hoop-poles over the centre and lined with a dark-green blanket, and having placed on board an abundant store of provisions and other comforts, committed us to the joint care of my brother Arthur and our faithful blacksmith, Mâtâ.

This latter was a tall, gaunt Frenchman, with a freckled face, a profusion of crisp, sandy hair, and an inveterate propensity to speak English. His knowledge of the language was somewhat limited, and he burlesqued it by adding an s to almost every word, and giving out each phrase with a jerk.

"Davids," he was wont to say to the little yellow fiddler, after an evening's frolic at the Interpreter's, "Davids, clear away the tables and the glasses, and play *fishes-hornspikes.*" (Fisher's Hornpipe.) He was a kind, affectionate creature, and his devotion to "Monsieur Johns" and "Madame Johns" knew no bounds.

Besides these two protectors, three trusty Indians, the chief of whom was called *Old Smoker,* were engaged to escort our party. The crew of the boat consisted entirely of French *engagés* in the service of the Fur Company. They were six gay-hearted, merry fellows, lightening their labour with their pipe and their songs, in which latter they would have esteemed it a great compliment to be joined by the ladies who listened to them; but our hearts, alas! were now too heavy to participate in their enjoyment.

The Fourth of July, the day on which we left our home, was a gloomy one indeed to those who departed and to the one left behind. Who knew if we should ever meet again? The experience which some of the circle had had in Indian warfare was such as to justify the saddest forebodings. There was not even the consolation of a certainty that this step would secure our safety. The Sauks might, possibly, be on the other side of us, and the route we were taking might perhaps, though not probably, carry us into their very midst. It was no wonder, then, that our leave-taking was a solemn one—a parting which all felt might be for this world.

Not *all*, however; for the gay, cheerful Frenchmen laughed and sang and cracked their jokes, and "assured Monsieur John that they would take Madame John and Madame Alum safe to the bay, spite of Sauks or wind or weather."

Thus, we set out on our journey. For many miles the fort was in sight, as the course of the river alternately approached and receded from its walls, and it was not until nearly mid-day that we caught the last glimpse of our home.

At the noon-tide meal, or pipe, of the *voyageurs*, an alarming discovery was made: no bread had been put on board for the crew! How this oversight had occurred, no one could tell. One was certain that a large quantity had been brought from the garrison-bakery for their use that very morning—another had even seen the sacks of loaves standing in Paquette's kitchen. Be that as it may, there we were, many miles on our journey, and with no provisions for the six Frenchmen, except some salted pork, a few beans, and some onions. A consultation was held in this emergency. Should they return to the Portage for supplies? The same danger that made their departure necessary, still existed, and the utmost dispatch had been enjoined upon them. We found upon examination that the store of bread and crackers with which our party had been provided was far-beyond what we could possibly require, and we thought it would be sufficient to allow of rations to the Frenchmen until we should reach Powell's, at the Butte des Morts, the day but one following, where we should undoubtedly be able to procure a fresh supply.

This decided on, we proceeded on our journey, always in profound silence, for a song or a loud laugh was now strictly prohibited until we should have passed the utmost limits of country where the enemy might possibly be. We had been warned beforehand that a certain point, where the low marshy meadows, through which the river had hitherto run, rises into a more firm and elevated country, was the border of the Menomonee territory, and the spot where the Sauks, if they had fled north of the Wisconsin towards the Chippewa country, would be most likely to be encountered.

As we received intimation on the forenoon of the second day that we were drawing near this spot, I must confess that "we held our breath for awe."

The three Winnebagoes were in the bow of the boat. Old Smoker, the chief, squatted upon his feet on the bench of the foremost rowers. We looked at him. He was gazing intently in the direction of the wooded point we were approaching. Our eyes followed his, and we saw three Indians step forward and stand upon the bank. We said in a low voice to each other, "If they are Sauks, we are lost, for the whole body must be in that thicket." The boat continued to approach; not a word was spoken; the dip of the paddle, and perhaps the beating hearts of some, were the only sounds that broke the stillness. Again, we looked at the chief. His nostrils were dilated—his eyes almost glaring.

Suddenly, with a bound, he sprang to his feet and uttered his long, shrill whoop.

"*Hoh! hoh! hoh! Neechee* (friend) *Muh-no-mo-nee!*"

All was now joy and gladness. Everyone was forward to shake hands with the strangers as soon as we could reach them, in token of our satisfaction that they were Menomonees and not Sauks, of the latter of whom, by the way, they could give us no intelligence.

By noon of that day, we considered ourselves to be out of the region of danger. Still, caution was deemed necessary, and when at the mid-day pipe the boat was pushed ashore under a beautiful overhanging bank, crowned with a thick wood, the usual vigilance was somewhat relaxed, and the young people, under the escort of Arthur and Mâtâ, were permitted to roam about a little, in the vicinity of the boat.

They soon came back, with the report that the woods were "alive with pigeons,"—they could almost knock them down with sticks; and earnestly did they plead to be allowed to shoot at least enough for supper. But no—the enemy might be nearer than we imagined—the firing of a gun would betray our whereabouts—it was most prudent to give no notice to friend or foe. So, very reluctantly, they were compelled to return to the boat without their game.

The next morning brought us to Powell's, at the Butte des Morts. Sad were the faces of the poor Frenchmen at learning that not a loaf of bread was to be had. Our own store, too, was by this time quite exhausted. The only substitute we could obtain was a bag of dark looking, bitter flour. With this provision for our whole party, we were forced to be contented, and we left the Hillock of the Dead, feeling that it had been indeed the grave of our hopes.

By dint of good rowing, our crew soon brought us to the spot where the river enters that beautiful sheet of water, Winnebago Lake. Though there was but little wind when we reached the lake, the

Frenchmen hoisted their sail, in hopes to save themselves the labour of rowing across; but in vain did they whistle, with all the force of their lungs—in vain did they supplicate La Vierge, with a comical mixture of fun and reverence. As a last resource, it was at length suggested by some one that their only chance lay in propitiating the goddess of the winds with an offering of some cast-off garment.

Application was made all round by Guardapié, the chief spokesman of the crew. Alas! not one of the poor *voyageurs* could boast a spare article. A few old rags were at length rummaged out of the little receptacle of food, clothing, and dirt in the bow of the boat, and cast into the waves. For a moment all flattered themselves that the experiment had been successful—the sail fluttered, swelled a little, and then flapped idly down against the mast. The party were in despair, until, after a whispered consultation together, Julian and Edwin stepped forward as messengers of mercy. In a trice they divested themselves of jacket and vest and made a proffer of their next garment to aid in raising the wind.

At first there seemed a doubt in the minds of the boatmen whether they ought to accept so magnificent an offer; but finding, on giving them a preparatory shake, that the value of the contribution was less than they had imagined, they, with many shouts and much laughter, consigned them to the waves. To the great delight and astonishment of the boys, a breeze at this moment sprang up, which carried the little vessel beautifully over the waters for about half the distance to Garlic Island. By this time the charm was exhausted, nor was it found possible to renew it by a repetition of similar offerings. All expedients were tried without success, and, with sundry rather disrespectful reflections upon the lady whose aid they had invoked, the Frenchmen were compelled to betake themselves to their oars, until they reached the island.

Two or three canoes of Winnebagoes arrived at the same moment, and their owners immediately stepped forward with an offering of some sturgeon which they had caught in the lake. As this promised to be an agreeable variety to the noon-tide meal (at least for the Frenchmen), it was decided to stop and kindle a fire for the purpose of cooking it. We took advantage of this interval to recommend to the boys a stroll to the opposite side of the island, where the clear, shallow water and pebbly beach offered temptation to a refreshing bath. While they availed themselves of this, under the supervision of Harry, the black boy, we amused ourselves with gathering the fine red raspberries with which the island abounded.

Our enjoyment was cut short, however, by discovering that the whole place, vines, shrubs, and even, apparently, the earth itself, was infested with myriads of the wood-tick, a little insect, that, having fastened to the skin, penetrates into the very flesh, causing a swelling and irritation exceeding painful, and even dangerous. The alarm was sounded, to bring the boys back in all haste to the open and more frequented part of the island.

But we soon found we had not left our tormentors behind. Throughout the day we continued to be sensible of their proximity. From the effects of their attacks, we were not relieved for several succeeding days; those which had succeeded in burying themselves in the flesh having to be removed with the point of a penknife or a large needle. After partaking of our dinner, we stepped on board our boat, and, the wind having risen, we were carried by the breeze to the farther verge of the lake, and into the entrance of the river, or, as it was called, the Winnebago Rapids.

On the point of land to the right stood a collection of neat bark *wigwams*—this was Four-Legs' village.

It was an exciting and somewhat hazardous passage down the rapids and over the Grand Chûte, a fall of several feet; but it was safely passed, and at the approach of evening the boat reached the settlement of the Waubanakees at the head of the Little Chûte. These are the Stockbridge or Brothertown Indians, the remains of the old Mohicans, who had, a few years before, emigrated from Oneida County, in the State of New York, to a tract granted them by the United States, on the fertile banks of the Fox River. They had already cleared extensive openings in the forest, and built some substantial and comfortable houses near the banks of the river, which were here quite high, and covered for the most part with gigantic trees.

It was determined to ask hospitality of these people, to the extent of borrowing a corner of their fire to boil our tea-kettle, and bake the short-cake which had been now, for nearly two days, our substitute for bread. Its manufacture had been a subject of much merriment. The ingredients, consisting of Powell's black flour, some salt, and a little butter, were mixed in the tin box which had held our meat. This was then reversed, and, having been properly cleansed, supplied the place of a dough-board. The vinegar-bottle served the office of rolling-pin, and a shallow tin dish formed the appliance for baking. The Waubanakees were so good as to lend us an iron bake-kettle, and superintend the cooking of our cake after Harry had carried it up to their dwelling.

So kind and hospitable did they show themselves, that the crew of the boat took the resolution of asking a lodging on shore, by way of relief after their crowded quarters in the boat for the last three nights. Arthur and Mâtâ soon adopted the same idea, and we were invited to follow their example, with the assurance that the houses were extremely neat and orderly.

We preferred, however, as it was a fine night, and all things were so comfortably arranged in the boat, to remain on board, keeping Edwin and Josette with us.

The boat was tightly moored, for the Little Chûte was just below, and if our craft should break loose in the rapid current, and drift down over the falls, it would be a very serious matter. As an additional precaution, one man was left on board to keep all things safe and in order, and, these arrangements having been made, the others ascended the bank, and took up their night's lodgings in the Waubanakee cabins.

It was a beautiful, calm, moonlight night, the air just sufficiently warm to be agreeable, while the gentle murmur of the rapids and of the fall, at no great distance, soon lulled our party to repose. How long we had slumbered we knew not, when we were aroused by a rushing wind. It bent the poles supporting the awning, snapped them, and, another gust succeeding, tent and blanket were carried away on the blast down the stream. The moonlight was gone, but a flash of lightning showed them sailing away like a spectre in the distance.

The storm increased in violence. The rain began to pour in torrents, and the thunder and lightning to succeed each other in fearful rapidity. My sister sprang to waken the Frenchman. "Get up, Vitelle, quick," cried she, in French, "run up the bank for Mâtâ and Mr. Arthur—tell them to come and get us instantly."

The man made her no reply, but fell upon his knees, invoking the Virgin most vociferously.

"Do not wait for the Virgin, but go as quickly as possible. Do you not see we shall all be killed?"

"Oh! not for the world, *madame*, not for the world," said Vitelle, burying his head in a pack of furs, "would I go up that bank in this storm." And here he began crying most lustily to all the saints in the calendar.

It was indeed awful. The roaring of the thunder and the flashing of the lightning around us were like the continued discharge of a park of artillery. I with some difficulty drew forth my cloak, and enveloped myself and Josette—sister Margaret did the same with Edwin.

"Oh! *madame*," said the poor little girl, her teeth chattering with cold and fright, "won't we be drowned?"

"Very well," said my sister to the Frenchman, "you see that Madame John is at the last agony—if you will not go for help I must, and Monsieur John must know that you left his wife to perish."

This was too much for Vitelle. "If I must, I must," said he, and with a desperate bound he leaped on shore and sped up the hill with might and main.

In a few minutes, though it seemed ages to us, a whole posse came flying down the hill. The incessant lightning made all things appear as in the glare of day. Mâtâ's curly hair fairly stood on end, and his eyes rolled with ghastly astonishment at the spectacle.

"Oh, my God, Madame Johns! what would Monsieur Johns say, to see you nows?" exclaimed he, as he seized me in his arms and bore me up the hill. Arthur followed with sister Margaret, and two others with Edwin and Josette. Nobody carried Vitelle, for he had taken care not to risk his precious life by venturing again to the boat.

On arriving at the cabin where Arthur and Mâtâ had been lodged, a fire was, with some difficulty, kindled, and our trunks having been brought up from the boat, we were at length able to exchange our drenched garments, and those of the children, for others more comfortable, after which we laid ourselves upon the clean but homely bed, and slept until daylight.

As it was necessary to ascertain what degree of damage the cargo of furs had sustained, an early start was proposed. Apparently, the inhabitants of the cottages had become weary in well-doing, for they declined preparing breakfast for us, although we assured them they should be well compensated for their trouble. We, consequently, saw ourselves compelled to depart with very slender prospects of a morning meal.

When we reached the boat, what a scene presented itself! Bedclothes, cloaks, trunks, mess-basket, packs of furs, all bearing the marks of a complete deluge! The boat ankle-deep in water—literally no place on board where we could either stand or sit. After some bailing out, and an attempt at disposing some of the packs of furs which had suffered least from the flood, so as to form a sort of divan in the centre of the boat, nothing better seemed to offer than to re-embark, and endure what could not be cured.

Our position was not an enviable one. Wherever a foot or hand was placed, the water gushed up, with a bubbling sound, and, oh! the state of the bandboxes and work-baskets! Breakfast there was none, for on examining the mess-basket everything it contained was found mingled in one undistinguishable mass. Tea, pepper, salt, short-cake, all floating together—it was a hopeless case.

But this was not the worst. As the fervid July sun rose higher in the heavens, the steam which exhaled from every object on board was nearly suffocating. The boat was old—the packs of skins were old—their vicinity in a dry day had been anything but agreeable—now it was intolerable. There was no retreating from it, however; so, we encouraged the children to arm themselves with patience, for the short time that yet remained of our voyage.

Seated on our odoriferous couch, beneath the shade of a single umbrella, to protect our whole party from the scorching sun, we glided wearily down the stream, through that long, tedious day. As we passed successively the *Kakalin*, the Rapids, Dickenson's, the Agency, with what longing eyes did we gaze at human habitations, where others were enjoying the shelter of a roof and the comforts of food—and how eagerly did we count the hours which must elapse before we could reach Fort Howard!

There were no songs from the poor Frenchmen this day. Music and fasting do not go well together. At length we stopped at Shanty-Town, where the boat was to be unloaded. All hands fell to work to transfer the cargo to the warehouse of the Fur Company, which stood near the landing. It was not a long operation, for all worked heartily. This being accomplished, the *voyageurs*, one and all, prepared to take their leave. In vain Mâtâ stormed and raved—in vain Arthur remonstrated.

"No," they said, "they had brought the boat and cargo to the warehouse—that was all of their job." And they turned to go.

"Guardapié," said I, "do you intend to leave us here?"

"*Bien, madame!* it is the place we always stop at."

"Does Monsieur John pay you for bringing his family down?"

"Oh, yes, Monsieur John has given us an order on the sutler, at the fort down below."

"To be paid when you deliver us safe at the fort down below. It seems I shall be there before you, and I shall arrange that matter. Monsieur John never dreamed that this would be your conduct."

The Frenchmen consulted together, and the result was that Guardapié with two others jumped into the boat, took their oars, and rather sulkily rowed us the remaining two miles to Fort Howard.

CHAPTER 34

Fort Howard—Our Return Home

We soon learned that a great panic prevailed at Green Bay on account of the Sauks. The people seemed to have possessed themselves with the idea that the enemy would visit this place on their way to Canada to put themselves under the protection of the British Government. How they were to get there from this point—whether they were to stop and fabricate themselves bark canoes for the purpose, or whether they were to charter one of Mr. Newbery's schooners for the trip, the good people did not seem fully to have made up their minds. One thing is certain, a portion of the citizens were nearly frightened to death, and were fully convinced that there was no safety for them but within the walls of the old dilapidated fort, from which nearly all the troops had been withdrawn and sent to Fort Winnebago some time previous.

Their fears were greatly aggravated by a report, brought by some traveller, that he had slept at night on the very spot where the Sauks breakfasted the next morning. Now, as the Sauks were known to be reduced to very short commons, there was every reason to suppose that if the man had waited half an hour longer, they would have eaten him; so, he was considered to have made a wonderful escape.

Our immediate friends and acquaintances were far from joining in these fears. The utter improbability of such a movement was obvious to all who considered the nature of the country to be traversed, and the efficient and numerous body of whites by whom they must be opposed on their entrance into that neighbourhood. There were some, however, who could not be persuaded that there was any security but in flight, and eagerly was the arrival of the *Mariner* looked for, as the anxiety grew more and more intense.

The *Mariner* appeared at last. It was early in the morning. In one hour from the time of her arrival the fearful news she brought had spread the whole length of the settlement—"the cholera was in this country! It was in Detroit—it was among the troops who were on their way to the seat of war! Whole companies had died of it in the River St. Clair, and the survivors had been put on shore at Fort Gratiot, to save their lives as best they might!" We were shut in between the savage foe on one hand and the pestilence on the other!

To those who had friends at the East the news was most appalling. It seemed to unman everyone who heard it. An officer who had exhibited the most distinguished prowess in the battlefield, and also in some private enterprises demanding unequalled courage and daring, was the first to bring us the news. When he had communicated it, he laid his head against the window-sill and wept like a child.

Those who must perforce rejoin friends near and dear, left the bay in the *Mariner*, all others considered their present home the safest; and so, it proved, for the dreadful scourge did not visit Green Bay that season.

The weather was intensely hot, and the mosquitoes so thick that we did not pretend to walk on the parade after sunset, unless armed with two fans, or green branches to keep constantly in motion, in order to disperse them. This, by the way, was the surest method of attracting them. We had somehow forgotten the apathetic indifference which had often excited our wonder in Old Smoker, as we had observed him calmly sitting and allowing his naked arms and person to become literally *grey* with the tormenting insects. Then he would quietly wipe off a handful, the blood following the movement of the hand over his skin, and stoically wait for an occasion to repeat the movement. It is said that the mosquito, if undisturbed until he has taken his fill, leaves a much less inflamed bite than if brushed away in the midst of his feast.

By day, the air was at this season filled with what is called the Green Bay fly, a species of dragon-fly, with which the outer walls of the houses are at times so covered that their colour is hardly distinguishable. Their existence is very ephemeral, scarcely lasting more than a day. Their dead bodies are seen adhering to the walls and windows within, and they fall without in such numbers that after a high wind has gathered them into rows along the sides of the quarters, one may walk through them and toss them up with their feet like the dry leaves in autumn.

As we walked across the parade, our attention was sometimes called to a tapping upon the bars of the dungeon in which a criminal was confined—it was the murderer of Lieutenant Foster.

It may be remembered that this amiable young officer had been our travelling companion in our journey from Chicago the preceding year. Some months after his arrival at Fort Howard, he had occasion to order a soldier of his company, named Doyle, into confinement for intoxication. The man, a few days afterwards, prevailed on the sergeant of the guard to escort him to Lieutenant Foster's quarters on the plea that he wished to speak to him. He ascended the stairs to the young officer's room, while the sergeant and another soldier remained at the foot, near the door.

Doyle entered, and, addressing Lieutenant Foster, said, "Will you please tell me, lieutenant, what I am confined for?"

"No, sir," replied the officer; "you know your offence well enough; return to your place of confinement."

The man ran downstairs, wrenched the gun from the sergeant's hand, and, rushing back, discharged it at the heart of Lieutenant Foster. He turned to go to his inner apartment, but exclaiming, "Ah me!" he fell dead before the entrance.

Doyle, having been tried by a civil court, was now under sentence, awaiting his execution. He was a hardened villain, never exhibiting the slightest compunction for his crime.

The commanding officer, Major Clark, sent to him one day to inquire if he wanted anything for his comfort.

"If the major pleased," he replied, "he should like to have a light and a copy of Byron's Works."

Some fears were entertained that he would contrive to make way with himself before the day of execution, and, to guard against it, he was deprived of everything that could furnish him a weapon. His food was served to him in a wooden bowl, lest a bit of broken crockery might he used as a means of self-destruction.

One morning he sent a little package to the commanding officer as a present. It contained a strong rope, fabricated from strips of his blanket, that he had carefully separated, and with a large stout spike at the end of it. The message accompanying it was, "He wished Major Clark to see that if he chose to put an end to himself, he could find means to do it in spite of him."

And this hardened frame of mind continued to the last. When he was led out for execution, in passing beyond the gate, he observed a quantity of lumber recently collected for the construction of a new Company's warehouse.

"Ah, captain, what are you going to build here?" inquired he of Captain Scott, who attended him.

"Doyle," replied his captain, "you have but a few moments to live—you had better employ your thoughts about something else."

"It is for that very reason, captain," said he, "that I am inquiring—as my time is short, I wish to gain all the information I can while it lasts."

★★★★★★★★★★★★★★★★

We were not suffered to remain long in suspense in regard to the friends we had left behind. In less than two weeks Old Smoker again made his appearance. He was the bearer of letters from my husband, informing me that General Dodge was then with him at Fort Winnebago, that Generals Henry and Alexander were likewise at the fort, and that as soon as they had recruited their men and horses, which were pretty well worn out with scouring the country after Black Hawk, they would march again in pursuit of him towards the head-waters of the Rock River, where they had every reason, from information lately brought in by the Winnebagoes, to believe he would be found.

As he charged us to lay aside all uneasiness on his account, and moreover held forth the hope of soon coming or sending for us, our minds became more tranquil.

Not long after this, I was told one morning that "*a lady*" wished to see me at the front door. I obeyed the summons, and, to my surprise, was greeted by my friend *Madame Four-Legs*. After much demonstration of joy at seeing me, such as putting her two hands together over her forehead and then parting them in a waving kind of gesture, laughing, and patting me on my arms, she drew from her bosom a letter from my husband, of which she was the bearer. It was to this effect—

"Generals Dodge and Henry left here a few days since, accompanied by Paquette; they met the Sauks near the Wisconsin, on the 21st. A battle ensued, in which upwards of fifty of the enemy were killed—our loss was one killed, and eight wounded. The *citizens* are well pleased that all this has been accomplished without any aid from *Old White Beaver*. (General Atkinson.) The war must be near its close, for the militia and regulars together will soon finish the remaining handful of fugitives."

The arrival of Lieutenant Hunter, who had obtained leave of absence in order to escort us, soon put all things in train for our return to Fort Winnebago. No Mackinac boat was to be had, but in lieu of it a Durham boat was procured. This is of a description longer and shallower than the other, with no convenience for rigging up an awning, or shelter of any kind, over the centre; but its size was better fitted to accommodate our party, which consisted, besides our own family, of Lieutenant and Mrs. Hunter, the wife of another officer now stationed at Fort Winnebago, and our cousin, Miss Forsyth. We made up our minds, as will be supposed, to pretty close quarters.

Our crew was composed partly of Frenchmen and partly of soldiers, and, all things being in readiness, we set off one fine bright morning in the latter part of July.

Our second day's alternate rowing and poling brought us to the Grande Chûte early in the afternoon.

Here, it is the custom to disembark at the foot of the rapids, and, ascending the high bank, walk around the fall, while the men pull the boat up through the foaming waters.

Most of our party had already stepped on shore, when a sudden thought seized one of the ladies and myself.

"Let us stay in the boat," said we, "and be pulled up the *chûte*." The rest of the company went on, while we sat and watched with great interest the preparations the men were making. They were soon overboard in the water, and, attaching a strong rope to the bow of the boat, all lent their aid in pulling as they marched slowly along with their heavy load. The cargo, consisting only of our trunks and stores, which were of no very considerable weight, had not been removed.

We went on, now and then getting a tremendous bump against a hidden rock, and frequently splashed by a shower of foam as the waves roared and boiled around us.

The men kept as close as possible to the high, precipitous bank, where the water was smoothest. At the head of the *cordel* was a merry simpleton of a Frenchman, who was constantly turning his head to grin with delight at our evident enjoyment and excitement.

We were indeed in high glee. "Is not this charming?" cried one. "I only wish——"

The wish, whatever it was, was cut short by a shout and a crash. "Have a care, Robineau! Mind where you are taking the boat!" was the cry, but it came too late. More occupied with the ladies than with his duty, the leader had guided us into the midst of a sharp, projecting tree that hung from the bank. The first tug ripped out the side of the boat, which immediately began to fill with water.

My companion and I jumped upon the nearest rocks that showed their heads above the foam. Our screams and the shouts of the men brought Lieutenant Hunter and some Indians, who were above on the bank, dashing down to our rescue. They carried us in their arms to land, while the men worked lustily at fishing up the contents of the boat, now thoroughly saturated with water.

We scrambled up the high bank, in a miserable plight, to join in the general lamentation over the probable consequences of the accident.

"Oh! my husband's new uniform!" cried one, and "Oh! the miniatures in the bottom of my trunk!" sighed another—while, "Oh! the

THE GRANDE CHÛTE, FOX RIVER.

silk dresses, and the ribbons, and the finery!" formed the general chorus.

No one thought of the provisions, although we had observed, in our progress to shore, the barrel of bread and the tub of ice, which Lieutenant Hunter had providently brought for our refreshment, sailing away on the dancing waves. Among the boxes brought to land, and "toted" up the steep bank, was one containing some loaves of sugar and packages of tea, which I had bought for our winter's supply from the sutler at the post. The young Indian who was the bearer of it set it upon the ground, and soon called my attention to a thick, white stream that was oozing from the corners. I made signs for him to taste it. He dipped his finger in it, and exclaimed with delight to his companions, when he perceived what it was. I then pointed to his hatchet, and motioned him to open the box. He did not require a second invitation—it was soon hacked to pieces.

Then, as I beckoned up all the rest of the youngsters who were looking on, full of wonder, such a scrambling and shouting with delight succeeded as put us all, particularly the boys, into fits of laughter. Bowls, dippers, hands, everything that could contain even the smallest quantity, were put in requisition. The squaws were most active. Those who could do no better took the stoutest fragments of the blue paper in which the sugar had been enveloped, and in a trice, nothing remained but the wet, yellow bundles of tea, and the fragments of the splintered box which had contained it.

By this time fires had been made, and the articles from the trunks were soon seen covering every shrub and bush in the vicinity. Fortunately, the box containing the new uniform had been piled high above the others, in the centre of the boat, and had received but little damage; but sad was the condition of the wardrobes in general.

Not a white article was to be seen. All was mottled; blue, green, red, and black intermingling in streaks, and dripping from ends and corners.

To add to the trouble, the rain began to fall, as rain is apt to do, at an inconvenient moment, and soon the half-dried garments had to be gathered out of the smoke and huddled away in a most discouraging condition.

The tent was pitched, wet as it was, and the blankets, wrung out of the water, and partially dried, were spread upon the ground for our accommodation at night.

A Hamburg cheese, which had been a part of my stores, was voted to me for a pillow, and, after a supper the best part of which was a portion of one of the wet loaves which had remained in a barrel too tightly wedged to drift away, we betook ourselves to our repose.

The next morning rose hot and sultry. The mosquitoes, which the rain had kept at bay through the night, now began to make themselves amends, and to torment us unmercifully.

After our most uncomfortable and unpalatable breakfast, the first question for consideration was, what we were to do with ourselves. Our boat lay submerged at the foot of the hill, half-way up the rapids. The nearest habitation among the Waubanakees was some miles distant, and this there was no means of reaching but by an Indian canoe, if some of our present friends and neighbours would be so obliging as to bring one for our use. Even then it was doubtful if boats could be found sufficient to convey all our numerous party back to Green Bay.

In the midst of these perplexing consultations a whoop was heard from beyond the hill, which here sloped away to the north, at the head of the rapids.

"There is John! that is certainly his voice!" cried more than one of the company.

It was, indeed, my husband, and in a moment, he was among us. Never was arrival more opportune, more evidently providential.

Not having learned our plans (for the unsettled state of the country had prevented our sending him word), he had come provided with a boat, to take us back to Fort Winnebago.

Our drying operations, which we had recommenced this morning, were soon cut short. Everything was shuffled away in the most expeditious manner possible, and in an incredibly short time we were transferred to the other boat, which lay quietly above the *chûte*, and were pulling away towards Winnebago Lake.

We had resolved to go only so far as the vicinity of the lake, where the breeze would render the mosquitoes less intolerable, and then to stop and make one more attempt at drying our clothing. Accordingly, when we reached a beautiful high bank near the Little Butte, we stopped for that purpose again, unpacked our trunks, and soon every bush and twig was fluttering with the spoils of the cruel waves.

Hardly had we thus disposed of the last rag or ribbon when the tramp of horses was heard, followed by loud shouts and cheers ringing through the forest.

A company of about twenty-five horsemen, with banners flying, veils fluttering from their hats, and arms glittering in the sun, rode into our midst, and, amid greetings and roars of laughter, inquired into the nature and reasons of our singular state of confusion.

They were Colonel Stambough and Alexander Irwin, of Green Bay, with a company of young volunteers, and followed by a whooping band of Menomonees, all bound for the seat of war. We comforted them with the assurance that the victories were by this time all won and the scalps taken; but, expressing the hope that there were yet a few laurels to be earned, they bade us *adieu*, and rapidly pursued their march.

We crossed Lake Winnebago by the clear, beautiful light of a summer moon. The soft air was just enough to swell the sail, and thus save the men their labour at the oar.

The witchery of the hour was not, however, sufficient to induce us to forego our repose after the heat and annoyances of the day—we therefore disposed ourselves betimes, to be packed away in the centre of the boat. How it was accomplished no one of the numerous company could tell. If any accident had occurred to disturb our arrangement, I am sure it would have been a Chinese puzzle to put us back again in our places. The men on the outside had much the best of it, and we rather envied those who were off watch, their ability to snore and change position as the humour took them.

We reached Powell's just in time to have gone ashore and prepare our breakfast had we had wherewithal to prepare it. We had hoped to be able to procure some supplies here, for hitherto we had been living on the remains of my husband's ample stock. That was now so nearly exhausted that when we found the mess-basket could not be replenished at this place we began to talk of putting ourselves on allowance.

The wet bread, of which there had remained an ample store, had, as may be readily imagined, soon fermented under the influence of a July sun. The tea, too, notwithstanding our careful efforts at drying it on newspapers and pieces of board, ere long became musty and unfit for use. There was, literally, nothing left, except the salted meat and a few crackers, hardly sufficient for the present day.

The men were therefore urged to make all the speed possible, that we might reach Gleason's, at Lake Puckaway, in good season on the following day.

At evening, when we stopped to take our tea at a beautiful little opening among the trees, we found our old enemies, the mosquitoes, worse than ever. It was necessary to put on our cloaks and gloves, and tie our veils close around our throats, only venturing to introduce a cracker or a cup of tea under this protection in the most stealthy manner.

The men rowed well, and brought us to Gleason's about eleven o'clock the next day. We were greeted with the most enthusiastic demonstrations by my old friend *La Grosse Américaine,* who had removed here from Bellefontaine.

"Oh, Mrs. Armstrong," cried we, "get us some breakfast—we are famishing!"

At that instant who should appear but our faithful Mâtâ, driving the old *calèche* in which we were in the habit of making our little excursions in the neighbourhood of the fort. He had ridden over, hoping to meet us, in the idea that some of us would prefer this method of reaching our home.

With provident thoughtfulness, he had brought tea, roasted coffee, fresh butter, eggs, etc., lest we should be short of such luxuries in that advanced stage of our journey.

His "Good-morning, Madame Johns! How do you dos?" was a pleasant and welcome sound.

We could not wait for our breakfast, but gathered round *La Grosse Américaine* like a parcel of children while she cut and spread slices of bread-and-butter for us.

After our regular meal was finished, it was decided that sister Margaret should take Josette, and return with Mâtâ to open the house and make it ready for our reception. It had been the headquarters of militia, Indians, and stragglers of various descriptions during our absence, and we could easily imagine that a little "misrule and unreason" might have had sway for that period.

We had yet seventy-two miles, by the devious winding course of the river, over first the beautiful waters of Lac de Boeuf, and then through the low, marshy lands that spread away to the Portage. An attempt was made on the part of one of the gentlemen to create a little excitement among the ladies as we approached the spot where it had been supposed the Sauks might pass on their way to the Chippewa country.

"Who knows," said he, gravely, "but they may be lurking in this neighbourhood yet? If so, we shall probably have some signal. We must be on the alert!"

Some of the ladies began to turn pale and look about them. After an interval of perfect silence, a low, prolonged whistle was heard. There was so much agitation, and even actual terror, that the mischievous author of the trick was obliged to confess at once, and receive a hearty scolding for the pain he had caused.

Just before sunset of the second day from Gleason's we reached our home. Everything was *radiant* with neatness and good order. With the efficient aid of our good Manaigre and his wife, the house had been whitewashed from the roof to the door-sill, a thorough scrubbing and cleansing effected, the carpets unpacked and spread upon the floors, the furniture arranged, and, though last not least, a noble supper smoked upon the board by the time we had made, once more, a civilized toilet.

Many of our friends from the fort were there to greet us, and a more happy or thankful party has seldom been assembled.

Chapter 35

Surrender of Winnebago Prisoners

The war was now considered at an end. The news of the Battle of the Bad Axe, where the regulars, the militia, and the steamboat *Warrior* combined, had made a final end of the remaining handful of Sauks, had reached us and restored tranquillity to the hearts and homes of the frontier settlers.

It may seem wonderful that an enemy so few in number and so insignificant in resources could have created such a panic, and required so vast an amount of opposing force to subdue them. The difficulty had been simply in never knowing where to find them, either to attack or guard against them. Probably at the outset every military man thought and felt like the noble old veteran General Brady. "Give me two infantry companies mounted," said he, "and I will engage to whip the Sauks out of the country in one week!"

True, but to whip the enemy you must first meet him; and in order to pursue effectually and *catch* the Indians, a peculiar training is necessary—a training which, at that day, few, even of the frontier militia, could boast.

In some portions of this campaign there was another difficulty—the want of concert between the two branches of the service. The regular troops looked with contempt upon the unprofessional movements of the militia; the militia railed at the dilatory and useless formalities of the regulars. Each avowed the conviction that matters could be much better conducted without the other, and the militia, being prompt to act, sometimes took matters into their own hands, and brought on defeat and disgrace, as in the affair of "Stillman's Run."

The feeling of contempt which the army officers entertained for the militia, extended itself to their subordinates and dependants. After the visit of the Ranger officers to Fort Winnebago, before the battle of the Wisconsin, the officer of the mess where they had been entertained called up his servant one day to inquire into the sutler's accounts, He was the same little "Yellow David" who had formerly appertained to Captain Harney.

"David," said the young gentleman, "I see three bottles of cologne-water charged in the month's account of the mess at the sutler's. What does that mean?"

"If you please, lieutenant," said David, respectfully, "it was to sweeten up the dining-room and quarters after them milish' officers were here visiting."

Black Hawk and a few of his warriors had escaped to the north, where they were shortly after captured by the One-eyed Day-kau-ray and his party, and brought prisoners to General Street at Prairie du Chien. The women and children of the band had been put in canoes and sent down the Mississippi, in hopes of being permitted to cross and reach the rest of that tribe.

The canoes had been tied together, and many of them were upset, and the children drowned, their mothers being too weak and exhausted to rescue them. The survivors were taken prisoners, and, starving and miserable, were brought to Prairie du Chien. Our mother was at the fort at the time of their arrival. She described their condition as wretched and reduced beyond anything she had ever witnessed. One woman who spoke a little Chippewa gave her an account of the sufferings and hardships they had endured—it was truly appalling.

After having eaten such of the horses as could be spared, they had subsisted on acorns, elm-bark, or even grass. Many had died of starvation, and their bodies were found lying in their trail by the pursuing whites. This poor woman had lost her husband in battle, and all her children by the upsetting of the canoe in which they were, and her only wish now was, to go and join them. Poor Indians! who can wonder that they do not love the whites?

But a very short time had we been quietly at home when a summons came to my husband to collect the principal chiefs of the Winnebagoes and meet General Scott and Governor Reynolds at Rock Island, where it was proposed to bold a treaty for the purchase of all the lands east and south of the Wisconsin. Messengers were accordingly sent to collect the principal men, and, accompanied by as many as chose to report themselves, he set off on his journey.

He had been gone about two weeks, and I was beginning to count the days which must elapse before I could reasonably expect his return, when, one afternoon, I went over to pay a visit to my sister at the Fort. As I passed into the large hall of one range of quarters, Lieutenant Lacy came suddenly in from the opposite direction, and, almost without stopping, cried,—

"Bad news, madam! Have you heard it?"

"No. What is it?"

"The cholera has broken out at Rock Island, and they are dying by five hundred a day. Dr. Finley has just arrived with the news." So, saying, he vanished, without stopping to answer a question.

The cholera at Rock Island, and my husband there! I flew to the other door of the hall, which looked out upon the parade-ground. A sentinel was walking near. "Soldier," cried I, "will you run to the young officers' quarters and ask Dr. Finley to come here for a moment?"

The man shook his head—he was not allowed to leave his post.

Presently Mrs. Lacy's servant-girl appeared from a door under the steps. She was a worthless creature, but where help was so scarce ladies could not afford to keep a scrupulous tariff of moral qualification.

"Oh! Catharine," said I, "will you run over and ask Dr. Finley to come here a moment? I must hear what news he has brought from Rock Island." She put on a modest look, and said,—

"I do not like to go to the young officers' quarters."

I was indignant at her hypocrisy, but I was also wild with impatience, when to my great joy Dr. Finley made his appearance.

"Where is my husband?" cried I.

"On his way home, madam, safe and sound. He will probably be here tomorrow." He then gave me an account of the ravages the cholera was making among the troops, which were indeed severe, although less so than rumour had at first proclaimed.

Notwithstanding the doctor's assurance of his safety, my husband was seized with cholera on his journey. By the kind care of Paquette and the plentiful use of chicken-broth which the poor woman at whose cabin he stopped administered to him, he soon recovered, and reached his home in safety, having taken Prairie du Chien in his route and brought his mother with him again to her home.

The Indians had consented to the sale of their beautiful domain.

Indeed, there is no alternative in such cases. If they persist in retaining them, and become surrounded and hemmed in by the white settlers, their situation is more deplorable than if they surrendered their homes altogether. This they are aware of, and therefore, as a general thing, they give up their lands at the proposal of government, and only take care to make the best bargain they can for themselves. In this instance they were to receive as an equivalent a tract of land, (a belt of land termed the Neutral Ground of the different opposing nations), extending to the interior of Iowa, and an additional sum of ten thousand dollars annually.

One of the stipulations of the treaty was, the surrender by the Winnebagoes of certain individuals of their tribe accused of having participated with the Sauks in some of the murders on the frontier, in order that they might be tried by our laws, and acquitted or punished as the case might be.

Wau-kaun-kah (the Little Snake) voluntarily gave himself as a hostage until the delivery of the suspected persons. He was accordingly received by the Agent, and marched over and placed in confinement at the Fort until the seven accused should appear to redeem him.

It was a work of some little time on the part of the nation to persuade these suspected individuals to place themselves in the hands of the whites, that they might receive justice according to the laws of the latter. The trial of Red Bird, and his languishing death in prison, were still fresh in their memories, and it needed a good deal of resolution, as well as a strong conviction of conscious innocence, to brace them up to such a step.

It had to be brought about by arguments and persuasions, for the nation would never have resorted to force to compel the fulfilment of their stipulation.

In the meantime, a solemn talk was held with the principal chiefs assembled at the Agency. A great part of the nation were in the immediate neighbourhood, in obedience to a notice sent by Governor Porter, who, in virtue of his office of Governor of Michigan Territory, was also Superintendent of the Northwest Division of the Indians. Instead of calling upon the Agent to take charge of the annuity money, as had heretofore been the custom, the governor had announced his intention of bringing it himself to Fort Winnebago and being present at the payment. The time appointed had now arrived, and with it the main body of the Winnebagoes.

Such of the Indians as had not attended the treaty at Rock Island

and been instrumental in the cession of their country, were loud in their condemnation of the step, and their lamentations over it. Foremost among these was Wild-Cat, the Falstaff of Garlic Island and its vicinity. It was little wonder that he should shed bitter tears, as he did, over the loss of his beautiful home on the blue waters of Winnebago Lake.

"If he had not been accidentally stopped," he said, "on his way to the treaty, and detained until it was too late, he would never, never have permitted the bargain."

His father, who knew that a desperate frolic, into which Wild-Cat had been enticed by the way, was the cause of his failing to accompany his countrymen to Rock Island, replied, gravely,—

"That he had heard of the chief's misfortune on this occasion. How that, in ascending the Fox River, a couple of kegs of *whiskey* had come floating down the stream, which, running foul of his canoe with great force, had injured it to such a degree that he had been obliged to stop several days at the *Mee-kan,* to repair damages."

The shouts of laughter which greeted this explanation were so contagious that poor Wild-Cat himself was compelled to join in it, and treat his misfortune as a joke.

The suspected Indians having engaged the services of Judge Doty to defend them on their future trial, notice was at length given that on a certain day they would be brought to the Portage and surrendered to their Father, to be by him transferred to the keeping of the military officer appointed to receive them.

It was joyful news to poor Wau-kaun-kah, that the day of his release was at hand. Every time that we had been within the walls of the fort, we had been saluted by a call from him, as he kept his station at the guard-room window:

"Do you hear anything of those Indians? When are they coming, that I may be let out?"

We had endeavoured to lighten his confinement by seeing that he was well supplied with food, and his father and Paquette had paid him occasional visits; but, notwithstanding these attentions and the kindness he had received at the Fort, his confinement was inexpressibly irksome.

On the morning of a bright autumnal day the authorities were notified that the chiefs of the nation would present themselves at the Agency to deliver the suspected persons as prisoners to the Americans.

At the hour of ten o'clock, as we looked out over the Portage road, we could descry a moving concourse of people, in which brilliant colour, glittering arms, and, as they approached still nearer, certain white objects of unusual appearance could be distinguished.

General Dodge, Major Plympton, and one or two other officers took their seats with Mr. Kinzie on the platform in front of the door of our mansion to receive them, while we stationed ourselves at the window where we could both see and hear.

The procession wound up the hill, and approached, marching slowly towards us. It was a grand and solemn sight. First came some of the principal chiefs in their most brilliant array. Next, the prisoners, all habited in white cotton, in token of their innocence, with girdles round their waists. The music of the drum and the *shee-shee-qua* accompanied their death-song, which they were chaunting. They wore no paint, no ornaments—their countenances were grave and thoughtful. It might well be a serious moment to them, for they knew but little of the customs of the whites, and that little was not such as to inspire cheerfulness. Only their father's assurance that they should receive strict justice, would probably have induced them to comply with the engagements of the nation in this manner.

The remainder of the procession was made up of a long train of Winnebagoes, all decked out in their holiday garb.

The chiefs approached and shook hands with the gentlemen, who stood ready to receive their greeting. Then the prisoners came forward, and went through the same salutation with the officers. When they offered their hands to their father, he declined.

"No," said he. "You have come here accused of great crimes—of having assisted in taking the lives of some of the defenceless settlers. When you have been tried by the laws of the land, and been proved innocent, then your father will give you his hand."

They looked still more serious at this address, as if they thought it indicated that their father, too, believed them guilty, and stepping back a little, they seated themselves, without speaking, in a row upon the ground, facing their father and the officers. The other Indians all took seats in a circle around them, except the one-eyed chief, Kau-ray-kau-say-kah (the White Crow), who had been deputed to deliver the prisoners to the agent.

He made a speech in which he set forth that, "although asserting their innocence of the charges preferred against them, his countrymen were quite willing to be tried by the laws of white men. He hoped they would not be detained long, but that the matter would be investigated soon, and that they would come out of it clear and white."

In reply he was assured that all things would be conducted fairly and impartially, exactly as if the accused were white men, and the hope was added that they would be found to have been good and true citizens, and peaceful children of their Great Father, the President.

When this was over, White Crow requested permission to transfer the medal he had received as a mark of friendship from the President, to his son, who stood beside him, and who had been chosen by the nation to fill his place as chief, an office he was desirous of resigning. The speeches made upon this occasion, as interpreted by Paquette, the modest demeanour of the young man, and the dignified yet feeling manner of the father throughout, made the whole ceremony highly impressive; and when the latter took the medal from his neck and hung it around that of his son, addressing him a few appropriate words, I think no one could have witnessed the scene unmoved.

I had watched the countenances of the prisoners as they sat on the ground before me, while all these ceremonies were going forward. With one exception they were open, calm, and expressive of conscious innocence. Of that one I could not but admit there might be reasonable doubts. One was remarkably fine-looking—another was a boy of certainly not more than seventeen, and during the transfer of the medal he looked from one to the other, and listened to what was uttered by the speakers, with an air and expression of even childlike interest and satisfaction.

Our hearts felt sad for them as, the ceremonies finished, they were conducted by a file of soldiers and committed to the dungeon of the guard-house until such time as they should be summoned to attend the court appointed to try their cause.

CHAPTER 36

Escape of the Prisoners

The Indians did not disperse after the ceremonies of the surrender had been gone through. They continued still in the vicinity of the Portage, in the constant expectation of the arrival of the annuity money, which they had been summoned there to receive. But the time for setting out on his journey to bring it was postponed by Governor Porter from week to week. Had he foreseen all the evils this delay was to occasion, he would, possibly, have been more prompt in fulfilling his appointment.

Many causes conspired to make an early payment desirable. In the first place, the Winnebagoes, having been driven from their homes by their anxiety to avoid all appearance of fraternizing with the Sauks, had made this year no gardens nor cornfields They had, therefore, no provisions on hand, either for present use or for their winter's consumption, except their scanty supplies of wild rice. While this was disappearing during their protracted detention at the Portage, they were running the risk of leaving themselves quite unprovided with food, in case of a bad hunting-season during the winter and spring.

In the next place, the rations which the agent had been accustomed, by the permission of Government, to deal out occasionally to them, were now cut off by a scarcity in the Commissary's department. The frequent levies of the militia during the summer campaign, and the reinforcement of the garrison by the troops from Fort Howard, had drawn so largely on the stores at this post that there was necessity for the most rigid economy in the issuing of supplies.

Foreseeing this state of things, Mr. Kinzie, as soon as the war was at an end, commissioned Mr. Kercheval, then sutler at Fort Howard, to procure him a couple of boat-loads of corn, to be distributed among the Indians. Unfortunately, there was no corn to be obtained from Michigan; it was necessary to bring it from Ohio, and by the time it at length reached Green Bay (for in those days business was never done in a hurry) the navigation of the Fox River had closed, and it was detained there, to be brought up the following spring.

As day after day wore on and "the silver" did not make its appearance, the Indians were advised by their father to disperse to their hunting-grounds to procure food, with the promise that they should be summoned immediately on the arrival of Governor Porter; and this advice they followed.

While they had been in our neighbourhood, they had more than once asked permission to dance the *scalp-dance*, before our door. This is the most frightful, heart-curdling exhibition that can possibly be imagined. The scalps are stretched on little hoops, or frames, and carried on the end of slender poles. These are brandished about in the course of the dance, with cries, shouts, and furious gestures. The women, who commence as spectators, becoming excited with the scene and the music which their own discordant notes help to make more deafening, rush in, seize the scalps from the hands of the owners, and toss them frantically about, with the screams and yells of demons.

I have seen as many as forty or fifty scalps figuring in one dance.

Upon one occasion one was borne by an Indian who approached quite near me, and I shuddered as I observed the long, fair hair, evidently that of a woman. Another Indian had the skin of a human hand, stretched and prepared with as much care as if it had been some costly jewel. When these dances occurred, as they sometimes did, by moonlight, they were peculiarly horrid and revolting.

★★★★★★★★★★★★★★★

Amid so many events of a painful character there were not wanting occasionally some that bordered on the ludicrous.

One evening, while sitting at tea, we were alarmed by the sound of guns firing in the direction of the Wisconsin. All started up, and prepared, instinctively, for flight to the garrison. As we left the house we found the whole bluff and the meadow below in commotion—Indians running with their guns and spears across their shoulders to the scene of alarm—squaws and children standing in front of their lodges and looking anxiously in the direction of the unusual and unaccountable sounds—groups of French and half-breeds, like ourselves, fleeing to gain the bridge and place themselves within the pickets so lately erected.

As one company of Indians passed us hurriedly, some weapon carelessly carried hit one of our party on the side of the head. "Oh!" shrieked she, "I am killed! an Indian has tomahawked me!" and she was only reassured by finding she could still run as fast as the best of us.

When we reached the parade-ground, within the Fort, we could not help laughing at the grotesque appearance we presented. Some without hats or shawls—others with packages of valuables hastily secured at the moment—one with her piece of bread-and-butter in hand, which she had not had the presence of mind to lay aside when she took to flight.

The alarm was, in the end, found to have proceeded from a party of Winnebagoes from one of the Barribault villages, who, being about to leave their home for a period, were going through the ceremony of burying the scalps which they and their fathers had taken.

Like the military funerals among civilized nations, their solemnities were closed on this occasion by the discharge of several volleys over the grave of their trophies.

★★★★★★★★★★★★★★★

At length, about the beginning of November, two months after the time appointed, Governor Porter, accompanied by Major Forsyth and Mr. Kercheval, arrived with the annuity money. The Indians were again assembled, the payment was made, and having supplied themselves with a larger quantity of ammunition than usual,—for they saw the necessity of a good hunt to remedy past and present deficiencies,—they set off for their wintering grounds.

We were, ourselves, about changing our quarters, to our no small satisfaction. Notwithstanding the Indian disturbances, the new Agency House (permission to build which had, after much delay, been accorded by government) had been going steadily on, and soon after the departure of the governor and his party, we took possession of it.

We had been settled but a few weeks, when one morning Lieutenant Davies appeared just as we were sitting down to breakfast, with a face full of consternation. "*The Indian prisoners had escaped from the black-hole!* The commanding officer, Colonel Cutler, had sent for Mr. Kinzie to come over to the fort and counsel with him what was to be done."

The prisoners had probably commenced their operations very soon after being placed in the black-hole, a dungeon in the basement of the guard-house. They observed that their meals were brought regularly, three times a day, and that in the intervals they were left entirely to themselves. With their knives they commenced excavating an opening, the earth from which, as it was withdrawn, they spread about on the floor of their prison. A blanket was placed over the hole, and one of the company was always seated upon it, before the regular time for the soldier who had charge of them to make his appearance. When the periodical visit was made, the Indians were always observed to be seated, smoking in the most orderly and quiet manner. There was never anything in their appearance to excite suspicion.

The prisoners had never read the memoirs of Baron Trenck, but they had watched the proceedings of the badgers; so, profiting by their example, they worked on, shaping the opening spirally, until, in about six weeks, they came out to the open air beyond the walls of the Fort.

That they might be as little encumbered as possible in their flight, they left their blankets behind them, and although it was bitter December weather, they took to the woods and prairies with only their calico shirts and leggings for covering. We can readily believe that hope and exultation kept them comfortably warm until they reached an asylum among their friends.

It would be compromising our own reputation as loyal and patriotic citizens to tell of the secret rejoicing this news occasioned us.

The question now was, how to get the fugitives back again. The agent could promise no more than that he would communicate with the chiefs, and represent the wishes of the officers that the prisoners should once more surrender themselves, and thus free those who had had the charge of them from the imputation of carelessness, which the government would be very likely to throw upon them.

When, according to their custom, many of the chiefs assembled at the Agency on New-Year's Day, their father laid the subject before them.

The Indians replied, that *if they saw the young men*, they would tell them what the officers would like to have them do. They could, themselves, do nothing in the matter. They had fulfilled their engagement by bringing them once and putting them in the hands of the officers. The government had had them in its power once and could not keep them—it must now go and catch them itself.

The government, having had some experience the past summer in "catching Indians," wisely concluded to drop the matter.

About this time another event occurred which occasioned no small excitement in our little community. Robineau, the striker from the blacksmith establishment at Sugar Creek, near the Four Lakes, arrived one very cold day at the Agency. He had come to procure medical aid for Mâtâ's eldest daughter, Sophy, who, while sliding on the lake, had fallen on the ice and been badly hurt. Her father was absent, having gone to Prairie du Chien to place his youngest daughter at school. Two or three days had elapsed since the accident had happened; a high fever had set in, and the poor girl was in a state of great suffering; it had therefore been thought best to send Robineau to us for advice and aid, leaving Turcotte and a friendly Indian woman from a neighbouring lodge to take charge of poor Sophy.

The commanding officer did not think it prudent, when the subject was laid before him, to permit the surgeon to leave the post, but he very cheerfully granted leave of absence to Currie, the hospital steward, a young man who possessed some knowledge of medicine and surgery.

As it was important that Sophy should have an experienced nurse, we procured the services of Madame Bellaire, the wife of the Frenchman who was generally employed as express to Chicago; and, as an aid and companion, Agathe, a daughter of Day-kau-ray, who lived in Paquette's family, was added to the party.

Of Agathe I shall have more to say hereafter.

The weather was excessively cold when Robineau, Currie, and

the two women set out for Sugar Creek, a distance of about forty miles. We had provided them with a good store of rice, crackers, tea, and sugar, for the invalid, all of which, with their provisions for the way, were packed on the horse Robineau had ridden to the Portage. It was expected they would reach their place of destination on the second day.

What, then, was our surprise to see Turcotte make his appearance on the fourth day after their departure, to inquire why Robineau had not returned with aid for poor Sophy! There was but one solution of the mystery. Robineau had guided them as ill as he had guided the boat at the Grande Chûte the summer before, and, although he could not shipwreck them, he had undoubtedly lost them in the woods or prairies. One comfort was, that they could not well starve, for the rice and crackers would furnish them with several days' provisions, and with Agathe, who must be accustomed to this kind of life, they could not fail in time of finding Indians, and being brought back to the Portage.

Still, day after day went on and we received no tidings of them. Turcotte returned to Sugar Creek with comforts and prescriptions for Sophy, and Colonel Cutler sent out a party to hunt for the missing ones, among whom poor Currie, from his delicate constitution, was the object of our greatest commiseration.

As the snow fell and the winds howled, we could employ ourselves about nothing but walking from window to window, watching, in hopes of seeing someone appear in the distance. No Indians were at hand whom we could dispatch upon the search, and by the tenth day we had almost given up in despair.

It was then that the joyful news was suddenly brought us, "They are found! They are at the fort!" A party of soldiers who had been exploring had encountered them at Hastings's Woods, twelve miles distant, slowly and feebly making their way back to the Portage. They knew they were on the right track, but had hardly strength to pursue it.

Exhausted with cold and hunger, for their provisions had given out two days before, they had thought seriously of killing the horse and eating him. Nothing but Currie's inability to proceed on foot, and the dread of being compelled to leave him in the woods to perish, had deterred them.

Agathe had from the first been convinced that they were on the wrong track, but Robineau, with his usual obstinacy, persevered in keeping it until it brought them to the Rock River, when he was obliged to acknowledge his error, and they commenced retracing their steps.

Agathe, according to the custom of her people, had carried her hatchet with her, and thus they had always had a fire at night, and boughs to shelter them from the storms; otherwise, they must inevitably have perished.

There were two circumstances which aroused in us a stronger feeling even than that of sympathy. The first was, the miserable Robineau's having demanded of Currie, first, all his money, and afterwards his watch, as a condition of his bringing the party back into the right path, which he averred he knew perfectly well.

The second was, Bellaire's giving his kind, excellent wife a hearty flogging "for going off," as he said, "on such a fool's errand."

The latter culprit was out of our jurisdiction, but Mons. Robineau was discharged on the spot, and warned that he might think himself happy to escape a legal process for swindling.

I am happy to say that Sophy Mâtâ, in whose behalf all these sufferings had been endured, was quite recovered by the time her father returned from the prairie.

Chapter 37

Agathe—Tomah

Agathe was the daughter of an Indian who was distinguished by the name of Rascal Day-kau-ray. Whether he merited the appellation must be determined hereafter. He was brother to the grand old chief of that name, but as unlike him as it is possible for those of the same blood to be.

The Day-kau-rays were a very handsome family, and this daughter was remarkable for her fine personal endowments. A tall, well-developed form, a round, sweet face, and that peculiarly soft, melodious voice which belongs to the women of her people, would have attracted the attention of a stranger, while the pensive expression of her countenance irresistibly drew the hearts of all towards her, and prompted the wish to know more of her history. As I received it from her friend, Mrs. Paquette, it was indeed a touching one.

A young officer at the fort had seen her, and had set, I will not say his heart—it may be doubted if he had one—but his mind upon her. He applied to Paquette to negotiate what he called a marriage with her. I am sorry to say that Paquette was induced to enter into this scheme. He knew full well the sin of making false representations to the family of Agathe, and he knew the misery he was about to bring upon her.

The poor girl had been betrothed to a young man of her own people, and, as is generally the case, the attachment on both sides was very strong. Among these simple people, who have few subjects of thought or speculation beyond the interests of their daily life, their affections and their animosities form the warp and woof of their character. All their feelings are intense, from being concentrated on so few objects. Family relations, particularly with the women, engross the whole amount of their sensibilities.

The marriage connection is a sacred and indissoluble tie. I have read, in a recent report to the Historical Society of Wisconsin, that, in former times, a temporary marriage between a white man and a Menomonee woman was no uncommon occurrence, and that such an arrangement brought no scandal, I am afraid that if such eases were investigated, a good deal of deceit and misrepresentation would be found to have been added to the other sins of the transaction; and that the woman would be found to have been a victim, instead of a willing participant, in such a connection.

At all events, no system of this kind exists among the Winnebagoes. The strictest sense of female propriety is a distinguishing trait among them. A woman who transgresses it is said to have "forgotten herself," and is sure to be cast off and "forgotten" by her friends.

The marriage proposed between the young officer and the daughter of Day-kau-ray, was understood as intended to be true and lasting. The father would not have exposed himself to the contempt of his whole nation by selling his daughter to become the mistress of any man. The Day-kau-rays, as I have elsewhere said, were not a little proud of a remote cross of French blood which mingled with the aboriginal stream in their veins, and probably in acceding to the proposed connection the father of Agathe was as much influenced by what he considered the honour to be derived as by the amount of valuable presents which accompanied the overtures made to him.

Be that as it may, the poor girl was torn from her lover, and transferred from her father's lodge to the quarters of the young officer.

There were no ladies in the garrison at that time. Had there been, such a step would hardly have been ventured. Far away in the wilderness, shut out from the salutary influences of religious and social cultivation, what wonder that the moral sense sometimes becomes blinded, and that the choice is made, "Evil, be thou my good!"

The first step in wrong was followed by one still more aggravated in cruelty. The young officer left the post, as he said, on furlough, but *he never returned.* The news came after a time that he was married, and when he again joined his regiment, it was at another post. There was a natural feeling in the strength of the "woe pronounced against him" by more tongues than one. "He will never," said my informant, "dare show himself in this country again! Not an Indian who knows the Day-kau-rays but would take his life if he should meet him!"

Every tie was broken for poor Agathe but that which bound her to her infant. She never returned to her father's lodge, for she felt that, being deserted, she was dishonoured. Her sole ambition seemed to be to bring up her child like those of the whites. She attired it in the costume of the French children, with a dress of bright calico, and a cap of the same, trimmed with narrow black lace. It was a fine child, and the only time I ever saw a smile cross her face was when it was commended and caressed by some member of our family.

Even this, her only source of happiness, poor Agathe was called upon to resign. During our absence at Green Bay, while the Sauks were in the neighbourhood, the child was taken violently ill. The house at Paquette's, which was the mother's home, was thronged with Indians, and of course there was much noise and disturbance. My husband had a place prepared for her under our roof, where she could be more quiet, and receive the attendance of the post physician. It was all in vain—nothing could save the little creature's life.

The bitter agony of the mother, as she hung over the only treasure she possessed on earth, was described to me as truly heart-rending. When compelled to part with it, it seemed almost more than nature could bear. There were friends, not of her own nation or colour, who strove to comfort her. Did the father ever send a thought or an inquiry after the fate of his child, or of the young being whose life he had rendered dark and desolate? We will hope that he did—that he repented and asked pardon from above for the evil he had wrought.

Agathe had been baptised by M. Mazzuchelli. Perhaps she may have acquired some religious knowledge which could bring her consolation in her sorrows, and compensate her for the hopes and joys so early blasted.

She came, some months after the death of her child, in company with several of the half-breed women of the neighbourhood, to pay me a visit of respect and congratulation on the advent of the *young Shaw-nee-aw-kee*. When she looked at her "little brother," as he was called, and took his soft, tiny hand within her own, the tears stood in her eyes, and she spoke some little words of tenderness, which showed that her heart was full. I could scarcely refrain from mingling my tears with hers, as I thought on all the sorrow and desolation that one man's selfishness had occasioned.

★★★★★★★★★★★★★★★★

Early in February, 1833, my husband and Lieutenant Hunter, in company with one or two others, set off on a journey to Chicago. That place had become so much of a town (it contained perhaps fifty inhabitants) that it was necessary for the proprietors of "Kinzie's Addition" to lay out lots and open streets through their property. All this was accomplished during the visit in question.

While they were upon the ground with a surveyor, the attention of my husband was drawn towards a very bright-looking boy in Indian costume, who went hopping along by the side of the assistant that carried the chain, mimicking him as in the course of his operations he cried, "Stick!" "stuck!" He inquired who the lad was, and, to his surprise, learned that he was the brother of the old family servants Victoire, Genevieve, and Baptiste. Tomah, for that was his name, had never been arrayed in civilized costume; he was in blanket and leggings, and had always lived in a *wigwam*. My husband inquired if he would like to go to Fort Winnebago with him and learn to be a white boy. The idea pleased him much, and, his mother having given her sanction to the arrangement, he was packed in a wagon, with the two gentlemen and their travelling gear, when they set forth on their return-journey.

Tomah had been equipped in jacket and trousers, with the other articles of apparel necessary to his new sphere and character. They were near the Aux Plaines, and approaching the residence of Glode (Claude) Laframboise, where Tomah knew he should meet acquaintances. He asked leave to get out of the wagon and walk a little way. When the gentlemen next saw him, he was in full Pottowattamie costume: although it was bitter winter weather, he had put on his uncomfortable native garb rather than show himself to his old friends in a state of transformation.

On his arrival at Fort Winnebago, our first care was to furnish him with a complete wardrobe, which, having been placed in a box in his sleeping-apartment, was put under his charge. Words cannot express his delight as the valuable possessions were confided to him. Every spare moment was devoted to their contemplation. Now and then Tomah would be missing. He was invariably found seated by the side of his little trunk, folding and refolding his clothes, laying them now lengthwise, now crosswise, the happiest of mortals.

Our next step was to teach him to be useful. Such little offices were assigned to him at first as might be supposed not altogether new to him, but we soon observed that when there was anything in the shape of work, Tomah slipped off to bed, even if it were before he had taken his supper. Some fish were given him one evening to scale; it was just at dark; but Tom, according to custom, retired at once to bed.

The cook came to inquire what was to be done. I was under the necessity of calling in my husband's aid as interpreter. He sent for Tomah. When he came into the parlour Mr. Kinzie said to him, in Pottowattamie,—

"There are some fish, Tomah, in the kitchen, and we want you to scale them."

"Now?" exclaimed Tom, with an expression of amazement. "It is very late."

A young lady, Miss Rolette, who was visiting us, and who understood the language, could not refrain from bursting into a laugh at the simplicity with which the words were uttered, and we joined her in sympathy, at which Tom looked a little indignant; but when he understood that it was the *white custom* to scale the fish at night, and put salt and pepper on them, he was soon reconciled to do his duty in the matter.

His next office was to lay the table. There was a best service of china, which was only used when we had company, and a best set of teaspoons, which I kept in the drawer of a bureau in my own room above-stairs. I was in the habit of keeping this drawer locked, and putting the key under a small clock on the mantel-piece. The first time that I had shown Tomah how to arrange matters for visitors, I had brought the silver and put it on the table myself.

Soon after, we were to have company to tea again, and I explained to Tomah that the best china must be used. What was my surprise, on going through the dining-room a short time after, to see not only the new china, but the "company silver" also, on the table! I requested our mother, who could speak with him, to inquire into the matter.

Tomah said, very coolly, "He got the silver where it was kept."

"Did he find the drawer open?"

"No—he opened it with a key."

"Was the key in the drawer?"

"No—it was under that thing on the shelf."

"How did he know it was kept there?"

This was what Mr. Tomah declined telling. We could never ascertain whether he had watched my movements at any time. No one had ever seen him in that part of the house, and yet scarcely an article could be mentioned of which Tomah did not know the whereabouts. If anyone was puzzled to find a thing, it was always,—

"Ask Tomah—he will tell you." And so, in fact he did.

He was a subject of much amusement to the young officers. We were to have a tea-party one evening—all the families and young officers from the fort. To make Tomah's appearance as professional as possible, we made him a white apron with long sleeves to put on while he was helping Mary and Josette to carry round tea—for I must acknowledge that Tomah's clothes were not kept in as nice order out of the trunk as in it.

Tom was delighted with his new costume, as well as with the new employment. He acquitted himself to perfection, for he had never any difficulty in imitating what he saw another do. After tea we had some music. As I was standing by the piano, at which one of the ladies was seated, Lieutenant Vancleve said to me, in a low tone,—

"Look behind you a moment."

I turned. There sat Tom between two of the company, as stately as possible, with his white apron smoothed down, and his hands clasped before him, listening to the music, and on the best possible terms with himself and all around him. Julian and Edwin were hardly able to restrain their merriment, but they were afraid to do or say anything that would cause him to move before the company had had a full enjoyment of the scene. It was voted unanimously that Tomah should be permitted to remain and enjoy the pleasures of society for one evening; but, with characteristic restlessness, he got tired as soon as the music was over, and unceremoniously took his leave of the company.

Chapter 38

Conclusion

What we had long anticipated of the sufferings of the Indians began to manifest itself as the spring drew on. Its extent was first brought to our knowledge by those who came in little parties begging for food.

As long as it was possible to issue occasional rations their father continued to do so, but the supplies in the Commissary Department were now so much reduced that Colonel Cutler did not feel justified in authorising anything beyond a scanty relief, and this only in extreme cases.

We had ourselves throughout the winter used the greatest economy with our own stores, that we might not exhaust our slender stock of flour and meal before it could be replenished from "below." We had even purchased some sour flour which had been condemned by the commissary, and had contrived, by a plentiful use of saleratus and a due proportion of potatoes, to make of it a very palatable kind of bread. But as we had continued to give to party after party, when they would come to us to represent their famishing condition, the time at length arrived when we had nothing to give.

The half-breed families of the neighbourhood, who had, like ourselves, continued to share with the needy as long as their own stock lasted, were now obliged, of necessity, to refuse further assistance. These women often came to lament with us over the sad accounts that were brought from the wintering grounds. It had been a very open winter. The snow had scarcely been enough at any time to permit the Indians to track the deer; in fact, all the game had been driven off by the troops and war-parties scouring the country through the preceding summer.

We heard of their dying by companies from mere inanition, and lying stretched in the road to the Portage, whither they were striving to drag their exhausted frames. Soup made of the bark of the slippery elm, or stewed acorns, were the only food that many had subsisted on for weeks.

We had for a long time received our own food by daily rations from the garrison, for things had got to such a pass that there was no possibility of obtaining a barrel of flour at a time. After our meals were finished, I always went into the pantry, and collecting carefully every remaining particle of food set it aside, to be given to some of the wretched applicants by whom we were constantly thronged.

One day as I was thus employed, a face appeared at the window with which I had once been familiar. It was the pretty daughter of the elder Day-kau-ray. She had formerly visited us often, watching with great interest our employments—our sewing, our weeding and cultivating the garden, or our reading. Of the latter, I had many times endeavoured to give her some idea, showing her the plates in the

Family Bible, and doing my best to explain them to her, but of late I had quite lost sight of her. Now, how changed, how wan she looked! As I addressed her with my ordinary phrase, "Tshah-ko-zhah?" (What is it?) she gave a sigh that was almost a sob. She did not beg, but her countenance spoke volumes.

I took my dish and handed it to her, expecting to see her devour the contents eagerly; but no—she took it, and, making signs that she would soon return, walked away. When she brought it back, I was almost sure she had not tasted a morsel herself.

★★★★★★★★★★★★★★★★

Oh! the boats—the boats with the corn! Why did they not come? We both wrote and sent to hasten them, but, alas! everything and everybody moved so slowly in those unenterprising times! We could only feel sure that they would come when they were ready, and not a moment before.

We were soon obliged to keep both doors and windows fast, to shut out the sight of misery we could not relieve. If a door were opened for the admission of a member of the family, some wretched mother would rush in, grasp the hand of my infant, and, placing that of her famishing child within it, tell us, pleadingly, that he was imploring "his little brother" for food. The stoutest man could not have beheld with dry eyes the heart-rending spectacle which often presented itself. It was in vain that we screened the lower portion of our windows with curtains. They would climb up on the outside, and tier upon tier of gaunt, wretched faces would peer in above, to watch us, and see if indeed we were as ill provided as we represented ourselves.

The noble old Day-kau-ray came one day, from the Barribault, to apprise us of the state of his village. More than forty of his people, he said, had now been for many days without food, save bark and roots. My husband accompanied him to the commanding officer to tell his story and ascertain if any amount of food could be obtained from that quarter. The result was, the promise of a small allowance of flour, sufficient to alleviate the cravings of his own family.

When this was explained to the chief, he turned away. "No," he said, "if his people could not be relieved, he and his family would starve with them!" And he refused, for those nearest and dearest to him, the proffered succour, until all could share alike.

The announcement, at length, that "the boats were in sight," was a thrilling and most joyful sound.

Hundreds of poor creatures were assembled on the bank, watching their arrival. Oh! how torturing was their slow approach, by the winding course of the river, through the extended prairie! As the first boat touched the land, we, who were gazing on the scene with anxiety and impatience only equalled by that of the sufferers, could scarcely refrain from laughing, to see old Wild-Cat, who had somewhat fallen off in his huge amount of flesh, seize "the Washington Woman" in his arms and hug and dance with her in the ecstasy of his delight.

Their Father made a sign to them all to fall to work with their hatchets, which they had long held ready, and in an incredibly short time barrel after barrel of corn was broken open and emptied, while even the little children possessed themselves of pans and kettles full, and hastened to the fires that were blazing around to parch and cook that which they had seized.

From this time forward, there was no more destitution. The present abundance was immediately followed by the arrival of supplies for the Commissary's Department; and, refreshed and invigorated, our poor children departed once more to their villages, to make ready their crops for the ensuing season.

In the course of the spring, we received a visit from the Rev. Mr. Kent and Mrs. Kent, of Galena. This event is memorable, as being the first occasion on which the gospel, according to the Protestant faith, was preached at Fort Winnebago. The large parlour of the hospital was fitted up for the service, and gladly did we each say to the other, "Let us go to the house of the Lord!"

For nearly three years had we lived here without the blessing of a public service of praise and thanksgiving. We regarded this commencement as an omen of better times, and our little "sewing-society" worked with renewed industry, to raise a fund which might be available hereafter in securing the permanent services of a missionary.

★★★★★★★★★★★★★★★★

Not long after this, on a fine spring morning, as we were seated at breakfast, a party of Indians entered the parlour, and came to the door of the room where we were. Two of them passed through, and went out upon a small portico—the third remained standing in the door-way at which he had at first appeared. He was nearly opposite me, and as I raised my eyes, spite of his change of dress, and the paint with which he was covered, I at once recognised him.

I continued to pour the coffee, and, as I did so, I remarked to my husband, "The one behind you, with whom you are speaking, is one of the escaped prisoners."

Without turning his head, Mr. Kinzie continued to listen to all the directions they were giving him about the repairing of their guns, traps, etc., which they wished to leave with the blacksmith. As they went on, he carelessly turned towards the parlour door, and replied to the one speaking to him. When he again addressed me, it was to say,—

"You are right, but it is no affair of ours. We are none of us to look so as to give him notice that we suspect anything. They are undoubtedly innocent, and have suffered enough already."

Contrary to his usual custom, their father did not ask their names, but wrote their directions, which he tied to their different implements, and then bade them go and deliver them themselves to M. Morrin.

The rest of our circle were greatly pleased at the young fellow's audacity, and we quite longed to tell the officers that we could have caught one of their fugitives for them, if we had had a mind.

****

The time had now come when we began to think seriously of leaving our pleasant home, and taking up our residence at Detroit, while making arrangements for a permanent settlement at Chicago.

This intelligence, when communicated to our Winnebago children, brought forth great lamentations and demonstrations of regret. From the surrounding country they came flocking in, to inquire into the truth of the tidings they had heard, and to petition earnestly that we would continue to live and die among them.

Among them all, no one seemed so overwhelmed with affliction as Elizabeth, our poor *Cut-Nose*. When we first told her of our intention, she sat for hours in the same spot, wiping away the tears that would find their way down her cheeks, with the corner of the chintz shawl she wore pinned across her bosom.

"No! I never, never, never shall I find such friends again," she would exclaim. "You will go away, and I shall be left here *all alone*."

Wild-Cat, too, the fat, jolly Wild-Cat, gave way to the most audible lamentations.

"Oh, my little brother," he said to the baby, on the morning of our departure, when he had insisted on taking him and seating him on his fat, dirty knee, "you will never come back to see your poor brother again!"

And having taken an extra glass on the occasion, he wept like an infant.

It was with sad hearts that on the morning of the 1st of July, 1888, we bade *adieu* to the long *cortége* which followed us to the boat, now waiting to convey us to Green Bay, where we were to meet Governor Porter and Mr. Brush, and proceed, under their escort, to Detroit.

When they had completed their tender farewells, they turned to accompany their father across the Portage, on his route to Chicago, and long after, we could see them winding along the road, and hear their loud lamentations at a parting which they foresaw would be forever.

Appendix

1

As I have given throughout the *Narrative of the Sauk War* the impressions we received from our own observation, or from information furnished us at the time, I think it but justice to Black Hawk and his party to insert, by way of Appendix, the following account, preserved among the manuscript records of the late Thomas Forsyth, Esq., of St. Louis, who, after residing among the Indians many years as a trader, was, until the year 1830, the Agent of the Sauks and Foxes. The manuscript was written in 1832, while Black Hawk and his compatriots were in prison at Jefferson Barracks:

"The United States troops under the command of Major Stoddard arrived here, (St. Louis, Mo.), and took possession of this country in the month of February, 1804. In the spring of that year, a white person (a man or boy) was killed in Cuivre Settlement, by a Sauk Indian Sometime in the summer following, a party of United States troops were sent up to the Sauk village on Rocky River, and a demand made of the Sauk chiefs for the murderer. The Sauk chiefs did not hesitate a moment, but delivered him up to the commander of the troops, who brought him down and delivered him over to the civil authority in this place (St. Louis).

"Some time in the ensuing autumn some Sauk and Fox Indians came to this place, and had a conversation with General Harrison (then Governor of Indiana Territory, and acting Governor of this State, then Territory of Louisiana) on the subject of liberating their relative, then in prison at this place for the above-mentioned murder.

"Quash-quame, a Sauk chief, who was the head man of this party, has repeatedly said, 'Mr. Pierre Chouteau, Sen., came several times to my camp, offering that if I would sell the lands on the east side of the Mississippi River, Governor Harrison would liberate my relation (meaning the Sauk Indian then in prison as above related), to which

I at last agreed, and sold the lands from the mouth of the Illinois River up the Mississippi River as high as the mouth of Rocky River (now Rock River), and east to the ridge that divides the waters of the Mississippi and Illinois Rivers; but I never sold any more lands.' Quash-quame also said to Governor Edwards, Governor Clarke, and Mr. Auguste Chouteau, Commissioners appointed to treat with the Chippewas, Ottawas, and Pottowattamies of Illinois River, in the summer of 1816, for lands on the west side of Illinois River,—

"'You white men may put on paper what you please, but again I tell you, I never sold any lands higher up the Mississippi than the mouth of Rocky River.'

"In the treaty first mentioned, the line commences opposite to the mouth of Gasconade River, and running in a direct line to the head-waters of Jefferson River, (there is no such river in this country, therefore this treaty is null and void—of no effect in law or equity, such was the opinion of the late Governor Howard), thence down that river to the Mississippi River—thence up the Mississippi River to the mouth of the Ouisconsin River—thence up that river thirty-six miles—thence in a direct line to a little lake in Fox River of Illinois, down Fox River to Illinois River, down Illinois River to its mouth—thence down the Mississippi River to the mouth of Missouri River—thence up that river to the place of beginning. See treaty dated at St. Louis, 4th November, 1804.

"The Sauk and Fox nations were never consulted, nor had any hand in this treaty, nor knew anything about it. It was made and signed by two Sauk chiefs, one Fox chief and one warrior.

"When the annuities were delivered to the Sauk and Fox nations of Indians, according to the treaty above referred to (amounting to $1000 *per annum*), the Indians always thought they were presents (as the annuity for the first twenty years was always paid in goods, sent on from Georgetown, District of Columbia, and poor articles of merchandise they were, very often damaged and not suitable for Indians), until I, as their agent, convinced them of the contrary, in the summer of 1818.

"When the Indians heard that the goods delivered to them were annuities for land sold by them to the United States, they were astonished, and refused to accept of the goods, denying that they ever sold the lands as stated by me, their agent. The Black Hawk in particular, who was present at the time, made a great noise about this land, and would never receive any part of the annuities from that time forward.

He always denied the authority of Quash-quame and others to sell any part of their lands, and told the Indians not to receive any presents or annuities from any American—otherwise their lands would be claimed at some future day.

"As the United States do insist, and retain the lands according to the treaty of November 4, 1804, why do they not fulfil *their* part of that treaty as equity demands?

"The Sauk and Fox nations are allowed, according to that treaty, 'to live and hunt on the lands so ceded, as long as the aforesaid lands belong to the United States.' In the spring of the year 1827, about twelve or fifteen families of squatters arrived and took possession of the Sauk village, near the mouth of the Rocky River. They immediately commenced destroying the Indians' bark boats. Some were burned, others were torn to pieces, and when the Indians arrived at the village, and found fault with the destruction of their property, they were beaten and abused by the squatters.

"The Indians made complaint to me, as their agent. I wrote to General Clarke, (Superintendent of Indian Affairs at St. Louis), stating to him from time to time what happened, and giving a minute detail of everything that passed between the whites (squatters) and the Indians.

"The squatters insisted that the Indians should be removed from their village, saying that as soon as the land was brought into market, they (the squatters) would buy it all. It became needless for me to show them the treaty, and the right the Indians had to remain on their lands. They tried every method to annoy the Indians, by shooting their dogs, claiming their horses, complaining that the Indians' horses broke into their cornfields—selling them whiskey for the most trifling articles, contrary to the wishes and request of the chiefs, particularly the Black Hawk, who both solicited and threatened them on the subject, but all to no purpose.

"The President directed those lands to be sold at the Land Office, in Springfield, Illinois. Accordingly, when the time came that they were to be offered for sale (in the autumn of 1828), there were about twenty families of squatters at, and in the vicinity of, the old Sauk village, most of whom attended the sale, and but one of them could purchase a quarter-section (if we except George Davenport, a trader who resides in Rocky Island). Therefore, all the land not sold, still belonged to the United States, and the Indians had still a right, by treaty, to hunt and live on those lands. This right, however, was not allowed them—they must move off.

"In 1830, the principal chiefs, and others of the Sauk and Fox Indians who resided at the old village, near Rocky River, acquainted me that they would remove to their village on Ihoway River. These chiefs advised me to write to General Clarke, Superintendent of Indian Affairs at this place (St. Louis), to send up a few militia—that the Black Hawk and his followers would then see that everything was in earnest, and they would remove to the west side of the Mississippi, to their own lands.

"The letter, as requested by the chiefs, was written and sent by me to General Clarke, but he did not think proper to answer it—therefore everything remained as formerly, and, as a matter of course, the Black Hawk and his party thought the whole matter of removing from the old village had blown over.

"In the spring of 1831, the Black Hawk and his party were augmented by many Indians from Ihoway River. This augmentation of forces made the Black Hawk very proud, and he supposed nothing would be done about removing him and his party.

"General Gaines visited the Black Hawk and his party this season, with a force of regulars and militia, and compelled them to remove to the west side of the Mississippi River, on their own lands.

"When the Black Hawk and party recrossed to the east side of the Mississippi River in 1832, they numbered three hundred and sixty-eight men. They were hampered with many women and children, and had no intention to make war. When attacked by General Stillman's detachment, they defended themselves like men; and I would ask, who would not do so, likewise? Thus, the war commenced.

****

"The Indians had been defeated, dispersed, and some of the principal chiefs are now in prison and in chains, at Jefferson Barracks....

"It is very well known, by all who know the Black Hawk, that he has always been considered a friend to the whites. Often has he taken into his lodge the wearied white man, given him good food to eat, and a good blanket to sleep on before the fire. Many a good meal has *the Prophet* given to people travelling past his village, and very many stray horses has he recovered from the Indians and restored to their rightful owners, without asking any recompense whatever....

"What right have we to tell any people, 'You shall not cross the Mississippi River on any pretext whatever'? When the Sauk and Fox Indians wish to cross the Mississippi, to visit their relations among the

Pottowattamies of Fox River, Illinois, they are prevented by us, b*ecause we have the power!*"

I omit the old gentleman's occasional comments upon the powers that dictated, and the forces which carried on, the warfare of this unhappy summer. There is every reason to believe that had his suggestions been listened to, and had he continued the Agent of the Sauks and Foxes, a sad record might have been spared—we should assuredly not have been called to chronicle the untimely fate of his successor, the unfortunate M. St. Vrain, who, a comparative stranger to his people, was murdered by them, in their exasperated fury, at Kellogg's Grove, soon after the commencement of the campaign.

2

It seems appropriate to notice in this place the subsequent appearance before the public of one of the personages casually mentioned in the foregoing narrative.

In the autumn of 1864 we saw advertised for exhibition at Wood's Museum, Chicago, "The most remarkable instance of longevity on record—the venerable Joseph Crély, born on the 13th of September, 1726, and having consequently reached, at this date, the age of *one hundred and thirty-nine years!*" Sundry particulars followed of his life and history, and, above all, of his recollections.

"Well done for old Crély!" said my husband, when he had gone through the long array. "Come, let us go over to Wood's Museum and renew our acquaintance with the venerable gentleman."

I did not need a second invitation, for I was curious to witness the wonders which the whirligig of time had wrought with our old *employé*.

We chose an early hour for our visit, that we might pay our respects to both him and the granddaughter who had him in charge, unembarrassed by the presence of strangers.

In a large room on the second floor of the building, among cages of birds and animals, some stuffed, others still living, we perceived, seated by a window, a figure clad in bright cashmere dressing-gown and gay tasselled cap, tranquilly smoking a *tah-nee-hoo-rah*, or long Indian pipe. His form was upright, his face florid, and less changed than might have been expected by the thirty-one years that had elapsed since we had last seen him. He was alone, and my husband addressed him at first in English:—

"Good-morning, M. Crély. Do you remember me?"

He shook his head emphatically. "*Je ne comprends pas. Je ne me ressouviens de rien—je suis vieux, vieux—le treize Septembre, mil sept cent vingt-six, je suis né. Non, non,*" with a few gentle shakes of the head, "*je ne puis rappeler rien—je suis vieux, vieux.*" (I do not understand. I remember nothing. I am very, very old—the thirteenth of September, 1726, I was born. No, no—I can recollect nothing. I am old, old.)

My husband changed his inquiries to the *patois* which Crély could not feign not to comprehend.

"Where is your granddaughter? I am acquainted with her, and would like to speak with her."

The old man sprang up with the greatest alacrity, and, running to a door in the wooden partition which cut off a corner of the room and thus furnished an apartment for the ancient phenomenon, he rapped vigorously, and called, in accents quite unlike his former feeble, drawling tones,—

"*Thérèse, Thérèse—il y a icite un monsieur qui voudrait vous voir.*" (Thérèse, there is a gentleman here who wishes to see you.)

The granddaughter presently made her appearance. She looked shyly at my husband from under her brows.

"Do you know me, Thérèse?" he asked.

"Yes, sir. It is Mr. Kinzie."

"And do you know me also?" I said, approaching. She looked at me and shook her head.

"No, I do not," she replied.

"What, Thérèse! Have you forgotten Madame John, who taught you to read—you and all the little girls at the Portage?"

"Oh, my heavens, Mrs. Kinzie!—but you have changed so!"

"Yes, Thérèse, I have grown old in all these years; but I have not grown old quite so fast as your grandpapa here."

There was a flash in her eye that told she felt my meaning. She hung her head without speaking, while the colour deepened over her countenance.

"Now," said I, in French, to the grandfather, "you remember me—"

He interrupted me with a protest, "*Non, non—je ne puis rappeler rien—je suis vieux, vieux—le treize Septembre, mil sept cent vingt-six, je suis né à Detroit.*"

"And you recollect," I went on, not heeding his formula, "how I came to the Portage a bride, and lived in the old cabins that the soldiers had occupied—"

"*Eh b'an! oui—oui—*"

"And how you helped make the garden for me—and how Plante and Manaigre finished the new house so nicely while Monsieur John was away for the silver—and how there was a feast after it was completed—"

"*Ah! oui, oui—pour le sûr.*"

"And where are all our people now?" I asked, turning to Thérèse. "Louis Frum *dit* Manaigre—is he living?"

"Oh, Madame Kinzie! You remember that—Manaigre having two names?"

"Yes, Thérèse—I remember everything connected with those old times at the Portage. Who among our people there are living?"

"Only Manaigre is left," she said.

"*Mais, mais, Thérèse,*" interposed the old man, "Manaigre's daughter Geneviève is living." It was a comfort to find our visit of such miraculous benefit to his memory.

"And the Puans—are any of them left?" I asked.

"Not more than ten or twelve, I think—" Again her grandfather promptly contradicted her:—

"*Mais, mais, je compte b'an qu'il y en a quinze ou seize, Thérèse;*" and he went quite glibly over the names of such of his red friends as still hovered around their old home in that vicinity.

He was in the full tide of gay reminiscence, touching upon experiences and adventures of long ago, and recalling Indian and half-breed acquaintances of former days, when footsteps approached, and the entrance of eager, curious visitors suddenly reminded him of his appointed role. It was marvellous how instantaneously he subsided into the superannuated driveller who was to bear away the bell from Old Parr and all the Emperor Alexander's far-sought fossils.

"*Je suis vieux, vieux—l'an mil sept cent vingt-six—le Treize Septembre, à Detroit—je ne puis rappeler rien.*"

Not another phrase could "*all the King's armies, or all the King's men,*" have extorted from him.

So, we left him to the admiring comments of the new-comers. I think it should be added, in extenuation of what would otherwise seem a gross imposture, that his granddaughter was really ignorant of Crély's exact age—that he, being ever a gasconading fellow, was quite ready to personate that certain Joseph Crély whose name appears on the baptismal records of the church in Detroit of the year 1726. He was, moreover, pleased with the idea of being gaily dressed and going on a tour to see the world, and doubtless rejoiced, also, in the prospect of relieving his poor granddaughter of a part of the burden of his maintenance. He was probably at this time about ninety-five years of age. There are those that knew him from 1830, who maintain that his age was a few years less; but I take the estimate of Mr. Kinzie and H.L. Dousman, of Prairie du Chien, who set him down, in 1864, at about the age I have assigned to him.

3
Indian Games

A very popular game or "*tau-tay*" with the Indians is the "*Moc-ca-sin-nay*" (*moccasin* game). It is not altogether unlike the English game of thimble rig. Four *moccasins* are placed upon the ground, in front of the performer who is seated with his opponent in front, and who holds in his hand a small rifle bullet. He commences to sing a little monotonous strain, "*hoop-hah-hoop-hah-hoop-hah-hoop!*" while he pats alternately on the ground with his hands, the latter against the *moccasins*, or against each other.

Suddenly he stops with a "*hoop!*" and calls upon the company to say under which *moccasin* he has left the ball. As it has been concealed during the performance of his motions and flourishes between two of his fingers, it is rather a matter of guess-work to determine its hiding-place, and the game is consequently one in which there are great chances of gain or loss.

It is, however, an exciting and very entertaining one. Instead of being played by only two competitors it is sometimes played by three or four on a side, who hide the ball by turns, and the greatest number of fortunate guessers on a side determines the success of the game.

Next to the horse-fights and card-playing, the favourite sports among the Indians are the different games of ball. Of these the game called by the French "*la Crosse*," but by the Chippewas, Pottowattamies and Ottawas, "*pau-kee-to-way*" is the principal. It is played in the following manner: A space from one to three miles is marked out, upon some level ground, at each extremity of which is planted a stake for a goal, while another is set in the centre, for a starting point. The players then choose sides, if the game is to be played by a single tribe or band. If, however, it is a trial of skill between rival tribes, an equal number of the best players of each is selected. Each player is provided with a "*crosse*" or "*pau-kee-to-way*," which is a slender stick about four feet in length, having at one end a shallow pocket of network fastened around a narrow rim of wood. With this he is to catch the ball when thrown and hurl it forward in the direction of the goal of his own party. The ball is about two and a half inches in diameter. It is made of deer skin stuffed with hair and frequently with a musket ball introduced to give it force and increase the momentum.

When all is ready the band of players take their stations by the starting-post in the centre. The ball is then thrown into the air and it is who can catch it in his "*crosse*" and send it in the direction of his own goal. It is seldom permitted to fall to the ground. Amid pushing, jostling, whooping, some happy player seizes it, shakes it in his "*crosse*" for a moment in triumph, and hurls it, perhaps in a direction the reverse of that in which all have until now been struggling forward. The object of each party is to send the ball beyond the opponents' goal! That once accomplished, the game is won.

The squaws have a game of ball called "*Pus-ko-way.*" It is played with two balls, attached by a cord of about eight inches in length, and these balls, instead of being round, are somewhat elliptical in form—they are called "*pus-kan-ween.*" The women use a stick without the racquet of net work—the style of the game is similar to that of the "*pan-kan-to-way,*" but the course of shorter extent, and something of additional amusement is afforded by the unusual manner in which the players stoop to gather up the balls as they fall, and the propensity of their "*matche cotees*" (which are seldom confined other than by lapping over in front) to fly back like the attire of the goddess Diana when vigorously engaged in the chase.

Another game of the Indian women is called "*Co-say-keen,*" or the Bowl. Two women, or perhaps four, two on each side, play at it. One chosen by the lot commences holding the bowl in which are placed a number of circular convex pieces of bone, of about three-fourths of an inch in diameter. They are nicely formed and polished and are painted red or black on one side, while the other retains its natural colour. They are called "*puk-kay-sun.*" Each individual, or pair chooses her colour. The one holding the bowl places the pieces within it, and with a dextrous movement tosses them in such a way that those of her chosen colour may fall uppermost.

Then one of the opposite side takes it and repeats the operation. The game is fixed at a certain number, and in this, as in many other games, the tally is kept by small sticks. The women gamble as enthusiastically as the men, staking their most valued trinkets on the chances of the game.

A Note

In compliance with the suggestion that some details of the life of Mr. and Mrs. John H. Kinzie should accompany this third edition of *Waubun*, the following brief sketch has been prepared:

Juliette Augusta Magill was born in Middletown, Conn., on the 11th of September, 1806. Her father, Mr. Arthur William Magill, was a prominent banker of that city; her mother was Mrs. Frances Wolcott Homans, the widow of Captain Thomas Homans, and a great-granddaughter of Governor Roger Wolcott.

Juliette Magill doubtless owed many of the characteristics which combined to make her a very remarkable woman, from these New England ancestors, who were prominent in its early history. From such men as Captain Job Drake, Colonel Samuel Partridge, Mr. Timothy Dwight, the Hon. Daniel Clark, the Hon. John Cushing and Governor Roger Wolcott she inherited the courage, the perseverance, the brilliant wit, the strong good sense and personal attractiveness for which she became so noted, and which made her a social power in Chicago for nearly forty years.

Her early life was spent in her native town, where her education, which was thorough, was conducted under the supervision of her mother—a woman of remarkable mental powers and great cultivation—while her course of reading was directed by her uncle, Dr. Alexander Wolcott, Jr. It was chiefly to the wise judgment and careful training of this relative that Juliette Magill owed the uncommon scope of her knowledge of books and her fine literary taste.

At the age of fifteen she was sent to a boarding school at New Haven, and from thence to Miss Willard's seminary in Troy, N.Y. About this time Mr. Magill met with severe pecuniary reverses, necessitating Juliette's return from school before the close of the first year. The family moved to Fishkill-on-the-Hudson, where Mr. Magill had invested what little property remained to him in some woollen mills. It was here that she met the quaint old Dutch characters depicted so graphically in her story of *Walter Ogleby*. Her studies were, however, by no means given up on her return from school.

During the next two years she prepared two of her brothers for college, coaching them especially in Latin. French, she spoke fluently, and she read Spanish and Italian with ease. In later years, in Chicago, she took up German, which she read, wrote and spoke with facility. She was an excellent musician, playing both piano and organ. She painted in water colours, and sketched from nature rapidly and accurately. All the illustrations in *Waubun* are from views she took on the spot.

Like all well-bred and carefully trained New England girls, she was an accomplished needlewoman, and could cut out and make a suit of gentleman's clothes as well as any tailor, while her embroidery was as exquisite as that of the French nuns from whom she learned the art. In combination with these accomplishments—I had almost said in spite of them—she was an admirable housekeeper. What she did not know about cookery was not worth knowing. Her recipes for jellies, cakes, cordials, etc., were always in great demand, and the combination of literary taste and practical housewifery, though novel, was in her case eminently successful, as all who enjoyed her conversation and hospitality could testify.

Mr. John H. Kinzie's life from his earliest years was intimately connected with the history of the Northwest. His mother's maiden name was Eleanor Lytle. At the time of her marriage to Mr. Kinzie she was a widow with one little daughter. Her first husband was Major McKillip, an officer in the British Army. Her daughter, Margaret McKillip, married Lieutenant Helm of the U. S. Army.

Mr. Kinzie married Mrs. McKillip at Amherstberg, Canada, in 1800. Their first son, John Harris Kinzie, was born at Sandwich, Upper Canada, July 7th, 1803. It was not by design that his birthplace was in the British dominions, for his mother was patriotic beyond most of her sex, but? having crossed the Detroit River to pass the day with her sister, Mrs. William Forsyth, it so happened that her eldest son drew his first breath on foreign soil. While still an infant he was carried in an Indian cradle on the shoulders of a French *engagé* to a place then called "*Parc aux Vaches*," but now the town of Bertrand, near Niles, on the St. Joseph River.

His father about this time purchased the trading establishment of a M. Le Mai at Chicago. He did not remove his family there, however, until the command of U. S. troops came in the following summer (1804) to construct and occupy Fort Dearborn. Children at these remote posts had at that day no advantages of education. Robert Forsyth, a cousin, who was then a member of Mr. Kinzie's family, undertook to teach young John to read, and a discharged soldier later on was engaged to instruct himself and sisters, along with the officers' children. His best friend, in these days, was Washington Whistler, who in after years became famous as a civil engineer, and who died in the

REPLICA OF FORT DEARBORN, CENTURY OF PROGRESS, 1933, CHICAGO

service of the Emperor of Russia. He was the son of the commanding officer who built Fort Dearborn.

At the time of the massacre Colonel Kinzie was nine years old. Of course, he preserved a distinct recollection of all the particulars that came under his observation; the discipline of those thrilling events doubtless helped to form in him that fearlessness and self-control of character for which he was noted in after years.

The Kinzie family took refuge after the massacre at Parc aux Vaches, whence they returned to Chicago in 1816.

In the year 1818, when he was but fifteen years of age, he was taken to Mackinac by his father and indentured to the American Fur Company, being the especial *protégé* of two old friends of the family, Mr. Ramsey Crooks and Mr. Robert Stewart. He lived in the family of the latter. His days during the five years of his engagement with the company were passed from five o'clock in the morning till dusk in the warehouses, or in superintending the numerous *engagés* and *voyageurs*, making up outfits for the Indian trade or in receiving and invoicing those which arrived. In the evenings he read aloud to his kind excellent friend Mrs. Stewart, who was unwearied in her efforts to supply the deficiencies which his unsettled and eventful life had made inevitable. To her explanations and judicious criticisms upon the books she put into his hands and to her patience in imparting knowledge from the treasures of her well-stored mind he was indebted for the ambition which surmounted early disadvantages and made him what his friends and society knew him.

In 1824, he was transferred from Mackinac to Prairie du Chien. While there he learned to speak Winnebago (which no white man before him had succeeded in doing), and he wrote a grammar of the language, which, after his death, was presented to the Chicago Historical Society. Mr. Kinzie at this time received an invitation from Gen. Lewis Cass, then Governor of Michigan, to become his private secretary. He accepted the appointment and went to Detroit, where he became a member of the Governor's family. A part of the time he was stationed near Sandusky, among the Wyandot and Huron Indians, whose language he learned, compiling a catalogue or grammar of it, as he had already done of the Winnebago. The traditions, legends and notices of the manners and customs of these people were all placed in the hands of his chief, and formed the basis of that famous article in the North American Review, which laid the foundation of General Cass' literary reputation.

Mr. Kinzie remained with General Cass until he received the appointment of Government Agent for the upper bands of the Winnebago Indians, in 1829, when he went to Fort Winnebago, near Portage City, making it his headquarters.

While residing in Chicago as Government Agent for the Indians, Dr. Alexander Wolcott, Jr., had married Mr. Kinzie's eldest sister. On one of his visits to his Boston home he was accompanied by his brother-in-law. Juliette Magill happened to be staying with her grandparents at the same time, and thus the young people met. It was a case of "love at first sight." They were married on the 9th of August, 1827.

Mr. Kinzie's influence with the Indians, like that of his father, was great and far-reaching, and enabled him to render effective service to the Government in many ways, more especially in holding back the Winnebagoes from joining in the Black Hawk war. They had unbounded faith in his integrity and just dealing, while his success in all their athletic games commanded their admiration. He was especially noted for his skill at *"La Crosse,"* and had beaten the swiftest runners of the Menomenees and Winnebagoes at foot-races. He spoke no less than thirteen different Indian languages.

Until the day of his death it was to him that the various deputations came on their way to interview their "Great Father" in Washington, in order that Shaw-nee-aw-kee, (the Silver-man), as they called Mr. Kinzie, might give them the benefit of his advice, make out their petitions properly, and arrange their transportation with free passes. It was no uncommon thing for a dozen or more Indians to be camped out on the grass in Mr. Kinzie's garden, smoking their pipes, or playing their favourite gambling game of *"moccasin."* (See description of Indian games in Appendix 3)

In 1834, the Kinzies returned to Chicago, with their little son Wolcott, and in that same year Mr. Kinzie and Mr. George W. Dole furnished the money to build St. James' Church, and Mr. Robert Kinzie donated the lot. The Rev. Isaac Hallam was called as rector. There were at this date but five communicants, viz.: Mr. and Mrs. John Kinzie, Mr. and Mrs. Dole and Mrs. Magill.

In 1835, the Illinois Legislature appointed a Board of Trustees for the "Village of Chicago," of which Mr. Kinzie was President. In 1836, he built the brick house on the corner of Cass and Michigan streets, in which they subsequently lived.

In 1838, little Wolcott Kinzie met with a sudden and tragic death. While playing with a party of other boys in an empty house a couple of blocks from home he found a bottle of corrosive sublimate on the hearth. He picked it up and took a drink of the contents. The agony was instantaneous. He rushed home, while all his little companions fled in dismay. Although three physicians were immediately summoned it was impossible to save his life. Mr. Kinzie was absent at Prairie du Chien and did not hear of his loss until he returned, to find his boy dead and buried.

Besides their own seven children, Mr. and Mrs. Kinzie adopted seven or eight nephews and nieces and cousins. Among these were Mrs. Joseph N. Balestier (grandmother of Mrs. Rudyard Kipling), Mrs. Mark Skinner of Chicago, Mrs. Samuel Barstow of Detroit, Mrs. Anne Meldrim Hamilton, Henry Wolcott, Edwin Helm and the late Julian Magill.

With all these young people in the family there was plenty of merry-making, and frequent and gay were the entertainments. The music for the dancing was furnished by Mrs. Kinzie, who presided at the piano, accompanied by Mr. Kinzie on the violin. It is safe to say no modern band ever sent forth more inspiring strains. Occasionally, by way of variety, Mr. Kinzie would steal away, array himself in full Indian costume, and coming with a bound, and a "*How—How—How*" into the drawing-room, would execute an Indian war-dance—to the delight of the young people and the terror of the nervous elderly guests.

Everyone who came to Chicago brought letters of introduction to the Kinzies. Their house was the headquarters and the rendezvous of all officers of the government, all the cultivated and intelligent people of our own and of foreign lands. Their hospitality, as bounteous as the winds, as beautiful as the waters of Lake Michigan, captivated the hearts and won the commendation of Frederica Bremer, Miss Martineau, Captain Marryatt, Charles Lever, poor Charles Fenno Hoffman, Mrs. Frances Kemble and many other eminent authors, artists and travellers.

The summers of 1844-45 Mr. Kinzie spent with a party of mining experts, looking into the mineral deposits of Lake Superior. He located the famous Ontonagen Mine, of which C. K. Green, George C. Bates and Mr. Kinzie were owners.

In 1848 President Taylor appointed Mr. Kinzie Registrar of the Land Office, and on the opening of the Illinois and Michigan Canal he was made Canal Collector, holding that office until he received his appointment as Paymaster in the Army in 1861.

The cholera raged in Chicago in 1850-51. Little Frank Kinzie was one of its earliest victims. There were no trained nurses in those days, and the only assistance to be had in cases of illness was through the voluntary aid of friends and neighbours. In spite of the danger of infection, Mr. and Mrs. Kinzie devoted all their time to nursing the sick, and kept the hospital supplied daily with huge caldrons of broth. This charitable work they continued during the two summers of the epidemic.

In the midst of a very busy life, Mrs. Kinzie found time for an immense amount of charitable and philanthropic work. Her liberality, her practical good sense, and her powers of organization made her a leader in such societies. She took an active part in the founding and equipping of that splendid institution, "St. Luke's Hospital," Chicago, and her interest in it terminated only with her life.

Mrs. Kinzie's first literary work was the account of the Massacre of 1812. She wrote this at the dictation of Mr. Kinzie's mother, and of his sister, Mrs. Helm, both of whom were eye-witnesses of all the facts they narrated. Mrs. Helm, who accompanied her husband. Lieutenant Helm, when the troops marched out of Fort Dearborn on that fateful day, was a participant in the fight. In view of some of the modern attempts to rewrite the story of the Massacre, and to characterize Mrs. Kinzie's account as "one which reads like a romance and was meant so to be read," it is most fortunate that the simple and graphic statements of the facts should have been given to posterity by actual eyewitnesses whose veracity was beyond question.

The story of the Massacre is embodied in *Waubun*, the first edition of which was published by Derby & Jackson (New York) in 1856. Their entire establishment was wiped out by fire a few years later, and all the plates to this edition, including the original illustrations from Mrs. Kinzie's drawings, were destroyed. A smaller edition, without illustrations, was issued by J. B. Lippincott & Sons (Philadelphia) after Mrs. Kinzie's death. This was soon exhausted, and copies of either edition are no longer in the market.

In 1869 Lippincott published Mrs. Kinzie's first novel, *Walter Ogleby*, the plot of which was laid among the scenes of her youth on the North River. It was favourably received by the public, and had a satisfactory sale.

At the time of her death Mrs. Kinzie was engaged in correcting the proofs of a novel called *Mark Logan*, founded on the tragic fate of the handsome and ill-fated Winnebago Chief, Red Bird. It was published by Lippincott & Co. in 1887, eight years after Mrs. Kinzie's death.

Col. Kinzie was appointed Paymaster in the Army with headquarters at Chicago, in 1861, with rank of major. In 1864 he was made lieutenant-colonel. His two eldest sons, John and Arthur, had volunteered at the commencement of the Civil War. John entered the navy. He was on the gunboat *Mound City,* under Admiral Davis, when an attack was made on a Confederate fort on the White River, Arkansas.

A hot shot penetrated the boiler of the *Mound City,* blowing her up and throwing ninety-seven men scalded and dying into the water. By order of the Confederate officer commanding the fort, General Frye, his sharpshooters picked out and shot the wounded men as they were struggling to reach the hospital boat sent to their rescue. Young Kinzie was shot through the legs and arms as he was being lifted into it. Hearing the shouts of the marines and learning that the fort had surrendered, he exclaimed, "Have we taken the fort? Then I am ready to die now."

The next morning (June 18, 1862,) just as the sun's first rays gilded the horizon his brave spirit took flight. He was just twenty-three years old, and left a young wife barely eighteen. His little daughter was born three months after his death. From this shock Col. and Mrs. Kinzie never recovered. Shortly after this bereavement their second son, Arthur, who was on General Washburn's staff, was captured by General Forrest, who made a raid into Memphis. Unfortunately, the youngest son, George, who was paying his brother a visit, was also captured along with the most of the officers at the headquarters. They were taken to Cahawba, Ala., but after a short imprisonment were exchanged by order of the President of the Confederacy, who was an old friend of the Kinzie family.

Mr. Kinzie's health now began to fail; heart trouble soon developed, and he obtained a leave of absence, and started for an Eastern health resort, accompanied by his wife, daughter and son Arthur. As the train approached Pittsburg a blind fiddler came into the car asking alms. Mr. Kinzie put his hand into his pocket to get his purse. Before he could draw it out again his head fell forward, and he died with a smile on his lips. His last act was an epitome of his whole life.

His death took place on June 21, 1865. In an obituary notice which appeared on June 23, the *Chicago Tribune* has the following:

> The last of his contemporaries, the death of Major Kinzie turns the final page in the first volume of the annals of this city and surrenders the last survivor of those who looked out on prairie

and woodland where Chicago was to stand.

It is rare that the sum of a single human life so honourably and usefully enshrines so much that pertains to human progress. To give the full details of such a life as his has been, would be to retrace the development of Chicago.

His widow survived him five years.

In 1870 Mrs. Kinzie joined her daughter and grandchildren, who were spending the summer at Amagansett, on Long Island. On the evening of September 14th, she sent to the local physician for some two-grain quinine pills. He sent morphine pills, instead of quinine, in a paper without a label. Mrs. Kinzie took one, and by the time the fatal mistake was discovered it was too late for the most powerful remedies to take effect. In four hours, she was dead. Her remains were brought to Chicago for interment, and she was laid beside her husband and children in Graceland Cemetery. A great crowd of the poor followed her to her last resting place, testifying their grief at the loss of one who had been so generous and sympathizing a friend.

The Rev. Dr. Clinton Locke, of Grace Church, Chicago, closed his beautiful tribute to her worth in the following words:

> As a member of St. James' Church, Mrs. Kinzie's name stands inscribed first upon its muster roll of women; and no soldier of the cross ever bore its arms or upheld its flag more triumphantly or more steadfastly than she did. In the early days of the Episcopal Church of Illinois, and under the teaching of that most pure, devout and holy of Christians, Bishop Chase, her house and home was the home of the church, and all who professed its creed, espoused its sublime liturgy, or partook of its communion, found welcome there. In the Sunday schools, mission schools, wherever work was to be done for the church, there was Mrs. Kinzie, ever active, zealous and faithful in every good work. To her energy, liberality and perseverance more than to all others, was the first Church of St. James indebted for its success and prosperity.
>
> No woman in the Northwest was more widely known than Juliette Kinzie, and when the future history of the early days of this magic city shall be written, her life and labours as a member of Christ's church, as a woman of the highest culture and most refined taste, as a faithful wife, devoted mother, kind and generous neighbour, and true American lady, will illuminate its

brightest pages.

"After life's fitful fever she sleeps well."

June, 1900.

Eleanor Kinzie Gordon.

The History of Fort Winnebago

By Andrew Jackson Turner

To the present generation, old Fort Winnebago (at Portage) is a tradition. To the older citizens of our State, who recall its whitened walls as they appeared above the stockade that enclosed them, and who retain a vivid recollection of many of its appointments and environments, it is a reminiscence; very few there are, now living, who dwelt in the fort from its first occupancy, and who had an acquaintance with those of its garrison who were subsequently illustrious in military and civil life. Of such, some passed their earlier years at the fort in comparative obscurity, awaiting an opportunity to prove their mettle on the sanguinary field of conflict, but these afterward left their impress on the pages of history.

Some of their names are still spoken; others who were here, of equal merit, are rarely or never mentioned, for the opportunity came not to them. Much that occurred here has been recorded in various public documents, volumes and papers, but nowhere, I believe, has it all been arranged in a convenient form. So, the old fort may be said to have had a history, but no historian. It is not my purpose to attempt an exhaustive history of the fort; but rather to collate what has already been written, but which is so scattered as to involve great research on the part of the student who desires to know as much as possible of its origin and history. I have incorporated in my account some things not found in any published matter, which I have heard related from the lips of those who were there as early as 1830, and who knew its innermost history. Some of it is of a minor character, but may possess sufficient local interest to warrant the recital.

Although the existence of the lead mines in Southwestern Wisconsin had been known for many years, it was not until about 1822 that they attracted general attention, when adventurers began coming in and commenced mining operations. The Indian title to the lands

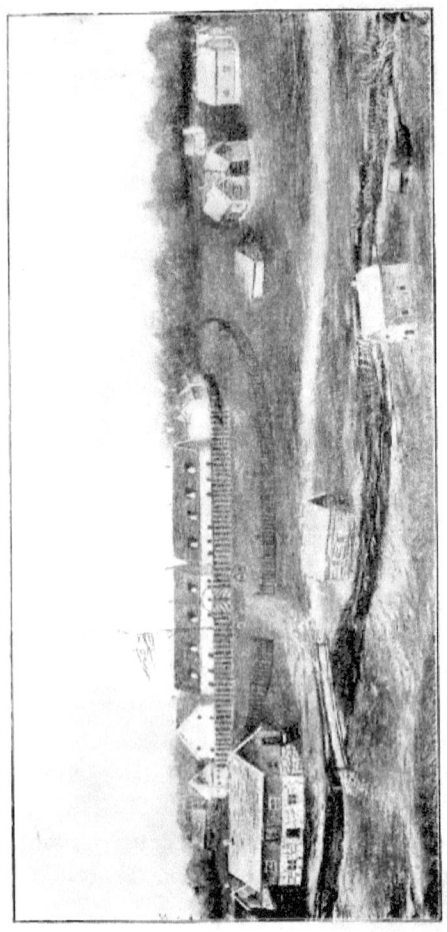

FORT WINNEBAGO IN 1834.

Reduced photographic facsimile of oil painting made by Ira A. Ridgeway, of Portage, in 1896, based with great care on contemporary plans, and recollections of early settlers. The view is from the southwest. The building to the right of the gate is the guardhouse; to the left, the armory. On the opposite side of the square, to the left, were the officers' quarters. The peaked-roof building at the left corner was a blockhouse, and a similar structure was in the corner diagonally opposite. The magazine appears in the corner diagonally opposite the guardhouse, and at the side of it to the right were soldiers' quarters. The chapel was in the corner diagonally opposite the magazine, but is not visible; as is also the case with some of the other smaller buildings. The log building near the end of the bridge over the Fox river, to the right, was Henry Merrell's sutler's store. The low structure a little to the east of it, was the ice cellar. A little farther along was the surgeon's headquarters (a portion of which is still standing), and a little to the right of it was the hospital. In the distance, looking between the hospital and surgeon's quarters, may be seen the old stone bakery; the blacksmith shop and the carpenter shop were close by, but do not appear on the painting. At the left of the bridge is a commissary building, which is still standing; just in the rear of it was Lowe's sutler's store, a portion of which only is discernible. Just beyond the fort, to the left (out of the above picture), was a log theatre. Still farther to the left, on an eminence, was the Indian Agency building.

in that section had not yet been extinguished, or was in dispute; and in any event the Indians were authorised to remain upon them "as long as the lands which are now ceded to the United States remain their property." The lands had not been brought into market and were not even surveyed. Nevertheless, "permits" to enter upon the lands claimed by the Indians were issued by certain government officials. This naturally irritated the savages whose lands had been invaded. The conduct of the adventurers toward the aborigines was frequently coarse and brutal, and disturbances were the inevitable result. In them we find the inciting causes that led to the establishment of old Fort Winnebago—so called because the lead region, as well as the Fox-Wisconsin portage, was in the territory of the Winnebagoes.

In 1827, Joseph M. Street, the Indian agent at Prairie du Chien, wrote to Governor Edwards of Illinois:—

> The Winnebagoes complained of the trespass of the miners, and the open violation of the treaty by the permits of Mr. Thomas, the agent. No notice was taken of it, and the diggings progressed. The Indians attempted force, which was repelled, and very angry feelings produced.

Col. Thomas L. McKenney, an officer in the regular army, who was superintendent of the Indian trade, also recorded his impressions of the condition of affairs in the lead regions, in this language:—

> The Winnebagoes were in a state of great excitement, caused by the intrusions of the whites on their lands. They had, after having remonstrated for a long time in vain, made up their minds to endure it no longer, and had so informed Mr. Courier, the sub-agent. A warning was circulated among the miners, who replied: 'We have a right to go just where we please.' Everything appeared threatening. Two thousand persons were said to be over the line, as intruders upon lands belonging to the Indians. The Indians had fallen back, and sent word to the sub-agent that they would see them no more—meaning, as friends. This overt act, this trespass upon their grounds, was the egg out of which the Black Hawk War was hatched. There was no necessity for that war, when, some four years after, it did break out.

For a time prior to 1826, Fort Crawford, at Prairie du Chien, had been occupied by a detachment of United States troops. In October of that year, they were ordered to Fort Snelling. When they left, they took with them two Winnebagoes, who had been confined in the guardhouse for some supposed offense of a trivial nature. The following spring a rumour was in circulation, and generally believed, that the two Indians had been turned over to the Chippewas, their enemies, to run the gauntlet through a party of the latter tribe, armed with clubs and tomahawks, and that the race for life had resulted in the killing of both of them.

Something like this occurred with reference to some Sioux prisoners at Fort Snelling, but the story had no truth as applied to the Winnebago captives. The report had its origin in the murdering of some Chippewas by a party of Sioux. Five of these Sioux were turned over to the United States forces at Fort Snelling to be dealt with by the Chippewas according to the aboriginal custom, and it was determined that they should run the gauntlet: the Chippewas being armed with rifles, instead of tomahawks and clubs, as stated in Smith's *History of Wisconsin* and some other accounts. The whole affair is graphically described by Mrs. Van Cleve, who was an eye-witness of the affair, in her little volume, *Three Score Years and Ten*. All of the Sioux were killed before reaching the goal.

★★★★★★★★★★

> Mrs. Charlotte Ouisconsin Van Cleve was born in Fort Crawford, July 1, 1819, and is said to have been the first white child born within the limits of Wisconsin. She is still living, (1898), at Minneapolis, Minn. Her book of reminiscences, *Three Score Years and Ten* (Minneapolis, 1895), is an interesting publication, ranking with Mrs. Kinzie's *Wau-Bun*, Folsom's *Fifty Years in the Northwest,* etc.

★★★★★★★★★★

Notwithstanding the falsity of the report, so far as it related to the Winnebagoes in confinement, it had its natural effect upon the disposition of our Indians, whose only creed is a life for a life; and it should not occasion surprise that it provoked retaliation and served to increase the difficulties which are the inevitable accompaniment of an advancing civilization. The whites, on the one hand, entertained nothing but contempt for "blanket Indians," strangely misjudged their disposition, and treated them as legitimate objects of plunder; the aborigines, on the other, sought to protect themselves in the only manner known to them, by taking revenge for imaginary or real wrongs, often committing excesses and cruelties in keeping with their savage nature.

And so, we read at the present day, with horror, of the murders of the family of Methode, at Prairie du Chien, in 1827; of Registre

Gagnier, and the scalping of his infant daughter by a noted Indian chief, Red Bird, and his accomplices of the Winoshic band. Of Red Bird and his subsequent dramatic surrender and death, I will speak further on.

As a component part of a general attack upon the whites, which doubtless had been planned, the keel-boat *Oliver H. Perry*, returning from a trip to Port Snelling with provisions for the troops at that station, was attacked by a band of Winnebagoes off the mouth of the Bad Ax, and a severe battle ensued, with a number of casualties on both sides.

He who reads Reynolds's *Life and Times* will find other explanations for the attack upon this boat, which would have justified almost any conduct upon the part of the Indians; but it is not my present purpose to attempt to locate the largest measure of blame for what was occurring. The idea will suggest itself, however, from the report of Maj.-Gen. Alexander Macomb (general-in-chief of the army) to the secretary of war the following year, stating that "from the restlessness evinced by the Winnebagoes and other tribes in the Northwest, partly arising from intrusion upon land in the mineral district claimed by them to be within their boundaries, by white people, etc.," he had found it necessary to establish a new military post at the Fox-Wisconsin portage; that due regard was not being given to the rights of the real owners of the soil, and that the whites were not wholly blameless in these matters. However, this may be, it had become apparent that an increased military force was necessary in this section. These occurrences have been referred to in historical works as the Winnebago "outbreaks," "disturbances," etc., and sometimes they are dignified as the Winnebago War.

Moses M. Strong, in his *History of the Territory of Wisconsin*, observes:—

> It may be thought that the results of this war are very meagre for the amount of force employed in it. If measured by the amount of blood shed after the murders at Prairie du Chien and on the keel-boat, the criticism is very correct. But if it be intended to suggest that there was no sufficient reason for apprehending that the Winnebagoes contemplated a general uprising against and a massacre of the whites, the thought and suggestion are the result of great ignorance of the intentions of the Winnebagoes, and of the facts in the case. There is satisfactory evidence

that the Pottawattomies were allied with the Winnebagoes, and that they were to fall upon and destroy the settlement at Chicago, and it is probable that but for the movements resulting from the efforts of General Cass, who was fortunately near the seat of war, the whole country would have been overrun with a general Indian outbreak.

It may be that this was an exaggerated view of what the Indians contemplated; but it appears clearly that there was abundant reason why General Macomb, in his report to the Secretary of War in November, 1828, should have thought it necessary to establish a military post at the portage, which opinion was communicated to the secretary in the following language:—

> From the restlessness evinced by the Winnebagoes and other tribes in the Northwest, partly arising from intrusion upon land in the mineral district claimed by them to be within their boundaries, by white people in search of lead; and in consequence of a belief entertained by these tribes, from the smallness of the military force in their neighbourhood, in comparison with what it had been several years before, the government might not find it convenient to increase it, and they might therefore with impunity resume the depredations which had led to the establishment of those posts in the first instance; therefore it was found necessary to establish a new post at the portage between the Fox and Ouisconsin Rivers and reoccupy Chicago. . . . . in order to effect these changes, the first regiment furnished the garrison of the post at the portage of the Ouisconsin and Fox Rivers, while it continued to occupy fort Crawford, at the Prairie du Chien, and Fort Snelling, at the junction of the St. Peters with the Mississippi.
>
> The second regiment, which heretofore occupied the posts at the Sault de St. Marie, Green Bay, and Mackinac, moved down to occupy the posts of forts Gratiot and Niagara, the residue of the regiment being at Houlton Plantations. The fifth regiment, which was stationed with the sixth at the school of instruction at Jefferson barracks, relieved the second at Green Bay, Sault de St. Marie, and Mackinac, besides furnishing two companies for the garrison at Chicago. The march of the fifth regiment by the way of Ouisconsin and Fox Rivers must have produced an imposing effect on the tribes of Indians through whose country

it passed; an effect which was contemplated by the movement. It will be seen by the accompanying map of the distribution of the troops that there is a complete cordon from Green Bay to the Mississippi, which must have a powerful influence over the Winnebagoes, and afforded protection to the Indian trade which passes in that direction; and there is every reason to believe that neither the Winnebagoes nor their confederates will attempt any hostilities so long as the troops maintain their present positions."

★★★★★★★★★★

As supplementary to and confirming General Macomb's report, the following extract is taken from the annual report of Peter B. Porter, Secretary of War, November 24, 1828: "In the course of the last year the Winnebagoes and other Indian tribes living in the neighbourhood of the posts which had been evacuated—emboldened probably by that circumstance—commenced a series of petty, but savage, warfare on the adjoining white population, and rendered it necessary to march a strong military force into the country, the effect of which was to quell, for a time at least, these disturbances. But in the course of the past spring and summer fresh symptoms of discontent and hostility were manifested by the Indians; and the people of Illinois, and more particularly the inhabitants of the lead mine district, became again so much alarmed as to suggest the necessity, not only of permanently garrisoning the former military post of Chicago and Prairie du Chien, but of establishing a new one in the centre of the Winnebago country, for the purpose of watching the movements of the Indians, and to serve as a connecting link between the chains of fortifications on the Mississippi and on the lakes." See *Senate Docs.*, No. 1, 20th Cong., 2nd sess., vol. i.—Original Ed.

★★★★★★★★★★

Executing the order of the Secretary of War, the Adjutant-General of the United States, under the direction of General Macomb, issued "Order 44," under date of August 19, 1828, which directed:

The three companies of the First regiment of Infantry, now at Fort Howard, to proceed forthwith under the command of Major Twiggs of that regiment to the portage between the Fox and Ouisconsin Rivers, there to select a position and establish a military post.

By command of Maj.-Gen. Macomb.

R. Jones, Adjt.-Gen.

An additional reason for the establishment of the fort is given in the *History of Columbia County*, not referred to in the official reports, which may contain many grains of truth:—

> There was necessity for some means of protection to the fur trade from Winnebago exactions; .... the general government at the solicitation of John Jacob Astor, who was then at the head of the American Fur company, and upon whose goods the Indians levied exorbitant tolls, authorised the erection of a post at portage.

It is true that the company had a post there, and it may be that heavy tolls were exacted; it is quite as likely, however, that with all the tolls that may have been exacted, the Indians were getting the worst of it, for it is not recorded, as far as I know, that that gigantic monopoly ever suffered many losses in their trades with the Indians.

September 7 following, Maj. David E. Twiggs reported his arrival at the fort which was to be established, as follows:—

> Fort Winnebago, September 7, 1828.
> Sir: I have the honour of reporting my arrival at the fort with my command this day. I have selected a position for the fort on the right bank of the Fox River, immediately opposite the portage. The Indians, I am told, are very much dissatisfied with the location of troops here; as yet I have not been able to see any of the chiefs, consequently cannot say with any certainty what their dispositions are.
>
> Very respectfully, your obedient servant,
>
> D. E. Twiggs,
> Major First Infantry.

****

Morgan L. Martin, in *Wis. Hist. Colls.*, xi, speaks of having met Maj. Twiggs at Butte des Morts, with three companies of soldiers in boats on their way to establish the garrison at Fort Winnebago. Jefferson Davis, just graduated at West Point, was one of his lieutenants.

****

The site selected for the fort was occupied by Francis le Roy, but satisfactory terms were made with him for its occupancy by the government. Macomb's request to have the lands selected for the fort withdrawn from market, was made January 10, 1835, and was approved by President Jackson, February 9 of the same year.

Twiggs reported December 29, 1828, what had been done in the matter of temporary buildings, for the shelter of his command, prior to the construction of the fort buildings proper; the report is here given in full:—

Fort Winnebago, 29 December, 1828.

General: I have not received any instructions relative to the construction of the permanent garrison at this place. After completing the temporary buildings, I commenced procuring materials for the quarters, etc., and soon will have square timber enough for two blockhouses. I have (and will continue through the winter) six saws, sawing flooring, weather boarding and other lumber. We have about twenty thousand feet of all kinds, and hope by spring to have sufficient to complete the buildings. The sash, blinds, etc., will be ready before the end of February. There will be wanting three or four yoke of oxen, and as many carts, the shingles and lime can better be furnished by contract; all the other materials the command can procure; all the buildings had better be frame—logs cannot be had, and if they could, frame is cheaper and much better; all the timber has to be brought from nine to eleven miles, but if the carts and oxen are furnished, and the lime and shingles got by contract, I can with ease complete the garrison by next November. I would be pleased to hear from you on the subject as soon as convenient.

I am, sir, very respectfully, your obedient servant,

D. E. Twiggs,
Major First Infantry.

To Gen, A. Atkinson, Commanding.

The temporary barracks were constructed of logs obtained principally on what is known locally as Pine Island, about six-miles west of Portage; they were probably a little east of the fort subsequently erected, and resembled the cabins which are always put up in logging camps for the use of the men; but nothing more definite concerning them is now obtainable. It is presumed that the instructions that Twiggs desired were not long delayed, for we know that active operations for the erection of the fort were soon in progress.

Lieut. Jefferson Davis, later the chieftain of the Confederacy, has recorded the fact that he went up the Yellow River, a tributary of the Wisconsin, some fifty miles distant, and got out the pine logs to be used in the construction of the fort, which were rafted down in the spring and hauled across the portage with teams and were wrought into proper form with whipsaw, broadax, and adz. (*Jefferson Davis—a Memoir, by his Wife*, vol. i, also. *Wis. Hist. Colls.*, viii.), Lumbermen still point out the foundations of Davis's dam, which was constructed for flooding out his rafts of timber for use in building the fort. Another party was detailed to get out the needed stone, of which a great quantity was used, at Stone Quarry Hill, the place where the most of the stone used in Portage for building purposes, has ever since been obtained. The bricks were manufactured near the present Wisconsin River bridge, at what we know as "Armstrong's brickyard." Lime was burned by another detail at or near Paquette's farm on the Bellefontaine, one of the best and most widely known farms in the State. (*Wis. Hist. Colls.*, xii)

An enormous well was sunk in the very centre of the square, around which the usual fort buildings were constructed, and it has continued from its never-failing fountain, to contribute to the comfort of the thirsty pilgrim until the present day; but a modern windmill now does the duty that was formerly so tedious and irksome. So, all hands were busy. Officers, who in after years became distinguished in the war with Mexico, the Florida and other Indian wars, and the great conflict involving the perpetuity of our Union, planned and wrought with the common soldier in bringing into form the fort and the necessary accompanying buildings. Stables, hospitals, bakeries, blacksmith shops, commissary buildings, ice-cellars (which were filled from Swan Lake), sutlers' stores, magazines, laundries, bathhouses, etc., rapidly sprang into existence. Gardens were also cleared, and old soldiers have recorded the fact that they could not be excelled in the matter of the quantity and quality of the vegetables produced.

A theatre was erected, and doubtless professional tragedians would have hidden their faces in confusion if they could have witnessed their own best efforts put to shame. A young lieutenant in the regular army, far removed from the confines of civilization, with the officers' wives and their guests, all cultured ladies, for an audience, would undoubtedly do his best when Macbeth or some other equally hair-lifting tragedy was on the boards, in the full glare of the pitch-pine fagots blazing from the fireplace in the rear, and shedding their effulgent rays over the brilliant assemblage.

While all this was going on, regular military duty was not neglected, and drills and parades were indulged in of course; the stars and stripes were regularly given to the breeze at the roll of the drum at guard mounting, and lowered with the same accompaniment at retreat; morning and evening guns were sounded, the *reveille* called the soldiers to duty in the grey light of the morning, and "taps" sent them to retirement in the blue twilight of the evening.

In the regular course of military movements, some of the companies first doing duty here were transferred to different posts, and their places were taken by others; and so, it happened that many whose names were enrolled on the scroll of fame in after years, were initiated into the science of war at Fort Winnebago. Perhaps the most prominent of them all was Lieut. Jefferson Davis, then subaltern of Capt. William S. Harney. To his honour, be it said, his services at Fort Winnebago were highly creditable. I have heard it remarked by those who knew him here, that he had no liking for the amusements to which officers, as well as private soldiers, resort to relieve the tedium of camp life; but that he was ever engaged, when not in active service, in some commendable occupation. His services in the lumber camps on the Yellow River, and his successful mission in bringing down fleets of lumber through the Dells of the Wisconsin, attest to his faithfulness as a soldier.

Next to Lieutenant Davis, should be mentioned Maj. David E. Twiggs, of the First Infantry, under whose immediate superintendence the fort was constructed, as already stated. Subsequently, Twiggs distinguished himself at the Battle of Monterey, in the Mexican War. He was dismissed from the federal service in February, 1861, for surrendering the United States stores in Texas, before that State had seceded, and was a Confederate general for a time. One of Twiggs's lieutenants here, was Captain Harney, who was brevetted a colonel for meritorious conduct in several engagements with hostile Indians in Florida, and became famous as an Indian fighter; he was also brevetted a brigadier-general for gallant service in the Battle of Cerro Gordo. He retired from active service in 1863, and in 1865 was brevetted a major-general for long and faithful service.

Col. William J. Worth—whose gallant services in the War of 1812, and who in the Mexican War disclosed abilities as a soldier which brought him into the public mind as a proper candidate for the presidency—was stationed here for a time.

Capt. E.V. Sumner, who became so renowned for his famous cavalry charge at the battle of Cerro Gordo, in which he was wounded, and who subsequently distinguished himself at Contreras, Churubusco, and Molino del Rey, in Mexico, was also here. Captain Sumner led an expedition against the Cheyenne Indians in Kansas; he commanded the left wing of the Federal Army at the siege of Yorktown; was in all of the Battles of the Peninsula, and was twice wounded; was again wounded at Antietam, and at the battle of Fredericksburg commanded the right grand division of the army. He was one of old Fort Winnebago's brightest jewels.

Lieut. Horatio Phillips Van Cleve went to the front early in the War of Secession as colonel of the Second Minnesota, and achieved distinction, retiring with the rank of major-general; he was one of the finest graduates of the old fort. At the battle of Stone River, Van Cleve was in command of a subdivision of the Army of the Ohio, and was severely wounded. Greeley's *History of the American Conflict* erroneously records him as killed. He recovered from his wounds, and served with distinction until the close of the war. Van Cleve married Charlotte Ouisconsin Clark, daughter of Maj. Nathan Clark, at Fort Winnebago in 1836, this lady having been born at Fort Crawford (Prairie du Chien) in 1819, said to be the first woman of pure white blood born within the present limits of Wisconsin. Her father, the major, died at Fort Winnebago and was buried in the old military cemetery, but his remains were subsequently removed to Cincinnati.

Lieut. Randolph B. Marcy was on duty at Fort Winnebago in 1837-40; captain in 1846, and in active service during the Mexican War, later being on frontier duty for many years. During the War of Secession, he was chief-of-staff under his son-in-law. Gen. George B. McClellan, in 1861-62, attaining the rank of inspector-general and brevet brigadier-general. *General Marcy was the author of several volumes descriptive of frontier life and service. (Exploration of the Red River of Louisiana in 1852; The Prairie Traveler, a Handbook for Overland Emigrants; Thirty Years of Army Life on the Border; Border Reminiscences.)*

Lieut. Nathan B. Rossell joined (1839) the Fifth Infantry at Fort Winnebago, his first post. He was with his regiment in the Mexican War, being severely wounded at Molino del Rey. He was brevetted for distinguished services and was presented by his native state, New Jersey, with a gold sword. He was in command at Fort Albuquerque, N. Mex., when the War of Secession broke out. He was ordered into active service, being killed while in command of the Third Infantry, at Gaines's Mill.

Lieut. Edward Kirby Smith, the dashing Confederate general who kept the Union forces so busy in the Southwest during the Rebellion, was also at the Fox-Wisconsin portage even prior to the establishment of the fort. A stray manuscript leaf from some of the army records left at the fort when it was evacuated, and now in possession of one of the citizens of Portage, contains the proceedings of a court-martial whereat the brevet lieutenant was tried for insubordination, being charged with having "refused to take orders from any d—d militia captain."

Dr. Lyman Foot, eminent as a surgeon and physician—who spent much of his early manhood at various military posts on the frontier, and who was greatly esteemed for his social qualities and professional attainments—was long remembered by early citizens of Portage.

Lieut. John Pegram, who became a distinguished Confederate general, and lost his life in one of the engagements near Petersburg; Lieut. John T. Collinsworth, who resigned in 1836 and became Inspector-General of the Republic of Texas, dying in 1837 at the age of 28; Col. James S. Mcintosh, who was mortally wounded at the Battle of Molino del Rey, in Mexico, in 1846; Lieut. John J. Abercrombie, who commanded the Union forces at the Battle of Palling Waters, one of the first engagements in the late war; Lieut. Alexander S. Hooe, who greatly distinguished himself at the Battles of Palo Alto and Resaca de la Palma, in the latter of which he lost an arm; Lieut. Pinkney Lugenbeel, who was brevetted for gallant and meritorious conduct in the Battles of Contreras, Churubusco and Chapultepec in the Mexican War, and served in the Army of the Potomac; Lieuts. Ferdinand S. Mumford and Samuel B. Hay man, who acquired honourable distinction in the War of Secession, and undoubtedly others of merit whose names do not occur to me, were here.

Little did these young officers, as they gathered around the festive board and sang:—

In the army there's sobriety,
Promotion's very slow,
We'll sigh o'er reminiscences of Benny Havens, O!
Old Benny Havens, O! Old Benny Havens, O!
We'll sigh o'er reminiscences of Benny Havens, O!

. . . . do more than dream of the promotion which was soon to be theirs; but the war with Mexico was near at hand, and promotion came to them very rapidly.

★★★★★★★★★★

Benny Havens was an army melody, very popular at our frontier posts sixty years ago. See "Grant's Appointment to West Point," *McClure's*

Magazine, January, 1897. "Benny Havens" was one of the institutions at West Point—a little tavern and bar on the riverbank, just outside of the reservation. It was considered very wild to slip down to Benny's and smoke a cigar and drink a glass of gin.

★★★★★★★★★★

Among the earliest to arrive at the fort was Capt. Gideon Low, who came here with his command from Green Bay in 1831. In the Black Hawk War, Capt. Low was ordered to Fort Atkinson; and after the danger was over there he returned to Fort Winnebago, where he remained on duty until 1840, when he resigned. Prior to his resignation he built the Franklin House, in 1838, which became so famous as a hostelry in the early days of Portage. Capt. Low died at the agency in 1850, and was buried in the cemetery at the fort; but subsequently his remains were removed to the burial lot of his son-in-law, Henry Merrell, in Silver Lake Cemetery.

Some of those who were not in the service directly, but who were at the fort in various capacities, and who afterward became prominent in public affairs, should be mentioned, as a history of Fort Winnebago would not be complete without recalling them.

The distinguished Hungarian political refugee. Count Agostin Haraszthy, was at the fort and had a contract with the government for supplying the garrison with fuel, his headquarters being on one of the "islands" in the marsh a few miles north of the fort. After leaving here he founded the village of Haraszthy, now called Sauk City, and subsequently removed to California, where he was a man of much prominence in public affairs, being a member of the legislature of that State. Later he directed his energies to affairs in Central America and lost his life there while crossing a lagoon, being drowned, or possibly pulled under by an alligator.

★★★★★★★★★★

Col. (or Count) Agostin Haraszthy was born in 1812, in the *comitat* of Bacska, Hungary, his family having been prominent in Hungarian annals for upwards of 700 years. Educated in the law, he was, at the age of 18, a member of Emperor Ferdinand's body guard (of nobles), later being chief executive officer of his (Haraszthy's) district, and then private secretary of the Hungarian viceroy. Upon the failure of the liberal movement of 1839-40, in which he was engaged, he was compelled to fly to the United States. After extensive travels over our country, he wrote a book (in Hungarian) intended to encourage his fellow countrymen to emigrate to America. In 1840-41 he settled in Wisconsin, near Portage, as related by Mr. Turner in the above text; here he had a large tract of land, which he improved at much cost, making necessary roads and ferries. Gaining permission to return temporarily to Hungary, to surrender certain important State papers to that government, he succeeded in saving $150,000 from his confiscated estates, together with a considerable amount of family plate and paintings.

With this fortune, he returned to Wisconsin (1842-43), and founded what is now Sauk City, where he planted the first hop-yard in our State, and encouraged others to do likewise; he was highly successful with this crop. He became the head of an emigrant association which brought to Wisconsin large and successful colonies of English, German, and Swiss. In 1848, he made considerable contributions of arms, supplies, and money to his revolutionary compatriots in Hungary. The following year (1849) he removed to California, being elected sheriff of San Diego County. He was for many years a prominent citizen of that State, holding important State and national offices.

He is called the Father of Viniculture in California, and published much on that subject—in 1861 being appointed by the governor as special commissioner to visit European vineyards and report thereon; the result of his report was the introduction of 400 distinct varieties of grapes into the Golden State. In 1868, he went to Nicaragua, where, at the head of a company of friends, he obtained valuable privileges for the manufacture of wines and spirits, sugar, and lumber—acquiring 100,000 acres of some of the best land in Central America. It was upon his plantation, the Hacienda San Antonio, near the port of Corinto, that he met his death (July 6, 1870), as stated above by Mr. Turner.

When Haraszthy returned to America in 1842-43, he was accompanied by his mother, who died at Grand Gulf, Miss., 1844-45; and his father (Charles), who, at the age of 80, was buried at sea on his return to San Francisco from Corinto (July 22, 1870). Colonel Haraszthy's wife (née Eleonora Dödinsky) died at Leon, Nicaragua, July 15, 1869; his son. Col. Gaza Haraszthy, died on the family plantation in Nicaragua, December 17, 1878, aged 45; his sons Attila F. and Arpad were born in Hungary and now (1898) live in California; another surviving son (Beba) was born in Sauk City, Wis.; of his two daughters, Ida was born in Peoria, Ill., and Otelia in Madison, Wis.—Original Ed.

****

Of those who were at the Fox-Wisconsin portage in early times, years before the fort had an existence, was Pierre Paquette. He was born at St. Louis in 1796, and married Thérèse Crelie, daughter of the noted Joseph Crelie. (See *Wis. Hist. Colls.*) His early manhood was spent among the Indians in the Far West, in the fur trade. Subsequently he became the agent of the American Fur Company at the portage, and was the agent of Joseph Rolette in the transportation business. He was slain by an Indian named Mauzamoneka (or Iron Walker), in 1836, with whom he had had some trouble, at a spot near the present site of the Catholic church in Portage. He was one of the best known men in the West, and his tragic death produced a sensation equal to what might be experienced if the most distinguished man in Wisconsin today should be assassinated; for he was a famous man in many ways, and was held in the highest esteem by both whites and Indians.

For years after his death, he was the most talked-about man in this section. At the time of his death, he was living across the river, where Judge Barden now resides, and some of the latter's farm buildings were erected by Paquette. His daughter, Thérèse, who is still living, (1898), and a resident of Caledonia, speaks of frequent visits to her father's place by Lieutenant Jefferson Davis and Captain Gideon Low.

Satterlee Clark in writing of him says:—

> He was the very best specimen of a man I ever saw. He was 6 feet 2 inches in height and weighed 200 pounds, hardly ever varying a single pound. He was a very handsome man, hospitable, generous and kind, and I think I never saw a better natured man. (*Wis. Hist. Colls* viii.)

Henry Merrell said of him:—

> He was a man of mild disposition, could neither read nor write, but had as true a sense of honour as any gentleman I ever knew, and all who knew him would take his word as soon as any man's bond. (*Wis. Hist. Colls v..*)

Most fabulous stories were often related of his remarkable strength.

Paquette was buried under the old log church which stood in about the centre of what is now Adams Street, near its junction with Conant Street. The church was burned about 1840, and his resting place was marked by a picket enclosure, after which his remains were removed to the lot in the rear of the present Baptist church, and were buried under the entrance to the "L" in the rear of it.

★★★★★★★★★★

> The church spoken of was the first church in Central Wisconsin, and was built by Paquette for a Dominican priest, Rev. Samuel Mazzuchelli, who came here occasionally to hold services among the Indians and half-breeds, and who in time became distinguished in his order, having founded Saint Clara Academy at Sinsinawa Mound, in Grant County.—A. J. T.

Cf. Moses Paquette's reference to the church built by Pierre Paquette, *Wis. Hist. Colls.*, xii.—Original Ed.

****

Another noted character hereabouts was Jean Baptiste Du Bay, whose trading post was on the hill opposite the fort and just east of the Indian Agency, having succeeded to the interest of Paquette, after the latter's death. He killed William S. Reynolds on the premises in 1857, during a land-title dispute, an event that attracted great interest at the time and which ever after clouded an otherwise honourable career. (*Wis. Hist. Colls. vii.*)

Henry Merrell was at the fort also; he was a sutler there in 1834, and afterwards became the agent of the American Fur Company, filling many positions of honour and trust; he was the first senator from this district when the State was organised, and his descendants have converted the site of the old military fort from its warlike appearance to the more peaceful one of a well-appointed farm. (See Merrell's *Pioneer Life in Wisconsin*, *Wis. Hist. Colls.*, vii.)

So also, Satterlee Clark, who was appointed a sutler by President Jackson in 1830; but being a minor he was unable to take charge of the position in his own name, and it was farmed out to Oliver Newbury of Detroit, Clark becoming his clerk. He devoted the most of his time, however, to the Indian trade. Clark was for many years a senator from Dodge County. He was an admirer of Jefferson Davis, and never suffered an opportunity to pass to sound his praises, even during the most exciting days of the War of Secession. So conspicuous was this habit, that he often found himself in controversy with others who were not in sympathy with him. On one occasion, when it fell to me to introduce him to a public assemblage in Portage, to lecture on early times at the fort, I remarked in a spirit of pleasantry:—

> Our friend who will address you tonight was a companion of Lieutenant Davis at the fort, and it is now impossible to say whether 'Sat' imbibed his secession ideas from 'Jeff,' or whether 'Jeff' obtained his from 'Sat.'

All of which was received by Clark with his accustomed good-nature.

With all of his peculiarities, and often extravagant expressions of speech, he was a most companionable man, and a true courtier to ladies, who admired him. (See his "Early Times at Fort Winnebago," *Wis. Hist. Colls.*, viii.) Clark was married at the old Indian Agency house on the hill just opposite the fort, and still standing, to a daughter of Mr. Jones, the sutler. And here it should be stated that this house was built for John H. Kinzie, the sub-Indian agent, who was a son of John Kinzie, whose name occupies so prominent a page in the early history of Chicago, he being a post-trader at Fort Dearborn at the time of the massacre of the garrison by the Indians in 1812. (Mrs. John H. Kinzie is the author of reminiscences of life at frontier posts, *Wau-Bun* included in this book.).

John H. Kinzie died on a Fort Wayne Railway train January 28, 1865, of heart disease.

When the Kinzies arrived at the fort, they found the Winnebagoes assembled there in anticipation of the arrival of Shawneeawkee (the Indian name for the agent), who was to pay them their annuities. (See *Wau-bun*). Mrs. Kinzie wrote:—

> The woods were now brilliant with many tints of autumn, and the scene around us was further enlivened by groups of Indians in all directions, and their lodges which were scattered here and there in the vicinity of the Agency buildings. On the low grounds might be seen the white tents of the traders, already prepared to send out winter supplies to the Indians, in exchange for the annuity money they were about to receive.
> Preparatory to this event, the great chief of the Winnebago nation, 'Four Legs' (Hootschope), whose village was on Doty's Island at the foot of Lake Winnebago, had thought proper to take a little carouse, as is too apt to be the custom when the savages come into the neighbourhood of a sutler's establishment. In the present instance, the facilities for a season of intoxication had been augmented by the presence on the ground of some traders, too regardless of the very stringent laws prohibiting the sale of liquor to Indians.
> Poor Four Legs could not stand this full tide of prosperity. Unchecked by the presence of his father, the agent, he carried his indulgence to such excess that he fell a victim in the course of a few days. His funeral had been celebrated with unusual pomp the day before our arrival, and great was my disappointment at finding myself too late to witness all the ceremonies.
> His body, according to their custom, having been wrapped in a blanket and placed in a rude coffin along with his guns, tomahawk, pipes, and a quantity of tobacco, had been carried to the

most elevated point of the hill opposite the fort, followed by an immense procession of his people, whooping, beating their drums, howling and making altogether what is emphatically termed a 'powwow.'

After the interment of his body a stake was planted at his head, on which was painted in vermillion a series of hieroglyphics, descriptive of the great deeds and events of his life. The whole was then surrounded with pickets of the trunks of the tamarack trees, and thither the friends would come for many successive days to renew the expression of their grief, and to throw over the grave tobacco and other offerings to the Great Spirit.

We might imagine that the bones of the great Four Legs repose there still, a little in the rear of the Agency building; but they probably do not, for the graves of the Indians were usually very shallow, and the tiller of the soil, as he "drove his team a-field, "would often turn their bones to the surface to be whitened in the sun; and it became in after years quite fashionable for white men to desecrate the Indian graves in pursuit of relics. Frequently no other covering than a roof of slabs, in the form of an upside-down **V** was given to them. The removal of a board would enable one to see the old Indian chief Choukeka or "Spoon Dekorra" sitting upright, with all of his funeral trappings surrounding him. (Not to be confounded with the Spoon Decorah of the next generation, whose narrative is given in *Wis. Hist Colls*, xiii.—Original Ed.) On one occasion, when two of our townsmen, prompted by the spirit of an overweening curiosity, made an inspection of Dekorra's rude mausoleum, to see how the old fellow was getting on, a rabbit was observed keeping vigil with the spirit of the old chieftain.

Continuing her narrative of events occurring at the fort immediately after their arrival, Mrs. Kinzie relates the "calls" they received from the principal chiefs, who had put on their best blankets, gaudiest feathers, and paint to receive their new "mother."

There was Nawkaw or Carrymaunee (The Walking Turtle), who, the principal chief of his tribe, was beside Tecumseh when he fell at the Battle of the Thames, and old "Daykauray,"—Schchipkaka (White War Eagle), as Mrs. Kinzie spells it, but which is always written, locally, "Dekorra."

****

The correct orthography undoubtedly is De Carrie, like that of his father the old chief, who was the reputed grandson of Sebrevoir De

Carrie, an officer in the French Army, who, after resigning his commission in 1729, became an Indian trader among the Winnebagoes, subsequently taking for his wife the head chief's sister. Morning Glory, spoken of as a most remarkable woman. De Carrie returned to the army and was mortally wounded at Quebec, April 28, 1760, and died of his wounds in a hospital at Montreal. Whether this genealogical tree has been correctly established or not, I will not undertake to determine. It is vouched for in Augustin Grignon's Recollections (*Wis. Hist. Colls.*, iii), and by John T. de la Ronde (*Id.*, vii), who was something of an expert in Indian genealogy; and so, let it be accepted as a fact. There certainly are some corroborating and extenuating circumstances to sustain it.

★★★★★★★★★★

Mrs. Kinzie spoke of her caller as:—

The most noble, dignified and venerable of his own, or indeed of any tribe. His fine Roman countenance, rendered still more striking by his bald head, with one solitary tuft of long silvery hair neatly tied and falling back on his shoulders; his perfectly neat, appropriate dress, almost without ornament, and his courteous demeanour, never laid aside under any circumstances, all combining to give him the highest place in the consideration of all who knew him. It will hereafter be seen, that his traits of character were not less grand and striking than were his personal appearance and deportment.

Mrs. Kinzie probably had in mind, when she penned the following paragraph, the time when the Indians were reduced to dire extremities for food. The game had been driven off by the troops and war parties the preceding summer, and soup made of slippery elm and stewed acorns was the only food that many of them had subsisted upon for weeks. Their condition was wretched in the extreme, and could only be relieved by the arrival of the stores that were expected to come up Fox River by the boat. While this condition of affairs existed, Mrs. Kinzie wrote:—

The noble old De-kau-ry came one day from the Barribault (Baraboo) to apprise us of the state in his village. More than forty of his people he said had now been for many days without food, save bark and roots. My husband accompanied him to the commanding officer to tell his story and ascertain if any amount of food could be obtained from that quarter. The result was the promise of a small allowance of flour, sufficient to alleviate the cravings of his own family. When this was explained to the chief, he turned away. 'No,' he said, 'if my people could not be relieved, I and my family will starve with them.' And he refused, for those nearest and dearest to him, the proffered succour, until all could share alike. When at last the boat arrived, the scene of exultation that followed was a memorable one. The bulky 'Wild Cat,' now greatly reduced in flesh from his long fasting, seized the aristocratic 'Washington Woman,' Madame Thunder, and hugged and danced with her in exuberance of their joy.

The old chief died in 1836, at what is known locally as Caffrey's Place, at the foot of the bluff in Caledonia, and was buried in Portage just in the rear of the old log Catholic church, nearly opposite J. E. Wells's residence, according to John T. de la Ronde; but Moses Paquette, in the *Wisconsin Historical Collections* (vol. xiii), states that his death occurred at the Pete-en-Well on the Wisconsin River. When the order was made to remove the bodies of all persons buried there, De-kau-ry's remains were bundled into some boxes promiscuously with others, and they now rest in the Catholic cemetery.

Among the Kinzies' other callers were Black Wolf, Talk English, Little Elk, Wild Cat, White Crow, and Dandy—a nephew of Four Legs, but not the Dandy known to so many of the housewives of Portage, who was omnipresent when pressed with hunger. His pretensions to noble lineage were distinctly repudiated by Yellow Thunder, who regarded his ancestry as tainted with uncertainty. Each of these distinguished callers could point to some special deed or traits of character that elevated him above the common herd, who could not point to so many scalps on their belts, or exhibit other evidences of prowess and greatness.

Among other callers, a little later, was the esteemed Mme. Yellow Thunder, who had been to Washington with Mr. Thunder, and was known by the other Indians as the "Washington Woman." Yellow Thunder had a reputation not a whit less honourable than Dekorra's. The good deeds related of him would fill a volume. His remains repose undisturbed on the west bank of Wisconsin River, a few miles below Kilbourn, where he lived and died, emulating, as well as he could, the virtues of his pale-faced brethren and eschewing their vices. At one time the government at Washington decided to remove him, with the rest of the tribe, to the Winnebago reservation near Omaha, and they did; but the old fellow got back even before the guard who escorted them thither, for he had decided to live in Wisconsin. (See *Wis. Hist. Colls.*, xii.—Ed.) He purchased a farm and became a tiller of the soil, swore allegiance to the government to which he had no occasion to feel grateful, and died at a great age in 1874.

The soldiers, apart from their garrison duties, were detailed to road-making. The old military highway between Fort Crawford (at Prairie du Chien) and Fort Howard (at Green Bay) was constructed wholly by them, and is still in use. Between times, some of the officers found time to go on the chase for deer in the neighbouring forest. An old Indian named Dixon, whose erect form is still frequently seen on Portage streets, loves to tell how he used to paddle a canoe on Swan Lake and in the rice fields for "two good officers" (meaning soldiers of rank) to shoot ducks. He does not remember their names, but one of them had an unusually red head, he assures you, and was always successful in his ducking expeditions. This was probably Lieut. Carter L. Stevenson, who enjoyed the distinction of having a very bright capillary adornment.

So, while old Fort Winnebago's history has not been distinguished by attacks, or massacres, or other stirring scenes, it has not been wholly uneventful.

During the Black Hawk War, which followed the suppression of the Winnebago outbreak, the garrison at the fort was assigned to more active duty. A portion of it was sent to Fort Atkinson to strengthen that post, under command of Captain Low. What remained was so meagre as to invite an attack from the Winnebagoes, of whose good intentions the inmates were not well assured. The approach of Black Hawk, in 1832, was heralded, and consternation prevailed. Satterlee Clark, in his reminiscences, states:—

> In the meantime, Black Hawk, learning from the Winnebagoes, who also promised to assist him, that only thirty men remained in Fort Winnebago, determined to burn it and massacre its inmates. They accordingly came and camped on the Fox River about four miles above Swan Lake, and about eight miles from the fort.

Clark probably meant Winnebagoes instead of Sacs, as some have inferred from his statement; for Black Hawk did not reach Columbia County. He detoured to the south with his braves, and was attacked and put to flight at what is known as the Battle of Wisconsin Heights, in the town of Roxbury, in Dane County, a short distance south of the town of West Point. Some amusing episodes occurred while the attack was in expectancy, but no serious catastrophe resulted.

Mrs. Van Cleve, in writing of her marriage and other occurrences at the fort, has recorded this incident, (*Three Score Years and Ten*):—

> During the following summer (1836) a detachment of troops in command of Col. Zachary Taylor, accompanied by General Brady, came up to Fort Winnebago in consequence of an Indian scare, which was entirely imaginary, and camped on the prairie, just outside the fort. Their coming was a very pleasant event, and the more so because there was not, and never had been, any danger from the Indians, who were very peaceable neighbours. But we enjoyed the visit exceedingly, and the officers were frequently entertained at our quarters, at their meals. Very opportunely for us, the strawberries were abundant, and the flowers, which were beautiful and fresh every morning, were more lovely as ornaments than elegant plate of silver or gold.

At the conclusion of the Black Hawk War, in 1832, a treaty stipulation was entered into for the cession of all the Indian lands south and east of the Fox and Wisconsin rivers. One of the stipulations of the treaty was the surrender of certain individuals of their tribe, accused of having participated with the Sacs in some murders. The men were surrendered, according to agreement, and were confined in the "black-hole," as it was called, being an enormous dungeon under one of the fort buildings, to await trial.

Although careful supervision was exercised, the Indians proceeded to plan their escape, and in about six weeks they had tunnelled their way out under the walls in almost the precise manner that a number of Union officers made their escape from Libby prison thirty years later. That they might be as little encumbered as possible in their flight, they left their blankets behind them; and although it was bitter December weather, they took to the woods and prairies with only their calico shirts and leggins for covering.

The question among the officers of the fort was, how to get the fugitives back. Kinzie, the agent, could promise no more than that he would communicate with the chiefs and represent the wishes of the officers that the prisoners should once more surrender themselves, and thus free those who had the charge of them from the imputation of carelessness, which the government would be very likely to throw upon them. When, therefore, according to their custom, the Winnebago chiefs assembled at the agency on New Year's Day, 1833, the agent laid the subject before them.

The Indians replied that if they saw the young men, they would tell them what the officers would like to have them do. They could themselves do nothing in the matter. They had fulfilled their engagement by bringing them once, and putting them in the hands of the officers. The government had had them in its power once, and could not keep them; it must now go and catch them.

The social amenities of life were not neglected in the least degree by the few ladies who gave grace by their refining presence to fort life. Calls were made and returned then as now, and a lady took her position in a canoe to make or return a call on an acquaintance—at Fort Crawford down the Wisconsin, 118 miles distant, or down the Fox to Fort Howard, about 175 miles away—with less ado and trouble in arranging her toilet for the occasion, than is sometimes experienced by our ladies of today in making a party call across the street. I have frequently heard a gentleman who was accustomed to escort ladies on such occasions, and paddle the canoe, and who made his bridal tour in that manner from the old Agency house to Green Bay, speak of the rare delight of these trips in a birchen canoe.

The venerable W. W. Haskin, who is spending the evening of his life at Pardeeville—one of the very few survivors of those who were at the fort when it was garrisoned—reverts with evident pleasure to an occasion when he chaperoned some ladies at the fort on some of their horseback gallopings in the oak openings about Stone Quarry Hill; and Mrs. Kinzie, a delicate young lady, and a stranger to life beyond the frontier, has told us most entertainingly in her *Wau-Bun*, of her trips to Green Bay by boat, and of her gallops to and from Chicago, sometimes in midwinter, following bridle paths through the forest, fording swollen streams (for of bridges there were none), riding across treacherous marshes and through swamps, braving storms and inclement weather, partaking of Indian diet in their lodges at times, and subsisting as best she might, and remembering it all as a pleasant part of life.

Miss Marcy, daughter of Lieutenant Marcy (she later became the wife of Gen. George B. McClellan), gave the garrison a joy with her childish antics, and I have heard habitues of the fort refer with pride to the times when they dandled the dear little miss on their knees.

The voice of Major Twiggs's daughter, Lizzie, first resounded in the fort in January, 1831, and so she is entitled to the distinction, as I suppose, of being the first white person born within the present limits of Columbia County. (She died at the age of five, in Washington, D. C.)

Mrs. Van Cleve has written:—

> The memory of the weekly musicals at John Kinzie's pleasant agency, and the delightful rides on horseback over the portage to the point where Portage City now stands, quickens my heart even now.

As Mrs. Van Cleve (then Charlotte Ouisconsin Clark) was shortly afterward married to Lieutenant Van Cleve, it is not difficult to guess who her escort was on these occasions. It is recorded that the ladies, ever foremost in good works, had a Sunday school in progress at the chapel, and let us feel well assured the lessons they taught were fruitful of good results.

Neither was education, temporal or spiritual, neglected, as we learn from W. C. Whitford's paper on "Early History of Education in Wisconsin" (*Wis. Hist. Colls.*, V), that Maj. John Green, commanding officer at Fort Winnebago, engaged, in 1835, Miss Eliza Haight as governess in his family; he allowed the children of other officers at the fort to attend the school. There were in all about a dozen pupils. In the spring of 1840, Rev. S. P. Keyes became both chaplain and schoolmaster of the fort, and taught about twenty children, some of them over twelve years of age.

In the spring of 1833, the garrison was excited over the arrival of a clergyman, the Rev. Aratus Kent, of Galena, who was accompanied by his wife. Mrs. Kinzie wrote:—

> This event is memorable as being the first occasion on which the gospel, according to the Protestant faith, was preached at Fort Winnebago. The large parlour of the hospital was fitted up for the service, and gladly did we say to each other:
> 'Let us go to the house of the Lord!' For nearly three years had we lived here without the blessing of a public service of praise and thanksgiving. We regarded this commencement as an omen of better times, and our little 'sewing society' worked with renewed industry to raise a fund which might be available hereafter in securing the permanent services of a missionary."

The efforts of the ladies in their religious work were sometimes

INDIAN AGENCY HOUSE, FORT WINNEBAGO.

Formerly occupied by Mrs. John H. Kinzie, author of *Wau-Bun*, and now the farm house of E. S. Baker.

turned in the direction of the Indians. Explaining the nature of their efforts to our old friend Dandy, he responded:—

> That is right; I am glad to see you doing your, duty; I am very religious myself and I like to see others so. I always take care that my squaws attend to their duties, not reading, perhaps, but such as the Great Spirit liked, and such as I think proper and becoming.

The chapel, after the evacuation of the fort, continued to be used as such, and the late Rev. William Wells and the late Rev. Isaac Smith were accustomed to officiate there. The building is now one of the farm buildings on the Helmann farm, a little east of the old fort.

The spirit of speculation was also abroad, and army officers and their thrifty friends invested in government lands, and laid out on paper many a promising village. One of these embraced a considerable tract of land adjoining the military reserve on the east, fronting in part on Swan Lake and extending back to Stone Quarry Hill, to which was given the pretentious name of "Wisconsinapolis". When the capital of the State was being located, the embryo city received six affirmative votes, to seven in the negative.

This proposition has been thought by some, unacquainted with its natural advantages, to have been a preposterous one; as a matter of fact, it was a most eligible and appropriate location for the capital. Another village, called "Ida," occupies the precise spot on Swan Lake, platted last year as Oakwood, which promises to become a popular resort. Another one on the south side of Swan Lake was called "Winnebago City," but better known in the east as "Swan Lake City," and now much better known as "Wardle's Farm."

While the officers hunted and fished, and speculated in wild lands and city lots by day, and indulged in games and festivities and theatricals at night, and the ladies knit and crocheted and did bead work and conducted Sabbath schools, and attended to their household duties as well as they could with their surroundings, the soldiers stood sentry, and between times visited the sutler's stores and trading posts, and made merry generally by day and sang "Benny Havens, O!" by night. In brief, army life at Fort Winnebago was very much like army life elsewhere. Athletics and theatricals, games and races, relieved the tedium; and discipline and demoralisation, vice and virtue went hand in hand.

****

The celebrated English writer, Frederick Marryat, journeyed through Wisconsin in 1837, and in his Diary in America (London, 1839, 2 vols.), vol. 1, records his visit to Fort Winnebago: "Fort Winnebago is situated between the Fox and Wisconsin Rivers at the portage, the two rivers being about a mile and a half apart, the Fox River running east, and giving its waters to Lake Michigan at Green Bay, while the Wisconsin turns to the west and runs into the Mississippi at Prairie du Chien. The fort is merely a square of barracks, connected together with palisades, to protect it from the Indians, and it is hardly sufficiently strong even for that purpose. It is beautifully situated, and when the country fills up will become a place of importance. Most of the officers are married and live a very quiet and secluded but not unpleasant life. I stayed there two days, much pleased with the society, and the kindness shown to me; but an opportunity of descending the Wisconsin to Prairie du Chien, in a keel boat, having presented itself, I availed myself of an invitation to join the party, instead of proceeding by land to Galena, as had been my original intention."

★★★★★★★★★★

The old fort, however, like all earthly things, had its day. The approaching war with Mexico had reached its threatening stage; and preparatory for it, orders for the evacuation were issued in 1845, the troops being sent to St. Louis to relieve those stationed at Jefferson Barracks, who had been ordered to the Gulf, and a little later they followed them to the sanguinary fields of Mexico. When the evacuation took place, the fort was left in charge of Sergeant Van Camp; but he died shortly after, when Capt. William Weir was placed in charge, he having been a soldier in the Florida War and afterward at the fort. Later, he was a soldier in the War of Secession. In 1853, the property was sold under the direction of Jefferson Davis, then secretary of war, who, as lieutenant in the army twenty-three years before, had assisted in the construction of the fort.

★★★★★★★★★★

The following is a copy of a letter from the secretary of war to the president, regarding the reservation at Fort Winnebago:

War Department, Washington, July 26, 1851.—Sir: By an order made on or before the 28th day of February and written upon a plat of the public lands adjacent to Fort Winnebago, the President directed that (among others) section 4 in township 12 north, and section 33 in township 13 north, range 9 east, be reserved for military purposes. At the time this order was made these sections had not been laid out in full, they were, as will appear by a copy of the plat bearing the president's order herewith marked D, situated on the western limit of the public domain and portions of them, if the lines had been run out, would have fallen within the country then belonging to an Indian tribe. The unsurveyed portions were, however, occupied for public purposes, and buildings were erected and one still standing thereon. By a treaty made in 1848 the Indians have ceded their land in that vicinity to the United States, and when it is surveyed and the lines of sections 4 and 33 completed, the portions of those sections lying within the newly acquired territory will be designated as fractional sections 4 and 33 lying west, etc., etc.

I am now advised by the commissioner of the general land office, in a letter herewith marked E, that agreeably to the understanding of his office the executive order as it now stands will not embrace these fractions; "but they will be subject to the operations of the general pre-emption law as other public lands as soon as they shall be surveyed, unless the President acting under advices to be given to that effect by the war department, shall deem it proper to add those portions to the existing reserve made for the use of the fort by President Jackson and in advance of the time of the survey of the same when the pre-emption right can legally attach to them."

Although I think it doubtful under the circumstances whether a pre-emption right could legally attach to these lands, embraced as they are by the terms of the President's order and actually occupied under it, yet to obviate any difficulty I deem it best to pursue the course suggested by the commissioner of the general land office and recommend that "the tract of land which when surveyed will be denominated fractional section 33 lying west of Fox River in township 13 north of range 9 east "and "fraction of section 4 lying west of claim No. 21 of A. Grignon in township 12 north, range 9 east," adjacent to Fort Winnebago, Wisconsin, be reserved from sale in fulfilment of the original order of President Jackson above cited.

Very respectfully, your obedient servant,

C. M. Conway,
Secretary of War.

To the President—(Approve)—Approved July 29, 1851, and ordered accordingly.

Millard Filmore.

****

Prior to the sale, the board of supervisors of Columbia County, January 7, 1852, formally adopted a memorial asking congress to grant the military reserve at Fort Winnebago for the benefit of the Fox and Wisconsin River improvement. Just why there should have been a desire to donate these lands to a private company, is hard to understand. If Congress had been asked to donate the reservation to the State,

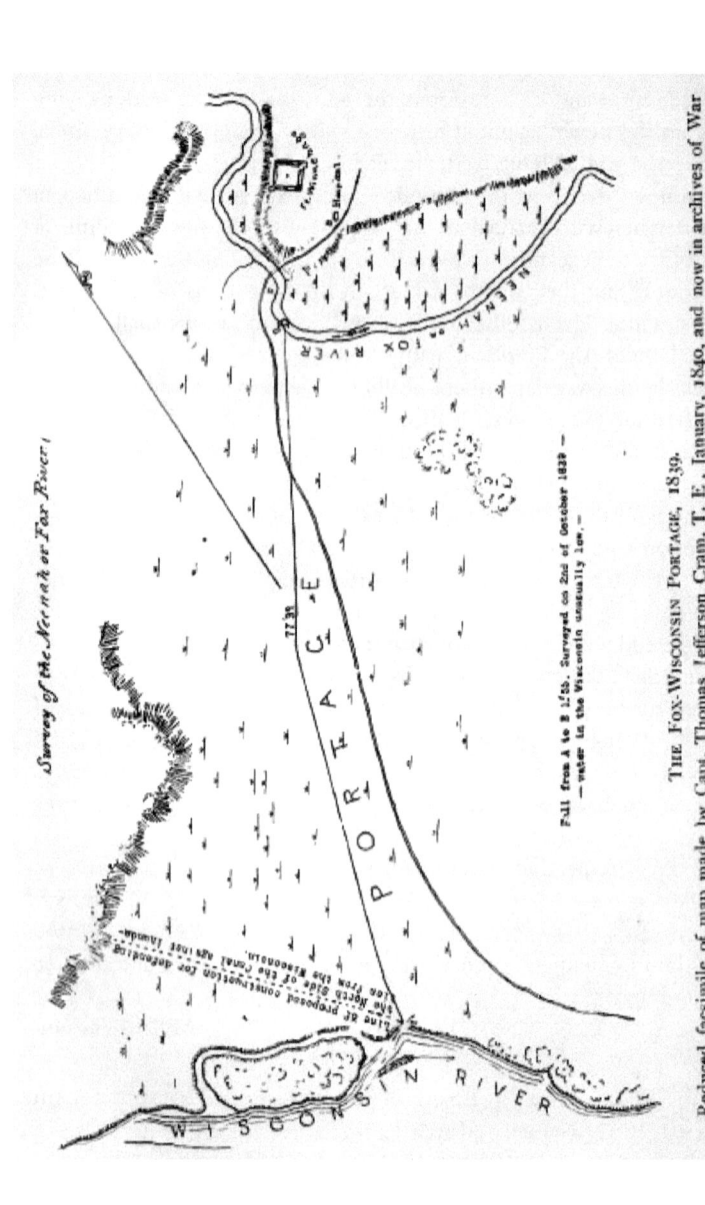

THE FOX-WISCONSIN PORTAGE, 1839.

Reduced facsimile of map made by Capt. Thomas Jefferson Cram, T. E., January, 1840, and now in archives of War Department, Washington. Survey made October 2, 1839, by Lieut. Webster, under direction of Captain Cram. The line from A to B, represents the route of the proposed government canal; the double line, is the old portage trail.

very likely it would have been done, as it is the practice of late years to donate abandoned military reservations to the States in which they are situated, for public purposes. It can only be regretted now that it had not been done in this instance. If it had been, the most important results might have followed.

It has been a matter of regret, often expressed, that the old fort should have been allowed to go to decay. (A destructive fire occurred in the officers' quarters, March 30, 1856, destroying one of the principal sections of the fort.) It certainly is to be regretted that the historic old spot could not have been donated to the State, but there was no reason why the fort should have been maintained. All occasion for it had passed forever, and in the natural order of events the buildings went to decay. H. D. Bath, editor of the Columbus Democrat, visited it in 1871, and gave his impressions of it as it then appeared, in an article published at the time:—

> Duration and desuetude have been busy upon it. Most of the buildings stand, but they are sadly dismantled and decayed. One of the small yet massive blockhouses was burned simultaneously with the line of buildings forming the end of the quadrangle just within the defences. The other remains, but it has been prostituted to bovine purposes. A domestic quadruped of that species shelters herself from the nightly attacks of the weather, in the strong enclosure built for refuge from the fury of the savage. On several of the edifices used for officers' quarters and similar accommodations, the massy roofing has descended almost to the ground, and barely depends, in crumpled decay, over the faces of the buildings, as when dilapidation seizes upon human ruins obtruding the tatters into their very eyes. The timbers were all of the best pine.
>
> The weather, however, if a slow hewer, is one that never rests and they must soon come down. The battered well with its forty feet of depth, and its never-failing waters, remains in the centre of the square, and answers the purpose. Yet the roofed curb and heavy roller, worn with much yielding of pure refreshment, appear about to make a grave of the shaft beneath it, and is in a condition to improvise a tomb for any drawer of water that gives it a call. The magazine wards off the worm as only stone can. Its safe interior has been transmitted into a *boudoir* for a new-milch cow. The stone bakery is also in a good

state of preservation; what use poverty, which makes men burrow wherever they can, has put this to, we did not observe.

The only human figure to be discerned about the premises was a red-shirted Celt, pantalooned in what might be the cast-off undress of some former *commandant* long since gone to glory, and the child he carried in his arms, though there were flitting in one of the better-preserved buildings, evidences of further family, present and future. He and his brood are the only life now in these former haunts, once so full of frontier life and military animation.

The outward walls are littered with posters, ruptured with winds and rains, and placarded with the names of firms telling you where to purchase watches, or adjuring you to buy some nostrum incompatible with debility or death. Silence and abandonment, two owls ancient and voiceless, brood over the place. Existence passes it, but seldom stops. Its early origin and associations attract you thither; then curiosity melts with sadness at its desolation, and you turn from the ruin with no care to visit it again."

The old ruins, however, so graphically described, have at last passed away. Fires destroyed some of them and the balance were razed by purchasers who have converted their timbers into barns and stables. The old commissary building, and a portion of the surgeon's quarters and of the hospital, still remain. Much of the land embraced within the reservation now comprises the stock farm of Merrell & Hainsworth, while the Merrell residence occupies the old fort premises. The well continues to do duty as of yore, and the stump of the old flag-staff is still pointed out to visitors.

Lieutenant Davis, in speaking of his career at the fort, once remarked to a former Portage lady, who met him at his home in Beauvoir, Miss., that to procure this staff was a matter of considerable anxiety to him. No timber entirely suitable for the purpose could be found near the fort. Two men, who had been consulted, informed them that the stick must be at least sixty feet in length, tapering gradually to a point, and so free from defects that it would sway gracefully when the flag was given to the breeze; and they were bargained with to bring such a one to the fort.

The fixtures and furniture left at the fort when it was evacuated, were disposed of at auction or carried away at will, and many a family in the vicinage can boast of some old fort relic; the famous "Davises" could have been found in the inventories of the household effects of some families, and they may be in existence somewhere yet, for aught I know. An old sideboard that was in service at the Agency, presumably Mrs. Kinzie's, is one of the treasures in James Collins's household; and a bureau and sideboard, which constituted a part of the furniture in one of the officer's quarters, is in possession of Mrs. O. P. Williams; as is also the old carved wooden eagle that was perched over the main entrance.

As a necessary adjunct to the fort, a cemetery was established. It was not largely populated from the garrison, and the graves of none of the soldiers who died there during its occupancy are marked by stones. Major Clark and Captain Low were buried there; but, as already stated, their remains were finally removed to family grounds elsewhere. Robert Irwin, Jr., the Indian agent, died there July, 1833. Sergt. William Weir and Private Henry Carpenter were buried there in after years, and their final resting places are appropriately marked.

****

The grave of one of the veterans, of the Revolution, who was buried there, is discernible, the stone marking it bearing this inscription: Cooper Pixley, Died, Mar. 12, 1855 Æ 86 y., 7 m., 26 D, Soldier of the Revolution.

****

The cemetery seems to have been made general for the public for a period, and not a few of the families of citizens, more or less prominent, were buried there; but finally, the national authorities took it directly in charge and built a substantial fence around it, and restricted its use to the military. Burials there in the future must be very few indeed; but it should be the duty of the national government to care for it more befittingly in the future.

The surrender of Red Bird and his accomplices in the Gagnier murder, heretofore referred to, may be said to have marked the close of the Winnebago War (1827). While the troops were in pursuit of the murderers, the old Indian chief, De-kau-ry, was seized as a hostage for the surrender of Red Bird, although he was charged with no offense himself. He was informed that if the offenders were not given up within a certain time, he would be executed himself. A messenger was sent out to inform the tribe of the situation, but no tidings came, and the time had nearly expired. Being in poor health, the old chief asked permission to go to the river and bathe, as he long had been accustomed to do.

He was informed by Colonel Josiah Snelling that if he would promise, upon the honour of a chief, that he would not leave, he might have his liberty until his time had expired; whereupon he gave his hand to the colonel and promised that he would not leave; then he raised both hands aloft, and in the most solemn manner promised that he would not go beyond the limits accorded to him, saying that if he had a hundred lives he would rather lose them all than forfeit his word. He was set at liberty, and was advised to make his escape, for there was no desire to shoot the old fellow, who had been guilty of no wrong himself. "No! Do you think I prize life above honour?" was his only reply. Nine of the ten days allotted to him had passed, and regularly at sunset of every day De-kau-ry reported to the colonel; but nothing was heard from the murderers. On the last day, General Henry Atkinson arrived with his troops, and the order for his execution was countermanded.

After the murder of Gagnier, Red Bird and the other Indians implicated in the affair, fled up the Wisconsin River, and a mounted force to operate against the Winnebagoes as a body scoured both sides of the river up to Portage. Maj. William Whistler, who was in command at Fort Howard (Green Bay), had been ordered by General Atkinson to go up the Fox to the portage, with any force at his disposal. A company of Oneida and Stockbridge Indians accompanied Whistler's troops, and were encamped on the bluff opposite the portage where Fort Winnebago was subsequently built, to await the arrival of the general.

In the meantime, the Winnebagoes to the number of several hundred were encamped on the ridge along where Cook Street now runs, west of the Catholic church. The Winnebagoes had heard of Atkinson's approach and Col. Henry Dodge's pursuit, before they were known to Whistler, and in a few days a great stir was discovered among the Indians. A party of thirty warriors was observed, by the aid of a field glass, on an eminence in the distance. It was Red Bird and his party, coming in to surrender. The details of the surrender of Red Bird have been most graphically described by the historians of the period. I would particularly advise the reader to examine the admirable account of the affair in Colonel McKenney's "The Winnebago War of 1827," in the *Wisconsin Historical Collections*, vol. v. The heroism of Red Bird and his friend We-kau was one of the most remarkable incidents in the annals of our Indian wars.'

The prisoners were sent to Prairie du Chien for trial, before Judge Doty. They were convicted, but for some cause sentence was deferred. While confined, Red Bird sickened and died—committed suicide, Mrs. Kinzie says, in *Wau-Bun*, in consequence of chagrin, the ignominy of his confinement being more than his proud spirit could bear; he had expected death. The historian, William R. Smith, who came to the Territory at a very early period, and was familiar with Indian character, speaking of the affair in his *History of Wisconsin*, states: —

> The delay of administering justice was to the Indian a matter not comprehended; they scarcely in any instance deny an act which they have committed, and do not understand why punishment should not be immediately inflicted on the guilty. The imprisonment of the body is to them a most insufferable grievance, and they look upon the act as cowardice on the part of the whites, presuming that they dare not inflict such punishment as the crime demands.

Red Bird's accomplices were subsequently sentenced to be hung December 26, 1828; but before that date they were pardoned by President Adams, one of the implied conditions being that the Indians should cede to the government the lands the miners had already appropriated to their use. Mrs. Gagnier was compensated for the loss of her husband and the mutilation of her infant. At the treaty in Prairie du Chien, in 1829, provision was made for two sections of land to her and her two children; and the government agreed to pay her the sum of $50 *per annum* for fifteen years, to be deducted from the annuity of the Winnebago Indians. This was the last act in the Winnebago outbreak.

The Winnebago War of 1827
By Charles R. Tuttle

THE WINNEBAGO OUTRAGES

In the early part of the year 1827, a party of twenty-four Chippewas, being on their way to Fort Snelling, at the mouth of St. Peter's River, were surprised and attacked by a war-party of the Winnebagoes; and eight of them were killed. The *commandant* of the United States troops at the fort took four of the offending Winnebagoes prisoners, and (certainly with great imprudence) delivered them into the hands of the exasperated Chippewas. who immediately put them to death. This act was greatly resented by a chief of the Winnebagoes, named Red Bird, and in addition to this source of enmity was to be added the daily encroachment of the whites in the lead-region; for at this time, they had overrun the mining-country from Galena to the Wisconsin River. In the spirit of revenge for the killing of the four Winnebagoes, Red Bird led a war-party against the Chippewas, by whom he was defeated, and thus, having been disappointed, he turned the force of his resentment against the whites, whom he considered as having not only invaded his country, but as having aided and abetted his enemies in the destruction of his people.

Sometime previously, a murder by the Winnebagoes had been committed in the family of a Mr. Methode, near Prairie du Chien, in which several persons had been killed. It was apparent that a spirit of enmity between the Indians and the whites had been now effectually stirred up; and, for the first time since the war of 1812, disturbances were daily looked for by the settlers and miners.

On the 28th of June, 1827, Red Bird, We-Kaw, and three of their companions, entered the house of Registre Gagnier, about three miles from Prairie du Chien, where they remained several hours. At last, when Mr. Gagnier least expected it. Red Bird levelled his gun, and shot him dead on his hearthstone. A person in the building, by the name of Sip Cap, who was a hired man, was slain at the same time by We-Kaw. Madame Gagnier turned to fly with her infant of eighteen months. As she was about to leap through the window, the child was torn from her arms by We-Kaw, stabbed, scalped, and thrown violently on the floor as dead.

The murderer then attacked the woman, but gave way when she snatched up a gun that was leaning against the wall, and presented it to his breast. She then effected her escape. Her eldest son, a lad of ten years, also shunned the murderers; and they both arrived in the village at the same time. The alarm was soon given; but, when the avengers of blood arrived at Gagnier's house, they found in it nothing living but his mangled infant. It was carried to the village, and, incredible as it may seem, it recovered.

Red Bird and his companions immediately proceeded from the scene of their crime to the rendezvous of their band. During their absence, thirty-seven of the warriors who acknowledged the authority of Red Bird, had assembled, with their wives and children, near the mouth of the Bad Axe River. They received the murderers with joy, and loud approbation of their exploit. A keg of liquor which they had secured was set abroach; and the red men began to drink, and, as their spirits rose, to boast of what they had already done and intended to do.

Two days did they continue to revel; and on the third the source of their excitement gave out. They were, at about four in the afternoon. dissipating the last fumes of their excitement in the scalp-dance, when they descried one of the keel-boats, which had a few days before passed up the river with provisions for the troops at Fort Snelling, on her return in charge of Mr. Lindsay. Forthwith a proposal to take her, and massacre the crew, was made, and carried by acclamation. They counted upon doing this without risk; for they had examined her on the way up, and supposed there were no arms on board.

Mr. Lindsay's boats had descended the river as far as the village of Wa-ba-shaw, where they expected an attack. The Dakotahs on shore were dancing the war-dance, and hailed their approach with insults and menaces, but did not, however, offer to obstruct their passage. The whites now supposed the danger over; and, a strong wind at that moment beginning to blow upstream, the boats parted company. So strong was the wind, that all the force of the sweeps could scarcely stem it; and, by the time the foremost boat was near the encampment at the mouth of the Bad Axe River, the crew were very willing to stop and rest.

One or two Frenchmen, or half-breeds, who were on board, observed hostile appearances on shore, and advised the rest to keep in the middle of the stream; but their counsel was disregarded as most of the crew were Americans, who, as usual with our countrymen, combined a profound ignorance of Indian character with a thorough contempt for Indian prowess. They urged the boat directly toward the camp with all the force of the sweeps. There were sixteen men on deck. It may be well to observe here, that this, like all keelboats used in the Mississippi Valley, was built almost exactly on the model of the Erie and Middlesex Canal boats.

The men were rallying their French companions on their apprehension, and the boat (named *Oliver H. Perry*) was within thirty yards of the shore, when suddenly the trees and rocks rang with the blood-chilling, ear-piercing tones of the war-whoop; and a volley of rifle-balls rained upon the deck. Happily, the Winnebagoes had not yet recovered from the effects of their debauch, and their arms were not steady. One man only fell from their fire. He was a little negro named Peter. His leg was dreadfully shattered, and he afterwards died of the wound. A second volley soon came from the shore; but, as the men were lying at the bottom of the boat, they all escaped but one, who was shot through the heart.

Encouraged by the non-resistance, the Winnebagoes rushed to their canoes, with intent to board. The whites, having recovered from their first panic, seized their arms; and the boarders were received with a very severe discharge. In one canoe, two savages were killed with the same bullet, and several were wounded. The attack was continued until night, when one of the party (named Mandeville), who had assumed command, sprang into the water, followed by four others, who succeeded in setting the boat afloat, and went down the stream.

Thirty-seven Indians were engaged in this battle, seven of whom were killed, and fourteen wounded. They managed to put six hundred and ninety-three bullets into and through the boat. Two of the crew were killed outright, two mortally, and two slightly wounded. The presence of mind of Mandeville undoubtedly saved the rest, as well as the boat. Mr. Lindsay's boat, the rear one, did not reach the mouth of the Bad Axe until midnight. The Indians opened a fire upon her, which was promptly returned; but, owing to the darkness, no injury was done, and the boat passed on safely.

The date of the attack on these keel-boats is stated by Judge J. H. Lockwood to have been June 26. Gen. Smith's *History of Wisconsin* says

June 30, on the authority of Judge Doty. It is, however, quite certain, that the murder of the Gagnier family, and the boat-attacks, were on the same day.

Great was the alarm at Prairie du Chien when the boats arrived there. The people left their houses and farms, and crowded into the dilapidated fort. An express was immediately sent to Galena, and another to Fort Snelling, for assistance. A company of upwards of a hundred volunteers soon arrived from Galena, and the minds of the inhabitants were quieted. In a few days, four imperfect companies arrived from Fort Snelling. The consternation of the people of the lead-mines was great, and in all the frontier settlements. This portion of the country then contained, as is supposed, about five thousand inhabitants. A great many of them fled from the country.

The Winnebago War

On the 1st of September, 1827, Major William Whistler, with government troops, arrived at the portage; and, while here, an express arrived from Gen. Atkinson, announcing his approach, and directing the former to halt and fortify himself at the portage, and wait his arrival. The object of the joint expedition of Gen. Atkinson from Jefferson barracks, below St. Louis, and of Major Whistler from Fort Howard, on Green Bay, was to capture those who had committed the murders at Prairie du Chien, and put a stop to any further aggression. At the opening of the council at La Butte des Morts, between the government and the Indians, the Winnebagoes were advised that the security of their people lay in the surrender of the murderers of the Gagnier family.

While Major Whistler was at the portage, he received a call in a mysterious way. An Indian came to his tent, and informed him, that, at about three o'clock the next day, "they will come in." In reply to the question, "Who will come in?" he said, "Red Bird and We-Kau."

After making this answer, he retired by the way he came. At three o'clock the same day, another Indian came, and took position in nearly the same place, and in the same way, when, to like questions, he gave like answers; and at sundown a third came, confirming what the two had said, adding that he had, to secure that object, given to the families of the murderers nearly all his property.

Col. McKenney in his *Tour of the Lakes*, 1827, who accompanied Judge Doty as one of the commissioners to meet the Indians at La Butte des Mort, and who was of Major Whistler's party, referring to this matter, says:—

There was something heroic in this voluntary surrender. The giving-away of property to the families of the guilty parties had nothing to do with their determination to devote themselves for the good of their people, but only to reconcile those who were about to be bereaved to the dreadful expedient. The heroism of the purpose is seen in the fact that the murders committed at Prairie du Chien were not wanton, but in retaliation for wrongs committed on this people by the whites. The parties murdered at the prairie were, doubtless, innocent of the wrongs and outrages of which the Indians complained; but the law of Indian retaliation does not require that he alone who commits a wrong shall suffer for it. One scalp is held due for another, no matter whose head is taken, provided it be torn from the crown of the family, or people who may have made a resort to this law a necessity.

About noon of the day following, says the same writer:—

There were seen descending a mound on the portage a body of Indians. Some were mounted, and some were on foot. By the aid of a glass, we could discern the direction to be towards our position. They bore no arms, and we were at no loss to understand that the promise made by the three Indians was about to be fulfilled. In the course of half an hour, they had approached within a short distance of the crossing of Fox River, when on a sudden we heard a singing. Those who were familiar with the air said, 'It is a death-song.' When still nearer, some present, who knew him, said, 'It is Red Bird singing his death-song.' The moment a halt was made, preparatory to crossing over, two scalp-yells were heard.

The Menomonees and other Indians who had accompanied us were lying carelessly about the ground, regardless of what was going on; but, when the 'scalp-yells' were uttered, they sprang as one man to their feet, seized their rifles, and were ready for battle. They were at no loss to know what these 'yells' were; but they had not heard with sufficient accuracy to decide whether they indicated scalps to be taken or given, but doubtless inferred the first.

Barges were sent across to receive, and an escort of military to accompany them within our lines. The white flag which we had seen in the distance was borne by Red Bird.

And now the advance of the Indians had reached half up the ascent of the bluff on which was our encampment. In the lead was Car-i-mi-nie, a distinguished chief. Arriving on the level upon which was our encampment, and order being called, Car-i-mi-nie spoke, saying, 'They are here. Like braves they have come in; treat them as braves; do not put them in irons.' This address was made to me. I told him I was not the big captain. His talk must be made to Major Whistler, who would, I had no doubt, do what was right. Mr. Marsh, the sub-agent, being there, an advance was made to him, and a hope expressed that the prisoners might be turned over to him.

For the remainder of the incidents connected with this surrender Mr. McKenney quotes from a letter addressed by him to Hon. James Barbour, Secretary of War:—

> The military had been previously drawn out in a line. The Menomonee and Wabanackie (Oneida) Indians were in groups, upon their haunches, on our left flank. On the right was the band of music, a little in advance of the line. In front of the centre, about ten paces distant, were the murderers. On their right and left were those who had accompanied thorn, forming a semicircle; the magnificent Red Bird and the miserable-looking We-Kau a little in advance of the centre.
>
> All eyes were fixed on the Red Bird, as well they might be; for, of all the Indians I oversaw, he is, without exception, the most perfect in form, face, and gesture. In height he is about six feet, straight, but without restraint. His proportions arc those of most exact symmetry; and these embrace the entire man, from his head to his feet. During my attempted analysis of this face, I could not but ask myself. Can this man be a murderer?
>
> He and We-Kau were told to sit down. At this moment the band struck up Pleyel's Hymn. Everything was still. Red Bird turned his eyes toward the band. The music having ceased, he took up his pouch, and, taking from it *kinnikinic* and tobacco, cut the latter in the palm of his hand, after the Indian fashion; then, rubbing the two together, filled the bowl of his *calumet*, struck fire on a bit of punk with his flint and steel, lighted, and smoked it. All sat, except the speaker. The subject of what they said was as follows:—
>
> They were required to bring in the murderers. They had no

power over any, except two: the third had gone away; and these had voluntarily agreed to come in, and give themselves up. As their friends, they had come with them. They hoped their white brothers would agree to accept the horses, of which there were, perhaps, twenty; the meaning of which was, to take them in commutation for the lives of their two friends. They asked kind treatment for them, and earnestly besought that they might not be put in irons, and concluded by asking for a little tobacco, and something to eat.

They were answered, and told in substance that they had done well thus to come in. By having done so, they had turned away our guns, and saved their people. They were admonished against placing themselves in a like situation in the future, and advised, when they were aggrieved, not to resort to violence, but to go to their agent, who would inform the Great Father of their complaints, and he would redress their grievances; that their friends should be treated kindly, and tried by the same laws by which their Great Father's white children were tried; that, for the present, Red Bird and We-Kau should not be put in irons; that they should all have something to eat, and tobacco to smoke.

Having heard this, Red Bird stood up; the commanding officer, Major Whistler, a few paces in front of the centre of the line, facing him. After a moment's pause, and a quick survey of the troops, he spoke, saying, '*I am ready.*' Then, advancing a step or two, he paused, saying, 'I do not wish to be put in irons. Let me be free. I have given away my life: *it is gone.*' (stooping, and taking some dust between his finger and thumb, and blowing it away), 'like that,' eying the dust as it fell and vanished from his sight, adding, 'I would not take it back: *it is gone.*'

Having thus spoken, he threw his hands behind him, and marched up to Major Whistler, breast to breast. A platoon was wheeled backwards from the centre of the line, when, the major stepping aside, Red Bird and We-Kau marched through the line, in charge of a file of men, to a tent provided for them in the rear, where a guard was set over them. The comrades of the two captives then left the ground by the way they had come, taking with them our advice, and a supply of meat, flour, and tobacco.

We-Kau, the miserable-looking being, the accomplice of Red

Bird, was in all things the opposite of that unfortunate brave. Never were two persons so totally unlike. The one seemed a prince, and as if born to command, and worthy to be obeyed; the other, as if he had been born to be hanged—meagre, cold, dirty in his person and dress, crooked in form, like the starved wolf, gaunt, hungry, and bloodthirsty; his entire appearance indicating the presence of a spirit wary, cruel, and treacherous. The prisoners were committed into safe keeping at Prairie du Chien, to await their trial in the regular courts of justice for murder.

In the course of the year, the people of the lead-mines increased in numbers and in strength, and encroached upon the Winnebago lands. The Winnebagoes complained in vain. The next spring the murderers of Methode and the other Indian prisoners were tried, convicted, and sentenced to death. A deputation of the tribe went to Washington to solicit their pardon. President Adams granted it on the implied condition that the tribe would cede the lands then in the possession of the miners. The Winnebagoes have kept their word, and Madame Gagnier has been compensated for the loss of her husband and the mutilation of her infant. At the treaty held at Prairie du Chien in 1829, provision was made for two sections of land to Madame Gagnier and her two children; and the government agreed to pay her the sum of fifty dollars *per annum* for fifteen years, to be deducted from the annuity to the Winnebago Indians.

Red Bird died in prison; and We-Kau died of the smallpox at the prairie, in 1836. In closing this account of the troubles at Prairie du Chien, we give an anecdote which places the Winnebago character in a more amiable light than any before related. The militia of Prairie du Chien, immediately after the affair of the boats, seized the old chief, De-kau-ray, and four other Indians; and he was informed, that, if Red Bird should not be given up within a certain time, he and the others were to die in his place. This he steadfastly believed. A messenger, a young Indian, was sent to inform the tribe of the state of affairs; and several days had elapsed, and no information was received of the murderers.

The dreadful day was near at hand; and De-kau-ray, being in bad state of health, asked permission of the officer to go to the river to indulge in his long-accustomed habit of bathing in order to improve his health; upon which Col. Snelling told him, if he would promise, on the honour of a chief, that he would not leave town, he might have his liberty, and enjoy all his privileges, until the day appointed for his execution. Accordingly, he first gave his hand to the colonel, thanking him for his friendly offer, then raised both hands aloft, and in the most solemn adjuration promised that he would not leave the bounds prescribed; and said, if he had a hundred lives, he would sooner lose them all than forfeit his word. He was then set at liberty. He was advised to flee to the wilderness, and make his escape.

"But no!" said he: "do you think I prize life above honour?" He then complacently remained until nine days of the ten which he had to live had elapsed, and still nothing was heard promising the apprehension of the murderers. His immediate death became apparent; but no alteration could be seen in the countenance of the chief. It so happened, that, on that day. Gen. Atkinson arrived, with his troops, from Jefferson barracks; and the order for the execution was countermanded, and the Indians permitted to return to their homes.

"There can be no doubt," says Judge Doty, "that the murder referred to was intended by the Winnebagoes as the first act of hostility in the commencement of a war upon the whites."

It is an error that many writers have fallen into, in saying that some of the Indians implicated in this tragedy were executed. This is not so: no one was executed.

This outbreak was generally termed the "Winnebago War," in contra-distinction to the Black Hawk war of 1832. This first outbreak was soon quieted. The restoration of tranquillity brought with it, as before remarked, an influx of miners and settlers in the lead-region; and an impulse was quickly given to a great portion of Western Wisconsin, which afforded every promise of future prosperity. The lake-shore and the interior of the Territory did not, as yet, in any considerable degree, receive the benefits of industrial immigration.

ALSO FROM LEONAUR
AVAILABLE IN SOFTCOVER OR HARDCOVER WITH DUST JACKET

A DIARY FROM DIXIE by *Mary Boykin Chesnut*—A Lady's Account of the Confederacy During the American Civil War

FOLLOWING THE DRUM by *Teresa Griffin Vielé*—A U. S. Infantry Officer's Wife on the Texas frontier in the Early 1850's

FOLLOWING THE GUIDON by *Elizabeth B. Custer*—The Experiences of General Custer's Wife with the U. S. 7th Cavalry.

LADIES OF LUCKNOW by *G. Harris & Adelaide Case*—The Experiences of Two British Women During the Indian Mutiny 1857. A Lady's Diary of the Siege of Lucknow by G. Harris, Day by Day at Lucknow by Adelaide Case

MARIE-LOUISE AND THE INVASION OF 1814 by *Imbert de Saint-Amand*—The Empress and the Fall of the First Empire

SAPPER DOROTHY by *Dorothy Lawrence*—The only English Woman Soldier in the Royal Engineers 51st Division, 79th Tunnelling Co. during the First World War

ARMY LETTERS FROM AN OFFICER'S WIFE 1871-1888 by *Frances M. A. Roe*—Experiences On the Western Frontier With the United States Army

NAPOLEON'S LETTERS TO JOSEPHINE by *Henry Foljambe Hall*—Correspondence of War, Politics, Family and Love 1796-1814

MEMOIRS OF SARAH DUCHESS OF MARLBOROUGH, AND OF THE COURT OF QUEEN ANNE VOLUME 1 by A. T. Thomson

MEMOIRS OF SARAH DUCHESS OF MARLBOROUGH, AND OF THE COURT OF QUEEN ANNE VOLUME 2 by A. T. Thomson

MARY PORTER GAMEWELL AND THE SIEGE OF PEKING by *A. H. Tuttle*—An American Lady's Experiences of the Boxer Uprising, China 1900

VANISHING ARIZONA by *Martha Summerhayes*—A young wife of an officer of the U.S. 8th Infantry in Apacheria during the 1870's

THE RIFLEMAN'S WIFE by *Mrs. Fitz Maurice*—*The Experiences of an Officer's Wife and Chronicles of the Old 95th During the Napoleonic Wars*

THE OATMAN GIRLS by *Royal B. Stratton*—The Capture & Captivity of Two Young American Women in the 1850's by the Apache Indians

---

AVAILABLE ONLINE AT **www.leonaur.com**
AND FROM ALL GOOD BOOK STORES

www.ingramcontent.com/pod-product-compliance
Lightning Source LLC
Chambersburg PA
CBHW030228170426
43201CB00006B/151